FRAGMENTS AND ASSEMBLAGES

FRAGMENTS AND ASSEMBLAGES

Forming Compilations of Medieval London

ARTHUR BAHR

THE UNIVERSITY OF CHICAGO PRESS

CHICAGO AND LONDON

ARTHUR BAHR is associate professor of literature at the
Massachusetts Institute of Technology.

The University of Chicago Press, Chicago 60637
The University of Chicago Press, Ltd., London
© 2013 by The University of Chicago
All rights reserved. Published 2013.
Printed in the United States of America

22 21 20 19 18 17 16 15 14 13   1 2 3 4 5

ISBN-13: 978-0-226-92491-5 (cloth)
ISBN-13: 978-0-226-92492-2 (e-book)
ISBN-10: 0-226-92491-2 (cloth)
ISBN-10: 0-226-92492-0 (e-book)

The University of Chicago Press gratefully
acknowledges the generous support of the
Massachusetts Institute of Technology toward
the publication of this book.

Library of Congress Cataloging-in-Publication Data
Bahr, Arthur, 1976–
Fragments and assemblages : forming compilations of medieval
London / Arthur Bahr.
    pages ; cm
Includes bibliographical references and index.
ISBN 978-0-226-92491-5 (hardcover : alkaline paper)—
ISBN 978-0-226-92492-2 (e-book)   1. English literature—Middle
English, 1100–1500—History and criticism. 2. English literature—
Middle English, 1100–1500—Manuscripts. 3. Manuscripts, Medieval—
England—London. 4. Horne, Andrew, d. 1328—Manuscripts.
5. Auchinleck manuscript. 6. Chaucer, Geoffrey, d. 1400. Canterbury
tales. 7. Gower, John, 1325?–1408—Criticism and interpretation.
I. Title.
    PR255.B27 2013
    820.9'001—dc23   2012027389

♾ This paper meets the requirements of
ANSI / NISO z39.48-1992 (Permanence of Paper).

CONTENTS

FIGURES

ACKNOWLEDGMENTS

My advisers in college and graduate school, Howell D. "Chick" Chickering and Anne Middleton, have shaped my critical sense and nurtured my love of reading; my life as a teacher, scholar, and person is enriched by their close and continued friendship. I also benefited immensely from the community of graduate medievalists at the University of California, Berkeley—the famous GMB ("Gumby")—who were and are one of the most remarkable aspects of that wonderful institution. Very special thanks to the Department of English at Haverford College and in particular to Maud McInerney, who helped keep me in this particular game.

I could not have finished this project without the energetic support and friendship of my colleagues at the Massachusetts Institute of Technology (MIT), whose vibrant community I feel deeply honored to have joined. I am grateful in particular to Joel Burges, Diana Henderson, Noel Jackson, and Shankar Raman for their helpful comments on this book's introduction. My work has benefited just as deeply, though more intangibly, from the personal and professional support of my entire department and of allies across MIT: they are legion and warmly appreciated. I have also found engaging interlocutors and good friends in the wider group of Boston-area medievalists and in particular the faculty and student members of Harvard University's Medieval Colloquium; I am especially grateful to James Simpson for his support. This project also received a big boost when Alexandra Gillespie reached out to me as a colleague, interlocutor, and friend. She has my lasting thanks.

Students at Berkeley, Haverford, and MIT have stimulated me intellectually and rewarded me pedagogically. I force myself to mention by name only thesis advisees Brittany Pladek and Jabe Ziino and research assistants Erin Fitzgerald and Joe Pokora because, if I allowed myself to begin listing all those whose brains, hearts, and guts have impressed me over the years, I would still be writing these acknowledgments. I also have to send a special shout-out to the Ancient and Medieval Studies cohort at MIT. Malory's *Morte d'Arthur* will never sound quite the same to me, and for that I am truly grateful.

I presented early versions of many of this book's key arguments at conferences and symposia, and I owe a correspondingly large debt of gratitude to the organizers and audiences of panels at the New Chaucer Society, Fordham University, Harvard University, the Medieval Academy, MIT, and the International Congress on Medieval Studies in Kalamazoo. An early version of chapter 4 appeared in *Studies in the Age of Chaucer*, and I am grateful for permission to use it here. Librarians and staff at Cambridge, Corpus Christi College, the British Library, and the National Library of Scotland helped me immensely during my research; I would like to single out Gill Cannell at Cambridge, Corpus Christi College, and Ulrike Hogg at the National Library of Scotland for special thanks. My thanks as well to MIT for the semester of sabbatical in spring 2010 that allowed me to conclude work on the book manuscript. The two anonymous readers for the University of Chicago Press made valuable suggestions that have strengthened this project, and my editor at the Press, Randy Petilos, has been a delight to work with.

My family is such that the traditional, blanket thanks to them is woefully insufficient. The following is not sufficient either, but I nevertheless thank my dad, whose support and enthusiasm cheer me; my mom, whose resilience and courage inspire me; and my beloved little sister, who will always be my best friend, each-other's-sentence-finisher without peer, and ultimate role model. This book, like everything I do, is dedicated to them.

Introduction

COMPILATION,

ASSEMBLAGE,

FRAGMENT

This book argues for the integral connection between the forms of matter and the matter of forms. Less elliptically put, it contends that we can productively bring comparable interpretive strategies to bear on the formal characteristics of both physical manuscripts and literary works. For the Middle Ages in particular, the distinction between material text and immaterial work is rarely clear-cut. Consequently, the complex ways that work and text inform and constitute one another in medieval manuscripts encourage us to develop a broader set of interpretive modes than such manuscripts have tended to receive. The hybridity of the surviving forms of medieval literature, that is, calls for a comparably hybrid methodology. In the chapters that follow, therefore, I unite close attention to the literary and the aesthetic, which has characterized a resurgent (and potentially "new") formalism, with Walter Benjamin's theory of constellations and the dialectical image for its perceptive account of how aesthetic works materialize or realize the past in the present. This approach seems especially powerful because, regarded properly as at once formal shapes and historical occurrences, medieval manuscripts expose as false the long-implied opposition between form and history.

I begin to make this case by adapting into my literary-critical project the codicological term *compilatio*, whose complex scholarly history amply demonstrates the challenges faced by anyone seeking, as I do, to set in meaningful conversation "literary creation and the physical layout of surviving manuscripts." In the sharply worded essay from which this quotation is drawn, the paleographers Richard and Mary

Rouse argue that the terminological inconsistency with which *compilatio* has sometimes been deployed (is it a literary form, a tangible artifact, or both?) demonstrates the futility of uniting criticism of literary works with that of physical objects: these, they insist, "are not the results of the same actions."[1] Even those skeptical of so neat a separation of the literary-imaginative from the historical-physical are often reluctant to see artistic significance in the arrangement of texts within medieval manuscripts, since their construction was frequently guided more by practical than by aesthetic considerations. The lexicon of intentionality thus underlies many of the binary oppositions used to describe such manuscripts: between "the planned and the random,"[2] for example, or between "exigencies of production and generic/topical arrangement."[3] Such binaries evoke the vexed concept of literariness—what it is and how to recognize it in particular textual or physical forms. Was it exemplar poverty or their beguiling thematic connections that led two texts to cohabit a given manuscript? Is a short poem positioned at the end of a quire because it subtly echoes the preceding, longer text or simply because it was at hand and fit the space the scribe had left? How completely do the answers to these often-unanswerable questions determine what literary interpretations

1. R. H. Rouse and M. A. Rouse, "*Ordinatio* and *Compilatio* Revisited," in *Ad Litteram: Authoritative Texts and Their Medieval Readers*, ed. Mark D. Jordan and Kent Emery Jr. (Notre Dame, IN: University of Notre Dame Press, 1992), 113–34 (quotation 124). For an important and cogent response to the Rouses' critique, see A. J. Minnis, "*Nolens Auctor Sed Compilator Reputari*: The Late-Medieval Discourse of Compilation," in *La méthode critique au Moyen Âge*, ed. Mireille Chazan and Gilbert Dahan (Turnhout: Brepols, 2008), 47–63.

2. Ralph Hanna, "Miscellaneity and Vernacularity: Conditions of Literary Production in Late Medieval England," in *The Whole Book: Cultural Perspectives on the Medieval Miscellany*, ed. Stephen G. Nichols and Siegfried Wenzel (Ann Arbor: University of Michigan Press, 1993), 37–51 (quotation 37–38). See further Hanna's more extended comments from later in the essay: "Although I used to think it an unduly mechanical explanatory procedure, in a precanonical period, exemplar poverty motivates much of the literary record. . . . Difficulties of textual supply . . . contribute to the miscellaneous, not to say random, appearance of many Middle English books" (ibid., 47).

3. Murray J. Evans, *Rereading Middle English Romance: Manuscript Layout, Decoration, and the Rhetoric of Composite Structure* (Montreal: McGill-Queen's University Press, 1995), 95. Evans is discussing the third booklet of the Auchinleck manuscript, my subject in chapter 2.

we can legitimately make of the physical arrangement of texts in their surviving manuscripts?

As this book will show, aligning codicological with literary evidence often reveals more extensive traces of intentionality than we would otherwise have. Such traces inform the arguments to follow; the author is, in my readings, not irrevocably dead. Even when they seem apparent, however, the intentions behind a given manuscript, or grouping of texts within one, cannot often or easily be reduced to the kinds of binaries outlined above. Nor do I believe that codicologically inspired literary arguments of the sort developed here derive their full force from the empirically demonstrable. In this introduction's first section, therefore, I define *compilation*, not as an objective quality of either texts or objects, but rather as a mode of perceiving such forms so as to disclose an interpretably meaningful arrangement, thereby bringing into being a text/work that is more than the sum of its parts. Our decision thus to "read compilationally" needs, of course, to be grounded in an object's historical specificity, in describable cues that can be physical, textual, or both. But our apprehension of those cues and the interpretive work to which we put them must ultimately be subjective. Compilational interpretation is interesting only as long as and to the extent that we can imagine a reasonable interlocutor disagreeing with us.

One important goal underlying *Fragments and Assemblages* is thus to provoke debate about how to regard the interactions between medieval texts and the manuscripts that contain and shape them. This aim can best be accomplished through specifics, so each of my four chapters offers a reading of a particular compilation: the corpus of manuscripts overseen by London City chamberlain Andrew Horn; booklet 3 of the famous Auchinleck manuscript; Chaucer's *Canterbury Tales*; and the so-called Trentham manuscript of short works by John Gower. Although I regard each of these as compilations in the sense outlined above—that is, as disparate texts whose assemblage into a larger structure is meaningfully interpretable—the form of each differs substantially from that of the others. We have, respectively, a group of manuscripts compiled by a single, historically identifiable figure; one booklet within a much larger manuscript, producer and patron(s) unknown; a hypercanonical literary text extant in multiple codicological arrangements; and (most traditionally) a single-author codex of texts from throughout a named poet's career. Despite their formal dissimilarities, however, they are all products of, and shed light on, the textual and social culture of fourteenth-century London, broadly defined. Furthermore, the second section of this introduction will show that their echoes of one another and shared concerns reveal more about the social, political, and textual life of the City than if we were to consider each as merely the sum of its constituent parts. They are thus four compilations *from* medieval London that, when assembled and apprehended together, become a compilation *of* medieval London.

The formal dissimilarities displayed by this particular concatenation of objects further allow us to test how the compilational methodology that I employ might respond to such disparate physical shapes. Yet it must also be underscored that each of these shapes is, crucially, fragmentary. Most famously, the *Canterbury Tales* (whose claim to be analyzed as a physical shape I take up in due course) does not complete its initiating storytelling ambitions, and a vocabulary of fragments has long constructed scholarly discussion of the poem.[4] Physical fragmentation bespeaks in turn the material condition of the other texts I examine. Many of Andrew Horn's works were disassembled and somewhat chaotically rebound in the sixteenth century, while others appear not to have survived. The Auchinleck manuscript, while still massive, has lost a great many leaves and texts and most of its miniatures. Even the Trentham manuscript, the most nearly intact of these compilations, has had one folio neatly excised and another exuberantly mutilated. The literal, physical fragmentariness of these objects usefully raises theoretical questions that I take up in the third and final section of this introduction. When, along with its originating intentions, the original physical shape of an object has likewise been lost, can we meaningfully interpret its surviving forms? How can we make fragments speak with a voice that is intelligible, if not unified? Such

---

4. In sometimes distorting ways, as shown in Robert Meyer-Lee, "Fragments IV and V of the *Canterbury Tales* Do Not Exist," *Chaucer Review* 45 (2010): 1–31.

questions get at the very heart of medieval studies since the period's literary record is dominated by fragmentary manuscripts, incomplete texts, and anonymous authors.

For perspective on how these broader questions touch on my particular compilations, and vice versa, I draw on Walter Benjamin's suggestive reflections about the presentness of the past, which usefully sharpen the theoretical questions raised by the historical situation of fourteenth-century London and its various cultural forms. For what is at stake is a method, necessarily both speculative (i.e., theoretical) and historical, that mediates between the occluded or lost original medieval intention and the subjective, contemporary apprehension of text and manuscript that informs their meaning, bringing intention into being as if for the first time. This meaning is contingent, I claim, on what Benjamin calls an "experience with the past" as opposed to a reconstruction of it, a past that is not mere masses of data but perceived in and across time.[5]

Indeed, from this perspective, the fragmentary forms of medieval manuscripts offer one of our best ways to counter the tendency for literary histories of medieval England to elevate named authors over the anonymous; English over French and Latin; Ricardian over any other period; and genial, ironic, relatable Chaucer over everyone and everything else. Compilations shake up such limited narratives. They compel texts to change their meanings in ways that a purely linear historicity cannot fully recover or anticipate, as a particular text's relation to its broader codicological forms makes us rethink or resee something that by itself might seem straightforward, uninteresting, or overfamiliar. Ultimately, then, *Fragments and Assemblages* shows that the individual texts and authors that it studies can be transformed,

---

5. In fact, we will see that other concepts central to Benjamin's theory and practice bear more closely on medieval manuscripts and compilational projects than one might think; terms like *constellation* and *Konvolut* that structure *The Arcades Project* are more than just etymologically related to the *compilation* that structures mine. Benjamin's subject in *The Arcades Project*—like mine, an urban, mercantile landscape in the throes of social and political change—highlights his deep acknowledgment of the pressures of history, while the multivalent effects of the *Konvolut* as a formal device mark his determination to avoid history's potentially hegemonic force.

not just by the medieval compilational structures in which they are preserved, but also by the modern one—this book—that sets them in newly resonant juxtaposition.

Compilation

The Latin term *compilatio* was popularized by Malcolm B. Parkes, who used it in conjunction with *ordinatio* to describe how manuscripts from the thirteenth century on evolved to facilitate the increasingly complex modes of thought demanded by scholastic philosophy.[6] Broadly speaking, Parkes characterizes *ordinatio* as those elements of the text's presentation and layout that make the reading process easier, such as *litterae notabiliores*, paraph marks, and running titles. He defines *compilatio* as a larger-scale, textual analogue of such small-scale visual aids: a repackaging, rearranging, or excerpting of authoritative texts that makes the resulting compilation more useful or comprehensible.[7] He also argued for the relevance of these concepts to literary texts, most famously with his contention that "the attitude of compiler seems to lie behind Chaucer's words in the General Prologue," specifically his insistence on being true to his sources by faithfully recording the pilgrims' stories:

> But first I pray yow, of youre curteisye,
> That ye n'arette it nat my vileynye,
> Thogh that I pleynly speke in this mateere,
> To telle yow hir wordes and hir cheere,
> Ne thogh I speke hir wordes proprely.
> For this ye knowen al so wel as I:
> Whoso shal telle a tale after a man,
> He moot reherce as ny as evere he kan

---

6. See Malcolm B. Parkes, "The Influence of the Concepts of *Ordinatio* and *Compilatio* on the Development of the Book" (1976), reprinted in *Scribes, Scripts, and Readers: Studies in the Communication, Presentation, and Dissemination of Medieval Texts* (London: Hambledon, 1991), 35–70. Parkes extends his arguments and applies them to manuscripts of Chaucer and Gower in Malcolm B. Parkes and A. I. Doyle, "The Production of Copies of the *Canterbury Tales* and the *Confessio Amantis* in the Early Fifteenth Century" (1978), reprinted in ibid., 201–48.

7. Parkes, "The Influence of the Concepts of *Ordinatio* and *Compilatio*," 52–58.

> Everich a word, if it be in his charge,
> Al speke he never so rudeliche and large,
> Or ellis he moot telle his tale untrewe,
> Or feyne thing, or fynde wordes newe.[8]

By itself, this passage might be taken as a straightforward and not necessarily compilational assertion of truth value, familiar enough from
a range of literary prologues. But a slightly later admission, not discussed by Parkes, in fact strengthens his argument:

> Also I prey yow to foryeve it me,
> Al have I nat set folk in hir degree
> Heere in this tale, as that they sholde stonde.
> (I.743–45)

The "I prey yow" formula repeated from line 725 combines with the
correlative "also" here to suggest that these two activities—faithfully
recording while unfaithfully rearranging—are somehow parallel. This
connection seems odd until we recall that these are in fact the two defining characteristics of the medieval *compilator*, who rearranged but
did not add to the material he inherited.[9]

Alastair Minnis has expanded on Parkes's theories, arguing that
Chaucer's identification with *compilatio* in fact extends well beyond
the *General Prologue*.[10] Thus, for instance, the famous passage in which
a supposedly sheepish Chaucer encourages his readers to "turne over
the leef and chese another tale" if they are offended by the Miller's
promised "harlotrie" (I.3176–80) is read by Minnis as reflecting an established compilational practice of respecting the reader's freedom
of choice.[11] The implication is thus that even less self-consciously

8. Ibid., 61–62, quoting *Canterbury Tales* I.727–36. For this and subsequent quotations of
the *Canterbury Tales*, I use *The Riverside Chaucer*, ed. Larry D. Benson et al., 3rd ed. (Boston:
Houghton Mifflin, 1987). Fragment and line numbers for subsequent citations are given parenthetically in the text.

9. Drawing on Bonaventure's definition, Parkes writes: "The compiler adds no matter of
his own by way of exposition (unlike the commentator), but compared with the scribe he is free
to rearrange (*mutando*)" ("The Influence of the Concepts of *Ordinatio* and *Compilatio*," 59).

10. A. J. Minnis, *Medieval Theory of Authorship: Scholastic Literary Attitudes in the Later Middle
Ages* (London: Scolar, 1984), esp. 190–210.

11. Ibid., 198–200.

literary and more straightforward compilations than the *Canterbury Tales* would have been understood as subject to the reader's imaginative intervention and physical manipulation. Moreover, as Ralph Hanna has demonstrated, no compilation can in fact be truly straightforward since the very process of selecting, excerpting, and arranging texts has authorial impact even if the compiler himself has written none of the texts in question.[12] Compilation, in other words, inevitably shades into a form of composition.[13]

It is therefore impossible to maintain the sharp distinction between "literary creation and the physical layout of surviving manuscripts" on which we earlier saw Richard and Mary Rouse insist. Nevertheless, their proposed separation of the literary (imaginative verbal composition) from the historical (physical construction of surviving artifacts) suggestively anticipates the tension between form and history that has especially exercised the so-called new formalist attempt to reclaim

---

12. See Ralph Hanna, "*Compilatio* and the Wife of Bath: Latin Backgrounds, Ricardian Texts," in *Latin and Vernacular: Studies in Late Medieval Texts*, ed. A. J. Minnis (Woodbridge: D. S. Brewer, 1989), 1–11. Noting that "the Wife's Prologue becomes marked as a compilation because so much of it . . . is pieced together of verbatim translations" (ibid., 1), Hanna asks us to consider how differently her compilation functions from those, like Jankyn's Book of Wicked Wives, that attempt to deny "personality to the compiler . . . [in order] to highlight the universal truth stated by the *auctores* whom the compiler has joined together" (ibid., 6). The Wife's exuberantly personality-constitutive compilation demonstrates that such a "depersonalization of the *compilator* is a rhetorical fiction" (ibid., 6–7) since the act of selection and resituation changes the meaning of the juxtaposed texts as surely as, e.g., translation into another language.

13. Vincent of Beauvais, another self-styled compiler cited by Parkes, seems to acknowledge the impossibility of pure or disinterested compilation when he equivocates as to just how much, if anything, he has added to his sources. He writes: "I have added little of my own, or nearly nothing. For theirs is the authority, while ours is solely in the arrangement of the parts." See Parkes, "The Influence of the Concepts of *Ordinatio* and *Compilatio*," 58–59. A similar recognition informs Emma Dillon's use of the term *author-compiler* to describe the producer of the longer, interpolated *Roman de Fauvel* manuscript. See *Medieval Music-Making and the Roman de Fauvel* (Cambridge: Cambridge University Press, 2002), esp. 65–121. Dillon argues, and I agree, that what we might call the *author function* can inhere, not just in the composition of text, but also in the arrangement of disparate materials (in her case, text, music, and illumination) and the physical design of the manuscript itself. Two other helpful book-length explorations of the intersections of authorship and codicological practice are Deborah McGrady, *Controlling Readers: Guillaume de Machaut and His Late Medieval Readers* (Toronto: University of Toronto Press, 2006); and Elizabeth J. Bryan, *Collaborative Meaning in Scribal Culture: The Otho Laȝamon* (Ann Arbor: University of Michigan Press, 1999).

for literary study some version of its "traditional address to aesthetic form."[14] Derek Pearsall argues, for example, that the poetic and formal qualities of Chaucer's writing have been unhelpfully sidelined by "those commentators with a predominant or more usually exclusive interest in political, social, or cultural history . . . [for whom] what is needful is paraphrasable meaning." He continues: "Poetry, as a form of 'literature,' exploits potentialities in language, especially metaphorical potentialities, that are not exploited by other forms of discourse. Words in poetry, *in the way they are chosen and arranged*, have a wider range of possible meaning than they have in ordinary discourse, and not in any way confined to denotation; the language is richer, more suggestive, more elusive, more open; meaning can be dwelt upon, and fresh meanings can emerge in the process of rereading, already there but newly discovered."[15] While I do not support Pearsall's implied reinscription of *literary* and *nonliterary* as straightforward, ontological categories, I enthusiastically endorse his broader point: that the aesthetic, and more particularly what we might call *literariness*, cannot be reduced to mere or transparent expression of external social and political facts.[16]

14. Marjorie Levinson, "What Is New Formalism?" *PMLA* 122 (2007): 558–69 (quotation 559). To Levinson's bibliography of new formalist work I would add *Representations*, vol. 104, no. 1 (2008), which is devoted to explorations of form, formalism, and aesthetics; and, for their particular address to medievalists, Peggy Knapp's *Chaucerian Aesthetics* (New York: Palgrave Macmillan, 2008); *Chaucer Review*, vol. 39, no. 3, which is devoted to Chaucer and aesthetics; and the forthcoming special issue of the *Chaucer Review* that Alexandra Gillespie and I are co-editing on the relation between form, aesthetics, and codicology.

15. Derek Pearsall, "Towards a Poetic of Chaucerian Narrative," in *Drama, Narrative, and Poetry in the Canterbury Tales*, ed. Wendy Harding (Toulouse: Presses Universitaires du Mirail, 2003), 99–112 (quotations 99–100; emphasis added).

16. Many commentators have recently made much the same argument, so I cite as metonymic the comments of John J. Joughin and Simon Malpas: "Aesthetic specificity is not . . . entirely explicable, or graspable, in terms of another conceptual scheme or discourse. . . . In other words, perhaps the most basic tenet that we are trying to argue for is the equiprimordiality of the aesthetic—that, although it is without doubt tied up with the political, historical, ideological, etc., thinking it as other than determined by them, and therefore reducible to them, opens a space for an artistic or literary specificity that can radically transform its critical potential and position with regard to contemporary culture" (introduction to *The New Aestheticism*, ed. John J. Joughin and Simon Malpas [Manchester: Manchester University Press, 2003], 3).

Pearsall's remarks also helpfully align aspects of this literariness with the codicologically grounded concept of *compilatio* since his emphasis on selection and arrangement (italicized in the passage quoted above) echoes the two roles of the *compilator* as defined by Parkes. This connection suggests how literary form and materialist history might be brought into more fruitful collaboration: this book's principal argument will be that the selection and arrangement of texts in manuscripts, like that of words in poetry, can produce those "metaphorical potentialities," discontinuities and excesses, multiple and shifting meanings, resistance to paraphrase, and openness to rereading that have deservedly become resurgent objects of critical value. In proposing this analogy between words in poetry and texts in manuscripts, I do not mean to suggest that manuscripts are inherently equivalent to poetry in either goal or effect. Not all medieval manuscripts readily offer those literary rewards that Pearsall eloquently describes. It is also the case, however—our now normalized passion for canon smashing notwithstanding—that not all medieval literature equivalently offers them either.[17] In short, neither words in poetry nor texts in manuscripts inherently produce such literary effects, but both have the potential to do so.

This, then, is my definition of a compilation: the assemblage of multiple discrete works into a larger structure whose formal interplay of textual and material parts makes available some version of those literary effects described above. Such objects are likewise assemblages of disparate historical moments: of their individual texts' composition and subsequent, often gradual evolution into the particular material form they now occupy, which itself often differs from its original, medieval form. How those historical vectors inform and complicate the formal arrangements that together compose the visible compilation, I argue, constitutes both a potential source of aesthetic reso-

17. Pearsall readily acknowledges this point, contrasting the "extremely workaday verse . . . that would later (for a reading audience) be in prose" with the "poetry" that offers the particular rewards that he describes and valorizes. He concludes by citing Coleridge's assertion that "a poem of any length neither can be, nor ought to be, all poetry" ("Towards a Poetic," 99, 112).

nance and an invitation to literary analysis. A compilation need not be a complete manuscript—I take up forms both larger and smaller in the following chapters—but it is always either literally or implicitly physical. (The *Canterbury Tales* qualifies in my terms because of its multiple invitations to imagine and treat it as a physical object.) I thus mean *compilation* to join terms like *anthology* and *miscellany* as modern ways of interpreting how disparate texts, assembled and juxtaposed, function as a whole.[18]

Whereas those terms seem to make claims about the essential nature of the objects they characterize, however, a compilation as I define it relies on the perspective of its readers, who must ultimately determine whether to interpret its given assemblage of texts in compilational terms, that is, whether to see in the sum of its parts some larger meaning, effect, or perspective.[19] By defining *compilation* as a way of apprehending and interpreting objects, rather than as an inherent quality of the objects themselves, I make central to my study the question of what constitutes a legitimate invitation to compilational reading, what makes it profitable interpretation rather than willfully idiosyncratic or anachronistic imposition. This issue of anachronism is particularly

18. In a brief but important article on British Library MS Harley 2253, Theo Stemmler defines a miscellany as "a somewhat arbitrary, casual collection of texts," to be contrasted with "an anthology, a careful collection selected as representative specimens of various genres." He characterizes the latter as "a middle course" between the randomness of a miscellany, on the one hand, and, on the other, "a well-wrought book made up of mutually corresponding parts." See "Miscellany or Anthology? The Structure of Medieval Manuscripts: MS Harley 2253, for Example," in *Studies in the Harley Manuscript: The Scribes, Contents, and Social Contexts of British Library MS Harley 2253*, ed. Susanna Fein (Kalamazoo, MI: Medieval Institute Publications, 2000), 111–21, 113.

19. We might further clarify by setting another term, *collection*, in opposition to the compilation as I have defined it. Textual collections may have a clear principle of inclusion, but they present their disparate textual items in a form that does not readily yield some larger meaning or effect. The contrast between the *Canterbury Tales* and the *Legend of Good Women* is illustrative: whereas the ordering of the individual fragments and tales is integral to the meaning of the whole, most readers would feel that one could swap the stories of Cleopatra and Thisbe, or add in another comparable narrative, or omit two, without materially changing the effect of the whole. Here too, however, the question involves subjective critical judgment; one sensitive reader might find in the *Legend* a compilational structure or meaning where others see a mere collection, and both perspectives can be valid to the extent that the arguments supporting them are compelling.

pressing since (as characterized by Parkes and others) medieval *compilatio* represented a practical rather than an aesthetic or literary form of textual engagement; its goal was to streamline difficult texts, making them "*readily* . . . [and] *easily* accessible"—and this in "systematic and convenient form."[20] I am arguing, by contrast, for an appreciation of the extent to which the forms of textual assemblages can resist such efforts, becoming compilations whose difficulty and complexity offer a fruitful intersection of historical textual practice, surviving material form, and contemporary critical engagement.

The questions that this intersection raises—how to interpret texts and objects from the past and what kinds of histories they can be said to embody and illumine—were likewise of vital concern to Walter Benjamin, to whom I now turn for perspective on the tension between form and history that Pearsall and others have evoked, as well as for two terms that are linked, etymologically and conceptually, to the compilation as I have defined it: the constellation that serves as his metaphor for the proper object of historical inquiry and the convolute that structures *The Arcades Project*, his vast, unfinished attempt to put his theories into practice.

One leitmotif throughout his work is the contrast between what Benjamin calls "historicism" and "historical materialism."[21] Near the end of "On the Concept of History," he writes: "The historical materialist cannot do without the notion of a present which is not a transition, but in which time takes a stand [*einsteht*] and has come to a standstill. For this notion defines the very present in which he himself is writing history. Historicism offers the 'eternal' image of the past;

20. Parkes, "The Influence of the Concepts of *Ordinatio* and *Compilatio*," 68 (emphasis added); Parkes and Doyle, "The Production of Copies," 228.

21. See, e.g., Walter Benjamin, "On the Concept of History," in *Selected Writings*, trans. Edmund Jephcott et al., ed. Howard Eiland and Michael W. Jennings, 4 vols. (Cambridge, MA: Belknap Press of the Harvard University Press, 2003), 4:389–400, "Paralipomena to 'On the Concept of History,'" in ibid., 401–11, and *The Arcades Project*, trans. Howard Eiland and Kevin McLaughlin (Cambridge, MA: Belknap Press of Harvard University Press, 1999), esp. the two versions of the exposé ("Paris, the Capital of the Nineteenth Century" [1935], 3–13; "Paris, Capital of the Nineteenth Century" [1939], 14–26) and convolutes C ("Ancient Paris, Catacombs, Demolitions, Decline of Paris," 82–100), H ("The Collector," 203–11), and N ("On the Theory of Knowledge, Theory of Progress," 456–88).

historical materialism supplies a unique experience with the past."[22] Rather than being swept along by an inexorably linear historicity, in other words, the historical materialist must make of the present a temporality in which to capture an experience of the past's relation with that present. The last sentence's subtle shifts in diction ("*'eternal'* image *of* the past" vs. "*unique* experience *with* the past") insist on both the inextricability of past from present and the danger of a history that makes claims to the eternal or universal.

A passage from *The Arcades Project* develops this distinction further through the key metaphor of the constellation: "It's not that what is past casts its light on what is present, or what is present its light on what is past; rather, image is that wherein what has been comes together in a flash with the now to form a constellation. In other words: image is dialectics at a standstill. For while the relation of the present to the past is a purely temporal, continuous one, the relation of what-has-been to the now is dialectical: is not progression but image, suddenly emergent."[23] This evocation of image and constellation insists that we regard the past, not as the endlessly progressing time line created by the historicist's mass of data, but rather as a picture fixed in time, though not isolated from it. Like the constellation, the compilation as I engage it is a collection of multiple, disparate pieces into a larger picture, a form that is meaningfully interpretable. This form is a tangible "standstill" of history's progression that prompts the profitable arrest and deployment of our own interpretive faculties, enabling that "tiger's leap into the past" on which Benjamin insists.[24] This past is not a single point on the eternal time line, however, but rather the set of multiple, intersecting temporalities created by the histories of a compilation's authors, scribes, patrons, and later handlers—the "manuscript matrix" of Stephen Nichols's seminal essay.[25]

22. Benjamin, "On the Concept of History," 396.

23. Benjamin, *The Arcades Project*, 462.

24. Benjamin, "On the Concept of History," 395. There, Benjamin cites the example of the French Revolution's fascination with ancient Rome as "a past charged with now-time, a past which he [Robespierre] blasted out of the continuum of history."

25. Stephen Nichols, "Introduction: Philology in a Manuscript Culture," *Speculum* 65 (1990): 1–10. For a compelling recent exploration of the concept of the manuscript matrix, see

The constellation is a helpful metaphor precisely because constellations do not exist objectively or transhistorically. Rather, they represent culturally inflected ways of interpreting how multiple members of a larger group of objects interrelate. I have likewise proposed the compilation as an entity both physical and perspectival, one that relies on its reader's mode of apprehension rather than on its existence as an ontological category. The question of subjective judgment entailed by this formulation also concerned Benjamin, who was no deconstructionist despite his distaste for positivist forms of historicism. Of the dialectical image visible in the constellation, he writes: "Its position is naturally not an arbitrary one. It is to be found, in a word, where the tension between dialectical opposites is greatest."[26] The compilations of this study embody such tensions, for they contain named and unnamed authors of wildly varying canonicity whose texts and projects evince a comparably wide range of relations to self-conscious literariness. Their texts are wholly English (the *Canterbury Tales*) and wholly non-English (the Horn corpus), exuberantly multilingual (Trentham) and suggestively near monolingual (Auchinleck). They include political, belletristic, historiographic, documentary, and other forms of verse, prose, and codicological "filler." Their versions of authorship range from self-conscious vernacular makers to the named and unnamed scribes, compilers, and later handlers who have given these compilations their various contemporary forms. These authors likewise vary markedly in the degree to which they actively and obviously seek to guide the reader's apprehension of how their multiple texts interrelate. The constructive potential of such tensions emerges, however, only when we regard form and history as complementary forces.[27]

Martha Rust, *Imaginary Worlds in Medieval Books: Exploring the Manuscript Matrix* (New York: Palgrave Macmillan, 2007).

26. Benjamin, *The Arcades Project*, 475 (N10a,3).

27. The expansive contrasts of this paragraph—particularly between canonical literary texts and the obscure, archival, and seemingly nonliterary—evoke the generic conventions of new historicism. Dissatisfaction with the potential emptiness of such conventions has given new formalism much of its drive and vigor, but as Marjorie Levinson emphasizes throughout "What Is New Formalism?" the most compelling versions of historicist scholarship in fact

The productive potential of this relation finds further expression in the *Konvolut*, the formal device that structures *The Arcades Project*. The German term designates a sheaf or booklet of materials designed to be read together, and Benjamin's project offers just such a compilation of minicompilations: forty-four convolutes whose topics range from the abstract ("Idleness") to the concrete ("Iron Construction") and from the self-consciously intellectual ("On the Theory of Knowledge, Theory of Progress") to the seemingly whimsical ("The Doll, the Automaton"). The dialectical oppositions created by these and other, comparable contrasts among their topics enact formally, at a large-scale level, the very theory of history that *The Arcades Project* advocates, whereby "the object constructed in the materialist presentation of history is itself the dialectical image."[28] Each individual convolute likewise takes in diverse material, typically quotations on its subject drawn from a formidable range of philosophical, literary, and historical works. Benjamin inserts his own thoughts and interpretations into these assemblages of quotations at very irregular intervals; often one can read for pages at a time without any explicit or sustained articulation of his perspective. As with the medieval compiler, however, Benjamin's activity—selecting, excerpting, and arranging an array of sources—has authorial impact even when he adds "little of my own, or nearly nothing," as Vincent of Beauvais put it. Moreover, even when Benjamin's own reflections do predominate, his style remains paratactic, as if he is taking care to present his own formulations as he does his sources, thus taking part in the history he studies rather than reconstructing it. This gambit also makes it possible to construct any number of logical relations between adjacent paragraphs within a convolute and between adjacent convolutes within the larger *Project*. The reader thus steps into a temporal nexus linking the moments of her reading, Benjamin's writing (which itself took place over many years), and the nineteenth-century Paris that his work addresses throughout.

---

work conspicuously with and toward an understanding of form. I place my own sympathetic relation with new formalism squarely in this tradition of deep engagement with the particularities of the past.

28. Benjamin, *The Arcades Project*, 475 (N10a,3).

Embracing multiple temporalities such as these is one way of re-specting the vastly different vantage point from which we must try to understand medieval art and artifacts; these are profitable anachro-nisms, to evoke Maura Nolan's compelling formulation.[29] *Compilatio* may originally have aimed to reduce the complexity of the difficult texts that it juxtaposes, but this was hardly its inevitable effect, even in the Middle Ages. The more we look at the *General Prologue*, for example, the more it seems that Chaucer has taken up the technical vocabulary of *compilatio* as a way of creating more rather than less com-plexity. He has set the pilgrim portraits in one order (and even that one not, he claims, "as that they sholde stonde" [I.745]) but their tales in another; even as he thematizes the pilgrims as professional entities, suggesting one organizational strategy, he gives them a range of other markers too: physical repulsiveness (Summoner, Cook), linguistic af-filiation (Prioress, Guildsmen and their wives),[30] entrepreneurial voca-tion (Merchant, Wife), and so on. This kaleidoscopic array of connec-tions enables us to take up the invitation in the "Miller's Prologue" to imagine juxtapositions of tales other than those authorized by either the headlinks or the surviving fragment structures. Because Fragment I self-consciously gives us the interpretive tools needed to construct alternate tale threads, the potential of such alternatives to radiate out-ward from the poem's initiating narrative becomes itself part of the form of the *Tales*.

The Horn corpus and the Auchinleck and Trentham manuscripts will show that such quintessentially literary forms of indeterminacy can be prompted by physical forms as well, even when (as with much of the Horn corpus and parts of the Auchinleck manuscript) their texts themselves do not seem to invite literary appreciation. Although An-

29. See Maura Nolan, "Making the Aesthetic Turn: Adorno, the Medieval, and the Future of the Past," *Journal of Medieval and Early Modern Studies* 34 (2004): 549–75. Nolan's is a corol-lary to Paul Strohm's insight that forms of "strategic *disrespect*" are necessary to provoke texts into that which they "cannot or will not articulate" for or about themselves. See *Theory and the Premodern Text* (Minneapolis: University of Minnesota Press, 2000), xiii.

30. The Prioress's French "of Stratford atte Bowe" (I.125) is often commented on. Less so is the fact that the wives of the Haberdasher, Carpenter, Weaver, Dyer, and Tapiser also find it "ful fair to been ycleped *madame*" (I.376), a point to which I will return in chapter 3.

drew Horn modeled some of his civic compendia on the streamlining organizational principles of classic *compilatio*, he also explored other modes of construction, and chapter 1 examines a range of odd textual juxtapositions from throughout his corpus that force the reader into complex and skeptical relation with seemingly utilitarian texts and manuscripts. The third booklet of the Auchinleck manuscript, my subject in chapter 2, shows that Paul Strohm's notion of a "textual unconscious" can also usefully apply to codicological structures;[31] this particular one uncannily evokes the structure of the manuscript as a whole in ways that elude demonstrable intention but nevertheless shed light on important literary and cultural relations among its texts. Chapter 4 will argue, meanwhile, that the Trentham manuscript's codicological form evokes the multiple intersecting histories of its many texts in ways that complicate and undercut the outward gaudiness with which it praises the Lancastrian accession. Just as the *Canterbury Tales* (the subject of chapter 3) is a literary text that provocatively presents itself as a manipulable physical object, then, so too the other manuscripts I take up here are physical objects whose form, content, and histories all prompt appreciation of their literariness.

My goal, however, is not simply to present isolated appreciations of four discrete codicological forms. I will further argue that these four particular compilations, here assembled and apprehended as a group, collectively attain compilational force, in the sense that their intersecting contrasts and continuities lead to a richer perspective on the life of the City that produced them than they would yield if analyzed individually. In the following section, I lay out first the historical basis for focusing on compilations from London and then some of the aspects of political, social, and economic history that will inform the following chapters. Along the way, I will offer brief, contextualizing introductions to the compilations I later take up, together with some of the historical claims that they have to be considered in conjunction with one another. I will also lay the groundwork for a key proposition that I advance across the following chapters: that the links between

---

31. See Strohm, *Theory and the Premodern Text*, 165–81.

social and textual identity were sufficiently strong in fourteenth-century London that it makes sense for us to read some of its textual assemblages as ways of engaging with the social imaginary.[32]

Assemblage

London's size and wealth made it one of the likeliest places in medieval England for texts, scribes, and patrons to coexist, but there are more than merely instrumental reasons for considering the social nexus of the City in relation to the textual nexus of the compilation. From the late thirteenth century on, both the lived reality and the idealized self-conception of London as a polity were becoming increasingly textual. The fourteenth century saw an explosion in the number of trade, craft, and parish guilds that were formally and thus textually registered with the City.[33] London's civic bureaucracy was also becoming increasingly large and complex, a process that had both social and textual ramifications.[34] Subtending these developments was Londoners' perennially insecure relationship with the Crown, whose goodwill

32. The most commonly cited studies of such interactions between the social and the textual tend to focus on modern and print cultures and, indeed, often claim for the medium of print a uniquely enabling function. They also tend to address national or transnational identity rather than civic identity, as here. See, e.g., Michael Warner, *The Letters of the Republic: Publication and the Public Sphere in Eighteenth-Century America* (Cambridge, MA: Harvard University Press, 1990); Homi Bhabha, ed., *Nation and Narration* (London: Routledge, 1990); and Benedict Anderson, *Imagined Communities: Reflections on the Origin and Spread of Nationalism* (London: Verso, 1983). On the dangers of thus privileging print culture and how it both relates to and obscures a more inclusive history of the book, see Alexandra Gillespie, "Analytical Survey 9: The History of the Book," *New Medieval Literatures* 9 (2007): 245–86.

33. Antony Black's *Guilds and Civic Society in European Political Thought from the Twelfth Century to the Present* (Ithaca, NY: Cornell University Press, 1984) is a good general introduction to the subject. Pamela Nightingale's *A Medieval Mercantile Community: The Grocers' Company and the Politics and Trade of London, 1000–1485* (New Haven, CT: Yale University Press, 1995) details one trade guild's history in medieval London, which in turn sheds considerable light on the relations between London guilds and other urban power structures. On literary reflections of social tensions produced by inter- and intraguild rivalries, see Marion Turner's *Chaucerian Conflict: Languages of Antagonism in Late Fourteenth Century London* (Oxford: Oxford University Press, 2007).

34. On the proliferation of textual and legal structures that was already beginning in thirteenth-century London, see Gwyn Williams's seminal *Medieval London: From Commune to Capital* (London: Athlone, 1963), esp. 76–105.

was necessary for the City to maintain those communal rights and privileges on which its wealth and power depended.[35] The most critical of these privileges were political and economic: self-governance by an annually elected host of civic bureaucrats, headed by a mayor who reported directly to the king,[36] and the franchise, a form of economic protectionism by which trade and craft monopolies severely restricted foreign and alien merchants' activities in the City.[37] English kings had good reason to dislike both provisions; the first seriously compromised their control over the kingdom's largest and wealthiest city, and the second complicated their access to the tax revenue offered by outside merchants. As a result, and particularly following Edward I's initiation of quo warranto hearings as a means of consolidating and extending royal power, Londoners' hopes of maintaining these and other rights rested largely on the scrupulous maintenance of their various documentary bases.[38] The panic that erupted in

35. Caroline Barron describes the dynamic nicely: "London was populous and wealthy but it was constantly thrown onto the defensive by a Crown served by eagle-eyed lawyers anxious to protect and enhance the rights of their royal master. In a series of charters from the twelfth century the Londoners had gained some important rights of self-government, judicial immunities, and economic advantages over other towns, but all these could be challenged, redefined, or simply withdrawn. . . . The city frequently had to defend its rights while the Crown was able to withdraw privileges or redefine them. . . . The citizens haggled and bargained and employed clever lawyers to pit their wits against the royal justices. . . . But in those struggles the two sides were not evenly matched" (*London in the Later Middle Ages: Government and People, 1200–1500* [Oxford: Oxford University Press, 2004], 41–42).

36. For the most thorough and helpful account of medieval London's complex civic bureaucracy—who elected it and how, what functions it served and why, and how these all changed over the period 1200–1500—see ibid., chaps. 6–9.

37. *Alien* and *foreign* have specific, technical meanings in discussions of medieval London's economic history, hence the initially startling impact of a title like T. H. Lloyd's seminal *Alien Merchants in England in the High Middle Ages* (New York: St. Martin's, 1982). An *alien* in this context was a non-Englishman, while *foreigns* were Englishmen from other parts of the country who had moved to London but had not gained the all-important citizenship that would allow them to operate freely in the City. See further the discussion in Williams, *Medieval London*, 43–49.

38. Ralph Hanna argues along these lines: "City history often appears a constantly renewed perception of threat to these legal arrangements, particularly from without. In this view, civic history is the preservation of ancient custom, and it depends upon a process fundamentally historical—legal memory. In part, such memory may be achieved by the preservation of evidences, which implies not just the Guildhall's locked chests that protect documents but equally their reproduction in writing as a guard against loss" (*London Literature, 1300–1380*

1314—when, challenged by the king's lawyers, London bureaucrats could not find the texts on which their interpretation of a decades-old writ depended—amply demonstrates the potentially dire practical consequences of textual disorganization.[39]

In Andrew Horn's extensive narration of that incident, it serves both as a point of pride (the City did eventually prevail) and as a cautionary reminder that London depended for its very survival on continuously shrewd and competent textual management. Horn had a uniquely intimate perspective on that reality, having served as City chamberlain through most of the 1320s, which saw both national and local political upheaval. Royal justices had stripped the City of nearly all its cherished autonomy at the Eyre of 1321,[40] and only in 1327, following Edward II's deposition and the coronation of his son Edward III, did London receive guarantees of its historic freedoms in the form of a new charter, read aloud to the assembled citizens by Horn himself.[41] The depiction of this episode in the *Annales Paulini* merits

---

[Cambridge: Cambridge University Press, 2005], 59). On Edward I's efforts, see Donald W. Sutherland, *Quo Warranto Proceedings in the Reign of Edward I* (Oxford: Clarendon, 1963). M. T. Clanchy also discusses the strategy in *From Memory to Written Record: England, 1066–1307* (Cambridge, MA: Harvard University Press, 1979; 2nd ed., Oxford: Blackwell, 1993), 35–43.

39. Hanna summarizes the episode, which Horn himself recorded at some length: "Edward I had issued a writ, modifying for the City, it was alleged, provisions of the problematic Statute of Gloucester, chapter 12 (*Statutes* I, 49, 52). But the justices remained skeptical, and faced with the loss of privilege, a two-year search ensued: where was the document which demonstrated the precedent on which the City based its interpretation? Once found and the City's understanding vindicated, the proper right was carefully re-entered, in both the rolls of Chancery and of the Common Bench so that it could never again be questioned. Equally, Horn had it written into his book, where it might remain part of civic record and, with the accompanying account of the research that led to its recovery, civic history" (*London Literature*, 59–60).

40. An Eyre or Iter is a judicial inquiry launched by royal justices making a tour (hence the original Latin) of a given area. Williams (*Medieval London*, 285–306) gives the fullest account of this particular one. As he puts it: "The Iter of 1321 was the last and the worst the city had to face. . . . Quo Warranto proceedings were launched against every franchise in the city. London's own liberties were combed through, clause by clause, and finally, many of the citizens' cherished privileges were suspended. . . . The summoning of officers, the daily service of juries, the closure of city courts, the endless hearings, paralyzed municipal life. The king seemed bent on prising every privilege and penny out of the city" (ibid., 286–87).

41. As described by Williams, this new charter "represented the widest measure of administrative freedom London had yet attained. All the ancient liberties, in their pre-1321 purity, were restored and confirmed" (ibid., 299).

consideration here because its formal structure suggests, not just the vital importance that Londoners placed on textual manifestations of social identity, but also the capacity of textual compilations to convoke disparate groups of people into a larger imagined community. It suggests a potential analogy, in other words, between textual and social forms of assemblage.

This is the relevant passage:

> Eodem anno, primo die mensis Februarii, videlicet die Dominica, dominus Edwardus filius Edwardi Regis et dominae Isabellae reginae primogenitus, anno aetatis suae quinto decimo, per communem electionem totius regni, et ex consensu Edwardi patris sui, ut dicebatur, apud Westmonasterium per archiepiscopum Cantuariensem fuit coronatus; aliis episcopis, videlicet Londoniensi et Wyntoniensi, ministrantibus circa solempnizationem coronationis; et omnes magnates regni officium suum secundum antiquam regni consuetudinem sine aliquo impedimento habuerunt.

> In praefato parliamento diversae petitiones cum responsionibus suis majori, aldermannis et communitati Londoniae per dominum regem Angliae sunt concessae, et sub magno sigillo cera viridi sigillatae; et vii idus Martii in Gihalda, coram majore, aldermannis et communitate ibidem congregatis, per Andream Horn camerarium Gilhaldae lectae et puplicatae ac in Anglico expositae, sub tenoribus qui sequuntur:

> "Edwardus Dei gratia rex Angliae, dominus Hyberniae et dux Aquitanniae. . . ."[42]

> In that same year, on the first day of the month of February, namely Sunday, the lord Edward firstborn son of Edward the king and the lady Isabella the queen, in his fifteenth year was crowned at Westminster by the Archbishop of Canterbury, by the common choice of the entire kingdom, and with the consent of his father Edward, as it was said; and other bishops, namely those of London and Winchester, participated in the ceremony of coronation; and all the magnates of the realm

---

42. William Stubbs, ed., *Annales Londonienses and Annales Paulini*, vol. 1 of *Chronicles of the Reigns of Edward I and Edward II*, Rolls Series, vol. 76.1 (London: Longmans, 1882), 324–25 (my translation).

performed their office without any impediment, according to the ancient custom of the kingdom.

In the aforementioned parliament various petitions, together with their responses, were granted to the mayor, aldermen, and commons of London by the lord king of England, and sealed under the Great Seal with green wax; and on March 9 at the Guildhall, in the presence of the mayor, with the aldermen and commons congregated there, they were read and made public by Andrew Horn, Chamberlain of the Guildhall, but explained in English, according to the following terms:

"Edward by the grace of God king of England, lord of Ireland, and duke of Aquitaine, greetings. . . ."

By juxtaposing its narration of the two events, this passage emphasizes the structural similarities between royal coronation and civic emancipation. Each is publicly performed in a specially sanctioned building (Westminster Abbey, the Guildhall) on a specified date, validated by the actions of key officers (ecclesiastical for the coronation, civic for the proclamation of the charter), and ratified by the presence of ranking representatives of those affected (the magnates for the realm as a whole, the assembled aldermen and commons for London). The annalist suggests a still stronger link between these two realms, the royal and the civic, by having a representative of London's government, Andrew Horn, ventriloquize the king himself as he reads the charter aloud.

This London chronicle's suggestion of parallels between Crown and City, two entities that were so often in sharp conflict, highlights a key historical node that will recur throughout this study: the question of what could serve as plausible representations of, and models for, London itself and the urban merchant elite that sought to control it. Despite or perhaps because of Londoners' constant struggles with the Crown, aristocratic models were deeply appealing. As the excerpt above implies, the civic government structure of mayor, aldermen, and sheriffs could be seen as a miniature aristocracy,[43] and, given the stark

---

43. Barron notes: "Within his small domain of three square miles, he [the mayor] was a king with many of the powers and some of the prestige of that office" (*London in the Later Middle Ages*, 147).

asymmetries of power that Londoners faced in their conflicts with the Crown, any advantage was attractive, however symbolic or rhetorical. From the thirteenth century on, aldermen had styled themselves barons,[44] and they also asserted a wide range of aristocratic privileges to complement their claims to political and economic autonomy.[45] Since the days of King John, moreover, baronial resistance to overweening royal authority had offered both model and means for London's citizens to extract new concessions from the Crown.[46] Indeed, the 1327 charter described above was granted precisely because of the City's pivotal support for the coup of Isabella and Mortimer.[47] This context will prove important for the following chapters' consideration of literary and cultural models that offer the potential for aristocratic performance or imitation by London's citizens.

Returning to the *Annales Paulini*, two other images further encourage us to make the connection I am suggesting between civic and royal realms—that is, to engage in the compilational reading of its two discrete, though juxtaposed, episodes as conveying more than the sum of their parts. These are the green wax and the Great Seal, whose vibrant physicality gives them an embossed prominence within the narration of the two episodes. They appear at the tangent point when the annalist links the "aforementioned parliament" of the first, royal ceremony with the date of the second, civic one. They thus "seal" in the reader's

44. As Williams (*Medieval London*, 3) points out, "mayor and barons" was the formulaic address.

45. These privileges included rights to extramural hunting, burial with baronial honors, and trial by a jury of peers. On the first two, see Hanna, *London Literature*, 59. On the third, see Williams, *Medieval London*, 3. Barron (*London in the Later Middle Ages*, 144–45) points out that such was the respect accorded aldermanic office that the theoretical penalty for striking an alderman was loss of the offending hand. No record that this provision was enforced exists, but imprisonment in Newgate, confinement in the stocks, or heavy fines could result from slandering these walking incarnations of civic privilege.

46. Hanna also notes Londoners' "logic for emulating, as well as making common cause with, fractious rural aristocrats" (*London Literature*, 59). Even royalist citizens tended to consider first the potential for civic advantage. "Almost in the same breath," as Williams puts it, the thirteenth-century civic historian Arnald fitz Thedmar "asserts the patriciate's loyalty to the king during the Barons' Wars and denounces the popular mayor for not wringing fresh loyalties from the prostrate Henry in 1264" (*Medieval London*, 203).

47. See Williams, *Medieval London*, 295–98.

mind the association between royal and civic performance and, in so doing, link the textuality that they represent and validate with the convocation that the narrative describes: the City united to hear the charter read aloud by Horn. The historical tableau of Horn reading aloud the same charter that the annals record invites later readers to imagine themselves there, a part of the polity assembled and reformed after years of chaos and distress. The stipulation that Horn spoke in English (*ac expositae anglice*), rather than the Latin given in the annals, prompts readers to hear in one language the text that they are reading in another, encouraging an imaginative participation that draws them further into the scene. The annals thus use a poetics of textual assemblage (here, two juxtaposed episodes linked by an arresting symbolic image) to create a convocation of citizens that reaches beyond those physically assembled on March 9, 1317. The episode gains its power by looking into the future even as it narrates the past, further indication that the sophisticated deployment of multiple temporalities is as much a medieval as a modern or postmodern concern.[48]

The social and political trauma that precipitated the assemblies recorded by the *Annales Paulini* finds vivid representation in texts throughout the Auchinleck manuscript, my subject in chapter 2. *The Simonie* is probably the most famous of its poems of social complaint, but a shorter text earlier in the manuscript, "The Sayings of the Four Philosophers," is more interesting than its critical neglect would suggest, for its prologue imagines textually the social dissolution that characterized Edward II's reign. Like the *Annales Paulini*, it juxtaposes images of wax, parliaments, and "wise men," though to very different effect:

> L'en puet fere & defere, ceo fait il trop souent;
> It nis nouþer wel ne faire, þerfore engelond is shent.
> Nostre prince de engleterre per le consail de sa gent,
> At Westminster after þe feire maden a gret perlement.
> La chartre fet de cyre ieo l'enteink & bien le crey
> It was holde to neih þe fire and is molten al awey.

---

48. For a provocative consideration of how such temporalities inflect the aesthetic theory of Theodor Adorno, see Nolan, "Making the Aesthetic Turn."

> Ore ne say mes que dire, tout i va a tripolay,
> Hundred, chapitle, court & shire, al hit goþ a deuel wey.
> Des plu sages de la tere, ore escoteʒ vn sarmoun,
> Of iiij wise men, þat þer were, whi engelond is brought adoun.[49]

Each sage then offers a diagnosis of England's grievous state, and the poem concludes with a prayer for better times. The charter, "molten al awey," presumably refers to the Ordinances of 1311, a set of restrictions placed on Edward II's authority by his restive barons. The ensuing struggles between the two parties exacerbated the dire social conditions that the rest of the poem describes.

Chapter 2 discusses "Four Philosophers" in the context of the Auchinleck manuscript's third booklet; here, my interest is in its image of the wax charter, "la chartre fet de cyre," whose melting is even more viscerally physical than the analogous green wax in the *Annales Paulini*. Just as crucially, it imagines the abuse of texts as tantamount to the failure of government. The Ordinances are represented as a communally produced document—made by an assembly of people (*gent*) convened at a *perlement*—and the result of Edward's failures is not just textual but social dissolution: the charter melts into nothingness, and the organizational units of the kingdom described two lines later are likewise destroyed. (The word *chapitle* reinforces this connection between textual and political entities since it can mean both the administrative body of ecclesiastical officials, clearly the primary meaning here, and the chapter of a text.)[50] The poem's introduction, in other words, suggests that, by dissolving the textual basis of social organization, Edward's failures have undone society itself. Indeed, this concern with making and unmaking is announced in the prologue's opening "fere et defere" (line 1).

49. *Historical Poems of the XIVth and XVth Centuries*, ed. Rossell Hope Robbins (New York: Columbia University Press, 1959), 140–43. While using Robbins's text, I have reproduced the long-line format of Auchinleck, with the result that, while only ten lines are reproduced here, they correspond to Robbins's lines 1–20. Line numbers for subsequent citations are given parenthetically in the text.

50. See *Middle English Dictionary*, ed. Hans Kurath et al. (Ann Arbor: University of Michigan Press, 1952–2000), s.v. *chapitle*.

In the body of the poem, each eponymous philosopher offers a set of gnomic statements that lead starkly into three lines of just two feet each. The second of these is representative:

> Nu on is two,
> Wel is wo,
> And frend is fo.
> (lines 39–41)

In their syllabic and linear brevity and oxymoronic content, these lines evoke the dissolution imaged by the macaronic introduction's molten wax. The poet, however, then contextualizes these statements by grafting each onto another clause in the next stanza:

> ffor on is two, þat lond is streinþeles;
> ffor wel is wo, þe lond is reuþeles;
> ffor frend is fo, þe lond is loueles.
> (lines 42–44)

By making each original line the dependent clause of a larger statement of causality, "Four Philosophers" partially undoes the fragmentation caused by the king's own failure at responsible textual management. Bleak as they are, these lines assert that England's wretched state is not as arbitrary or meaningless as the preceding stanza might suggest. And, while the prescriptions that conclude the poem are thoroughly conventional (to love God [line 81], be steadfast [line 87], and so on), the poem arrives at them—and at the equally conventional tail-rhyme stanza form in which they are presented—only after metaphorically reassembling the textual integrity that Edward's violation of the Ordinances helped destroy.

These two examples display what we might call a *poetics of assemblage*, which goes beyond merely the textual representation of social phenomena in order to use textual assemblages of varying sizes to think through how analogously disparate social entities are productively called together or, just as relevantly, laid bare as prone to collapse. Precisely this connection between the textual and the social underwrites my discussion of the *Canterbury Tales* in chapter 3. We have already considered how the *General Prologue* evokes the technical lexicon of *compilatio*. This vocabulary complements the language of social *felaweshipe* that David Wallace has emphasized, by which Chaucer shifts from characterizing the pilgrims as "hem" and "they" and ends up including himself as one of the "we" who set out on "oure pilgrimage."[51] Wallace is right to argue that the oaths and technical terms by which the Canterbury pilgrims organize themselves and their tale-telling competition establish them as a miniature polity,[52] while Marion Turner, Ardis Butterfield, and others have properly insisted on its substantial London associations.[53] The pilgrims' participation in such a sociopolitical structure, however, is coterminous with the textual structure that both their tales and their characters, as examples of an established literary tradition, constitute.[54] Chaucer's joking invitation in the "Miller's Prologue" (I.3176–80) that we treat his poem as a physical, textual object—turning over the leaf, picking a different genre from the assembled construct—is funny rather than absurdist only if the activity it proposes is in fact comprehensible. The extended dramas of Fragment I's headlinks help ensure that we will read that selection of tales in the order presented, even as their acknowledgment of alternate possibilities (not just Geffrey's invitation but the Miller's own, immediately preceding disruption of the Host's proposed Knight-Monk ordering) enables us to construct a wide range of other compilational threads extending out from the initiating

51. See David Wallace, *Chaucerian Polity: Absolutist Lineages and Associational Forms* (Stanford, CA: Stanford University Press, 1997), 65–103.

52. Ibid., 66–72.

53. Wallace dismissed London as an "absent city" in Chaucer's work (this is the title of chap. 6 of *Chaucerian Polity*), but his position cannot be maintained in the face of Turner's *Chaucerian Conflict* and Ardis Butterfield's collection *Chaucer and the City* (Cambridge: D. S. Brewer, 2006), to name just two recent and substantial studies.

54. Here, I follow the field-altering demonstration of Jill Mann (*Chaucer and Medieval Estates Satire* [Cambridge: Cambridge University Press, 1973]) that, as part of the well-established estates-satire genre, the pilgrim portraits are more typological than psychological; because nearly all their characteristics are drawn from a preexisting literary tradition, the pilgrims are fundamentally textual constructions. As Mann wisely acknowledges, however, the genius of the portraits lies in Chaucer's emphasis of the pilgrims' typological characteristics even as his use of authenticating details "give[s] us an extraordinarily vivid *impression* of their existence as individuals" (ibid., 16). In other words, the pilgrims manage to appear simultaneously textual and human, such that, in gathering them together, Chaucer is promising both a textual compilation and a social convocation in the body of the tales that follow.

storytelling of the *Knight's Tale* and, likewise, to imagine what the various sociocultural associations of such threads might reveal about the London-based polity in which they are produced and consumed. That Chaucer could present such a speculative poetics of assemblage as an already comprehensible form of textual play suggests that the *Tales* is at least as vitally informed by the tradition of compilational construction and interpretation embodied by the Horn corpus and Auchinleck as by the range of Continental models with which he has more usually been associated.

Like Chaucer, Gower was based in the metropolis. Moreover, while the Trentham manuscript is not marked as Londonian, like some of his earlier poems or the other compilations studied here,[55] it was produced by two London scribes, and as a textual assemblage it queries the potential for an analogous, though larger-scale, social cohesion: how and whether Henry IV, the new monarch whom it repeatedly addresses, can unite the nation that has, like London itself, repeatedly been ravaged by the bitter politics of faction. In Trentham, that larger significance is made clear, not just by the political focus of numerous individual texts like *In Praise of Peace*, but also by the trilingual character of the manuscript as a whole. This multilingualism, which the manuscript self-consciously emphasizes, does more than give the lie to a simplistic "triumph of English"-type interpretation of the linguistic trajectory of Gower's three longest poems, all of which Trentham substantially postdates. It is in itself political since for Gower the very fact of multilingualism is inextricably linked with Babel, as the moment when linguistic and political unity alike were shattered into *divisioun*.[56]

---

55. The City is a vibrant presence in Gower's earliest long work, *Mirour de l'Omme*, which devotes its entire eighth section to satiric depictions of "l'estat des Marchantz, Artificers et Vitaillers," and in *Vox Clamantis*, where London is famously imagined as a widowed New Troy, laid bare to the ravages of the 1381 Rising. Gower's connections with the City are biographical, too. Robert Epstein argues that, as an urban lawyer, Gower "may have found an important early audience through his connection to the legal culture of Chancery Lane." See "London, Southwark, Westminster: Gower's Urban Contexts," in *A Companion to Gower*, ed. Siân Echard (Cambridge: D. S. Brewer, 2004), 43–60 (quotation 44).

56. On this connection, see Mary Catherine Davidson, *Medievalism, Multilingualism, and Chaucer* (New York: Palgrave Macmillan, 2009), chap. 2; Tim William Machan, "Medieval

Gower frequently decries this human affliction even as his exuberantly multilingual textual production constantly evokes it. Discussions of his multilingualism have tended to center on his Latin glosses to the English *Confessio Amantis*, with some critics regarding the Latin as stabilizing a dangerously slippery vernacular[57] and others arguing that its attempts at semantic control inevitably fail in ways Gower must have understood and possibly intended.[58] Comparatively little work, however, has been done on Gower's tri- as opposed to bilingual literary production or how this trilingualism works across specific manuscripts as discrete occurrences of codicological form.[59] I take up these key issues in chapter 4.

By rewriting, resituating, and alluding to texts from throughout Gower's career, the Trentham manuscript looks back to the reign of Richard II even as it addresses his successor/usurper (one text celebrating Henry even quotes extensively from a version of the *Vox Clamantis* praising Richard). It thus offers striking similarities with the Auchinleck manuscript, which likewise was written early in the reign of a new king whose deposed predecessor retains a powerful hold on the textual imagination of the compilation itself and the audience it assumes. Differences naturally exist: Trentham's allusions to Richard are veiled, while a number of Auchinleck's texts refer to Edward II

Multilingualism and Gower's Literary Practice," *Studies in Philology* 103 (2006): 1–25; Diane Watt, *Amoral Gower* (Minneapolis: University of Minnesota Press, 2003), 21–37, esp. 32–35; and Rita Copeland, *Rhetoric, Hermeneutics, and Translation in the Middle Ages* (Cambridge: Cambridge University Press, 1991), 213–20. As Machan puts it: "Sociolinguistically, language change and variation originated because of human pride and in this sense testify, like all moral failures, to our fallen condition" ("Medieval Multilingualism," 2).

57. This broadly is the conclusion of Derek Pearsall, "Gower's Latin in the *Confessio Amantis*," in Minnis, ed., *Latin and Vernacular*, 13–25.

58. Thus, e.g., Watt argues: "[Gower] must . . . have been aware that his own poetic discourse had become a hybrid. A mixing of 'high' and 'low,' prestige and vernacular languages, it was itself a cacophony, a confusion of voices, a veritable Tower of Babel" (*Amoral Gower*, 33). See also Siân Echard, "With Carmen's Help: Latin Authorities in the *Confessio Amantis*," *Studies in Philology* 45 (1998): 1–40.

59. One recent, valuable exception is Elizabeth Dutton, John Hines, and R. F. Yeager, eds., *John Gower, Trilingual Poet: Language, Translation, and Tradition* (Woodbridge: D. S. Brewer, 2010).

directly; and, whereas Trentham's celebration of Henry is frequent and explicit, Auchinleck makes only brief and glancing allusions to Edward III. Nevertheless, the parallel is one of a larger set of historical commonalities that lead this book's particular set of compilations to emerge with what Benjamin might call *constellational* clarity. In each case, we have one piece of a pairing (the Horn corpus and the *Canterbury Tales*) that dates from and responds to the last decade of a troubled monarch's reign; another (Auchinleck and the Trentham manuscript) dates from the first years of the deposed king's successor and looks back at those darker days with a mixture of nervousness and relief. The similarities between the two periods, noted as well by late fourteenth-century commentators,[60] will set in clearer relief the ways in which authors and compilers grappled textually with social and political conflicts.

Of the two historically contiguous pairings, Horn-Auchinleck has recently been shown to have striking points of overlap in terms of production practices, content, and audience,[61] and Ralph Hanna suggests that Horn's largely legal-civic corpus and the primarily literary texts of Auchinleck also share substantial thematic concerns: "a nexus that joins legal precedent, the historicist insistence upon temporally descending antique right, with a fictive mode of thought that has often

---

60. Turner (*Chaucerian Conflict*, 9) alludes to these comments as part of a broader discussion of Richard II's attempts to stop unfavorable gossip about him.

61. Similarities of production include the manuscripts' physical size and ambition, reflected in their vast number of texts; their *mise-en-page*, with double-column format boasting a comparable number of lines per column (thirty-nine and forty-two in Horn's two largest custumals, forty-four in Auchinleck); and their illuminating artists, who were part of the "Queen Mary Psalter Group" of illuminators that worked on upward of twenty-five, mostly prestige manuscripts in the first third of the fourteenth century. See further Hanna, *London Literature*, 74–97, esp. 80–82; and Lynda Dennison, "'Liber Horn,' 'Liber Custumarum,' and Other Manuscripts of the Queen Mary Psalter Workshops," in *Medieval Art, Architecture, and Archaeology in London* (Conference Transactions, no. 10), ed. Lindy Grant (London: British Archaeological Association, 1990), 118–34. Hanna points out that their artistic programs suggest still closer ties between the Horn corpus and Auchinleck: "Painting in Horn's books appears most prominently in illustrations of kings in attitudes of authority or judgment. . . . This is a presentation exactly analogous, so far as one can tell, to that of Auchinleck, where painting occurs at the heads of individual romances, depictions of heroes in action" (*London Literature*, 82).

proved troubling to more legally inclined scholars."[62] *Troubling* understates the furious indignation that *Mirror of Justices*, one of the principal texts I consider in chapter 1, inspired in its most distinguished commentator, the great legal historian F. W. Maitland. Yet the terms in which Maitland denigrates the work—it will be called "fancy," "romance," and the "art-work of the future," its author "a young man ambitious of literary fame"—suggest that he recognized the aesthetic allure of this supposedly legal text. Indeed, his outrage seems to stem as much from being faced with a work that refuses to adhere to a clear and consistent generic identity as from the frequent legal misstatements that he so fiercely documents. Both the Horn corpus and the Auchinleck manuscript thus offer sets of texts in which legal, historical, and literary modes overlap as a matter of both historical record and modern apprehension.

The audiences of Horn's corpus and Auchinleck were likewise comparable. I begin chapter 1 by considering Andrew Horn's will, which leaves a series of volumes to the London Guildhall. This bequest, to a place rather than a person, highlights the role of the Guildhall as the nerve center of mayoral and civic power; Horn could be certain that any citizen who might in future be charged, as he was, with the defense of London's prerogatives would have access to his texts. In its own way, then, his will is a convocational gesture akin to his reading of London's charter as narrated in the *Annales Paulini*: it imagines his assembled volumes (most of these themselves codicological assemblages of considerable size and ambition, as we will see) as equal to the task of helping his fellow citizens, physically assembled in the Guildhall, fend off royal and alien encroachment alike. Precisely this kind of goal seems to have been at the heart of an exercise organized by Mayor Richer de Refham in 1310 and narrated approvingly in the portion of the *Annales Londonienses* most likely written by Horn:

> Hic antiquas consuetudines et libertates in rotulis et libris camerae civitati fecit persecutari, et, congregatis sapientioribus, potentioribus, una cum aldermaniis, coram eis fecit legi et pupplicari.

62. Hanna, *London Literature*, 74.

He [de Refham] caused the ancient customs and liberties in the rolls and books of the chamber of the city to be thoroughly searched [*persecutari*], and, the wiser and more powerful men having been assembled, together with the aldermen, he had them read and made public in their presence.[63]

The passive construction of this sentence deemphasizes the mayor and puts the focus instead on a succession of ablatives: the *rotulis et libris* that are thoroughly searched and the City's good and great assembled by this exercise (*congregatis sapientioribus* . . .). The following *eis* thus gains a nice hint of ambiguity, for it recalls both the assembled *sapientioribus* etc. whose liberties are at issue and the *rotulis et libris* in which those liberties are contained. *Rotulis* and *sapientioribus* alike are *congregatis*, the mutual reinforcement that textual and social assemblages offer here made visible grammatically as well.

This example of a communally owned textual collection is instructive too for consideration of the Auchinleck manuscript, long thought to have been produced for a wealthy member of London's merchant elite.[64] Timothy Shonk and Thorlac Turville-Petre both imagine Auchinleck as destined for a household rather than an individual,[65] and I would go still further and hypothesize some sort of collective confraternal or civic ownership of the manuscript. The evidence of the London *puy*, a mercantile poetic society whose statutes were recorded by Horn, makes it clear that London's prominent citizens valued liter-

63. Stubbs, ed., *Annales*, 175 (my translation).

64. There has been near unanimity on this point since the publication of Laura Hibbard Loomis's influential "The Auchinleck Manuscript and a Possible London Bookshop of 1330–1340," *PMLA* 57 (1942): 595–627. Noting that secular books owned by the aristocracy tend overwhelmingly to be in French or Latin rather than the English that Auchinleck almost exclusively contains, Loomis imagined a commissioner from one of London's "large numbers of literate 'civil servants'" (ibid., 601), a class populated substantially by wealthy merchants like Andrew Horn and his associates. Although her theories of the manuscript's production have been largely discredited, her conclusions about its audience have been echoed in A. I. Doyle, "English Books in and out of Court from Edward III to Henry IV," in *English Court Culture in the Later Middle Ages*, ed. V. J. Scattergood and J. W. Sherborne (London: Duckworth, 1983), 163–82; Timothy Shonk, "A Study of the Auchinleck Manuscript," *Speculum* 60 (1985): 71–91; and Hanna, *London Literature*, 1–147 passim.

65. See Shonk, "A Study of the Auchinleck Manuscript," 90; and Thorlac Turville-Petre, *England the Nation: Language, Literature, and National Identity* (Oxford: Clarendon, 1996), 136.

ary consumption, while Cambridge, Magdalene College, MS Pepys 2498 is a comparable example of a large textual collection that seems likely to have been produced for a communal audience.[66] Despite containing many fewer leaves than Auchinleck, this manuscript of homiletic works squeezes in considerably more text, partly by avoiding the ample margins that characterize both Auchinleck and Horn's custumals, a "white space" that Ralph Hanna describes as aspiration "to aristocratic opulence—here a form of superfluous waste."[67] We have already seen that London's elite citizens fancied themselves barons entitled to a range of aristocratic privileges. Auchinleck's emphasis on narratives that posit imitation as a means of narrowing the distance between mercantile and aristocratic identity complements such aspirations and suggests an audience from among the City's most prosperous guilds, like the mercers prominently involved in supporting the London *puy*.[68]

Chaucer's own family biography illustrates how this literate class of wealthy merchants and civil servants evolved into the audience and social milieu that inform the *Canterbury Tales*. In the first half of the fourteenth century, a range of his ancestors were associated with three of the luxury trades—mercers, pepperers, and vintners—who dominated London's mercantile elite throughout the thirteenth century and into the fourteenth.[69] His father, John, a vintner, became deputy to the king's chief butler in 1347, overseeing shipments of wine from Bordeaux, and he remained prominent in London affairs until his death, probably around 1366. Geoffrey Chaucer, of course, served in a range

66. See Hanna, *London Literature*, 148–221. Hanna (ibid., 199–202) suggests that the manuscript may have been produced for one of the parish guilds that were founded in great numbers from the 1330s on.

67. Ibid., 153.

68. See Anne Sutton, *The Mercery of London: Trade, Goods, and People, 1130–1578* (Aldershot: Ashgate, 2005), 67–72.

69. Chaucer's ancestor Robert moved from Ipswich to London, where he apprenticed himself to a mercer and gained substantially from his will in 1302 (he may also have gained the name Chaucer from him). Robert married the widow of a pepperer, her son by a previous marriage was already a vintner, and on Robert's death she married his cousin Richard Chaucer, likewise a vintner. Their son John, Chaucer's father, also became a vintner. For these biographical details, I have followed Derek Pearsall, *The Life of Geoffrey Chaucer* (Oxford: Blackwell, 1992), 12–17.

of even more prominent royal and civic positions, as a high-ranking customs official, member of Parliament, and clerk of the king's works. Chaucer and his audience thus radiate outward from earlier forms of urban merchant culture whose textual interests and sophistication my first two chapters will document. Indeed, if Linne Mooney's conclusions about Chaucer's connections with Adam Pinkhurst (a regular employee of the Mercers' Company of London) are correct, then the latter's "mercantile affiliations" suggest that Chaucer was even more proximate than has been generally supposed to "the factional squabbles in London" that we see implied throughout the Horn corpus.[70]

Although Gower's texts were mediated by a comparable urban literary culture, their explicit audience, at least, was more likely than Chaucer's to be very highly placed figures like Archbishop Arundel, the recipient of a dedicated *Vox* manuscript,[71] Richard II, the supposed patron of the earliest recension of *Confessio Amantis*, and Henry IV, to whom (in his earlier guise as *comes Derbiae*) the *Confessio* was famously rededicated.[72] As I will argue in chapter 4, however, the veneer of obviousness that these moves convey belies the real complexity of Gower's relation with royal power. Trentham has long been assumed to have been either itself presented to Henry IV or else the plainer draft of a lost presentation copy; indeed, the showiness of its early texts' direct addresses to Henry, which praise the politically healing effects of his recent coronation, makes such conclusions understandable. Yet, while Gower is constantly implied as Trentham's architect, the codicological evidence is too fragmentary and ambiguous to establish him firmly as such. Similarly, the intention of the manuscript itself seems less securely celebratory and Henrician when we examine how its in-

---

70. Linne Mooney, "Chaucer's Scribe," *Speculum* 81 (2006): 97–138 (quotation 98).

71. This is All Souls College, Oxford MS 98, which in addition to the *Vox* includes a considerable number of shorter Latin poems and the *Traitié* that also appears in Trentham, where its codicological context gives it a very different overall effect. For a complete description of the manuscript and its contents, see John Gower, *The Complete Works of John Gower*, ed. G. C. Macaulay, 4 vols. (Oxford: Clarendon, 1899–1902), 4:lx–lxii.

72. R. F. Yeager proposes that we add Edward III or his close associates to this list as the likely audience of the bulk of *Mirour de l'Omme*. See "Gower's French Audience: The *Mirour de l'Omme*," *Chaucer Review* 41 (2006): 111–37.

dividual poems evoke both their own complex textual histories and Gower's authorial history, as well as how Trentham's broader codicological form presents a physical matrix of those multiply intersecting histories. From "Gower" and "Henry," then, we move to conceptions of authorship and audience considerably more complex.

Trentham's longest text, the unique copy of Gower's *Cinkante Balades*, also presents the manuscript's richest concatenation of form and history. Its dedication shifts back and forth between Latin and French, prose and verse, and amatory and political registers; its genre, French *forme fixe* lyric, recalls that Gower has represented himself giving up such *fols ditz d'amours* not once but twice, at the end of both *Mirour de l'Omme* and *Confessio Amantis*.[73] The *Balades'* centrality to Trentham and dedication to Henry, however, suggest that this amatory Continental verse form has not just a political register but also the potential for a socially unifying function: as Gower has gathered up these disparate *balades*, and as Trentham packages them and its other texts in an elaborately wrought codicological form, so too will Henry unite his hitherto fractious country. (The reality behind all these propositions will, as I have suggested, prove less straightforward.) In this, the *Balades* forms part of another key historical node that will recur throughout this study: London's fascination with literary and cultural models from the Franco-Flemish Low Countries.[74] This fascination

---

73. "Fols ditz d'amours" is Gower's characterization at *Mirour de l'Omme* line 27340, as part of a broader confession of a sinful youth (lines 27337–49). The *Confessio* of course is neither French nor *forme fixe*, but Gower's famous farewell to love in that poem follows his address to Venus of an epistle that consists of twelve rhyme-royal stanzas, a form that is markedly at odds with that of the rest of the poem but that dominates the *Cinkante Balades*; it is this lament, self-consciously poetic (he both "write[s]" and "endite[s]" the stanzas), that brings Venus to him and prompts both her rejection and his consequent farewell to love.

74. In her introduction to the excellent collection *England and the Low Countries in the Late Middle Ages* (ed. Caroline Barron and Nigel Saul [Bodmin: Sutton, 1995], 2), Caroline Barron characterizes *Low Countries* as a "convenient, but vague term used to describe, in the medieval period, a multitude of political units . . . in the low-lying areas stretching from the river Somme in the south-west to the Zuider Zee in the north-east. . . . At the heart of this area lay the county of Flanders . . . dominated by the great weaving towns of Ypres, Ghent and Bruges. To the north-east of Flanders lay the separate counties of Holland, Zeeland and Guelders, and to the east the duchy of Brabant . . . and the county of Hainault, and to the south-west Artois and Picardy." By *Franco-Flemish*, I mean to include Flanders, Hainault, Artois, and Picardy: the

dates back to the Horn corpus, which includes two sets of statutes for the London *puy*, a mercantile poetic society that flourished in cities like Arras, Lille, Douai, and Valenciennes. There, the *puy* was one of a host of civic *festes* that offered urban merchant elites a means of demonstrating their cultural savoir faire by taking part in a wide range of typically aristocratic activities.[75] Such festivals' narrowing of the distance between aristocratic and bourgeois identity, however partial and provisional, helps explain their appeal to the Londoners whose *puy* statutes Horn records; as we have seen, London's merchant elite eagerly asserted an aristocratic station that could complement or even advance its strong sense of political and economic entitlement. (Here, the imitation must also have been strongly adversarial: anything you interloping Continental merchants can do, we Londoners can do better.)

The London *puy* itself seems almost certain to have died out well before either Chaucer or Gower was writing,[76] but the Continental *puys* and their associated *festes* would have remained in such Ricardian poets' imaginative ambit because they were within London's immediate commercial and cultural context.[77] The joke that Sir Thopas was

---

territories described by Barron whose cultural inclinations were francophone even as their political allegiances in the long-running wars between England and France varied widely. While the vernacular in these locales likewise varied, the language of the region's rulers was French, and much of its aspirational merchant class cultivated the language too.

75. See the discussions in Juliet Vale, *Edward III and Chivlary: Chivalric Society and Its Context, 1270–1350* (Woodbridge: Boydell & Brewer, 1982); Evelyne van den Neste, *Tournois, joutes, pas d'armes dans les villes de la Flandre à la fin du Moyen Age* (Paris: École des Chartes, 1996); and Malcolm Vale, *The Princely Court: Medieval Courts and Culture in North-West Europe, 1280–1380* (Oxford: Oxford University Press, 2001).

76. On this point, see Anne F. Sutton, "Merchants, Music and Social Harmony: The London Puy and Its French and London Contexts, circa 1300," *London Journal* 17 (1992): 1–17; and Ardis Butterfield, "French Culture and the Ricardian Court," in *Essays on Ricardian Literature in Honor of J. A. Burrow*, ed. A. J. Minnis, Charlotte C. Morse, and Thorlac Turville-Petre (Oxford: Clarendon, 1997), 82–120.

77. This point is conclusively established in Vanessa Harding, "Cross-Channel Trade and Cultural Contacts: London and the Low Countries in the Later Fourteenth Century," in Barron and Saul, eds., *England and the Low Countries*, 153–68, which shows particularly nicely that "late-fourteenth century London was in constant contact with the trading community, language, native products, and everyday culture of the Low Countries" (ibid., 163). The connections are also literary: Jean Froissart composed poems that were crowned at a number of *puys*

born "in fer contree, / In Flaundres, al biyonde the see" (VII.718–19) is funny only if the Low Countries are in fact just around the corner. The *Tale of Sir Thopas* is of course English Geffrey's representation of a Flemish would-be knight, but, as I argue in chapter 3, Chaucer brings the relevance of the tale's multiple inadequacies (of Thopas's chivalric performance, within the tale; of Geffrey's literary performance, on the pilgrimage) back to an English and specifically London audience, most obviously via the poem's famous catalog of romances that populate the Auchinleck manuscript. Like the Squire, a practicing poet who has traveled "in Flaundres, in Artois and Picardye" (I.86) but whose tale is interrupted well before its conclusion, the *Tale of Sir Thopas* comes to England and fails. These failures are intimately connected to the short-circuiting of the London-based *Cook's Tale*, whose protagonist, Perkyn Revelour, unites a wide range of *Flaundrish* associations. Francophilic literary composition imported from the Continent, which is literally central to Trentham's imagination (however contingent) of a new political future, is within Chaucer's Canterbury polity a recipe for literary implosion and social animus.

As this wide-ranging discussion suggests, the four compilations of this study do not enable construction of a tidy literary history of fourteenth-century London (though they do empower vital revisions to other, too-tidy literary histories). Rather, these compilations' overlapping textual, cultural, and physical relations are more rhyzomic than linear, something akin to the book assemblage as described by Gilles Deleuze and Félix Guattari: "A book . . . is made of variously formed matters, and very different dates and speeds . . . [with] lines of articulation or segmentarity, strata and territories; but also lines of flight, movements of deterritorialization and destratification. Comparative

---

throughout the region before coming to England in the service of Edward's queen, Philippa, where he became almost as influential on English literary culture as he was on the Continent. Butterfield ("French Culture and the Ricardian Court," 85–88) has shown that his *Chroniques* in particular made him "more than merely a contemporary French counterpart to Chaucer, but an author whose last great work, notwithstanding its Frenchness, becomes as much of an English cultural icon as Chaucer's poetic *oeuvre*." See further the more recent Helen Cooper, "London and Southwark Poetic Companies: 'Si tost c'amis' and the *Canterbury Tales*," in Butterfield, ed., *Chaucer and the City*, 109–25.

rates of flow on these lines produce phenomena of relative slowness and viscosity, or, on the contrary, of acceleration and rupture. All this, lines and measurable speeds, constitutes an *assemblage*. A book is an assemblage of this kind."[78] This articulation of the book as an object always in motion, both temporally and in the interrelation of its assembled parts, is congruent with my understanding of how medieval compilations attain historical and aesthetic force and of how I have sought to assemble my analysis of the four particular compilations I treat here. Deleuze and Guattari's deconstructive turn also usefully reminds us that no assembled object, and especially no materially fragmented medieval manuscript, can fully sustain whatever unifying impulses might have inspired its construction. In the next, concluding section, I address some of the theoretical ramifications of this fact by analyzing particular instances of fragmentation in the four compilations of this study.

Fragment

The best efforts of civic-minded writers like Andrew Horn could not and cannot conceal the fact that, as Ralph Hanna puts it, "London always presents a *fractured* landscape, a locality irreconcilably *plural*, whatever the apparent glories of its legal status or the aggressiveness of its claims against outsiders."[79] In other words, London was desperate to present itself as tranquil and united precisely because it was typically just the opposite, its often violent displays of faction giving the Crown pretexts for seizing control of civic government. Marion Turner has recently addressed the comparable social fragmentation evoked by the *Canterbury Tales*, usefully complicating a critical tradition that has focused largely on the congenial, unifying aspects of the pilgrims' endeavors.[80] We have seen a similar kind of social dissolution figured textually within Auchinleck's "Sayings of the Four Philoso-

---

78. Gilles Deleuze and Félix Guattari, *A Thousand Plateaus: Capitalism and Schizophrenia*, trans. Brian Massumi (Minneapolis: University of Minnesota Press, 1987), 3–4.

79. Hanna, *London Literature*, 57 (emphasis added).

80. See Turner, *Chaucerian Conflict*, passim.

phers," whose macaronic prologue might be read as an effort either to rejoin disparate pieces of human experience or to evoke Babelian *divisioun*—shades of the ambiguity that critics have likewise seen in Gower's multilingual practice. Debbie Cannon, commenting on the grandest of Horn's custumals, writes that "the city of London is a *fragmented* but consistent presence in the *Liber regum*."[81] This fragmentation is implied by the custumal's vast range of texts, which detail the equivalently daunting array of disparate persons and interests at work in London, unintentionally evoking the difficulty of convening these social f(r)actions into a stable and coherent whole.[82]

The question then becomes how to link these metaphoric forms of fragmentation within each compilation's medieval temporality to its contemporary status as a literally fragmentary object: damaged, incomplete, or both in ways that are impossible to have been masterminded by a single, all-intending author. Joining these notions of fragmentation across temporal distances might liberate these texts and objects from a universal, totalizing historicity, the reductive form of historicism that we considered earlier. Yet such links are difficult to establish conclusively. Howell D. Chickering, commenting on the kinds of criticism to which the Old English *Judith* has recently been subject, acknowledges that, "if one takes the text as a fragment, which it certainly is, one can hypothesize about the lost whole, or can treat its fragmentation and the fragmentation of Holofernes as metaphorically interchangeable," but he goes on to point out that such critical moves allow "interpretive possibilities [to] flower like an exotic jungle."[83] Chickering's curiously

81. Debbie Cannon, "London Pride: Citizenship and the Fourteenth-Century Custumals of the City of London," in *Learning and Literacy in Medieval England and Abroad*, ed. Sarah Rees Jones (Turnhout: Brepols, 2003), 179–98 (quotation 189; emphasis added).

82. A very partial list includes statutes governing the behavior of merchants from Lorraine, Amiens, Cologne, and Provence, among many other places; the ordinances of lorimers, joiners, saddlers, woad dealers, poulterers, and bakers, to name just a few; and a wide range of even more disparate kinds of texts (royal decrees, records of disputes between mayors and sheriffs, centuries-old laws) that in turn call attention to other forms of conflict, potential and actual, across the City.

83. Howell D. Chickering, "Poetic Exuberance in *Judith*," *Studies in Philology* 106 (2009): 119–36 (quotation 119–20). Maura Nolan has recently argued along comparable lines: "In order to genuinely grasp the historicity of a medieval poem we must first identify its excesses,

ambivalent simile rightly suggests that the problem lies in knowing how vigorously to prune: too little, and we risk being swallowed up in a jungle of undersubstantiated readings that obscure or distort rather than clarify or delight; too much, and we are left with a desert of data and dry contextualizations that risk denying the spirit of interpretive play that brought so many of us to literary study in the first place.[84] In concluding this introduction, I discuss a few concrete instances of literal fragmentariness in my compilations that raise questions of how, and how far, to push the boundaries of interpretation. Without becoming "metaphorically interchangeable" with other forms of fragmentation, as Chickering puts it, they suggest how such details of codicological form, accidentally produced or otherwise, can productively obtrude on our literary-critical consciousness, profitably frustrate our ability to construct overly neat literary-historical narratives, and help us see the outlines of other, less limiting histories.

The fragments of the *Canterbury Tales* are of course codicologically attested tale groupings. A number of tales, however, are themselves fragments in the sense of being incomplete, usually interrupted

---

the ways in which it solicits meanings that seem, at first glance, to be unauthorized or illicit, and to exceed the brief of the manuscript or the words on the page. Those excesses have to be evaluated, of course, and some we must reject as fanciful, or fundamentally alien to the Middle Ages, or the poet; some we must admit are mere castles in the air built by our own modern preoccupations. Others, however, exist in the spaces between past authority and present desire, and these meanings are perhaps the most significant, and the best indices to the power of the aesthetic within history and culture" ("Lydgate's Worst Poem," in *Lydgate Matters: Poetry and Material Culture in the Fifteenth Century*, ed. Lisa H. Cooper and Andrea Denny-Brown [New York: Palgrave Macmillan, 2007], 71–87 [quotation 82]). Although the tone with which they are presented differs, Chickering's overlush jungle and Nolan's "excesses" both suggest the need for an interpretive freedom that somehow avoids becoming license.

84. This spirit is eloquently on display in an essay by Samuel Otter on *Moby-Dick* that emphasizes the role of history in helping us see the excess that, like Maura Nolan, he identifies as a key component of the literary. He insists that we remain "alert to the humor, the *excess*, and the complexities of both history and text" and later, discussing Ishmael's parenthetical aside from which he draws his title, argues that the parentheses themselves "point to the relationships between the words inside and outside of their borders and on and off the page," again drawing attention to "varieties of literary *excess*, in whose pursuit I have sought to articulate a literary historicism." By interpreting the visual shape of the parentheses themselves, moreover, he demonstrates that codicological form can have aesthetic resonance even in postmedieval literature. See "An Aesthetic in All Things," *Representations* 104 (2008): 116–25 (quotations 121–23; emphasis added).

by another pilgrim, as with the *Squire's Tale* and *Tale of Sir Thopas*, which I take up in chapter 3. The *Cook's Tale* is unique in that it provides no such narrative context for its abrupt end after just over fifty lines.[85] What it does have is a note in the Hengwrt manuscript by the scribe now identified as Adam Pinkhurst: "Of this Cokes tale maked Chaucer na moore." This tantalizing assertion is an addition to the tale, an excrescence that draws attention to the fragmentary nature of what has come before. In so doing, it presents an interpretive crux both codicological and literary. The codicological aspects of the problem have been persuasively analyzed by Stephen Partridge and Simon Horobin.[86] Even if (as they and I believe) Chaucer left the *Cook's Tale* in its current, very fragmentary form, however, the note in Hengwrt can be read in at least two different ways: as a neutral admission that Pinkhurst has been unable to find any more of the tale to copy and that, as far as Hengwrt is concerned, there is "na moore" of it (this is what Horobin proposes);[87] or, in a more active sense, as an assertion that the tale's incompleteness is its point and substance, that the "na moore" it offers, as much as the narrative that exists, is in fact what Chaucer "maked."[88] We are thus presented with a codicological detail whose attempts to shut down further reading—there's no more,

85. Many scribes, however, did so by substituting the non-Chaucerian *Gamelyn*. As Stephen Partridge writes in his detailed and readable account: "[There is no] persuasive evidence that *Gamelyn* has any connection with Chaucer. . . . *Gamelyn* does not appear in most of the manuscripts which are generally considered most reliable, such as Hengwrt, Ellesmere, Gg.4.27, Dd.4.24, and Egerton 2726. Thus it appears that an early scribe or 'editor' inserted *Gamelyn*, largely unmodified, to repair a perceived deficiency in a copy of the *Tales* which turned out to be the archetype of a large number of the surviving codices" ("Minding the Gaps: Interpreting the Manuscript Evidence of the *Cook's Tale* and the *Squire's Tale*," in *The English Medieval Book: Studies in Memory of Jeremy Griffiths*, ed. A. S. G. Edwards, Vincent Gillespie, and Ralph Hanna [London: British Library, 2000], 51–85 [quotation 55]).

86. In addition to Partridge's "Minding the Gaps," see Simon Horobin's more recent examination of the line in the context of Mooney's identification in "Chaucer's Scribe" of Pinkhurst as Hengwrt's scribe and her consequent proposition that Pinkhurst likely had inside knowledge as to Chaucer's desired arrangement of the *Tales*: "Adam Pinkhurst, Geoffrey Chaucer, and the Hengwrt Manuscript of the *Canterbury Tales*," *Chaucer Review* 44 (2010): 351–67. The note at the end of the Hengwrt *Cook's Tale* comes up at ibid., 358–60.

87. Horobin, "Adam Pinkhurst," 359.

88. I will argue for a version of this conclusion in chapter 3. Jim Casey alludes to comparably interpretive readings of the *Cook's Tale*'s abrupt cessation (but takes no position of his

so stop looking—actually encourage it, not unlike the cop shooing people away with a "show's over folks, nothing to see here." No comment more effectively creates onlookers. The host of other, broader questions that this episode raises about Chaucer's inherently shifting and fragmentary magnum opus (e.g., should this note inform interpretations of the *Cook's Tale* generally, as opposed to just its Hengwrt incarnation?) ought to make us skeptical of any literary history that would make Chaucer either its stable, universalizing center or its inevitable, teleological conclusion.

The Horn corpus has been subjected to massive codicological intervention, which chapter 1 will explore in depth. Here, I highlight just one moment: the addition of one quire to the much larger *Liber regum*, sometime after the custumal's initial construction around 1321 but before a list of its contents was drawn up during the fifteenth century since the quire's texts were included in that list. All comment of which I am aware treats this quire as added by Horn himself, a fact that invites interpretive speculation: was the quire added later because it was a mere afterthought or because its importance was such that its inadvertent omission from the final product had at all costs to be rectified? Either way, its texts gain added prominence today, for the existence of this "curious section containing Henry of Huntingdon's description of Britain, Fitz Stephen's description of London, and the extracts from the *Trésor*" is inserted into Jeremy Catto's description of *Liber regum* just as the quire itself was inserted into the physical object—indeed, Catto describes its contents with far greater specificity than he does the rest of the massive volume.[89] This prominence then gets picked up and reinforced by Ralph Hanna, who in the next substantial critical discussion of Horn's custumals devotes a full paragraph to the contents of this quire and several pages to the relevance of its texts.[90] My point is not that this notice is unwarranted or these analyses illegitimate; on

---

own) in "Unfinished Business: The Termination of Chaucer's *Cook's Tale*," *Chaucer Review* 41 (2006): 185–96.

89. Jeremy Catto, "Andrew Horn: Law and History in Fourteenth-Century England," in *The Writing of History in the Middle Ages: Essays Presented to Richard William Southern*, ed. R. H. C. Davis and J. M. Wallace-Hadrill (Oxford: Clarendon, 1981), 367–91 (quotation 377).

90. Hanna, *London Literature*, 87–88, 96.

the contrary, I also devote considerable attention to the quire's contents in chapter 1. My point is rather that a codicological occurrence whose impetus we cannot securely know (how planned? how random?) has shaped the textual significance of this vast, unwieldy compilation in ways that highlight the interpenetration of codicological form and history. *When* the quire was added becomes part of the contemporary form of *Liber regum* quite as much as *that* it was added, and later critical discussions (this one included) contribute to its growing prominence. At the same time, the quire's disparate contents remind us that the custumal into which it was inserted is also an assemblage of vastly numerous small textual pieces that do not present a coherent whole—a fact that its medieval title, *Liber legum antiquorum regum*, seems to seek with grandiloquence to paper over.

Pinkhurst's note and the Latini quire are codicological additions, whether textual as in Hengwrt or physical as in *Liber regum*. They are fragmentary bits that draw attention (explicitly, with the *Cook's Tale*; implicitly, with *Liber regum*) to the comparably fragmentary nature of what surrounds them. My next two examples are of absences: literal, physical subtractions from the original codicological form that constitute a more obvious kind of fragmentation but one less securely open to interpretation since arguments from absence are inherently difficult to substantiate. Yet we will see that setting aside our lack of knowledge as to the cause of such absence can yield surprising interpretive payoffs.

Take, for example, the Auchinleck manuscript's loss of what were probably its first five texts, such that *The Legend of Pope Gregory*, labeled the sixth by the contemporary numerator, now begins the surviving manuscript. The *Legend* cannot have had in the original Auchinleck this same structural prominence, but the new form that historical accident has bequeathed the manuscript has likewise given new prominence to already extant textual connections: in this case, between the now manuscript-initial *Legend of Pope Gregory* and the romance *Sir Degaré*, which appears later. Despite their purportedly different modes (homiletic and romance, respectively, distinctions that we will discover to be far from absolute), they share almost exactly the same plot for the first two-thirds of their narratives. When they do diverge, it is because of a seemingly insignificant detail, and even there they echo one another. The role of this random, inexplicable chance in both poems' denouements (does a mother happen to recognize that the cloth her son is now wearing is the same one she left with him as a foundling?) parallels within the original temporality of the manuscript the comparably random chance that has, by shaving off Auchinleck's first five texts, led these two poems' thematic connections thus to emerge with particular clarity. The significance of this coincidence resists easy characterization: the textual echoes that it highlights are real and meaningful, and the uncanniness of the analogy that it creates has a kind of aesthetic force in itself, so to say that the coincidence is random, while doubtless literally true, seems nevertheless not to capture its full meaning.

The Trentham manuscript is my most nearly complete compilation, but it too has been physically damaged in two crucial places. The first is the exuberant, oval-shaped tear through the middle of folio 12 at the beginning of the *Cinkante Balades*, which has seriously compromised one of the two dedicatory balades, the incipit of the sequence proper, and the first poem of that sequence. That textual opening may well have contained a miniature, which would offer a perfectly logical explanation for the mutilation (a similar motivation appears to underlie many of Auchinleck's losses). Whatever the motive, however, the loss of these lines has obscured the ways in which Trentham's recipient and intent were framed: the incipit now reads, "Ci apres sont escrites en françois Cinkante balades, quelles . . . *d* fait pour les . . . *ment* desporter." The questions that these lacunae create for modern readers become still more pointed when we reach the second damaged element of the manuscript: the loss of an entire folio between the surviving folios 33 and 34. This missing page also contained the beginning of a text, here the *Traitié*, so miniature thieves may explain this loss as well. But we have also been robbed of any initiating interpretive context that Trentham might have provided as to what such a set of cautionary poems about misbehaving rulers might be doing in a manuscript that addresses Henry IV, a king who by many lights had substantially misbehaved his way to the throne. I do not interpret these absences as metaphoric *indicators* of ambivalence on the part of Gower or Trentham (it is unclear just who is in charge and where) concerning the Lancastrian accession. Whatever historical accidents produced these aspects of the manuscript's contemporary codicological form, however, they both parallel and help lead to the broader textual and historical arguments that I present in chapter 4 concerning the ambiguity of Trentham's allegiance to its supposed recipient. In that sense, these absences are paradoxically integral to how Trentham as a (fragmentary) whole creates meaning.

These vignettes have explored a range of codicological forms, from scribal notes and quire construction within manuscripts to those manuscripts' manipulation and defacement by later hands. The following chapters adopt a similarly broad understanding of what codicological form can be and mean, but they focus particularly on the sequence of texts within manuscripts, both because this aspect of codicological form foregrounds the intersection of textual with physical concerns and because it was the questions that such sequences pose (is an evocative textual juxtaposition planned or random, can we tell, and how should that matter?) that first inspired this project. Both the vignettes that I have just offered and the more sustained arguments of the following chapters, however, attempt to grapple with the kinds of meaning that may inhere in or be illumined by seemingly unrelated, random, or inconsequential formal details.

One powerful spur to this effort has been the provocative recent injunction by Christopher Cannon that we read for form even, and especially, when faced with objects that seem to resist such ministrations: "Middle English texts are more likely than most to *have* a form only in situations . . . where we are willing to insist that every aspect of every 'line' *must* relate to every other such aspect, and that, whatever the obfuscating complexities, all such details can be brought together as the parts of a shape that discloses an originating, if complex, thought."[91] Cannon is discussing texts, not manuscripts, and, having

91. Christopher Cannon, "Form," in *Middle English* (Oxford Twenty-First Century Approaches to Literature), ed. Paul Strohm (Oxford: Oxford University Press, 2007), 175–90 (quotation 184). Cannon writes further: "The forms of Middle English writing were almost never progressive in this careful way [i.e., through "a certain formal logic . . . pressed upon any observer by means of the careful and precise articulation of each and every formal level"], and, even though they were equally rich, they tended toward the opposite of such transparency,

returned to my earlier words-in-texts/texts-in-manuscripts analogy, I would emphasize once more that I do not regard manuscripts' various textual dispositions and codicological attributes as inherently or necessarily literary. With old distinctions between *literary* and *nonliterary* texts now largely and productively effaced, however, there seems little reason to insist on the comparably rigid categories *text* and *manuscript* when determining what can profitably receive literary analysis. That is, if even alchemical lists and medieval recipes for ointments and culinary dishes can yield a "poetics of practicality," as Lisa H. Cooper compellingly suggests,[92] then it seems comparably legitimate to read the intended and unintended shapes of medieval manuscripts in terms of their literary and aesthetic potential.

In this context, the comments of Jonathan Loesberg on Marcel Duchamp's *Fountain*, likewise a physical art object, offer suggestive echoes of Cannon's earlier words on the interpretability of Middle English texts:

> Its claim [that of symbolic embodiment], whether such a thing is possible or not, is that the meaning occurs entirely, and without remainder, in the surface display, the body that does the embodying. Thus one may explicate the meaning of a work only by recounting *all* of its features. This is its own kind of formalism, I think, but it differs from what I am calling experiential formalism in that this latter attends only to those aspects of appearance that have aesthetically pleasing effect. Experiential formalism claims that these pleasing features are the only aesthetic features of an artwork. But Duchamp's *Fountain* counters that claim.

Loesberg himself concedes the possibility that "no object can be such a perfect embodiment,"[93] but the similarity between these lines and

---

usually employing governing logics so unusual that they have remained virtually invisible to critical analysis, often appearing to such analysis in the guise of their opposite, the very absence of structure" (ibid., 184).

92. See Lisa H. Cooper, "The Poetics of Practicality," in Strohm, ed., *Middle English*, 491–505. Cooper limits herself to texts "whose explicit goal is to assist their readers to *make* something in the world beyond the page (a book, a culinary dish, an ointment, an object)," asking whether they "might be said to have a poetics and, if so, in what that poetics might be said to consist" (ibid., 492).

93. Jonathan Loesberg, *A Return to Aesthetics: Autonomy, Indifference, and Postmodernism* (Stanford, CA: Stanford University Press, 2005), 92.

Cannon's above is suggestive all the same. And, if Duchamp's *Fountain*—a signed, upside-down urinal presented as art that has subsequently disappeared and now exists only in photographs and as a concept—seems initially of doubtful relevance to medieval English literature or codicology, consider how frequently medievalists must grapple with productions, like *Fountain*, that are fragmentary or lost and whose aesthetic bona fides have been challenged or dismissed.

We are now in a position better to understand how my concepts of fragment and assemblage relate to the idea of compilation with which I began. The complexity of medieval compilations' past histories is made visible by the fragmentariness of their contemporary forms, both of which (the assembled form and the fragments within it) are variously authorial and accidental, intended and serendipitous. Those lacunae then become spaces for current and future interpretive activity since their "true" cause is often as unknowable as the "true," originary form that their existence has altered. A "fragment" is thus an intentional incompleteness (like the *Cook's Tale?*), an accidentally or mechanically produced absence (like the *Cook's Tale?*), and that which, by reinforcing our frequent inability to be certain which of these we are beholding (like the *Cook's Tale*), generates the kind of critical engagement that keeps such objects lively and vital. Interpreting compilations thus involves a temporal paradox: in order to discuss such forms at all, we must isolate them at a moment in time, but their form at every moment includes their multiple retrospective and prospective histories. This dizzying array of temporal vectors, paralleled by the host of other contrasts and oppositions we have considered, complicates efforts to assemble anything meaningful out of fragments like those I have gathered together in this study.

As Benjamin well knew, however, such fragments are precisely the materials out of which we must construct an understanding of the past.[94] "It is important," he writes, "to differentiate the construction

---

94. Beatrice Hanssen has pointed out that, for Benjamin, the fragment is itself "the figure that explodes the continuity of universalizing conceptions of history" (*Walter Benjamin's Other History: Of Stones, Animals, Human Beings, and Angels* [Berkeley and Los Angeles: University of California Press, 1998], 66).

of a historical state of affairs from what one customarily calls its 're-construction.' The 'reconstruction' in empathy is one-dimensional. 'Construction' presupposes 'destruction.'"[95] Rather than attempting to re-create the organic unity of a fragment's originary state—and from there the as-it-really-was of its creation—construction here involves assembling a vision at once contemporary and temporally distant. The destruction that Benjamin cites as a precondition to such construction enables new forms of meaning and interpretation to emerge, as we saw in the brief analyses of codicological form above. The construction that follows on this creative destruction thus cannot claim for itself absolute truth value; other historical visions could be assembled out of other or, indeed, the same constellations of objects from the past.

This fact is vital for those of us who seek a wider range of literary histories for medieval England, broadly defined, than the one that dominated for so long: of the triumph of English over French and Latin (to say nothing of Welsh and Irish and others); of named authors over anonymous scribes and makers; of the Ricardian period over the supposedly "dull" fifteenth century and implicitly primitive "Early Middle English"; and especially of the genial, ironic, and relatable Chaucer over all others. Chaucer's poetry is an equal participant in and neither the end point nor the vital center of the literary history that this book explores. Chaucer joins the obscure (Horn), the anonymous (Auchinleck's compilers and poets), and the denigrated (as Gower almost universally was until quite recently) as one but only one member of this constellation. Such a constellation demonstrates that making manuscripts central to the literary histories we assemble need not constitute a futile "mourn[ing] for the alienated physical labor of the medieval scribal craft, the scribe's writing hand," as Kathleen Biddick asserts.[96] On the contrary, taking seriously the current, fragmen-

---

95. Benjamin, *The Arcades Project*, 470 (N7,6).

96. Kathleen Biddick, *The Shock of Medievalism* (Durham, NC: Duke University Press, 1998), 43. For a powerful response to this critique, see Andrew Taylor, *Textual Situations: Three Medieval Manuscripts and Their Readers* (Philadelphia: University of Pennsylvania Press, 2002), 197–208.

tary states of medieval manuscripts offers one way of disrupting the linear historicism that would ignore their lost scribes and unknown makers.

By *assemblage*, then, I designate not just my focus in the previous section, that is, the historically documentable efforts of medieval scribes and authors to create complex textual groupings that press on comparably difficult questions of social cohesion. I also mean something akin to construction in the Benjaminian terms I have outlined: later and contemporary attempts, my own included, to construct out of the precise forms of such assemblages (in their current, fragmentary states) an understanding of the multiple pasts that created them. The more specific historical nodes articulated by my assembled group of objects (links and tensions between Crown and City; the appeal and limitation of francophone and aristocratic imitation to London's merchant elite; theories of the relation between law and kingship) emerge both through their textual contents and through the codicological forms that contain and create them. My interest in form thus has both historical and theoretical facets. I explore the historical evidence of how and why manuscripts like Auchinleck or Trentham were physically formed and what their construction suggests about how London's textual culture participated in wider social, political, and economic worlds. In so doing, I necessarily explore as well the interpretive benefits and challenges, the pleasures and dangers, that attend any reader's efforts to perceive in such objects a conceptual, interpretive, or argumentative form that either complements or complicates that physical shape. Both modes of forming medieval compilations, the historical-physical and the literary-conceptual, are necessary in order to understand, not just the what of medieval London's literary culture, but also how and why it matters, then and now. It is thus a temporally fragmented, radically reassembled audience of modern and medieval readers who must join with the authors and scribes of the Middle Ages to give form, in both senses and most fully, to the compilations to come.

Chapter One

CIVIC COUNTERFACTUALISM
AND THE ASSEMBLAGE OF LONDON

The Corpus of Andrew Horn

The broad argument of this chapter will be that, despite their generally utilitarian appearance, both the codicological form and the textual
contents of the manuscripts superintended by Andrew Horn partici-
pate in and help create an urban, mercantile reading culture in which
compilational interpretation formed one crucial facet of a broader
textual competence necessary to protect London's civic liberties from
abrogation. Despite the fine scholarship that aspects of these manuscripts have recently received, the corpus as a whole remains relatively
unfamiliar, and the manuscripts' codicological situation moreover is
dauntingly complex.[1] I will therefore give a brief summary of both,
along the way flagging texts and issues that I take up later, before sum-
marizing more thoroughly the particular arguments that the chapter
advances.

---

1. A relative flurry of scholarly activity in the past twenty years, following the virtual
silence of the preceding decades, is most encouraging. This work includes Hanna, *London
Literature*, esp. chaps. 2 (which deals centrally with Horn) and 3 (which links legally based
textual productions like Horn's to romance-centered ones like the Auchinleck manuscript and
Bodleian Library, Laud 622); Cannon, "London Pride"; David J. Seipp, "*The Mirror of Justices*,"
in *Learning the Law: Teaching and the Transmission of Law in England, 1150–1900*, ed. Jonathan A.
Bush and Alain Wijffels (London: Hambledon, 1999), 85–112; Sutton, "Merchants, Music and
Social Harmony"; and Dennison, "'Liber Horn,' 'Liber Custumarum.'" These works complement the older but still essential Catto, "Andrew Horn"; and Neil Ker, "Liber Custumarum,
and Other Manuscripts Formerly at the Guildhall" (1954), reprinted in *Books, Collectors, and
Libraries: Studies in the Medieval Heritage*, ed. Andrew G. Watson (London: Hambledon, 1985),
135–42.

The 1328 will of Andrew Horn includes this bequest:

Item lego camere Gildaule London[ie] unum magnum librum de gestis anglorum in quo continentur multa ultilia, et unum alium librum de veteribus [word omitted] anglorum cum libro vocato Bretoun et cum libro vocato speculum Justic,' [sic] et alium librum compositum per Henricum de Huntingdon[ia]. Item alium librum de statutis Anglorum cum multis libertatibus et aliis tangentibus civitatem.

Item: I leave to the London Guildhall one great book containing the ancient deeds of the English in which are contained many useful things, and one other book concerning the ancient English [laws] with a book called Bretoun and with the book called the Mirror of Justices, and another book composed by Henry of Huntingdon. Also another book concerning the statutes of the English with many liberties and other matters pertaining to the city.[2]

The first of these books is the most complex, and I will consider it last. Concerning the rest, scholarly consensus is that the volume by Henry of Huntingdon has been lost and that the last book named, "concerning the statutes of the English," refers to the *Liber Horn* still held in the Corporation of London Record Office; it is a comprehensive collection of the statutes of Henry III and Edward I together with some thirteenth-century legal treatises.[3] The second book Horn describes as a collection that includes within it (hence the repeated *cum libro* formulation) two other self-contained works, "Bretoun" and "speculum Justic." These titles indicate that the original volume was subsequently separated into the two manuscripts now shelved as Cambridge, Corpus Christi College MSS 70 and 258. These contain the so-called London Collection, a version of the legal text *Quadripartitus* that owes its sobriquet to interpolations that glorify the City and its various civic liberties;[4] *Britton* ("Bretoun"), a well-attested redaction of some of the

2. Cited in Catto, "Andrew Horn," 370–71 (my translation). We will see that context justifies reading *legibus* for the missing word.

3. *Liber Horn*, Custumal 2. For further details, see Ker, "Liber Custumarum," 137–39; Catto, "Andrew Horn," 371–72; and Cannon, "London Pride," 183–85.

4. The London Collection was edited by Felix Liebermann as *Über die Leges Anglorum saeculo XIII ineunte Londoniis collectae* (Halle, 1894). See also Felix Liebermann, "A Contemporary

more important laws of the first half of Edward I's reign;[5] and *Mirror of Justices* ("speculum Justic"), an idiosyncratic legal treatise that now survives only in this copy.[6] The strangeness of *Mirror*, and of its juxtaposition with the far more conventional *Britton*, will form the first argumentative node of this chapter.

The first of the books in Horn's will, the only one that he calls "great," probably refers to one of the two massive custumals that he compiled over the course of his tenure as City chamberlain, *Liber custumarum* and *Liber legum antiquorum regum*.[7] The good news is that these two monumental volumes have mostly survived, the bad that they have done so in singularly confusing fashion. Jeremy Catto's narration is tartly succinct: "The two custumals fell into the hands of Sir Robert Cotton, who divided them into more than twenty different fragments, reassembled them into three piles, returned one to the Guildhall (the modern *Liber Custumarum*), kept another (British Library MS Cotton Claudius D.ii), and gave the third to Sir Francis

---

Manuscript of the 'Leges Anglorum Londoniis collectae,'" *English Historical Review* 28 (1913): 732–45. *Quadripartitus* itself is a vexatiously complicated production that consists basically of two parts (only half of the four implied by its title were ever produced): first, a translation into Latin of Anglo-Saxon laws that constituted a main medieval source for English laws from the Anglo-Saxon kings through the reign of Henry I and, second, a continuation of legal material into the reign of Henry. Broadly and simplistically speaking, the first part is historically accurate, the second full of mythohistorical interpolations, though we will discover this binary to be substantially unhelpful for actually interpreting Horn's texts. On *Quadripartitus*, see Patrick Wormald, "*Quadripartitus*," in *Law and Government in Medieval England and Normandy: Essays in Honor of Sir James Holt*, ed. George Garnett and John Hudson (Cambridge: Cambridge University Press, 1994), 111–72. (Wormald's essay includes an appendix by Richard Sharpe on the *Quadripartitus*'s prefaces.) The London Collection appears to have been written by a Londoner working during the reign of King John; he included a great many more historical interpolations.

5. *Britton*, ed. and trans. Francis Morgan Nichols (Oxford: Clarendon, 1865; reprint, Holmes Beach, FL: W. W. Gaunt, 1983).

6. *The Mirror of Justices*, ed. William Joseph Whittaker, with an introduction by F. W. Maitland (London: Selden Society, 1895). Subsequent citations are given parenthetically in the text.

7. Catto considers the evidence in detail and reaches "the tentative conclusion . . . that the original *LLAR* [*Liber legum antiquorum regum*], a large volume incorporating an English chronicle, a collection of ancient laws, and charters, statutes, and London ordinances of current application, is likely to have been the volume bequeathed by Andrew Horn" ("Andrew Horn," 378).

Tate (Oriel College, Oxford MS 46)."[8] Catto's reference to "the modern *Liber Custumarum*" indicates a feature of contemporary nomen-
clature that frustratingly compounds this already complex situation:
the volume called *Liber custumarum* in the Middle Ages corresponds
only in part and nonsequentially with the volume now housed at the
Guildhall under that title (the first of the "three piles" cited by Catto),
which was pieced together from fragments of both medieval custumals. Fortunately, fifteenth-century tables of contents survive for both
custumals, which allowed Neil Ker to summarize the codicological
situation as follows (note that his "MS C" represents the contents of
the original, medieval *Liber custumarum* and his "MS D" that of the
original *Liber regum*; by "Liber Custumarum" in the following descriptions he designates the current, modern volume so named):

> MS C. Guildhall, Liber Custumarum fo[l]s. 103–172, 187–284 + Oriel
> Coll., Ox 46 fo[l]s. 1–108 + Brit. Mus., Cotton Claudius D.ii fo[l]s.
> 116–123.

> MS D. Guildhall, Liber Custumarum fo[l]s. ii, 1–102, 173–186 + Claudius
> D.ii fo[l]s. 30–40, 42–115, 124–135, 266–277 + Oriel Coll. 46 fo[l]s.
> 109–211.[9]

Hereafter, my use of the terms *Liber custumarum* and *Liber regum* refers
to their medieval forms as orchestrated by Horn and pieced together
above. The second argumentative node of this chapter will concern a
few texts that are unique to *Liber regum*. Like *Mirror of Justices*, they are
thematically consonant with what surrounds them, but they create
juxtapositions that both imply and encourage more complex modes
of reading than the predominantly practical and archival nature of
Liber regum suggests.

    In addition to these surviving texts, Horn appears to have written
portions of the *Annales Londonienses* originally found in Cotton Otho

---

8. Ibid., 376.
9. Ker, "Liber Custumarum," 135. For the fifteenth-century lists, see *Liber custumarum*,
ed. Henry Thomas Riley, vols. 2–3 of *Munimenta Gildhallae Londoniensis: Liber albus, Liber custumarum, et Liber Horn*, Rolls Series, vol. 12 (London: Longmans, 1859–62), 2:488–90 (for Ker's
MS C); and Ker, "Liber Custumarum," 140–42 (for Ker's MS D).

B.iii, whose depiction of Mayor Richer de Refham's exercise in collective civic research I considered in the introduction.[10] This manuscript having been mostly destroyed in a fire, the annals survive only in an eighteenth-century transcript. They begin acephalously with the year 1194 and proceed until 1293, relying largely on Matthew Paris's *Flores Historiarum*, as well as other chronicles not now identifiable, but freely excerpting and adding material that might particularly interest a London audience.[11] The annals from 1293 to 1301 are lost, and it is for the portion of the work from their resumption in 1301 to their conclusion in 1316 that Horn has been posited as author.[12] The most detailed of these cover the years 1307–12, from the coronation of Edward II to his dramatic appeal to Londoners following the murder of Piers Gaveston. Likewise now apparently lost is whatever was designated as "Summa Legum per Andream Horne" in the list of manuscripts held by Westminster Abbey included in Bernard's *Catalogi Manuscriptorum Angliae et Hiberniae*.[13]

10. Stubbs, ed., *Annales*, 1–282. See also Antonia Grandsen, *Historical Writing in England, c. 1307 to the Early Sixteenth Century* (Ithaca, NY: Cornell University Press, 1982), 3, 23–25. Catto ("Andrew Horn," 377) speculates, and Cannon ("London Pride," 187) agrees, that *Liber regum* may originally have contained the *Annales Londonienses*, as well (i.e., before the fifteenth-century table of contents was assembled). It is partly on this basis that Catto believes the first book mentioned in Horn's will to refer to *Liber regum*.

11. Grandsen speculates on the basis of "the numerous references to St. Paul's . . . that the author also used a chronicle compiled in the cathedral" (*Historical Writing in England*, 23–24).

12. William Stubbs was the first to argue for Horn's authorship, citing three main points. First, the annal for 1305 includes a notice of the birth, and death twelve weeks later, of one John, son of Andrew Horn; it is hard to imagine that the event could have been of much interest to anyone but the father. Second, many of the documents included in the annals are also found in the *Liber Custumarum*, of which Horn is the undisputed compiler. Third, the author of the *Liber Albus*, a custumal of 1419, quotes portions of the annals from 1285 to 1293 and cites as his source the "Chronicles of the greater Liber Horne." Stubbs leaves the association with Horn a mere possibility, introducing it with engaging understatement as "a conjecture which, in the absence of any competing theory, need not be regarded as rash" (Stubbs, ed., *Annales*, xxiii). Over a century after Stubbs wrote, however, no such competing theory has emerged, and, in the most recent sustained consideration of Horn's association with the annals, Catto ("Andrew Horn," 374–76) agrees with Stubbs, citing the same evidence and presenting it as far more conclusive.

13. See Catto, "Andrew Horn," 380. Catto's reference is brief and unhelpfully vague: "The manuscript was presumably burnt in 1694. As it is not mentioned in the 1672 catalogue, its sojourn there [in Westminster Abbey] must have been brief." Since *Mirror of Justices* is introduced

Already this is an extraordinary amount of knowledge to possess
about the contents and disposition of so substantial a textual corpus.
We can further deduce a good deal about the order in which these
volumes were produced and the uses to which some of them, at least,
were put. The originally conjoined Corpus MSS 70 and 258 and *Liber
Horn* appear to have been produced relatively early in Horn's career
as a compiler, for a note in the former cuts short an announced set of
statutes of Edward I with the following announcement:

> Ista statuta quorum prohemia superius hic intitulantur in libro isto non
> scribentur nec Registrum, quia alibi habeo et quia intendo ex libro isto
> et aliis impostrum deo dante magnum codicem componere, quia utile
> duxi posteris presentia temporum nostrum exprimere.

> Neither these statutes [their rubrics are given above] nor the register of
> documents shall be written in this book, because I have them elsewhere
> and because I intend to compile, with God's grace, from that book and
> others a great codex of those things I think useful to portray to posterity
> the circumstances of our days.[14]

Ralph Hanna has plausibly speculated that the "elsewhere" referred
to here is *Liber Horn*, while the *magnum codicem* anticipates the production of *Liber regum* or *Liber custumarum* in the 1320s.[15] This hypothesis
fits the dates: a colophon partway through *Liber Horn* identifies as it
Horn's and dates it to 1311, though a continuation (which is considerably larger than the original collection) adds material through 1319. By
this time, a table of contents had been provided for the entire manuscript, which appears to have served as a practical, working copy;
notes added throughout indicate sources for various documents held
in other Guildhall volumes, leading Debbie Cannon to the conclusion that "the Liber Horn seems to have been designed to function as
a kind of unofficial referencing system to its [London's] rapidly ex-

---

as a *summa legum* in its sole surviving manuscript, it seems quite possible that this was a copy
of that text, now lost.

14. Cited in Hanna, *London Literature*, 68.

15. Ibid.

panding collection of documents at the beginning of the fourteenth century."[16]

Of Horn's two large custumals, *Liber regum* can be dated to 1321 or just afterward and *Liber custumarum* to between 1324 and 1327.[17] Both draw substantially, though not wholly, on *Liber Horn*; the words *hic incipe* and *non scribe* have been written next to portions of *Liber Horn* that do and do not, respectively, get copied into the later volumes.[18] *Liber custumarum*, meanwhile, also includes material from *Liber regum*; Hanna describes both of these as containing "(a) a Latin collection of pre-Statute law, extending from Ine of Wessex to Richard I (the logic for entitling one of the volumes 'Liber legum antiquorum regum'); (b) an extensive collection of *Statuta Anglie*, the latest items from *c.* 1321; (c) another extensive collection, in this case of London legal materials (the 'custume')."[19] While their largely historical, legal, and civic contents look broadly similar to those of *Liber Horn*, however, these volumes display important differences of presentation and visual impact, which in turn draw attention to some of the idiosyncratic, less obviously practical texts within *Liber regum* that I take up in this chapter. Ker anointed *Liber regum* "the finest of the city books, admirably written and illuminated,"[20] while Hanna notes both custumals' "opulent page layouts."[21] Lynda Dennison, meanwhile, has demonstrated that their border and figure illuminations were influenced by the Queen Mary Psalter Group of illuminators, who worked on a great number of prestige manuscripts.[22] While *Liber Horn* also boasts substantial decoration, its quality is less impressive than that which

16. Cannon, "London Pride," 185.

17. See Catto, "Andrew Horn," 376–79; and Cannon, "London Pride," 186.

18. See Cannon, "London Pride," 190; and Hanna, *London Literature*, 69.

19. Hanna, *London Literature*, 69.

20. Ker, "Liber Custumarum," 137.

21. Hanna, *London Literature*, 69.

22. Dennison, "'Liber Horn,' 'Liber Custumarum,'" 120–24. Confusingly, Dennison refers to the original *Liber regum* (Ker's MS D) as *Liber custumarum* throughout, doubtless because a substantial portion of *Liber regum*'s original contents are now found in *Liber custumarum*. The distinction that she maintains is between MS D (the original *Liber regum*) and MS C (the original *Liber custumarum*).

distinguishes *Liber regum*,[23] and whereas *Liber Horn* was apparently used as a practical guide, assembled over the course of nearly a decade, *Liber regum* appears to have been constructed all at a go.[24] It seems designed, as Cannon puts it, both "as a complete reference work, and as a showpiece item, rather than as an ongoing notebook. Its contents are dignified by the visual impressiveness of the book in which they are contained."[25] Hanna concurs, deeming both it and *Liber custumarum* "expressions for posterity . . . tailor-made for the City as its communal records of memory."[26]

It is clear, moreover, that Horn himself had a sense of the grandeur that books could possess; he uses the word *magnum* twice to describe the *codicem* that he plans to assemble, first in the note in the *Mirror* codex quoted earlier, and later in his will to designate one of the volumes left to the Guildhall. Even if we cannot establish definitively that *Liber regum* is that volume, as Catto proposes,[27] it clearly merits the adjective both for its size and for its performative and practical power. For its collective owners, it offered the aesthetic delight of its many decorations, a sense of civic pride at owning so monumental a physical tokening of London's greatness, and the peace of mind of knowing that the documentary basis of the city's rights lay securely within. By making available to the City both these massive and beautiful volumes and his other, more modest and personal books, Horn convenes his fellow Londoners, present and future, as the reading community that will need to understand and use all these documents in defense of civic prerogative, just as he himself did. His carefully orchestrated textual productions implicitly urge comparably detailed contemplation of their contents, in a process not unlike that undertaken by Mayor Richer de Refham in 1310:

23. Ibid., 124–25. *Liber Horn* features two artists with unrelated styles. Of these, Artist A exhibits a style totally unrelated to the Queen Mary workshop, "and although by a competent artist the work is not of the highest quality." Artist B, meanwhile, displays "a highly competent imitation of the style current at the time" that is nevertheless "derivative stylistically" (ibid.).

24. Ibid., 122.

25. Cannon, "London Pride," 187.

26. Hanna, *London Literature*, 69.

27. Catto, "Andrew Horn," 376–78.

Hic antiquas consuetudines et libertates in rotulis et libris camerae civitati fecit persecutari, et, congregatis sapientioribus, potentioribus, una cum aldermaniis, coram eis fecit legi et pupplicari.[28]

He [de Refham] caused the ancient customs and liberties in the rolls and books of the chamber of the city to be thoroughly searched [*persecutari*], and, the wiser and more powerful men having been assembled, together with the aldermen, he had them read and made public in their presence.

It is actions like these, Horn continues, by which Refham "was seen to preserve and reform the king's city in its former and unblemished dignity and authority."[29] Texts here are imagined capable of convening London's citizens (*congregatis*) and thus literally re-forming (*reformare*) their beloved city.

The suggestion that such reform is necessary, however, hints that all this grandeur could in fact be read as evidence of the City's precarious position, since only those whose privileges are in jeopardy need to protect them so ostentatiously.[30] This proposition is further strengthened by the fact that the grandest of all the volumes, *Liber regum*, was produced in or just after 1321, the year of the great Eyre and of London's consequent civic dismay. In this context, the Horn corpus's obsessive doubling and even trebling of contents across its various manuscripts starts to look like a sign of insecurity. Horn had good cause to worry that London would fall short of high-minded ideals of civic harmony in the future, as it had in the past,[31] and that relations between City

28. Stubbs, ed., *Annales*, 175 (my translation).

29. Ibid., 175–76 (my translation): "sic regis civitatem ad pristinam dignitatem et indempnem visus est servare et reformare." *Dignitas* suggests "authority" as well as "dignity," a suggestion that I imagine Horn was going for.

30. We might recall along these lines Hanna's observation, concerning the ubiquity of *Statuta* manuscripts: "[Such a] proliferation of legal materials testifies . . . not to respect for law, but to a situation quite the opposite. People only need the law in situations where social unrest requires just dealing to be imposed by litigation" (*London Literature*, 53).

31. On Horn's debt to the thirteenth-century civic historian Arnald fitz Thedmar's text and its exhortations to civic unity in the face of contemporary manifestations of anything but, see ibid., 63–68. On fitz Thedmar more generally and more extensively, see Williams, *Medieval London*, 196–242.

and Crown would continue to be rocky. We will see further evidence of all this in the evocations of London within the *Canterbury Tales* that I examine in chapter 3. Horn's volumes thus celebrate London's civic liberties while implying their essential fragility; to borrow the terms of my title, they are at once literal assemblages of London's privileges yet also reminders of how quickly those privileges, and the City that they define and protect, could be fragmented.

In this chapter, I argue that a comparable ambivalence underlies some of the odder texts, and textual juxtapositions, within Horn's corpus of manuscripts. I first consider the eccentric legal text *Mirror of Justices* and, in particular, the strangeness of its juxtaposition with the following, infinitely more conventional legal treatise *Britton*. That pairing, to which a marginal note draws our attention, prompts us to read *Mirror* for more than merely its frequently erroneous statements of legal practice; it is the codicological form of the *Mirror* codex, in other words, that helps determine *Mirror's* meaning. I then turn to a set of texts from *Liber regum*: William fitz Stephen's *Description of London*; a creatively edited set of excerpts from Brunetto Latini's *Livres dou Tresor*; and two sets of statutes for the London *puy* (which we briefly considered in the introduction). None of these is straightforwardly practical after the fashion of the laws, statutes, and charters that make up most of *Liber regum*, and each therefore encourages more creative forms of interpretation, particularly given the broader context of the *Mirror-Britton* juxtaposition, where such interpretation was necessary in order to make sense of *Mirror*. Each of these texts in *Liber regum* proposes a model for London that comes at some distance, whether geographic, temporal, or both. I argue that both individually, as discrete texts, and cumulatively, through their broader codicological situation within the custumal, they suggest a complex mixture of civic pride and insecurity, aspirationalism and nostalgia.

Assembling Meaning and
Constructing Justice in the *Mirror* Codex

Only a handful of the few to have considered *Mirror of Justices* have taken it at all seriously. David J. Seipp opens his essay on the text by collecting some of the nasty things that have been said about it since its publication by the Selden Society in 1895, of which the following are a choice but representative few: "hopelessly unpractical nonsense . . . no authority for the law of the thirteenth or any other century . . . wholly unworthy of credit . . . a multitude of groundless fabrications . . . so much improbable trash."[32] As these derogations from eminent historians of English law would suggest, *Mirror* does indeed regularly misrepresent medieval English legal history and practice. The strong indications that its author had read widely in the legal tradition, however, make these misstatements unlikely to be the result simply of ignorance. In his influential introduction to the text, for instance, Frederic Maitland argues that its author was conversant with *Bracton*, arguably the most influential thirteenth-century English legal treatise,[33] which makes it impossible to suppose that he believed that all or even most of the legal principles he cites would stand up to judicial scrutiny. Indeed, many of *Mirror*'s claims directly contradict some of the more important developments in English common law over the fifty to seventy-five years before it was written.[34]

In legal as in historical writing of the Middle Ages, however, sharply drawn binaries of *truth* and *falsehood* do not get us very far, and *Mirror* is not the random or nonsensical work that some of its detractors suggest. Clear and serious themes emerge over the course of the text, prime among them the idea that the true law of the realm is being perverted by both the king and his corrupt judges. The final book of the work, a long list of "Abuses," identifies as "first and sovereign" of these the false notion that the king is above the law.[35]

---

32. Seipp, "*The Mirror of Justices*," 85–87. See further Seipp's plausible (and amusing) speculation that some scholars formed such opinions, "not from reading the *Mirror* itself, but from trying to outdo Maitland's witty and malicious introduction to it" (ibid., 88). His goal is to rehabilitate *Mirror* as a document worthy of serious consideration by legal historians, but Seipp also readily acknowledges that "the author projected some of his ideals onto current law and others onto the law of England's distant past . . . [and that] all of the references in the *Mirror* to times before the thirteenth century are, so far as I can tell, completely made up" (ibid., 105).

33. *The Mirror of Justices*, xxxv.

34. See Seipp, "*The Mirror of Justices*," 97; and *The Mirror of Justices*, xliii–xliv.

35. "La premere et soverein abusion est qe li Roi est outre la lei, ou il dust estre subject" (*The Mirror of Justices*, 155).

Subsequent abuses are handled relatively quickly until the author arrives at abuse no. 108: "Abusion est qe justices et lur ministres qi occient la gent par faus jugement ne sunt destruz al foer dautres homicides."[36] The author notes approvingly that in one year King Alfred executed forty-four such wicked justices, and he goes on to describe individually each instance of righteous vengeance, complete with suitably Anglo-Saxon-sounding names and often with an extended vignette of a paragraph or more.[37] Indeed, this theme of unjust punishment opens the work, for it is while wrongly imprisoned by the king's justices that *Mirror*'s unnamed narrator claims to have unearthed the legal precepts that constitute his text: "Je persecutor de faus juges e par lur exsecucion fausement enprisone, les privileges le Roi e les vieuz roulles de sa tresorie, dount amis me solacerent en mon soiour, cerchai, e le foundement e la nessaunce des usages dEngleterre donez por lei, oveqe les gueredouns de bons jugez e la peyne des autres i trovai, e a plus bref qe jeo savoie la necessite mis en remenbraunce, a quoi compaignons meiderent destudier el viel testament, el novel, el canon e en lei escrist."[38] This theme of wicked judges complements internal evidence that *Mirror* was written ca. 1285–90,[39] for Edward I instituted

---

36. "It is an abuse that justices and their officers who slay folk by false judgments are not destroyed like other murderers" (ibid., 166).

37. Ibid., 166–71.

38. "I, the prosecutor of false judges, and by their doing falsely imprisoned, have searched the privileges of the king, and the old rolls of his treasury, with which my friends consoled me in my sojourn, and found there the foundation and the origins of the customs of England given as law, together with the rewards due good judges and the punishment due others, and as briefly as I knew how have set the essentials in remembrance, toward which end my companions aided me in studying the Old and New Testaments, the canon and written law" (ibid., 2).

39. The text ends with a largely chronological list of statutes to which the author objects; the last of these is the Statute of Merchants of 1285, which he describes as "new" (ibid., 199). He does not, however, mention the *Quia Emptores* of 1290 or any others from the 1290s that, as Maitland puts it, "would have afforded him abundant materials for criticism and cavil" (ibid., xxiv). Maitland further argues convincingly that "the Edward the second" mentioned in the text (ibid., 141) is not necessarily the one we know as Edward II, noting: "His contemporaries might call him the first, second, third, or fourth, according to the extent of their historical knowledge. Few, perhaps, would remember Edward the Elder or Edward the Martyr, but all men had heard of Saint Edward" (ibid., xxiii). He then notes that the "Edward the Second" cited in *Mirror* is criticized for changing the punishment for rape from mutilation to death.

a purge of such false judges after he returned from Gascony in 1286.[40] The misbehavior of so many justices at the time of *Mirror's* writing hints at a satiric or critical purpose behind its various misstatements of actual legal practice, and the work's title subtly supports this theory: when *Mirror* was written, a true "mirror" of justices would indeed contain unattested legal principles and arbitrary bases for judgment, since the plural, human, corrupted *justices* were spectacularly failing to be a mirror of the *justice* they were sworn to execute.[41]

Events around 1290 would have suggested such a bitterly ironic reading of the text to a London audience in particular, since the City had been stripped of its liberties in 1285 and would not see them restored until 1297; Gwyn Williams writes that "perhaps never had the city been so subject, in such detail, to the royal power."[42] The legal basis for the king's move was the technicality that the mayor had resigned his office to protest an earlier royal slight.[43] While the king may have had the letter of the law on his side, however, it would have been easy for a partisan London audience to deduce from these events, and the judicial scandal just a few years later, that the law was not just

---

This was carried out in the Statute of 1285, other provisions of which show up throughout the text. Since *Mirror's* author clearly did know of Saint Edward (ibid., 81), Maitland reasons that his "Edward the Second" must have been our Edward I, allowing him to arrive at his date of around 1290.

40. On this drama, see Paul A. Brand, "Edward I and the Judges: The 'State Trials' of 1289–93," in *Thirteenth Century England I*, ed. P. R. Cross and S. D. Lloyd (Woodbridge: D. S. Brewer, 1986), 31–40. My thanks to David Seipp for this reference.

41. Compare the comment by Seipp that "the mirror reflected the judges' own defaults and defects so that they could see them and the mirror showed the judges their law and themselves as they should be" ("*The Mirror of Justices*," 97).

42. Williams, *Medieval London*, 257.

43. See the narration of the event in the 1285 entry in Stubbs, ed., *Annales*, 94. The problem began when the mayor was summoned to the Tower for questioning without the forty days' notice required according to London's "ancient liberties" (*antiquas libertates*). Accordingly, he resigned the mayoralty in protest so that in answering the summons he would be doing so in his own person but without conceding that he could be thus summoned in his person as mayor. On learning all this, however, the royal treasurer, John de Kirkby, seized the mayoralty into the king's control "because the City found itself without a mayor" (*quia civitas inveniebatur sine majore*)—even though the mayor had in fact left the City seal with a subordinate. The civic fascination with royal forms of authority is clearly visible here in the "mayor's two bodies" type of reasoning being used, which would in turn make the specific nature of the royal power grab—the assertion of mayorlessness (*sine majore*)—particularly stinging.

powerless in the face of wrongdoing but could also hurt those who trusted its guarantees. Seipp emphasizes throughout his essay that *Mirror*'s pronouncements are not so consistently outlandish as Maitland implies; such moments of reasonableness, and the righteous indignation that the author summons in defense of those unjustly preyed on by corrupt legal practice, make all the more startling such patently untrue statements as, for example, the claim that debtors cannot be distrained by their movable goods.[44] Such topsy-turvy, careening shifts drive Maitland to distraction[45] but help create a broader satiric message: that quick, unexpected, and arbitrary changes in legal practice and premise in fact constitute a "mirror of the justices" in charge of English courts. *Mirror*'s grounding in legal literature, consistent interest in serious themes of topical relevance, and at least occasional presentation of reputable legal statements thus combine to suggest a deeper significance to the text's often strange contents.

Consider, for example, the Boethian resonance of *Mirror*'s opening vignette, quoted earlier, in which the unjustly imprisoned narrator discovers and commits to writing wisdom that eludes those on the outside.[46] Just as Boethius was consoled by philosophy, so too the *Mirror* narrator is consoled (*solacent*) by the friends with whom he discovers the true English law that his text records. But that plural verb creates a wrinkle: it is a host of unnamed friends who comfort *Mirror*'s narrator, recalling the fact that in the *Consolation* Boethius is visited first by the Muses, whom Philosophy angrily dismisses for offering

44. "E dunt si rente, suite ou autre service soit arere a ascun segneur de son fieu pur ceo nest mie li tenant destreignable de ses biens moebles . . ." (*The Mirror of Justices*, 129). Maitland cites this example as one statement, not just false, but "obviously and notoriously false" (ibid., xxxvii).

45. After marveling at the example above and several others, Maitland concludes: "When once we know his character [the author's], we shall begin to suspect that those passages in his book which successfully stand a comparison with plea rolls and honest treatises are the most deceptive, having been designed for the very purpose of inducing us to swallow the fables that lurk amongst them" (ibid., xxxviii).

46. This opening has a clear analogue in *Fleta*, a roughly contemporary (ca. 1290) legal treatise that takes its name from Fleet Prison, where its author was supposedly imprisoned while writing, but the *Mirror* author's handling of the conceit is considerably more sophisticated.

sweet poisons instead of true consolation. Two distinct yet complementary meanings thus emerge from this literary allusion. On the one
hand, the good law of *Mirror*, unrecognized in English courts, parallels
the unjustly neglected Philosophy. Precisely because the courts do not
recognize *Mirror*'s status, however, going into a courtroom armed with
its legal facts and principles is a recipe for earthly disappointment; like
the blandishments of the Muses, they may make you feel better but
will not help. The generic play of *Mirror*'s opening thus suggests that,
as a legal treatise, it is a seductive illusion; as philosophy or statement
of ideals, by contrast, it offers the truth. Even Maitland seems open to
this possibility when he contends that the author "deliberately stated
as law what he knew was not law, if by law we mean the settled doc-
trines of the king's court."[47] Seipp pounces on that dependent clause,
pointing out that, "if we mean something else by 'law' . . . something
more closely connected with an idealized, universal conception,"[48]
then *Mirror of Justices* begins to look far more comprehensible. If we
read past Maitland's wonderfully cutting quips about the text, we find
that he too, albeit provisionally, comes round to this view.[49]

47. *The Mirror of Justices*, xxxvii.

48. Seipp, "*The Mirror of Justices*," 97. Seipp continues: "Maitland told us to insert a 'not' in
every sentence. We would be better served by replacing the 'is' with a 'should be.' "

49. The comments toward the end of the introduction suggest that Maitland has softened a
bit toward the *Mirror*'s author and its claims: "What our author seems to detest most is any rule
that puts the king or any of his subordinates outside the ordinary course of common justice.
Writs should run against the king himself. The punishments that have been denounced as late
against official oppressions are inadequate; those who are guilty of them are simply perjurers
and larceners, and should be treated as such. May we not guess that here, if anywhere, our
author is really in earnest, and that a good deal of the rest of his book is but a cloud in which
he wraps up his dangerous opinions—opinions, I mean, that may bring him into danger? . . .
Here, more definitely than anywhere else, we can connect the *Mirror* with a political program
that many will accept. Again, if we suppose that the book was written about the year 1289,
the talk of 'false judges,' the hints that the chancery and the exchequer are full of perjurers
and thieves, are not without point and truth." Acknowledging that "all confidence in the official oracles of the law had vanished," he asks rhetorically and, to my ears, approvingly: "Was
not there an opening here for a fanciful young man ambitious of literary fame?" (*The Mirror of
Justices*, xlix). It is almost as if he remembers himself at the very end, however, shakes his head
free of such fancies, and concludes sternly: "Once more let it be repeated that, if this book was
meant to be read and copied, it was a miserable failure" (ibid., li). He continues: "If ever we are

Crucially informed by the late thirteenth century of its composition, *Mirror* uses the safely distant Anglo-Saxon past as a blank slate for its topically resonant concoction of fantastic laws and anecdotes. I turn now to the question of how its meaning changes with the addition of yet a third temporality, the early fourteenth century of its inclusion in Horn's *Mirror* codex, and what that inclusion suggests about the reading habits that Horn imagined among the fellow citizens to whom he would subsequently bequeath the volume. Our first indication comes in the form of some cryptic Latin verses that immediately precede the text:

> Hanc legum summam si quis vult iura tueri
> Perlegat et sapiens si vult orator haberi
> Hoc apprenticiis ad barros ebore munus
> Gratum iuridicis utile mittit opus.
> Horn michi cognomen Andreas est michi nomen.[50]

> If anyone wishes to consider the laws or be held a wise orator,
> let him thoroughly read this collection of laws.
> To apprentices at the bar this work sends a pleasant gift of ivory,
> to justices something useful.
> Horn is my last name, Andrew is my first.

The content of the first four lines is strange enough, but the fifth adds codicological elements to the puzzle. It is in a different hand and a different color (red; the four verses are in black), and it does not read at first like poetry or seem to add anything to the preceding lines that clearly are. The fact that this line appears elsewhere in Horn's corpus as a kind of ex libris (including once earlier in the London Collection portion of the *Mirror* codex),[51] and that here it causes the scribe to ex-

---

tempted to accept any statement made in the *Mirror* and not elsewhere warranted, we shall do well to ask ourselves whether we believe that an Englishman called Nolling was indicted for a sacrifice to Mahomet, and to speculate as to what may happen if six centuries hence *The Comic Blackstone* is mistaken for the work of a great commentator" (ibid., lii). Maitland's introduction, a marvelous literary production in its own right, deserves fuller analysis and appreciation than I can give it here.

50. Ibid., xx (my translation). The lines appear on fol. 1r of what is now Corpus MS 258.

51. See the bottom of fol. 101r of Corpus MS 70. The hand, moreover, appears to be the same as the one that wrote the fifth line here.

tend into the margin, suggests that it could have been an afterthought (see fig. 1).[52]

The name verse thus looks like codicological filler, wholly distinct from the preceding, literary lines. As Maitland points out, however, those four lines are extremely obscure by themselves. Why would "a pleasant gift of ivory" be contrasted with "something useful," and why would they be associated, respectively, with "apprentices at the bar" and "justices" already in practice? Only in reading these four lines together with the last, seemingly straightforward one announcing Horn as the owner or compiler of the manuscript does the significance of the enigmatic reference to ivory emerge: in classical mythology, false dreams passed through an ivory gate, true dreams through one of horn.[53] This allusion explains the distinction between youthful apprentices and their more experienced colleagues. To the former, who know little of the law, *Mirror* is an ivory dream since many of its legal statements are false, but to those who recognize the work's untruths as just that they are doubly useful, both as condemnation of the current state of the law and as an idealized vision of what it ought to do: rein in the king and neutralize his corrupt justices.[54] (It also suggests a coyly self-aggrandizing assertion on the part of Horn—I am the mouthpiece of true visions—rendered charming by its obliqueness.)

Both *Mirror* and its introductory verses thus offer deeper significance than they seem to at first: despite its many factual misstatements, *Mirror* grapples with serious social and legal concerns, while the verses conceal an allusive riddle that hints at the satiric theme of *Mirror* itself. These textual pieces—the first four verses with rubricated name

52. In the manuscript, what I have reproduced as five lines are written out as three long lines, with the final line's last word, *nomen*, extending into the margin. See further fig. 1.

53. Virgil, Horace, and Statius all carry on this tradition, which ultimately goes back to Homer. See, e.g., *Aeneid* 6.894–97.

54. Maitland saw the connection between horn and ivory as well, imagining the last three lines saying effectively: "Here for the apprentices at the bar are pleasant visions of the law that are not too true; here for their seniors are profitable things that are not so pretty. Horn is my name, but you have Ivory also here" (*The Mirror of Justices*, xxi). He never explains clearly what these "profitable things" are, however, and, as we have seen, is deeply ambivalent about the possibility of *Mirror*'s being in any respect worthy of serious study.

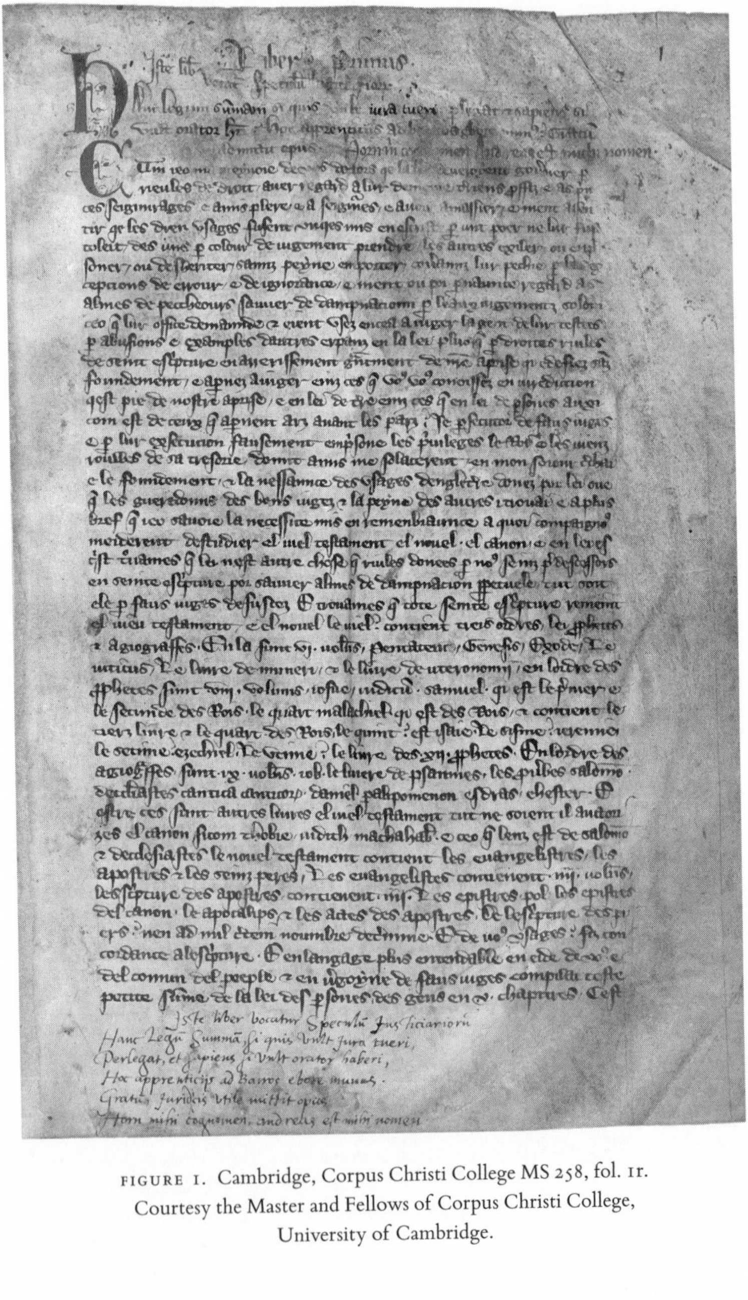

FIGURE I. Cambridge, Corpus Christi College MS 258, fol. 1r.
Courtesy the Master and Fellows of Corpus Christi College,
University of Cambridge.

verse and those five taken together, then juxtaposed with the following *Mirror*—gain their full force only when assembled; allusive and indirect meaning starts small and seemingly insignificant (some odd lines of Latin; a rubricated ex libris) and extends outward to *Mirror* itself and, I will propose momentarily, from there to that text's juxtaposition with *Britton*. Each element of these gradually emerging structures reinforces and deepens the others: just as the strangeness of the first four verses prompts us to look for meaning in the seemingly straightforward name verse, and just as the riddling play of the assembled five lines in turn encourages us to read *Mirror* for more than its statements of actual legal practice, so too *Mirror*'s eccentricities and puzzlements prompt us to return to the verses and read them more carefully if we originally dismissed them as merely announcing the owner-compiler of the manuscript. Derek Pearsall's encomium of poetic meaning is worth recalling here: poetry exploits "metaphorical potentialities," its significance is "not confined to denotation," and the whole is "more suggestive, more elusive" than ordinary language, allowing "fresh meanings [to] emerge in the process of rereading, already there but newly discovered."[55] Only a tiny fraction of the *Mirror* codex is in fact literally poetic, but its pieces offer a poetics of assemblage for the careful reader.

My point here is twofold: first, that the poetic play of the first four verses prompts us to find in a piece of codicological data ("my name is Andrew Horn") and a bizarre legal treatise comparably literary forms of allusive and elusive meaning and, second, that our discovery of this literary game depends on what I have called *compilational reading*, our decision to regard an assembled whole as more than the sum of its parts. Like all really satisfying play, this game is also serious: it represents not just an invitation to such interpretation but also a challenge to Horn's colleagues and successors, those to whom he bequeathed this volume and who in the years to come would be responsible for the legal—which is to say textual—defense of London's prerogatives. Will they be savvy enough readers to tell ivory from horn? The answer to this question doubtless varied, but we have evidence that at least one

55. Pearsall, "Towards a Poetic," 100.

FIGURE 2. Cambridge, Corpus Christi College MS 258, fol. 1r (details). Courtesy the Master and Fellows of Corpus Christi College, University of Cambridge.

later reader did indeed interpret Horn's puzzle correctly: all five lines have been recopied at the bottom of the same page, lineated as poetry, in the same ink, and with no indication that Horn's name verse should be construed as distinct from the preceding four (see fig. 2). Here, we see the multiple temporalities that compilational meaning both depends on and produces, for that meaning is contingent not just on a given reader's willingness to reread in terms of larger structures (to reconsider *Mirror*'s introductory verses in light of that text's strangeness or the name verse in light of the puzzle posed by the preceding four); it is also highlighted for us by a later reader's manipulation of codicological form, here a visual reformulation of extant text at the bottom of a single folio.

    This complicated context has the potential to make the text that follows *Mirror*, the legal treatise *Britton*, less straightforward than it would be if read in isolation. Indeed, even though *Mirror* is eccentric while *Britton* is reliable and well attested, Horn has been at some pains to juxtapose them for his readers and even to emphasize their similarities. On the same page as the note cutting short the statutes of Edward I and forecasting his plans to construct a *magnum codicem* in the future, he offers this note:

Non erit plus nunc, quia satis habes in ij. Libris subsequentibus, videlicet libro vocato Speculum Iusticiariorum et altero libro vocato Brethun. Sed not sunt libri sigillati per Regem. Attamen taliter placitabantur temporibus Regum Edwardi filii Regis Henrici III et Edwardi filii Regis Edwardi.

No more of this now, for you have enough in the two following books, namely the book called Mirror of Justices and the second book called Britton. These books are not sealed by the king, but in such a way were things pleaded in the times of Edward son of King Henry III [i.e., Edward I] and Edward son of King Edward [i.e., Edward II].[56]

Not just here, but also in his will, where he used the same *cum libro vocato* formulation for each, Horn prompts us to consider the two treatises as part of the same codicological structure, even as *Britton*'s presence begs the question of what *Mirror* is doing in the manuscript in the first place. If the principal purpose of the *Mirror* codex as a whole were simply to put forth uncomplicated and practical statements of legal fact and precedent—to be a collection not unlike *Liber Horn*, for example, where excerpts from *Britton* also appear and *Mirror* does not—then *Mirror* would have no place in it. By emphasizing the juxtaposition of *Mirror* with *Britton*, Horn's notes and characterizations of the two texts press readers both to look for more complex modes of apprehension in the preceding *Mirror* and even to read *Britton* itself as other than the purely utilitarian legal document that it seems.

We have already considered *Mirror*'s prologue, in which a loyal citizen, imprisoned by the king's wicked judges, discovers the true law of the land hidden in the royal treasury. This opening assumes added significance retroactively, after we have read *Britton*, for that text announces itself in the voice of Edward I himself, the very king who so scandalously allowed such wicked justices free reign. Indeed, *Britton*'s modern editor claims that "the royal authority under which the book assumes to be promulgated" constitutes one of its chief interests today and a principal reason for its wide dissemination in the Middle Ages.[57]

56. Quoted in *The Mirror of Justices*, xvi.

57. *Britton*, xxviii. *Britton* is, broadly speaking, an attempt to render the massive *Bracton* shorter and more manageable and, in this effort, is comparable to *Fleta* and *Thornton* (ibid.,

Though they are roughly contemporaneous and, unusually for legal treatises, in French rather than Latin, a comparison of their openings indicates how radically these two texts differ in their imagination of legal authority:

Mirror: Cum jeo maperceyvoie devers de qe la lei deveroyent governer par rieules de droit, aver regard a lur demeine terriens proffiz, e as princes seignurage e amis plere, e a seinuries e avoir amassier, e nient assenter qe les dreiz usages fusent unqes mis en escrist . . . je persecutor de faus juges e par lur exsecucion fausement enprisone, les privileges le Roi e les vieuz roulles de sa tresorie, dount amis me solacerent en mon soiour, cerchai, e le foundement e la nessaunce des usages dEngleterre donez por lei, oveqe les gueredouns de bons jugez e la peyne des autres i trovai, e a plus bref qe jeo savoie la necessite mis en remenbraunce, a quoi compaignons meiderent destudier el viel testament, el novel, el canon e en lei escrist.[58]

Britton: Edward, par la grace Deu, Roi de Engleterre, Seignur de Hyrelaunde, et Duk de Aquitayne, a touz ses feaus et sugez de Engleterre et de Hyrelaunde pes et grace de sauvacioun. Desirauntz pes entre le poeple qe est en nostre proteccioun par la suffaunce de Deu, la quele pes ne poet mie ben ester sauntz ley, si avoms les leys qe hom ad usé en noster reaume avaunt ces hores fet mettre en escrit solum ceo qe cy est ordeyné. Et volums et comaundums qe par tut Engleterre et tut Hyrelaunde soint issi usetz et tenuz en touz poyntz, sauve a nous de repeler les et de enoyter et de amenuser et de amender a totes les foiz qe nous verums qe bon serra, par le assent de nos Countes et Barouns et autres de noster conseyl, sauve les usages a ceux qe par prescripcioun de tens ount autrement usé en taunt qe lour usages ne soynt mie descordauntz a dreiture.[59]

---

xxv). Nichols attributes *Britton*'s vastly greater number of surviving manuscripts (the other two, like *Mirror*, are extant in only one) to its having been written in French rather than Latin (it is "the first great treatise upon our law written in the vernacular language of the courts" [ibid., xxviii]) and to the "sanction of the royal name" (ibid.).

58. *The Mirror of Justices*, 2. For the translation, see n. 38 above.

59. *Britton*, 1–2: "Edward, by the grace of God king of England, lord of Ireland, and duke of Aquitaine, to all his faithful people and subjects of England and Ireland: peace and the grace of salvation. Desiring peace among the people whom God has suffered to be placed in our protection, which peace cannot prosper without law, we have accordingly caused to be put into writing the laws that have been practiced in our realm before now, as is here ordained. And we desire and command that throughout England and Ireland they be so used and held in all

The *Mirror* narrator emphasizes his solitary stand against a host of wicked justices: his singular *jeo* is the only one who perceives (*maperceyvoie*) their legal perversions, the only one who seeks out and finds the realm's true law in the king's treasury (*cerchai . . . trovai*; his *amis* offer consolation, but the action verbs remain singular). The opening of *Britton*, by contrast, uses royal power to create plurals: the multiple lands (England, Ireland, Aquitaine) over which Edward's regally plural persona rules and the many laws (*leys*) that govern them. *Mirror*'s narrator also speaks of the law, but always in the singular: as such, the word *ley* recurs thirteen times within and is also the word that concludes the work's relatively brief prologue. This small difference in diction enacts in miniature two fundamentally different legal theories. According to *Britton*, it is the royal prerogative to repeal, extend, restrict, and amend the laws at each and every moment the king sees fit; *a totes les foiz* emphasizes by expanding (a simple *quant* would have sufficed) and making plural the occasions on which he is imagined exercising this royal power. The list of actions to which he can subject the laws, meanwhile, is so exhaustive as to rhetorically neuter the subsequent, pro forma commitment to listen to his barons and respect local usage. In any event, the preamble ends not with this promise to defer to local custom but with the proviso that he will do so only inasmuch as these customs satisfy his inherently subjective sense of their accordance with *dreiture*. The 1285 imposition of royal wardens, however, had given Londoners little reason to trust Edward's parsing of this word, with its slippery meaning of "right" or "justice."

In *Mirror*, by contrast, the law is inherently singular and transcends the desires of any particular king who happens to be on the throne at the time—particularly, we may suppose, one who like *Britton*'s royal narrator has overseen such rampant judicial corruption. These juxtaposed legal treatises thus implicitly question whether the readily pluralizable laws of *Britton* in fact constitute a mirror of justice as it should

---

points, save that we may repeal, extend, restrict, and amend them at any point when we shall see that to be good, by the assent of our earls and barons and others of our counsel, save those customs for those who by the prescription of time have been practiced differently, insofar as their customs are in no way contrary to the law."

be, however accurately it states the laws that obtain in the courts. Indeed, *Mirror*'s entire premise is that an unnamed prisoner knows better than the king or his justices what the true law of the land really is. He acquired this knowledge, moreover, by carefully searching "les privileges le Roi et les vieuz roulles de sa tresorie," a process that recalls the 1310 exercise sponsored by Mayor Richer de Refham that we considered earlier. Even the language is echoic: de Refham saw to it that the City's ancient liberties were "thoroughly searched" (*persecutari*) in the Guildhall's books and rolls (*rotulis*; cf. the *roules* of *Mirror*). The Latin prefix *per-* with its implication of thoroughness likewise recalls the introductory verses to *Mirror*, with their exhortation that we "thoroughly read" (*perlegat*; i.e., for more than its surface meaning?) the legal collection (*summam*) that we are holding. These echoes across three elements of Horn's textual corpus—prose annals, allusive verses, legal treatise—implicitly unite London's citizens from the past (of the 1310 Guildhall exercise) and those of the future (who will read the *Mirror* codex after Horn's death) with the fictional narrator of *Mirror of Justices*. Together, they propose that textual mastery safeguards the law, just as texts themselves define it.

This vision differs radically from that of *Britton*'s preamble, which asserts a performative legal theory in which the king's personal pleasure (*a totes les foiz qe nous verums qe bon serra*) defines the scope, nature, and amendment of the laws. By offering such a contrast even as it presents both with first-person verbs, the *Mirror/Britton* juxtaposition emphasizes the rhetorical character of royal power and thus the ways in which it is open to imitation, parody, and deconstruction (even unnamed prisoners, apparently, can freely root around in the king's treasury). It thereby hints, and hopes, that being king may not always be sufficient unilaterally to create the law. Through its juxtaposition with *Mirror of Justices* and the riddling verses that introduce that text, then, *Britton* becomes a fundamentally different work than it would be by itself or accompanied by other, more conventional texts and contexts—but only if we accept the manuscript's invitation to read compilationally, in terms of the larger structures created by these assembled texts. Individually, *Mirror*'s opening verses are just confusing, the text itself just bizarre, and *Britton* just a conventional treatise. As we have seen, however, at least one reader did indeed put the four literary verses together with Horn's name verse, recopying them as an assembled block at the bottom of the page, and Horn has explicitly instructed us to read *Mirror* and *Britton* together, as part of a larger physical structure that might yield an analogously broader and more complex range of meanings.

In the *Mirror* codex, such invitations are quite pointed. In the *Liber regum*, by contrast, the vastly greater number of texts combines with the lack of sly poetic introductions or name verses to place more of the initial interpretive onus on the reader. One crucial aspect of Horn's corpus, however, is the cumulative effect of its invitations to think of its texts in terms of and against one another: the elaborate cross-referencing system in *Liber Horn* to other volumes in the Guildhall already extant and its implicit projection (the *hic incipe* and *non scribe* comments) of future textual production; the self-conscious announcements of nonproduction that we saw in the *Mirror* codex (*non erit plus nunc*; *ista statuta . . . non scribentur*) and equally self-conscious, even self-aggrandizing claims to future production (*intendo . . . magnum codicem componere*); and of course the retrospective look back on Horn's past texts, rhetorically assembled in his will and physically assembled in the Guildhall to which he bequeathed them. These gestures combine to suggest that Horn's volumes themselves add up to more than the sum of their parts, that they all take part in a vast, complex project—a multimanuscript corpus as compilation—that it is up to us to unpack and comprehend. The relevance of the *Mirror* codex's complexity and allusiveness thus extends beyond the physical boundaries of that particular manuscript because they prompt us to consider how other parts of Horn's corpus, too, might be interpretively legible in such creative terms.

Distant Ideals of Civic Harmony in *Liber regum*

We have already seen that parts of Horn's project are thoroughly practical. *Liber Horn*, for example, functions like a *compilatio* as Parkes defines it, systematically taming multiple complex authorities so as to make them "easily accessible."[60] Yet *Liber Horn* is far from Horn's last word in textual production. *Liber regum* and its descendant *Liber custumarum* represent considerably more than a mere expansion of *Liber Horn*'s texts and statutes into the 1320s; the impressiveness of their decorative schemes and physical size assert London's majesty even as their obsessive textual acquisitiveness implies the City's fundamental insecurity. Precisely this mixture of pride and self-doubt emerges from the juxtaposition of two pairs of texts within *Liber regum*: William fitz Stephen's *Description of London* and excerpts from Brunetto Latini's highly influential *Livres dou Tresor*, which appear in the inserted quire that we considered in the introduction, and two sets of statutes for a mercantile poetic society called the *puy*, which was modeled on institutions of the same name that flourished in northern France and the Low Countries.[61] Each of these pairs—Fitz Stephen and Latini and the two sets of *puy* statutes—creates through juxtaposition interpretive complexity akin to what we saw in the *Mirror* codex. Read and interpreted together, these pairs yield deeper meaning than their elements would if considered in isolation.

60. Indeed, Don C. Skemer has proposed that academic *compilatio* of the sort described by Parkes and Minnis was a model for the organizational structure of *Statuta* manuscripts, which would, as we have seen, been thoroughly familiar to Horn. He writes: "Standard elements in statute books from all periods were the orderly division of important component texts in parts and the addition of specialized reference tools to enhance access. . . . These tools should be understood as part of the proliferation of practical texts and other academic reference tools that had developed since the thirteenth century in a new and more public age of reading and teaching" ("Reading the Law," in Bush and Wijffels, eds., *Learning the Law*, 113–31 [quotation 122–23]).

61. Anne F. Sutton has written two illuminating articles on the London *puy*: "The *Tumbling Bear* and Its Patrons: A Venue for the London Puy and Mercery," in *London and Europe in the Later Middle Ages*, ed. Julia Boffey and Pamela King (London: Centre for Medieval and Renaissance Studies at Queen Mary and Westfield College, University of London, 1995), 85–110, and "Merchants, Music and Social Harmony." The London *puy* also figures briefly in her recent and compendious study of the City's mercers (*The Mercery of London* [Aldershot: Ashgate, 2005], 67–72), though these pages add little to the earlier articles. Of Continental *puys* in this period, that of Arras is the best attested (and was apparently the model for London's). See Ardis Butterfield, *Poetry and Music in Medieval France* (Cambridge: Cambridge University Press, 2002), 133–70; and Roger Berger, *Littérature et société arrageoises au XIIIème siècle* (Arras: Editions Université de Paris, 1981). Other cities with prominent *puys* include Lille, Douai, Valenciennes, and Amiens.

Fitz Stephen's *Description of London* marks the last of a series of texts that center on England: it follows Henry of Huntingdon's *Description of Britain* and the long series of English laws from which the *Liber legum antiquorum regum* presumably derives its original name. Its praise, however, compares London to cities that are geographically or temporally other, thus initiating the themes of historical and spatial distance that the following excerpts from Latini's *Livres dou Tresor* continue to explore. From there, much of *Liber regum* is devoted to detailing economic and legal arrangements governing the many groups of alien merchants active in the City, whom Londoners like Horn and his Guildhall colleagues hated and feared as increasingly successful challengers to their own protectionist impulses. Yet the Latini extracts and, later, the two sets of *puy* statutes suggest a more complicated attitude toward the mercantile urban centers with which those texts were associated: northern Italy and the Franco-Flemish Low Countries, respectively. On the one hand, by imitating the political and cultural forms of those merchants' cities, these texts suggest an attitude of jealous admiration, mixed perhaps with the hope that Latini's political theory or the cultural performance of the *puy* might bring Londoners a comparable degree of civic power and autonomy. Such aspirations, however, were as phantasmal as *Mirror*'s presentation of the law as it should be instead of the law as it stands since, as we have seen in the introduction, Londoners operated under a strong central authority that aggressively sought to curtail their loftiest political and economic aspirations. These elements of *Liber regum* optimistically posit imitative models by which London's citizens might defend their privileges and autonomy, even as they implicitly recognize the challenges Londoners faced in so doing; they thus parallel the ambivalence that we have seen from the compilation, and Horn's corpus, as a whole.

William fitz Stephen's *Description of London* clearly owes its presence in *Liber regum* partly to its encomiastic quality; it describes London as "felix . . . aeris salubritate, Christiana religione, firmitate munitionum" and so on.[62] Its position in the manuscript, immediately

---

62. "Happy in the healthfulness of its air, its Christian religion, the security of its defenses . . ." (*Liber Custumarum*, 2, pt. 1:2). All translations of *Liber Custumarum* are my own. Subsequent

following Henry of Huntingdon's *Description of Britain*, suggests that London is the jewel in Britain's crown, as in the text's opening:

> Inter nobiles urbes orbis quas fama celebrat, civitas Londonia, regni Anglorum sedes, una est quae famam sui latius diffundit, opes et merces longius transmittit, caput altius extollit. (2, pt. 1:2)

> Among the noble cities of the world celebrated by fame, the city of London, seat of the kingdom of the English, is one who spreads her renown very widely, sends her influence and wealth to great distances, and raises her head very high.

This personified London unites her potentially fractious groups and interests into a single body politic, the metaphor reinforced by the image of her head raised high with justified pride. London's expansiveness is central to Fitz Stephen's praise: she extends laterally (*latius, longius*) and vertically (*altius*), forcing the other "nobiles urbes orbis" to acknowledge her. (And, lest we detect a hint of overavailable female sexuality in London's eager spreading of her wealth, a Langlandian Lady Mede *avant la lettre*, Fitz Stephen reassures us that "urbis matronae ipsae Sabinae sunt" ["the matrons of the city are very Sabines" (2, pt. 1:5)].) In extending outward, London draws others irresistibly to her: "ad urbem hanc ex omni natione quae sub coelo est, navalia gaudent institores habere commercia" ("to this city from every nation that is under the sun, commercial docks rejoice to have brokers and goods" [2, pt. 1:9]). Fitz Stephen implicitly links this mercantile prowess to London's antiquity, claiming in this same chapter that "urbe Roma, secundum Chronicorum fidem, satis antiquior est" ("London is a fair amount older than the city of Rome, according to the authority of the Chronicles" [2, pt. 1:9]) and that London's laws and institutions

---

citations are given parenthetically in the text. On the *Description* as an example of the genre of *encomium urbis*, see John Scattergood, "Misrepresenting the City: Genre, Intertextuality, and William fitzStephen's *Description of London* (c. 1173)," in Boffey and King, eds., *London and Europe in the Later Middle Ages*, 1–34. C. David Benson also devotes a few pages to the text. See "Some Poets' Tours of Medieval London: Varieties of Literary Urban Experience," *Essays in Medieval Studies* 24 (2007): 1–20, esp. 2–5.

are equally venerable.[63] By proceeding from praise of London's commercial might to praise of its antiquity and thence to praise of its civic and legal institutions, Fitz Stephen provides precisely the links between wealth and fame, history and the law, that the rest of *Liber regum* seeks to reinforce and that animate the Horn corpus more broadly.

Fitz Stephen's evocation of delight in this mercantile context (*navalia gaudent institores habere*) anticipates his extended description of Londoners' many recreations: Passion and miracle plays, hawking and hunting, bear- and boar-baiting, and cockfighting and ice skating make up only a partial list. His extensive descriptions of these *ludi* give texture to his suggestion that the fame and respect Londoners have gained abroad owe as much to their recreations as to their more serious pursuits: Fitz Stephen writes that "non expedit utilem tantum et seriam urbem esse, nisi dulcis etaim sit et jocunda" ("it is worth little for a city to be so practical and serious unless it is also sweet and pleasant" [2, pt. 1:10]). He thus links the commercial aspects of London that precede this sentence with the subsequent description of its recreations; we will see this emphasis on the symbiotic relation between ludic performance and civic prominence further intimated in the *puy* statutes later in *Liber regum*. Fitz Stephen's phrase also recalls the juxtaposition of "pleasant . . . ivory" and "something useful" from *Mirror*'s introductory verses; just as full meaning there depended on reading for both the playful and the serious, so too here Fitz Stephen implies that London is such a paragon because it unites business with pleasure.

Fitz Stephen also takes care to associate these games with their respective seasons: cockfighting takes place just before Lent, mock battles during Lent, quintain games during Easter, and so on. This gambit is consonant with his broader interest in history and time; this chapter and the *Description* as a whole conclude with a return to the mythohistorical realm by alluding to London's Trojan origins and citing Constantine as one of the city's famous natives. Fitz Stephen then

---

63. "unde et adhuc antiquis eisdem utuntur legibus et communibus institutis" ("from which time they use the same ancient laws and common institutions even still" [2, pt. 1:9]).

links the antique with the (for him) present, extending his list *mod-
ernis temporibus* with the Empress Matilda and Saint Thomas Becket.
London as presented by Fitz Stephen is, on the one hand, a contemporary, living place; he describes in detail the disposition of its buildings, fields, and markets, reinforcing this immediacy by constructing
his account of its recreations as a year in the life of the ludic citizen. Yet he is also concerned with establishing for the City an antique
pedigree that transcends time: when he compares London to Rome,
it is to the Rome of Caesar, not that of the Middle Ages, and he repeatedly quotes Virgil while name-dropping more exotic figures like
Heraclitus and Zeno.[64] This dual emphasis is not inherently remarkable: the antiquity of a city is a natural element of praise for an *encomium urbis* like Fitz Stephen's, and London's putative Trojan origins
had been well established since the time of Geoffrey of Monmouth.[65]
It is important, however, because it parallels Horn's larger goal of using the antiquity of the City's laws and customs as a way of ensuring
its continuing prosperity. Here, the *Description*'s position within the
compilation is significant, for it follows a progression of laws from
the Anglo-Saxon kings to Henry II, and, after the Latini excerpts that
immediately follow it, *Liber regum* continues with a series of charters
going back to the original one of William the Conqueror.[66] London's
antiquity, then, secures its privileges, while the sense of immediacy
that Fitz Stephen also conveys aims to fix the relevance of those privileges to two different historical presents: that of his own writing, ca.
1170, and through the text's inclusion in *Liber regum* the 1320s of the
custumal's compilation.

As we have seen, however, such multiple temporalities rarely re-
main straightforward, and wrinkles emerge here when we recall that
Fitz Stephen's *Description* deals with a very different city from Horn's:
London, to be sure, but the London of the late twelfth century rather

64. On such instances of "obvious and ostentatious literariness," see Scattergood, "Misrepresenting the City," 16–28 (quotation 17).
65. See, e.g., Sylvia Federico, *New Troy: Fantasies of Empire in the Late Middle Ages* (Minneapolis: University of Minnesota Press, 2003).
66. See Ker, "Liber Custumarum," 140.

than the early fourteenth. In the intervening 150 years, London's population grew at a staggering rate, the very economic prowess that Fitz Stephen praised drawing immigrants from other parts of England and abroad.[67] This growth profoundly altered the City's landscape as the newcomers first stretched and then shattered London's structural capacities; deeds and royal inquiries from throughout the thirteenth century record "continuous subdivision" of existing buildings[68] as well as accusations that new construction encroached on common land and blocked public rights of way.[69] The inevitable result was suburban expansion: southern and western suburbs grew rapidly in the thirteenth century, producing "new units of jurisdiction, the extra-mural appendages of intra-mural wards."[70] By the time Horn was constructing *Liber regum*, then, London had been fundamentally transformed from the city Fitz Stephen described.[71]

Horn's inclusion of this encomium in his custumal thus represents a counterfactual gesture, much like the legal idealism we saw in *Mirror of Justices*. The reality was that, by transforming its geography, London's

67. Williams (*Medieval London*, 18–20, 315–17) suggests that, between 1200 and 1300, London doubled in population from 20,000 to 40,000, but even his striking estimate probably understates the case. More recently, Nightingale (*A Medieval Mercantile Community*, 18) has proposed a figure of 60,000 in the early fourteenth century, while Barron (*London in the Later Middle Ages*, 238) argues that 50,000 was "the minimum size" for London's 1300 population, that "the likely size was nearer to 80,000," and that it "may have been as high as 100,000."

68. "One communally owned tenement rented at 10s. early in the reign of Edward I had become two shops at £1 each by 1304, and this was typical" (Williams, *Medieval London*, 17).

69. See ibid., 17–20; and Barron, *London in the Later Middle Ages*, 238–39.

70. Williams, *Medieval London*, 18. See further Martha Carlin, *Medieval Southwark* (London: Hambledon, 1996), 19–44; and Kevin McDonnell, *Medieval London Suburbs* (London: Phillimore, 1978), 119–32.

71. I do not mean to imply by this that the *Description of London* is the purely and transparently factual record of the City that it is suggested to be in, e.g., Antonia Grandsen, "Realistic Observation in Twelfth-Century England," *Speculum* 46 (1972): 29–51. Scattergood is right to insist: "[Fitz Stephen] is not simply describing what he sees. . . . He seeks through praise to establish fame" ("Misrepresenting the City," 19). My point is not to deny the counterfactual idealism that inhered in the original but rather to observe that the many ways in which the *Description* does appear to have been an accurate depiction of the City (even Scattergood acknowledges that the text "is valuable on the level of simple information if one treats it as a conscientious attempt to describe the physical appearance of London in 1173 or thereabouts" [ibid., 33]) would have been transformed out of all recognition by the time it came to be included in *Liber regum*.

exploding population had created serious social and political conflict. Matthew Paris, for example, complained in the thirteenth century that the City was "overflowing" with all sorts of alien merchants,[72] whom Londoners deeply resented for their erosion of civic liberties. Violent protests against the Crown's perceived coddling of such aliens constituted one of the major forms of lawlessness that often enabled the king to seize control of the City.[73] Immigrants from other parts of England had also flocked to London, and, like the alien merchants, these foreigns threatened long-established social norms by which citizenship and its attendant rights were acquired through years of apprenticeship, for they either bought citizenship or else set up shop on the margins of London society, undercutting the citizens' privileges.[74] This historical context puts a distinctly different spin on Fitz Stephen's celebration of London's ability to attract merchants from far-flung lands. As imagined by the *Description*, these merchants come to London ("ad urbem hanc") but do not themselves transform the City. By Horn's day, they either did or were trying to and, as a result, deeply complicated Londoners' ability to imagine themselves as a unified polity with the power to resist encroachment from outside.

Within *Liber regum*, then, Fitz Stephen's *Description of London* can be read in two distinctly different ways. On the one hand, it praises

72. Quoted in Williams, *Medieval London*, 12.

73. Barron (*London in the Later Middle Ages*, 35) points out that, in general, "the most serious threat to the city's right to govern its own affairs through officers chosen by the citizens, was posed by the problems of lawlessness and disorder." Conflict could break out among Londoners, but frequently the targeted groups were aliens like Jews, Cahorsins, Italians, and Flemings. Nightingale notes, moreover, that the consequences of Londoners' resentment could extend beyond the alien merchants themselves: "It was conflicts . . . in which the Crown appeared to join with alien interlopers in threatening the livelihood of the retailers and the craftsmen, which helped to win for de Montfort the fervent support of all but the Court purveyors and the aldermen" (*A Medieval Mercantile Community*, 79).

74. These threats became particularly acute in the 1280s and 1290s. Nightingale points out that despite citizens' attempts "to close ranks and organize themselves so as to exclude from their trade all who were not freemen . . . the increasing numbers of redemptioners who were able to buy citizenship threatened to swamp the market." Those who were not able to buy citizenship, meanwhile, could live in the suburbs and there "take lower prices for their goods, work at night, or reduce standards and quality to undercut the freemen" (*A Medieval Mercantile Community*, 111).

the City by emphasizing its antiquity, legal structures, and economic prowess and its citizens' socially reinforcing enjoyment of their many recreational activities.[75] Other elements of *Liber regum* confirm that fourteenth-century Londoners still relied on these to assert their civic rights. For this same readership of the 1320s, however, all these elements had been thrown into question. The City's *antiquas libertates* were proving no defense against royal attempts to rescind its privileges—the Eyre of 1321, the very year of *Liber regum*'s likely compilation, had made that painfully clear—and rather than benefiting from the alien and foreign merchants attracted to its markets, as imagined by Fitz Stephen, Londoners were suffering socially from their radical transformation of London's topography and economically from their ability to undercut Londoners' cherished protectionism. The historical distance between Fitz Stephen's London and Horn's thus turns the *Description* into a nostalgic and counterfactual statement as much as a laudatory one: the City has fundamentally changed in population and geography, and those changes have turned the harmonious games described by Fitz Stephen into the fierce competition of rival factions.

This more ambivalent resonance of the *Description* deepens when we consider its juxtaposition with the following text, a series of excerpts from Brunetto Latini's much-copied *Livres dou Tresor*.[76] Like Fitz Stephen's *Description of London*, the Latini excerpts highlight one form of counterfactualism underlying Londoners' self-aggrandizement in the early fourteenth century, this time geographic rather than historical. Horn's adaptation of the political sections of the *Tresor* optimistically implies that the political power of the Italian city-states that Latini was writing about could be translated into London's very different political culture, just as he literally translates Latini's *seignor* (lord) into the *meire* (mayor) appropriate to the City. Yet in adapting the *Tresor* to the particularities of his own locale, as Latini's text itself

---

75. Compare Benson's comments that the *Description*'s emphasis on local recreations "creates a strong sense of an inclusive community. . . . [T]he result is as joyous, convivial, and communal as any Bahktinian could wish" ("Some Poets' Tours of Medieval London," 5).

76. *Li livres dou tresor*, ed. Spurgeon Baldwin and Paul Barrette (Tempe, AZ: Arizona Center for Medieval and Renaissance Studies, 2003). *Tresor* is cited by volume, chapter, and page numbers.

encourages, Horn emphasizes its cautionary rather than celebratory elements. Juxtaposed as they are with Fitz Stephen's *Description*, another text whose praise of London becomes skeptical when read for more than its superficial content, the Latini extracts further highlight the remove at which London finds itself from the optimistic ideals being presented; importing such Continental political theory will not in fact enable London to match the autonomy of an Italian city-state, and Horn's selection and arrangement of the extracts suggest that he recognized as much. Taken together, then, Fitz Stephen and the Latini extracts do in the civic sphere what the conjoined *Mirror of Justices* and *Britton* did in the legal: present ideals that, however attractive, are fundamentally at odds with the reality of London as Horn and his audience experienced it.

The excerpts that Horn has chosen to include in *Liber regum* all come from the final section of the *Tresor*, in which Latini outlines the proper method of choosing a city's lord and how that lord should govern. Critically, however, Horn is not simply copying relevant sections of the text; he has rearranged them substantially, dividing and reassembling the chapters, and providing different chapter headings.[77] He is thus orchestrating a compilation (the Latini extracts) within a compilation (*Liber regum*). The result is a text that, compared to Latini's, emphasizes the role of the citizens in the political contract rather than focusing on their governor.[78] Two analogous chapter headings that precede substantially identical text illustrate this difference:

---

77. *Liber regum* gives a table of eight chapters, prefaced by the heading "Incipiunt capitula titulorum inspiciendorum in electione cujuscunque superioris." Each of these chapters has its own Latin title, some of which are reproduced in French before the corresponding chapter in the text. The eight chapters correspond, respectively, to *Tresor* chaps. 74–75, 75, 75, 102, 104, 97, 96, and 96 of vol. 3. Baldwin and Barrette specify that the chapter headings and titles that they reproduce and that I cite from are attested in the manuscripts (*Tresor*, li). Since we cannot know the form in which Horn knew the *Tresor*, we cannot be absolutely certain that he was not simply consulting a particularly idiosyncratic manuscript that included the unusual chapter divisions, ordering, and titles found in *Liber regum*. In the absence of any evidence for such a manuscript, however, it seems reasonable to assume that they were adapted by their English compiler. For the text, see *Liber Custumarum*, 2, pt. 1:15–25.

78. On this point, see also Lynn Staley, *Languages of Power in the Age of Richard II* (University Park: Pennsylvania State University Press, 2005), 34–36.

Tresor: "Ci dit des choses que li sire doit consirer & faire en sa seignorie."

Liber regum: "La maniere coment chescun bon Meire se devra porter entre
ses sougis, duraunt le temps de sa Mayrie."[79]

Tresor: "Ci dit des choses que li sire doit fere le derenier jor de son
office."

Liber regum: "La maniere coment le Meir se deit avoir et porter envers
ceus qil aura en sa subjectioun, au darreyn jour de sa seignourie, quaunt
il devra prendre de eus soun counge."[80]

By mentioning the mayor's "subjects" where the *Tresor* does not, the
Liber regum version emphasizes that, while one party is in charge, he
does not rule in a vacuum. Horn further reinforces that the mayor's
power is temporary: his "duraunt le temps de sa Mayrie" highlights
the office's finite nature more than the *Tresor*'s "en sa seignorie." The
second example is even more emphatic, adding an entire clause stipu-
lating that the mayor must vacate his office after a specified time, and
using an additional verb of obligation (*devra*) to draw attention to his
departure. The right to replace their mayors annually was one of Londoners' most cherished privileges, a crucial safety valve to ensure that
the mayor could not become a mere puppet of the king, and these
changes to Latini's text highlight this power. Yet thus emphasizing
the finite and defined terms of mayoral office inevitably recalls the
royal wardens who had seized control of the City so often in the past
and were to do so again in 1321. As royal officers serving at the king's
pleasure, they had no such fixed term of office, and, as we saw in our
consideration of *Mirror of Justices*, London had endured over a decade
of this form of royal control in living memory, from 1285 to 1297.
Horn thus insists on a civic prerogative that was crucial to London's
governance; in so doing, however, he recalls the fact that the City had

79. *Tresor*, 3, chap. 97:386: "It speaks here of the things that the lord must consider and do
during his lordship." *Liber Custumarum*, 2, pt. 1:21: "The manner in which every good mayor
must conduct himself among his subjects, during the time of his mayoralty."
80. *Tresor*, 3, chap. 104:391: "It speaks here of the things that the lord must do on the last
day of his office." *Liber Custumarum*, 2, pt. 1:20: "The manner in which the mayor must maintain and conduct himself toward those whom he has in his protection, on the last day of his
lordship, when he must take his leave of them."

frequently been stripped of this right—and would be again in what may well have been the very year of *Liber regum*'s construction.

The omissions from Latini's text are just as significant as his rearrangements and retitlings: Horn includes chapters on how the mayor must be elected and then leave office but omits the many chapters from the *Tresor* that deal with the lord's actual governance.[81] *Liber regum*'s excerpts, in other words, are less about proper rulership than about the transitions and definitions that should properly circumscribe rulership: the criteria and mechanisms for election; how the lord should assume and leave office; the distinction to be made between king and tyrant. Besides highlighting the active role that Horn took in manipulating the original text of the *Tresor*, these interventions recall Latini's frequent acknowledgment that differences between cities mean that local custom will help determine what actions to take in a given case. After describing in detail how the lord of a city should be chosen and how he should govern, for example, Latini concludes thus:

> Par les ensegnemens de ces livres puet bien chiascun qui droitement le regarde governer la cite a tens de pais & de guerre, a l'aide de Dieu & de bon conseil. & ja soit ce que il ait asés des enseignemens, neporquant il a es seignories tant de diversités & des choses que nus hom vivant ne le poroit escrire ne dire de bouche. Mais en sonme il doit sivre la loi comune & la loi et us de la ville a foi, & conduire son office selonc la costume dou pais. Pour ce que li villain dit: quant tu es a Roume, vive come a Roume, car de tels terres, tel pors.[82]

This emphasis on the primacy of local custom is of course thoroughly consonant with Londoners' insistence that their city's uniqueness and ancient rights be respected. Horn goes further than this, however, by actively manipulating Latini's text in the ways we have seen,

---

81. See *Tresor*, 3, chaps. 77–95:367–84.

82. Ibid., 3, chap. 101:389–90: "By the instructions in this book each person who looks at it carefully can govern the city in time of peace or war, with the help of God and good counsel. Although there are many instructions, nevertheless there is in lordship such a variety of things that no man alive could write them down or tell them; but in short he must follow the common law and the customs of the city in faith, and conduct his office according to the custom of the country. This is the reason for the popular expression: when you are in Rome, do as the Romans, for each land has its own customs."

adapting it to London's particular situation by emphasizing the role of the citizens and civic custom, rather than the power of the lord himself. In so doing, he effectively claims that he and his city are Latini's target audience and that the *Tresor* is just as adaptable to London as it was to the Italian city-states about which it was written.

Yet like Fitz Stephen's *Description of London*, Horn's adaptation of Latini's text invites a darker interpretation as well, for he has chosen to highlight the admonitory and elide the celebratory aspects of the *Tresor*'s vision of civic power. He has taken the section of the *Tresor*'s volume 3, chapter 75, that attacks electors for selecting rulers based on their *rischesces* and *ados* rather than their *mours* and *vertues*, for example, and made it its own chapter in *Liber regum*; in the table of contents, moreover, it is entitled "De Discordiis et Atyiis ortis in Civitatibus per Custodum negligentias." Similarly, at the end of the excerpts, he has broken up Latini's volume 3, chapter 96, into two separate chapters, titling his last "La Différence entre Rey et Tyraunt." This emphasis on the tyrannical tendencies of rulers, and on the frequency with which citizens themselves make poor choices of governors, accords with London's negative experience of authoritarian kings, wardens, and mayors, but it also gives the lie to the notion that Londoners' capacity for civic harmony could lead to a degree of civic autonomy comparable to that of thirteenth-century Italian cities.[83] As translated into Londonese by Horn, in other words, the *Tresor* insists on the importance of active citizen involvement in urban politics even as it alludes to Londoners' poor track record in this area,[84] right around the

---

83. I mean to imply, not that urban life in thirteenth-century Florence was wholly rosy, or that Latini's ideals were fully realized there, but merely that the city's civic structures and relation to centralized feudal authority were radically different from London's and that the how and why of Florence's own failure to live up to these ideals were therefore likewise different.

84. The political chaos and factionalism that characterized London politics ca. 1299–1319, as summarized by Williams (*Medieval London*, 264–84), were in fact quite typical. The reforming mayor Richer de Refham (whose sponsorship of the 1310 *antiquas libertates persecutari* exercise we have already considered) was ousted in 1311 following a conflict with his fellow mercers, and John de Gisors III succeeded him. Gisors, however, lost the support of the commons, which "won control over the executive service, the personnel of city administration, and vital sectors of the revenue" (ibid., 271). Gaveston's return in 1312 furthered the reformist impulse, but his murder allowed the king to regain Londoners' loyalty following his dramatic appeal to

moment in which the City's relative impotence had been highlighted by the 1321 Eyre. The effect of this geographic counterfactualism—London is not, after all, an Italian city-state—is heightened by being juxtaposed with the historical counterfactualism of Fitz Stephen's *Description* that we have already considered. Taken together, the two texts depict ideals of civic autonomy and harmony that they simultaneously suggest are unlikely ever to be fully realized.

The *Tresor* extracts of *Liber regum* implicitly point to the Italian city-states that Latini was principally writing about as a worthy but ultimately not fully imitable model of civic power. Latini's text was also widely popular in another area of Europe renowned for urban prosperity and autonomy: the cities of the Franco-Flemish Low Countries. Julia Bolton Holloway has drawn attention to the many *Tresor* manuscripts that can be traced to Arras;[85] given the strong trading and cultural links between London and the Low Countries, this may well be how Horn came to know of Latini's text. Part of the *Tresor*'s particular appeal to a Franco-Flemish audience was doubtless the fact that, like Latini's Florence, their cities were characterized by urban merchant elites whose economic prowess afforded them a considerable degree of political autonomy. Horn's *Liber regum* also records another, much more mimetic attempt to imitate the cultural prestige that was an outward manifestation of this power: two sets of statutes for the London *puy*, a homegrown version of the mercantile poetic society of the same name that flourished in such cities. As we will see, Horn's contextualization of the two *puy* statutes within *Liber regum*

---

them narrated in Horn's *Annales Londonienses*. Meanwhile (1312–13), the crafts were attempting to gain power outside the structure of the commonalty and, in so doing, allied the fractious trade guilds against them. These guilds, who supported the anti-Edwardian baronial movement headed by Thomas of Lancaster, used that support (combined with the propagandist value of the Bannockburn disaster of 1314) to crush the reformists by 1316. At this point, the technocratic mayor John de Wengrave took charge, but there arose around him a faction, detested by the commons, that would ultimately be convicted of conspiracy at the 1321 Eyre. This summary, drawn entirely from Williams's engagingly readable account, usefully highlights how fractiously (to be generous) Londoners used their substantial political autonomy when they were able to exercise it.

85. See Julia Bolton Holloway, *Brunetto Latini: An Analytic Bibliography* (London: Grant & Cutler, 1986), 40.

as a whole makes a counterfactual gesture similar to those we have seen in the *Mirror/Britton* and *Description/Tresor* pairings; here, however, Horn links more explicitly the ideals of civic power and cultural play that were adumbrated in Fitz Stephen's description of Londoners' recreations.

As we saw in the introduction, the *puy* was one of a wide range of civic festivals at which the merchant elite of Franco-Flemish cities sought to display their social and cultural prestige. In the case of the *puy*, the annual occasion for this display was a poetic competition, whose winner was crowned *prince du puy* and typically sponsored a lavish feast. This condition effectively made mercantile success a prerequisite for cultural recognition: full acknowledgment of one's poetic talents depended on having the wealth to offer a suitably grand repast. In their original Continental context, the *puys* appear to have offered a space in which a wide range of competitive tensions (social, economic, political) could be expressed and then released through the sublimated medium of a literary contest. Arras, for example, whose celebrated *puy* was a likely model for London's own, featured a "notoriously mixed" social character, with two distinct and potentially competing jurisdictions, la Cité and la Ville, and two poetic societies (the *puy* and the less socially exclusive *carité des ardents*) that testify to "the complexity and multiplicity of social relations."[86] These various tensions, however, would ultimately be contained, or at least contextualized, by the socially cohesive activity of feasting (we might think ahead to the comparable feast promised but never enjoyed in the *Canterbury Tales*). The *puys* featured participants from across the social spectrum, with kings and aristocrats joining both professional poets like Adam de la Halle and far humbler merchants and bankers as composers and judges alike.[87] The "court" of the *puy* thus offered Franco-Flemish merchants

---

86. See Butterfield, *Poetry and Music in Medieval France*, 133–35. On the intersection of play and power in Arras more generally, see Carol Symes, *A Common Stage: Theater and Public Life in Medieval Arras* (Ithaca, NY: Cornell University Press, 2007).

87. At the *puy* of Arras in 1263, e.g., the judges included the future Edward I of England and Charles of Anjou, the future king of Sicily and uncle of the Count of Artois. That *jeu parti* is recorded as no. 104 in the *Recueil général des jeux-partis français*, ed. Arthur Långfors (Paris: Edouard Champion, 1926). Among the recorded aristocratic composers of *jeux partis* are

an opportunity to hobnob with, and play at being, aristocrats; one favored literary form (and that specified for the *puy* of London) was the *chant royal*, and of course the eventual winner was crowned *prince*. This imitative aristocratic play took place in a setting that enhanced mercantile prestige and, at the feast, mirrored the harmony across the city's social and political structures that would, in turn, allow its urban elite to exercise their economic might most productively. This enterprise appears to have been successful, for it was while the *puy* of Arras was at its most spectacular in the late thirteenth century and contributing to the city's reputation as "the greatest urban literary center in Europe," as Ardis Butterfield deems it,[88] that Arras was also growing fabulously wealthy as the most important banking center in Northern Europe. Cultural, economic, and political power were all mutually fulfilling.

It was about this time, during the 1270s, that Londoners probably founded their own *puy*.[89] Its most extensive surviving records are the two sets of statutes contained in *Liber regum*; two others are slight but revealing. The first of these is an annuity of five marks given to the Brethren of the Puy in 1299 by Henry le Waleys, past mayor of London (1273–74, 1280–83) and Bordeaux (1275) and trusted lieutenant of Edward I.[90] The second is a 1304 judgment secured by the commonalty of the mercers and Roger de Paris, a wealthy mercer and sheriff (1304–5), against one John le Mirourer in the amount of twenty pounds, of which one hundred shillings were to be paid toward works of the Chapel of Our Lady of the Puy; a later record from that same

---

Geoffrey, Count of Brittany (1169–86), and Thibaut, Count of Champagne (1201–53). See further Butterfield, *Poetry and Music in Medieval France*, 135–37; and Sutton, "Merchants, Music and Social Harmony," 9–11.

88. Butterfield, *Poetry and Music in Medieval France*, 133.

89. See Sutton, "Merchants, Music and Social Harmony," 5. Sutton argues that London's society was based on the *puy* of Arras, partly because Londoners chose the *chant royal* for their competition, and this form was popularized by Adam de la Halle, a composer, poet, and member of the Arras *puy*. During the 1270s, Arras was at its most powerful, and the still flourishing trading contacts between the city and England would have encouraged cultural imitation of the sort Sutton imagines.

90. *Memorials of London and London Life in the XIIIth, XIVth, and XVth Centuries, 1276–1419*, ed. Henry Thomas Riley (London: Longmans, Green, 1868), 42; *Calendar of the Letter Books of the City of London, E*, ed. R. R. Sharpe (London: Corporation of the City of London, 1903), 1–2.

year confirms payment.[91] One further name can be adduced from the *puy* statutes themselves, which identify John de Cheshunt, a wealthy vintner, as "le tierz prince, [qui] douna la primere chaundoile."[92] Such names indicate that the *puy* enjoyed the membership and patronage of the upper echelons of London society. Mercers and vintners were among the most prominent and powerful London trades through the end of the fourteenth century, and the society's mayoral supporters included, not just Henry le Waleys, but also Richer de Refham,[93] whose push to codify London's liberties we have already considered.

The London *puy* thus seems for a time to have functioned like its Continental models, uniting prosperous merchants and both royalist and more civic-minded mayors. Yet, while we have no record of its dissolution and it must still have existed in some form when the mercers secured funds for its chapel in 1304, there is good reason to agree with Sutton's assessment that the society had been defunct some while by the time its statutes were included in *Liber regum* around 1321.[94] As will we see shortly, the second set of statutes preserved by Horn strongly suggests that the society was suffering from internal dissension.[95] This second, cautionary set presumably predates 1299 since it identifies the appointment of a chaplain as a desideratum not yet attained, yet Henry le Waleys's gift of that year was to precisely that end. It is therefore reasonable to suppose that, by our last mention of the society as an active institution in 1304, it was in serious trouble. Since Sutton is surely right to argue that "the economic problems, civil war

91. Sutton, "Merchants, Music and Social Harmony," 4.

92. *Liber Custumarum*, 2, pt. 1:219. The candle of this passage refers to a collective obligation of the *puy* membership cited earlier in the statutes: to provide annually a fifty-pound wax candle to the Lady Chapel of Saint Martin le Grand. Cheshunt figures centrally in the speculative reconstruction of the day-to-day activities of the *puy*'s membership in Sutton, "The *Tumbling Bear* and Its Patrons."

93. Refham was among those listed as witnesses to the mercers' action against John le Mirourer that resulted in the grant to the society's chapel.

94. Sutton suggests that the society "did not long survive 1300" ("Merchants, Music and Social Harmony," 2). More recently, she has suggested that the *puy* existed "perhaps as long as *c.* 1270–1310" (*The Mercery of London*, 69).

95. Compare Riley's suggestion that "the society would appear, at the date of its Second Series of regulations, to have already contained within itself the germs of dissolution" (*Liber Custumarum*, 2, pt. 1:lii).

and capricious tyranny of Edward II's reign did not provide a good environment" for a society premised on leisure and conspicuous consumption,[96] we can conclude that the society was either actually or practically defunct by around 1310.

The question then becomes why in the 1320s, at least a decade after the *puy*'s likely dissolution, Horn would include its statutes in a collection composed principally of more obviously practical texts. Horn himself might have been a member of the society, of course, and its statutes' inclusion thus have been a nod to his former company, a personal touch not unlike the inclusion of his son's death in his portion of the *Annales Londonienses*.[97] That tantalizing possibility aside, the ideals of the *puy* as stated in the statutes' preamble accord with the custumal's general praise of the City, with moves that recall the *encomium urbis* of Fitz Stephen's *Description of London*: "En le honour de Dieu, Madame Seinte Marie, touz Seinz, et toutes Seintes; e en le honour nostre Seignour le Roy e touz les Barons du pais; e por loial amour ensaucier. Et por ceo qe la ville de Lundres soit renomee de touz biens en tuz lieus; et por ceo qe jolietes, pais, honestez, douceur, deboneiretes, e bon amour, sanz infinite, soit maintenue."[98] The comfortably vague conventionality of the final list of goals should not dull our notice of the more pointed aim that the city of London be renowned for all good things (*de touz biens*—presumably trade goods as well as the listed intangibles) in all places. Like Fitz Stephen's *Description*, then, the London *puy* looks both inward and outward: it seeks the glorification of the City and its merchants above all, but its intended relevance is much wider, a kind of advertisement to the rest of the world of Londoners' gracious qualities. The *puy* thus imagines its members taking their place on the world stage of great international cities marked by powerful mercantile elites. The statutes' harmonious ideal, moreover,

---

96. Sutton, "Merchants, Music and Social Harmony," 11.

97. Stubbs, ed., *Annales*, 137.

98. *Liber Custumarum*, 2, pt. 1:216: "In the honor of God, Our Lady Saint Mary, and all saints male and female; and in the honor of our lord the king and all the barons of the country; and for the increasing of loyal love. And to the end that the city of London may be renowned for all good things in all places; and so that delight, peace, honesty, sweetness, gaiety, and good love may be maintained without end."

extends beyond its members to the entire "ville de Lundres" and offers a vision, not just of mercantile power, but also of the elusive civic unity that was necessary to keep an encroaching Crown at bay.

The second set of statutes, however, does not sustain this idealism. Three times as long as the first set, these statutes' provisions indicate a host of ways in which the society was failing to meet its lofty goals as initially conceived: they demand more rigorous accounting of the society's funds, for example, to make sure that each member pays his fair share, and limit the amount that the *prince du puy* can spend on the society's annual feast. Such amendments suggest that members had become more interested in upstaging each other and avoiding payment than in performing the *bon amour* promised in the statutes' preamble. Sutton argues that the second set of statutes "showed how . . . follies and sins . . . had undermined these ideals [of the first set]—the pride of the rich and the resulting quarrels and jealousies which had presumably destroyed the Puy by the time Horn recorded it."[99] Her conclusion is plausible, but it does not address why, if Horn intended the statutes to provide a glimpse of the ideal world that would result from an emancipated civic government, as Sutton also argues,[100] he would include evidence that London's merchants had failed to produce that harmony even among themselves, much less in London at large.

I believe that we can best understand the second set of statutes as a warning by Horn to both his contemporaries and those who would read his books in the future to avoid any display of disunity that might give the Crown an opportunity to deprive the City of its liberties, and I suspect that he was thinking particularly of Edward I's seizure of city government from 1285 until 1297—the very time, if we accept Sutton's dating, that the London *puy* was in full force and that *Mirror of Justices* was written. In that case, royal encroachment was enabled by Londoners' failure to control factional violence within the City,[101]

---

99. Sutton, "Merchants, Music and Social Harmony," 12.

100. Ibid., 14–17.

101. For a zestful and detailed account, see Williams, *Medieval London*, 248–57, of which the following is a brief summary. In 1281, rising crime rates led Londoners to elect as mayor the strongly authoritarian Henry le Waleys, but they soon grew leery of some of his harsher pronouncements in the name of civic order—not least, we may suppose, because a 1283 writ by

the consequence of which was Edward I's declaration in June 1285 that the area around Saint Paul's had become the haunt of vagabonds and thieves; he went so far as to empower the cathedral to enclose and take over the area.[102] In fact, this was precisely the site of London's ancient civic assemblies, the Folkmoot and the Muster. Although both assemblies were practically defunct by the early fourteenth century, his rhetorical attack struck at the heart of Londoners' sense of how they had from time immemorial convened themselves into an autonomous polity. Indeed, Gwyn Williams argues that Edward's insult (that London's traditional assemblies are assemblies of criminals) and threat (that the cathedral could take control of that symbolically important space) were strategically chosen to produce something like the results that we have already considered in the context of *Mirror of Justices*: the mayor's resignation in protest, which allowed Edward to appoint a royal warden, dismantle the City's franchise, and control civic government through his wardens until 1297.[103]

The continuing resonance of this traumatic episode for texts as dissimilar as the *puy* statutes and *Mirror* highlights the long reach of history for both Horn and London's civic culture more broadly. Horn's use of Fitz Stephen's *Description of London* likewise demanded historical acuity from the reader in order to understand both London's grandeur (the City is even older than Rome) and its insecurity (the complex and fractious London of today is not the idealized London of Fitz Stephen). Each element of the Horn corpus that I have considered, then, juxtaposes counterfactual idealism with stern depictions of the consequences of failing to meet these inherently impossible ideals. In *Mirror*, we saw both the idealism and the attack on its failure combined

---

the king encouraged the new mayor in such measures. In October 1284, they booted le Waleys and restored the more traditionalist Gregory de Rokesle. The city's rejection of his chosen mayor would have angered Edward anyway, but it did so the more for occurring shortly after a long-running feud between two prominent Londoners, Ralph Crepyn and Laurence Ducket, concluded in bloody scandal, with a claim of sanctuary violated and a murder disguised as suicide in the church of Saint Mary le Bow.

102. Williams (*Medieval London*, 254) cites the "thieves and vagabonds" line from the deeds and wills of Saint Paul's Cathedral Chapter Library, A/70/1756.

103. Williams, *Medieval London*, 254.

in the same work, the satire made legible by the introductory verses and reinforced by its juxtaposition with *Britton*. In the Latini quire, the complementary counterfactualisms (one historical, one geographic) of the *Description* and *Tresor* excerpts combined to warn Horn's audience of the difficulty of translating their ideals into contemporary London. With the *puy* statutes, the first set expresses the idealism, and the second gives the warning. Read with this larger resonance in mind, the conclusion of the second set of statutes sounds almost apocalyptic: "Saunz ces Estatuz ci escriz navera jammes le gentil Pui de Loundres pouer de estre honoure ne meintenu a soun avenaunt en due manere. E si li Estatuz ne seient bien garde et renablenent [*sic*] tenu, tote la confraternite descherra saunz doute, en bref temps; qe Dieu defende par sa douce merci."[104] By including the statutes even after the society they governed had disbanded, Horn projects the *puy* as a synecdoche for the entire London merchant class: just as factionalism threatened to and ultimately did destroy the *puy*, so too it might easily shatter the larger convocation (*confraternite*) of Londoners out of that elusive unity that civic writers had long been seeking to effect.

In this context, even one of the reforms instituted in the second set of statutes seems to have the society's dissolution written into it: "Ke xii des mieux vaillaunz, suffisaunz, et reseiaunz en la cite de Lundres de la compaignie, qe sachent, voelent, et puissent, a les bosoignes du Pui entendre, soient nomez et eslu par assent des compaignouns, le jour du grant siege du Pui, pur la confraternite governer et consailler, en eide du prince; enci qe li princes rien ne face qe touche la compaignie sanz la presence de ii ou de iii de cele dozime, qi puissent ses fetz tesmoigner."[105] This excerpt, together with the limitations on the

---

104. *Liber Custumarum*, 2, pt. 1:223: "Without these statutes written here, the gentle *puy* of London will never have the power to be honored or maintained according to its graciousness in due manner. And if the statutes are not well kept and reasonably held, the entire confraternity will fall apart without doubt, in a short while; which God in his sweet mercy forbid."

105. Ibid., 220: "That twelve of the most valiant and competent members of the company residing in London, who know how, wish, and are able to see to the business of the *puy*, should be named and elected by assent of the companions, on the day of the great seat of the *puy*, in order to govern and counsel the confraternity, in aid of the Prince; so that the Prince may do nothing touching the company without the presence of two or three of the twelve, who can witness his acts."

expenditure for the annual feast, suggests that one of the society's problems involved *princes* who concentrated too much power in themselves, draining the treasury, and turning the *puy* into a vehicle for the display of personal rather than communal prestige. While perhaps a necessity given such abuses, however, this provision institutionalizes precisely the divisions and factions that threatened the society—and Londoners' relations with the king—in the first place. It thereby displays Londoners' ambivalent relation with royal authority: while everyone wants to be crowned *prince* following a competition of *chants royaux*, the prince's fellows immediately become suspicious of his power. We have only to consider the case of Henry le Waleys to see that overambitious mayors could become as much of a threat as the king himself. As we have seen, he was a benefactor of the *puy* whom Londoners elected mayor, but his authoritarian tendencies led them to remove him, thus beginning the sequence of events that led to Edward I's 1285 suspension of civic liberties. In the context of the entire *Liber regum*, then, the *puy* statutes serve some of the same functions as the *Tresor* excerpts: to hold up an ideal of emancipated civic government imported from the Continent while querying the translation of that ideal to London's urban culture, defined as it was by the uncomfortable reality of a strong monarchy.

In suggesting a relation between festive literary play and harmonious civic unity, the *puy* statutes recall Fitz Stephen's extended description of Londoners' various *ludi*. The first, idealistic set of statutes figures literary production and consumption as the model of and means to civic harmony. While the second set might seem to imply (and the society's failure prove) that literary games like the *puy* will never be equal to managing London's strife and uncertainty, in fact they suggest a more complex attitude, for their reforming provisions are literary as well as social: they specify, for example, that the *chants royaux* must be strictly composed and sung (per the name) rather than spoken. The social decay implied by the rest of the statutes thus has a literary manifestation, in the form of improper poetic composition and performance. This parallel offers at least the hint that a more proper or well-executed form of literary play might have positive social consequences. In the introduction, we saw a comparable relation between literary performance and social well-being implied in the "Sayings of the Four Philosophers" of the Auchinleck manuscript, my subject in the following chapter. But I would like to conclude the current discussion by returning to the subject of history: Horn's marshaling of obsolete texts for contemporary purposes, his curious construction of historical narrative, and how the postmedieval histories of his now fragmentary corpus and of our own academic disciplines complicate our ability to assemble quite so coherent a set of narratives about this fascinating figure as our wealth of data might suggest we could.

Obsolescence, Performance, and the Forms of History

As a prominent member of London's increasingly powerful bourgeoisie, Andrew Horn would have been unlikely to sympathize politically with members of the Frankfurt school. His sophisticated deployment of no longer or never applicable texts within an otherwise practical corpus and career, however, demonstrates that he understood well the substance of Adorno's comments to Benjamin: "With the vitiation of their use value, the alienated things are hollowed out and, as ciphers, draw in meanings. . . . Dialectical images are constelled between alienated things and incoming and disappearing meaning."[106] *Mirror of Justices* makes expansive claims about Anglo-Saxon legal history, but as a legal treatise it would have had no "use value" in either that period or Horn's own, and precisely this fact gives it the new, satiric significance that we have considered. The *Description of London* and *puy* statutes do appear once to have had the use value that they assert: Fitz Stephen's text was a broadly accurate (if lovingly rendered) picture of the London of his day, and the *puy* statutes describe the activities of an externally verifiable society. Their subjects had been transformed or disbanded by the time these texts were included in *Liber regum*, however, and this obsolescence contributes vitally to the meanings

---

106. Quoted as a "letter from Wiesengrund of August 5, 1935," in Benjamin, *The Arcades Project*, 466 (N5,2).

they achieve in this particular manuscript. I have emphasized the significance of these texts' position as members of a juxtaposed pair (Fitz Stephen with Latini and the two sets of statutes); my argument has been that this version of codicological form is complemented by the force of history to yield meanings that are complex, allusive, and metaphoric—*poetic*, in Pearsall's sense of the word.

Moreover, the sharp oppositions that these obsolete texts create within their broader codicological structure—the bizarre *Mirror* juxtaposed with the conventional *Britton*; the obsolete statutes of an arguably frivolous literary society within a compendium largely devoted to practical and serious matters—help turn these larger objects, *Liber regum* and the *Mirror* codex, into versions of the dialectical image that Adorno describes above. Horn had already included portions of *Britton* in a different compendium, the *Liber Horn*, where its function appears to have been far more straightforward; when repeated in the *Mirror* codex, however, it becomes a functionally different text, despite its still intact use value, for its meaning changes when cheek by jowl with the "alienated thing" that precedes it. Constraints of space and time (versions, yet again, of form and history) have prevented me from considering the London Collection, which once preceded both *Mirror* and *Britton*, or working with more than a handful of the vast range of texts included in *Liber regum*, but I would be surprised if some of them, too, did not gain radically different meanings when read in light of the obsolete texts whose manuscripts they cohabit.

We can see differently inflected versions of some of these relations—between literary form and social history, civic play and political harmony, obsolescence and repetition—in the portion of the *Annales Londonienses* apparently written by Horn in which he narrates, twice, the birth of the crown prince and future Edward III in 1312. The first episode is quite terse:

> Ad festum Sanctorum Simonis et Judae Johannes Gisors eligitur in majorem civitatis Londoniarum. Item xiii die Novembris, regina peperit filium qui vocatur Edwardus.[107]

---

107. Stubbs, ed., *Annales*, 219.

On the Feast of Sts. Simon and Jude, John Gisors was elected mayor of the City of London. And on the thirteenth day of November, the queen bore a son who was called Edward.

Horn's construction of these sentences subtly downplays a normally joyous occasion by identifying the date of Gisors' election with a religious feast day yet failing to do the same with the crown prince's birthday (it fell on the feast of Saint Brice, as we will see), suppressing any hint of celebratory content. So matter-of-fact a description gains retroactive force after we read the much fuller narration of the same event later in that annal:

> Eodem anno in festo Sancti Bricii, videlicet xiii die Novembris, natus est Edwardus primogenitus regis Edwardi apud Wyndeshore, toto regno gaudium conferens permaximum. Cum rumor ejusdem nativitatis civibus Londoniensibus pervenisset, major cum aldermannis per totam civitatem, diebus et noctibus continuis, choream duxerunt, et quaelibet contubernia civium catervatim prae nimio gaudio hoc idem fecerunt: sed et piscenarii, contra adventum dominae reginae Westmonasterio se praeparantes, inaestimabilem ordinaverunt choream.[108]

That same year, on the feast of St. Brice, that is to say on the thirteenth day of November, Edward the firstborn son of King Edward was born at Windsor, bringing very great joy to the entire kingdom. When news of his birth circulated among the citizens of London, the mayor led a procession with the aldermen through the entire City for days and nights at a time, without stopping; and all sorts of groups of citizens did the same, in throngs, on account of their exceedingly great joy at this: and the fishmongers too, preparing for the arrival of the lady queen at Westminster, ordered an indescribable [*inaestimabilem*] procession.

Since we learn here that November 13 is the feast of Saint Brice, the omission of that detail in the first narration of Edward's birth seems significant, particularly given the contrast of the feast day's being named for Gisors' election. Besides the second description's superabundance of joyful intensifiers (*gaudium permaximum, nimio gaudio*, and so on), which contrast sharply with the unadorned, detached

108. Ibid., 220.

first description, there are other, subtler differences. In the first narration, the queen gives birth to a son who is named only incidentally,
in a dependent clause, and whose status as crown prince is nowhere
mentioned. In the second, by contrast, the baby Edward is the subject
of the sentence, and he is immediately identified as the firstborn son
of the reigning king. The second description, in other words, enacts
discursively the royal succession that it was a principal duty of every
ruler to ensure, right down to the chiastic symmetry of the two identi-
cally named male figures (*Edwardus primogenitus regis Edwardi*). The first
description prevents any such display of royal power by making the
agent a woman who is merely consort, not monarch, and neglecting
to mention either the reigning king or the newborn infant's status as
heir to the throne.

These radically contrasting narrations of the royal birth suggest the
role of a contented London populace in the happy acknowledgment
of the succession on which royal power depends. Although the second
description informs us that Prince Edward's birth brought joy to the
entire kingdom, all agency belongs to the citizens of London, who are
the only ones we hear rejoicing. When they are silenced, omitted from
the narrative as they are in the first description, that unadorned statement of fact likewise suppresses the crucial information that not just
a son but a crown prince has been born. Once London's citizens are
involved, however, their joy is literally unstoppable, from the round-
the-clock celebratory procession of the mayor and aldermen (*diebus et
noctibus continuis*) to the fishmongers' preparations for the queen's arrival, which begin in November 1312 and culminate in a lavish parade
the following year. The section quoted above continues as follows:

> . . . sed et piscenarii, contra adventum dominae reginae Westmonasterio
> se praeparantes, inaestimabilem ordinaverunt choream. Igitur die Domi-
> nica proxima post Purificationem beatae Mariae, pridie nonas Februarii,
> rege et regina Westmonasterium pervenientibus, dicti piscenarii induti
> sindone depicta ex auro, de armis regum Angliae et Franciae, per me-
> dium civitatis equitabant versus Westmonasterium; coram quibus praei-
> bat quaedam navis, quodam mirabili ingenio operata, cum malo et velo
> erectis, et depictis de supradictis armis et varietate plurima; et sic coram
> regina karolantes, et per medium praedictae civitatis ante reginam equi-

tantes, conducendo ipsam versus Heltham, omnibus intuentibus, inauditum praemonstraverunt solatium.[109]

> . . . and the fishmongers too, preparing for the arrival of the lady queen at Westminster, ordered an indescribable procession. Accordingly on the next Sunday after the Purification of St. Mary, the day before the nones of February [i.e., February 4, 1313], once the king and queen had arrived at Westminster, the aforementioned fishmongers, bedecked in muslin adorned with the arms of England and France in gold, rode through the middle of the City toward Westminster; in front of them a certain ship led the way, operated by a certain marvelous device, raised up with a mast and sail, and adorned with the arms mentioned before, and with splendid fabric; and caroling thus in the presence of the queen, riding also before the queen through the middle of the aforementioned City, they demonstrated unheard-of delight [*inauditum praemonstraverunt solatium*] by leading her toward Eltham, with everybody looking on.

The intensity of these preparations overrides the annals' traditional formula for a new year's events: "Anno Domini," followed by the year in question. This disruption of strict annalistic form both emphasizes the impressiveness of the fishmongers' pageant and encourages readers to interpret the next event as a further outgrowth of that pageant:

> Eodem anno ante festum Natalis Domini iterum convenerunt quidam ex parte regis et comitum tractaturi de pace reformanda sic: "Ceo est le tretiz de la pees sur aucouns rancours et irrour qe le roi avoit consceu contre les contes de Lancastre, Hereforde et Warewik et ascuns autres gentz de seon roiaume, pur ascuns certeyns enchesons. . . ."[110]

> In the same year, before Christmas, certain parties of the king and the barons came together to discuss renewing the peace, in this way: "This is the treaty of peace concerning the indignation and anger that the king had conceived for the counts of Lancaster, Hereford, and Warwick, and certain other people of his kingdom, for various reasons. . . ."

The long agreement that follows lays out the terms of the barons' submission and the king's pardon, putting to rest (for now, at least) *l'affaire*

Gaveston, which had consumed so much of the annals to this point. By juxtaposing the pageant and the peace agreement, Horn hints that the fishmongers' performance, watched by everybody (*omnibus intuentibus*), provided a model of the loyal love that could lead to royal and baronial reconciliation.[111] This is an even more dramatic version of the kind of civic amity that the *puy* statutes imagined the London merchant class performing among themselves and using to make the City itself "renomee de touz biens en tuz lieus." This episode thus imagines another, potentially more salutary form of the usually tense relation between Crown and City. Whereas much of the Horn corpus implicitly imagines the two entities as adversaries, the success of the fishmongers' pageant suggests that king and barons alike might learn from the merchants' successful modeling of *bon amour*.

The importance of this moment is twofold. First, it depicts a communal focus on play and spectacle as socially reinforcing, with the implicit power to effect positive change even in weighty political affairs. Second, this import emerges only when we read the various episodes of the annals compilationally, as meaningfully arranged in a way that extends beyond the literal. By using the fishmongers' procession to disrupt strict annalistic organization, and by giving us two very different narrations of the same single event, Horn hints at precisely this more flexible and interpretive form of reading. He cannot come out and say as much, not least because it sounds definitely silly, probably insubordinate, and possibly dangerous (this is the irascible Edward II, we recall) seriously to propose a fishmongers' parade as a model for peace between the king and his barons. For precisely this reason I find significant his frequent use of the inexpressibility topos: the mayor's and fishmongers' processions alike are *inaestimabilis* and the joy inspired by the latter *inauditus*. Horn was a rigorous defender of London's pre-

---

111. The word Horn chooses to describe what the fishmongers provide, *solacium*, strengthens this interpretation, for it can mean both "recreation" or "relaxation" (presumably the primary meaning here) and "comfort" or "consolation." To the extent that Horn has rhetorically linked the fishmongers' performance and the king's reconciliation with his magnates, that performance was also a comfort since the entire kingdom had been suffering from their hostility.

rogatives and a sometimes unscrupulous businessman himself,[112] but this chapter has shown that he also understood the power of strange juxtapositions and obsolete texts to convey complex, allusive forms of meaning; *inaestimabilis* is, after all, another way of saying "resistant to paraphrase."

The Horn corpus is a perfect storm. We know so much about its compiler, contents, and contexts that it seems possible even the Rouses might admit the legitimacy of offering close readings of some of its codicological forms, as I have here.[113] This very fact, however, makes it dangerous to my broader goal of encouraging literary interpretation of codicological form. In the first place, the embarrassment of contextual riches that the Horn corpus presents makes it natural for us to want comparably full (if complex) forms of knowledge before embarking on comparably adventurous interpretations of other compilations. Horn has the potential to become, as Hoccleve and Christine de Pizan are for the Rouses, the exception that proves the more general rule of codicology's aesthetic inapplicability. It is therefore worth pausing a moment to consider how the Horn corpus, too, will always resist wholly conclusive, empirically demonstrable forms of argumentation. Quite apart from the literal fragmentation of the corpus, which we have already considered in detail, there is the capaciousness of the manuscripts, which ensures that arguments about their contents will always be fragmentary in two important senses. First, if they are of publishable length, they will take in only a tiny fraction of Horn's texts and, thus, always be open to revision, counterargument, and other forms of dialogic scholarly play. Second, if they grapple with his

112. Hanna points out: "Horn appears in his text as trade-protectionist, pleading for his own very prominent company of Fishmongers against poorer men. . . . And civic record reveals that in 1307 . . . he judicially revealed himself as profiteer in the sale of basic foodstuffs" (*London Literature*, 72).

113. Rouse and Rouse acknowledge "exceptions and qualifications" to their starkly categorical distinction between literary and codicological production. "Some authors," they admit, "did take a lively interest in how their texts would be presented physically. And a few [they specify Hoccleve and Christine de Pizan] . . . even took steps to ensure that the physical appearance of their texts conformed to their wishes" ("*Ordinatio* and *Compilatio* Revisited," 124). They imply that the manuscript situation of such texts becomes part of their authorially sanctioned meaning and equally amenable to literary interpretation.

codicological forms in anything approaching their full range—as his corpus, in my view, strongly encourages them to—they will expose the comparably fragmentary knowledge of the commentator. I am not equally a specialist in medieval law, Franco-Flemish urban culture, civic historiography, London's historical topography, and the works of Brunetto Latini (or, equally, the accretions of scholarly context that each of these areas of study has inevitably accumulated), but the contemporary academy's valorization of niche specialties helps ensure that no one else is either. Andrew Taylor makes much the same point in describing his attempts to grapple with Royal 10.E.4, acknowledging that "the sheer range of material, from medical texts to hawking manuals and from musical pieces to political satires, will defeat any single scholar," and I would strongly second his conclusion that "as medievalists we need to establish protocols for much more extensive collaboration."[114] Such collaboration might allow Horn's corpus once more to perform its convocational function, reaching across the centuries and oceans to yield a community of readers and teachers, *congregatis coram rotulis et libris*.

114. Taylor, *Textual Situations*, 7.

Chapter Two

FRAGMENTARY FORMS OF
IMITATIVE FANTASY

Booklet 3 of the Auchinleck Manuscript

The Auchinleck manuscript is suffused with fantasy and desire. Part of this nimbus is textual, since the Middle English romances for which Auchinleck is best known are marked by the union of the fantastic with a wide range of desires: marvelous elf queens, magical castles, and bleeding lances serve as focal points for narratives structured by the quest for identity, love, or patrimony. Perhaps partly because of these associations, the manuscript has occupied an analogous position for generations of medievalists. Tantalizing in its massive uniqueness, it begs to be analyzed as more than the sum of its many parts, and we have obliged, reading it as (among other things) evidence of an entire, lost network of urban scriptoria,[1] as a self-consciously nationalistic blow struck for literature in English as opposed to French or Latin,[2] and even as a direct, talismanic connection to Geoffrey Chaucer.[3]

---

1. Loomis raised this possibility in an influential series of articles, the chief of these being "The Auchinleck Manuscript and a Possible London Bookshop." Though since largely discredited by subsequent scholarship from the mid-1980s, Loomis's arguments exerted a defining influence on study of Auchinleck.

2. This is the central argument of the chapter on Auchinleck in Turville-Petre, *England the Nation*, 108–41.

3. That Chaucer consulted or even owned Auchinleck is the beguiling argument of Laura Hibbard Loomis's "Chaucer and the Breton Lays of the Auchinleck MS," *Studies in Philology* 38 (1941): 14–33. For a recent and nuanced reassessment of Loomis's argument, see Christopher Cannon, "Chaucer and the Auchinleck Manuscript Revisited," *Chaucer Review* 46 (2011): 131–46.

Another part of the appeal is codicological, however, since our ability to construct such varied roles for Auchinleck has depended on the vast yet fragmentary nature of the manuscript itself. While still boasting an impressive 334 folios and forty-four surviving texts (many of these their earliest extant versions), it has lost most of its many miniatures, eighty or more of its original leaves, and at least fourteen texts, including the first five.[4] Like the Horn corpus, Auchinleck is big enough that no scholarly treatment of publishable length can fully grapple with all its texts and contexts, so we are free to focus on those most congenial to our own interests and interpretations. Even as it denies us the possibility of ultimate proof for our theories, moreover, its fragmentariness likewise prevents their being conclusively disproved either; it *could* always be the case that Auchinleck's lost texts, or miniatures, or circumstances of production, or scribal identities, or owners (you get the idea) would fit just right, establishing us as the protagonist of our own academic romance. In this sense, the Auchinleck manuscript as it stands today is structurally akin to one of the medieval romances for which it is so famous: dauntingly long yet incomplete, episodic and paratactic yet deceptively subtle in its organization, and with the ever-deferred prospect of closure (here its academic analogue: certain knowledge) prompting us to keep reading and writing. As modern scholars, then, we play out forms of the fantasies that so many medieval romances and their manuscripts inspire. Comparable versions of such imitative fantasies animate the Auchinleck manuscript's relationship to its original, medieval audience, and this chapter's main argument will be that the codicological elements of booklet 3—its internal structure, relation to the rest of the manuscript, and codicological details like catchwords and page layout—both complement and complicate its texts' literary explorations of such fantasies.

---

4. For a detailed description of its size, texts, and booklet and gathering structures, see the introduction to *The Auchinleck Manuscript: National Library of Scotland Advocates' MS. 19.2.1,* ed. Derek Pearsall and I. C. Cunningham (1977; reprint, London: Scolar, 1979). This work draws on the groundbreaking A. J. Bliss, "Notes on the Auchinleck Manuscript," *Speculum* 26 (1951): 652–58.

Auchinleck's Booklet 3:
Codicological Feature and Literary Entity

Such an argument must be prepared for by a few words both practical and theoretical about Auchinleck in general, booklet 3 in particular, and how the two are linked. When it can be determined that large manuscripts have been constructed as a series of booklets, analyzing the structure of those booklets can tell us a great deal about the production history, patronage, and readership of such compendia, and Auchinleck has been fortunate in the excellent scholarship that it has attracted on precisely those topics. Taking such studies as my point of departure, I ask in this chapter what interpretive purchase we gain by electing to perceive such booklets, not just as the codicological units that they undoubtedly and importantly are, but also as aesthetic and literary entities. Such an enterprise is less wholly anachronistic than it might sound. It is, to be sure, a discovery of modern codicology that the manuscript was produced as fascicles that were only later bound and assembled into what is now called the Auchinleck manuscript.[5] There is, moreover, no reason to suppose that Auchinleck's third or any other booklet would have been perceptible as such to its medieval readers or meaningful as a literary unit even if it were. Yet it was *produced* as such, overseen by the so-called Scribe 1, who has been identified as the effective editor in chief of the whole production.[6]

The booklets of Auchinleck, then, have at least three different formal identities, depending on when we encounter them. Created first

5. I do not mean by this that Auchinleck's booklets circulated independently or ever enjoyed public status as self-contained entities, although I. C. Cunningham and J. E. C. Cunningham have suggested that booklet 3 might have. See "New Light on the Signatures of the Auchinleck Manuscript," *Scriptorium* 36 (1982): 280–92. Likewise, Hanna speculates: "Perhaps even on multiple occasions at various stages of production, portions of the book may have passed from scribe 1, not just to the illuminator (which we would expect), but to the client for his or her use" (*London Literature*, 77). These possibilities would add a fascinating wrinkle to the multiple forms and temporalities of the manuscript that I explore here.

6. This view was first put forth in the groundbreaking Shonk, "A Study of the Auchinleck Manuscript." Shonk uses the word *editor* of Scribe 1 (ibid., 73, 82) and the word *editorial* to describe his duties (ibid., 87). This characterization has since been broadly accepted and further substantiated by subsequent treatments of the manuscript.

as self-contained entities, they then become part of the Auchinleck manuscript as initially assembled, their integrity transformed into "merely" a series of folios and texts in a much larger object.[7] Today, the booklets recall both those medieval forms. Their distinctiveness once more perceptible, they nevertheless remain part of their larger whole. Because Auchinleck itself is now fragmentary, however, the relation between booklet and manuscript has necessarily changed, effacing some textual connections while bringing others to new prominence. Like the manuscript of which it is part, booklet 3 is both an assemblage and a fragment: by design one part of a larger whole and by unrecoverable historical accident a fragmentary version of the shape it once had.[8] We will see, furthermore, that such parallels between booklet and manuscript run deeper still. Even to speak of the singular "form" of the Auchinleck manuscript therefore seems unsatisfying; its forms are multiple, created by and reflecting the various temporalities of its many moving parts. Auchinleck thus reminds us that form becomes visible only through the intentions and accidents alike of history, even as it highlights the inability of any single, linear historicity fully to account for or contain the meaning of booklet 3, Auchinleck as a whole, or the relation of either to the London mercantile community, for which the manuscript was almost certainly produced.[9]

---

7. The most detailed and plausible hypothetical reconstructions of how and in what order Auchinleck was constructed are offered in Hanna, *London Literature*, 75–77; and Shonk, "A Study of the Auchinleck Manuscript," 74–77.

8. The entirety of gathering 15, in the facsimile reconstruction (*The Auchinleck Manuscript*), has been lost. This gathering corresponds to the last roughly 1,050 lines of *Seven Sages of Rome* and the first roughly 350 lines of *Floris and Blauncheflur*. The pages containing the first lines of "The Assumption of Our Lady" and *Seven Sages of Rome* have also been cut out, possibly because they once contained miniatures.

9. On the evidence for this proposition, see my introduction. The most notable dissent has come from Turville-Petre (*England the Nation*, 137ff.), who argues for an audience of rural aristocrats. Taking as a premise the supposedly unsophisticated nature of Auchinleck's contents (rural aristocrats, he asserts, "have never been distinguished by their refined taste" [ibid., 138]), he points out that the London *puy* demonstrates a mercantile appetite for francophone cultural and literary pastimes; London's merchant class, he implies, was too sophisticated to have appreciated Auchinleck. This argument, however, fails to account for the rediscovery in the past decade or so of substantial reservoirs of sophistication in Middle English romance, the strong London interests of the additions and reworkings to the *Anonymous Short English Metrical Chronicle* (on which, see, surprisingly enough, Turville-Petre, *England the Nation*, 111), or the

Indeed, the many ways in which booklet 3 looks out of place within Auchinleck make it a useful site for exploring how Paul Strohm's concept of a *textual unconscious* might apply to codicological groupings as well as literary texts,[10] for various aspects of booklet 3 are in fascinating tension with one another.[11] On the one hand, it is the only multitext booklet that lacks any copying by Scribe 1, the so-called editor in chief who is responsible for over 70 percent of the manuscript's extant work. Even here, however, his supervisory role continued, for he has added catchphrases, titles, and numerations throughout.[12] The booklet's principal scribe, Scribe 3, is the only one in the entire manuscript other than Scribe 1 to copy an extended series of texts; all other "subsidiary scribes copied only full single texts in isolated sections of the manuscript."[13] Despite this prominence, however, Scribe 3

---

fact that the *puy*'s onetime popularity did not necessarily indicate a monolithic preference for French as a literary language, either during its heyday or during the decade of Auchinleck's production.

10. Broadly speaking, Strohm defines this as the notion that a text can be usefully prodded into revealing aspects about which it is itself reticent and that one necessary job of the literary critic is to encourage it to do precisely that. See Strohm, *Theory and the Premodern Text*, 165–81.

11. This tension can be seen in the terms in which critics have discussed booklet 3, typically acknowledging its strangeness, yet nevertheless proposing meaningful organizational strategies for it. Evans treats booklet 3 at some length in his study of what the codicological situation of various Middle English romances reveals about how their genres were perceived in the Middle Ages. See *Rereading Middle English Romance*, 82–96. There, after concluding that there is a "loose rationale, but rationale nonetheless, for the Auchinleck context of" *Sir Degaré*, he backtracks slightly, writing that "the presence of the *Sayings* [*of the Four Philosophers*] and the list of barons as the last two items . . . suggests a compromise between exigencies of production and generic/ topical arrangement" (ibid., 95–96). But he immediately follows this concession by contending that the booklet "has generic coherence" that smooths out the manuscript's broader transition from homiletic to romance material and from booklet 3's last two texts to the "martial romances" of the next two booklets. H. M. Smyser is more blunt in discussing the "Battle Abbey Roll," admitting frankly: "[As to why it] should have been copied into the Auchinleck MS. I am at a complete loss to explain" ("The List of Norman Names in the Auchinleck MS. [Battle Abbey Roll]," in *Mediaeval Studies in Honor of Jeremiah Denis Matthias Ford*, ed. U. T. Holmes Jr. and A. J. Denomy [Cambridge, MA: Harvard University Press, 1948], 257–87 [quotation 271]). Like Evans, however, he cannot accept the idea that it was truly serendipitous, and he suggests quite sensibly that it may relate to the immediately preceding "Sayings of the Four Philosophers." I will argue for a version of this proposition later in this chapter.

12. See Shonk, "A Study of the Auchinleck Manuscript," 82–87.

13. Hanna, *London Literature*, 76.

appears not to have consistently understood what he was copying, for he frequently substitutes yogh for thorn, even where the sense clearly requires the latter.[14] Elsewhere in the manuscript, Scribe 1 takes almost complete responsibility for the shortest texts and those that conclude booklets,[15] orchestrating the final look of a given booklet whose main text(s) may have been selected or at least proposed by the patron. The absence of any copying by him in booklet 3 is therefore especially puzzling.

Moreover, booklet 3's shape differs markedly from that of other surviving booklets: unlike the "top-heavy" structure identified by Ralph Hanna as typical (i.e., with the most substantial text coming first),[16] it presents a crescendo, opening with short texts, and offering its longest at almost its exact midpoint before concluding with shorter texts. It is also the only booklet to bear the hand of three different scribes, one of whom, Scribe 4, shows up here alone to copy surely the most enigmatic work in the entire manuscript, a completely uncontextualized list of names subsequently identified as the earliest extant version of the "Battle Abbey Roll," a list of the Norman knights who supposedly came to England with William the Conqueror. The fact that Scribe 3 seems to have been uncomfortable or unfamiliar with texts in English makes it quite unlikely that he orchestrated a booklet of texts in that language for inclusion in a manuscript whose resolute Englishness is so remarkable.[17] Scribe 4, too, is hardly likely to have

14. See *The Seven Sages of Rome*, ed. Karl Brunner, Early English Text Society, O.S. 191 (London: Oxford University Press, 1933; reprint, New York: Kraus, 1971), ix, where Brunner attributes this feature to the scribe having been a "French Norman" not fluent in English and further notes: "He is also very irregular in writing the symbol for the gutteral fricative. Instead of the usual ȝ or *gh* he uses also *gȝ, g, þȝ, w.* . . ."

15. Other than in booklet 3, subsidiary scribes copy only longish texts of around ten folios or more; the shortest are *Speculum Gy de Warewyke* (Scribe 2, fols. 39r–48r) and *Reinbrun* (Scribe 5, fols. 167r–175v). *Reinbrun* is also the only booklet-final text copied by anyone other than Scribe 1.

16. Hanna, *London Literature*, 76. This pattern holds for booklets 4, 5, 8, 9, and 10, all of which open with their longest text.

17. Bliss ("Notes on the Auchinleck Manuscript," 653) detected hints of Chancery training in the length of Scribe 3's cursive *f, r,* and long *s*; this, in conjunction with his confusion of the English-specific characters thorn and yogh, strongly suggests that he worked principally on texts in other languages.

gone rogue by copying so odd a text as the "Battle Abbey Roll"—
quite the opposite of the anodyne filler that frequently concludes
booklets, in Auchinleck and elsewhere—without receiving definite
instruction from somebody; and it is hard to come up with another
source of such a directive than Scribe 1 (possibly transmitting some set
of desires from the patron). Scribe 1 thus hangs over the booklet like
a ghostly not-quite-author whose presence can be inferred but not
proved, and the many ways in which booklet 3 seems at odds with the
rest of the manuscript thus press us to look more deeply into what,
coining Strohm, we might call its *codicological unconscious*. Doing so
yields some remarkable findings.

In the first place, although its structure is atypical of Auchinleck's
other booklets, booklet 3 uncannily reflects that of the surviving manuscript in both length and genre of text. Its crescendo (short early
works, the longest in the middle, and short texts at the end) parallels
that of Auchinleck as a whole: others have noted the broad move in
Auchinleck from homiletic works early on, to (mostly) romance in the
middle, and finally to (again, mostly) political or historical texts at the
end.[18] A comparable trajectory obtains in booklet 3: its first three texts
are short religious works; the central three are longer romances (the
longest of these in the middle); and the final two works are explicitly
political ("The Sayings of the Four Philosophers") or implicitly historical ("Battle Abbey Roll"). Table 1 illustrates the similarity between
booklet 3 and the manuscript as a whole (a full list of contents, scribes,
and booklets can be found in app. 1 at the end of this chapter). Absolute terms like these—*religious, romance, political, historical*—are blunt
instruments that do not honor fully the nuances of many medieval
texts, Auchinleck's included, but they nevertheless help us sketch
broad outlines. In fact, the positioning of some texts that particularly
resist easy generic classification (e.g., *Amis and Amiloun* and *Richard
Coer de Lyon*) near the junctures of the manuscript's broad genre groupings suggests an effort either to smooth out the generic transitions
of the manuscript as a whole or to play with generic boundaries and

18. See Turville-Petre, *England the Nation*, 112–13; and Hanna, *London Literature*, 104–5.

TABLE 1. Generic Trajectory of the Auchinleck
Manuscript and Its Third Booklet

Auchinleck as a Whole	Booklet 3	Principal Mode
Booklets 1–2 (texts 1–16)	Texts 14–16	Religious
Booklets 3–9 (texts 17–39)	Texts 17–19	Romance
Booklets 10–12 (texts 40–44)	Texts 20–21	History

expectations,[19] and we will see comparable effects within booklet 3 as well.[20] To the modern observer, then, booklet 3 emerges as a *mise-en-abyme* of Auchinleck as a whole.

Of course, the structural relation between booklet and manuscript would presumably have looked different when Auchinleck was presented to its original patron(s), and this disjunction between its medieval and its modern forms makes Benjamin's distinction between construction and reconstruction of the past especially useful. *Reconstructing* Auchinleck would complicate and perhaps efface the analogues between booklet 3 and the manuscript as a whole that I have identified; the impossibility of engaging in such a reconstruction therefore, and somewhat paradoxically, forces on us a *constructive* interpretive freedom when we perceive such echoes and resemblances. This freedom poses challenges, to be sure; Auchinleck's shifting and fragmentary forms can make it difficult to feel secure even in the object of one's interpretations, much less in their content. Nor do I mean to suggest

19. Romance's links to homiletic and hagiographic material, on the one hand, and historiographic texts, on the other, are well documented; critics like Susan Crane and Ojars Kratins have coined terms like *pious romances* and *secular hagiography* to discuss texts like *Amis and Amiloun*, while John Finlayson has emphasized that many works generally considered romances, such as the various Alexander poems and *Richard Coer de Lyon*, seem to have been read in the Middle Ages at least as much as history as romance. See Susan Crane, *Insular Romance: Politics, Faith, and Culture in Anglo-Norman and Middle English Literature* (Berkeley and Los Angeles: University of California Press, 1986), 92–133; Ojars Kratins, "Middle English *Amis and Amiloun*: Chivalric Romance or Secular Hagiography," *PMLA* 81 (1966): 347–54; and John Finlayson, "*Richard, Coer de Lyon*: Romance, History, or Something in Between?" *Studies in Philology* 87 (1990): 156–80.

20. See also Evans, *Rereading Middle English Romance*, 95–96.

that the discovery of what now fragmentary manuscripts once looked like, where possible, ought to be avoided as a matter of principle. I have gratefully taken advantage of our ability to piece together the original forms of *Liber regum* and *Liber custumarum*, for example, although in so doing I aimed to turn such *codicological* reconstructions to constructive rather than reconstructive *interpretive* ends. The Horn corpus and the Auchinleck manuscript thus pose different interpretive challenges. So much recoverable data swim in and around the many texts and contexts of Horn's manuscripts that it is easy to take refuge in (inevitably incomplete) reconstructions rather than constructions of the past, valorizing empiricist demonstration at the expense of more creative interpretive modes. With Auchinleck, by contrast, the challenge lies in grounding our interpretive constructions, in assembling out of the manuscript's fragments a meaningful understanding of them. Here, as throughout this study, form and history combine to offer a way forward. The uncanny formal and thematic resemblances between booklet 3 and Auchinleck as a whole create the kind of arresting constellation that we have seen Benjamin cite as the ideal locus for historical inquiry—a "unique experience with the past" rather than the always illusory " 'eternal' image of the past."[21] The manuscript's demonstrated links with the producers and audience of Horn's manuscripts, meanwhile, crucially ground the interpretations that follow.

Booklet 3, I will argue, looks inward at itself as a closed system with its own formal coherence, outward to the larger manuscript of which it is part, and outward still further to the historical antagonisms between Crown and City that we first considered in the introduction and then saw animate portions of the Horn corpus. Booklet 3 and Auchinleck both open with religious texts that dramatize the imitation of spiritually wholesome figures and practices, setting up the question of whether this imitative model can be effectively transferred into the secular context that the following romance materials introduce. Auchinleck thus continues to press on the cultural question that we saw explored in the Latini extracts and *puy* statutes of Horn's *Liber regum*: what could serve as effective models for the self-representation

21. Benjamin, "On the Concept of History," 396.

and self-conception of London's merchant elite? *Sir Degaré* and *Floris and Blauncheflur*, the two romances that bracket booklet 3's longest text, suggest complementary yet opposed answers to this question, evocative of the codicological mirror image that they constitute.

The booklet's final two texts likewise raise similar issues in opposed modes: "Sayings of the Four Philosophers" is explicitly political and tries painstakingly to reassemble the severed links between past, present, and future, while the "Battle Abbey Roll" dispenses with narrative altogether, presenting rather a wall of names that it implicitly challenges its audience to contextualize and understand. *Seven Sages of Rome*, meanwhile, booklet 3's longest and literally central text, queries the social and political value of fictional discourse and, thus, by extension that of both Auchinleck and literary societies like the *puy* memorialized by Horn. These challenges are sharpened by *Seven Sages'* many other outward-looking gestures: both its allusion to the recent politics of Edward III's accession and its status as a generically mixed collection of stories (like booklet 3, like Auchinleck) that allude to key elements of other texts within the booklet, whether the number 7 (central to both of the booklet's first, short religious works) or the trope of wise men offering advice to a hapless king (taken up in "Sayings of the Four Philosophers").

Booklet 3 and Auchinleck enable such interpretations (even as certain of their texts call such interpretive acts into question) by encouraging a key element of what we would call literary analysis: rereading that attends to allusions, echoes, and motifs of plot and image. The precise nature of the close reading performed by contemporary literary critics is of course culturally constructed and thus hardly transhistorical, but the manuscript seems likely to have prompted comparable forms of repeated engagement in its original audience. Its great size and the comparably daunting length of many of its texts make Auchinleck something you have to sit down with more than once, then and now; like its long romances, it is the kind of object you get lost in, and such wandering has a way of yielding unexpected discoveries and connections, as any number of chivalric knights discovered. Auchinleck is also an object that a medieval mercantile audience would have *wanted* to sit down with frequently, not least because it offered

tangible proof of the economic might behind its commission; its codicological similarities to the more monumental elements of the Horn
corpus, likewise designed for grandeur and display, are worth recalling in this regard. And, while its few surviving illuminations are not
especially luxurious, their presence—rare in vernacular English manuscripts—testifies to the care its production received and the aesthetic
appeal it must have commanded as a finished object. These physical
incitements to rereading complement the pleasures of the manuscript's
many varied literary offerings and mean that the precise and subtle
concatenations of theme and image across Auchinleck's texts, compellingly uncovered by a wide range of modern critics, become part of
the manuscript's overall project.[22]

Booklet 3's Opening: Religious and Chivalric Imitation

I will turn to booklet 3's participation in that larger project momentarily. First, I must set the stage for the religious themes of its opening texts by considering more broadly the leitmotif of spiritual imitation that runs through what we might call Auchinleck's "religious
overture," texts 1–16, a form of imitation that we are encouraged to
contemplate applying to the world of (more) secular romance heroism
that will dominate the central portion of both Auchinleck and booklet

---

22. Loomis ("The Auchinleck Manuscript and a Possible London Bookshop," 613–21) argued that various connections between different texts suggested some sort of unifying impulse
in the manuscript as a whole, pointing to precise similarities of phrase between the stanzaic
Guy of Warwick and *Amis and Amiloun*. Turville-Petre (*England the Nation*, 112) notes that many
of the additions that make the *Liber Regum Anglie* unique provide additional, (pseudo)historical
context for the legendary heroes depicted in earlier romances: Guy of Warwick, King Arthur,
Beues of Hampton. Meanwhile, Finlayson ("*Richard, Coer de Lyon*," 162ff.) concurs with Ewald
Zettl's argument that the author of the Auchinleck version of the chronicle both knew and
referred to a copy of *Richard Coer de Lyon* in making his additions to his text about Richard's
exploits. Zettl makes his argument in the introduction to his edition, *An Anonymous Short
English Metrical Chronicle*, Early English Text Society, O.S. 196 (London: Oxford University
Press, 1935). Finlayson ("*Richard Coer de Lyon*," 160) also argues for the textual interrelation of
Sir Tristrem, Horne Child and Maiden Rimnild, and *Amis and Amiloun*, while E. B. Lyle detects
parallels between *Sir Orfeo* and *Guy of Warwick*. See "*Sir Orfeo* and the Recovery of Amis from
the Otherworld in *Guy of Warwick*," *Neuphilologische Mitteilungen* 80 (1979): 65–68. This is,
moreover, a sampling rather than an exhaustive list.

3. The first booklet's "Life of Adam and Eve" (text 3) introduces this theme of imitation with Eve's command that Seth commit his parents' story to writing so that future readers "mowe take ensaumple of ous."[23] The dream vision of purgatory variously called *Saint Patrick's Purgatory*, *Owayne Miles*, and *Sir Owain* (text 6) then links this concept of religious imitation to chivalric identity, thus anticipating a range of texts crucial to booklet 3 and Auchinleck as a whole.[24] In the poem, Owain enters purgatory through Saint Patrick's shrine on Lough Derg, where he undergoes the same trials as the souls inside in order to atone for his sins as a knight. His success in undergoing a spiritually cleansing imitation of the affective suffering of purgatory's souls encourages the text's audience to imitate his model of pilgrimage and atonement. Many people did so: the shrine was so popular that pilgrimages continued well after its suppression by Pope Alexander VI in 1497.[25]

Like the more famous *Amis and Amiloun*, *Sir Owain* straddles the homiletic and romance traditions, as the contrasting generic associations of its various modern titles suggest. In the introduction to his edition, Edward E. Foster seems to make calling the poem *Sir Owain* (instead of the more traditional *Saint Patrick's Purgatory*) part of a broader assessment of its overall generic identity: he asserts that *Sir Owain* is "a didactic religious poem struggling to become a romance" and that, by the end, "tract has become romance."[26] In fact, the movement of the text's narrative is quite the reverse since Owain goes from a typical romance hero to a penitent whose voluntary suffering is de-

23. "Life of Adam and Eve," in *The Apocryphal Lives of Adam and Eve*, ed. Brian Murdoch and J. A. Tasioulas (Exeter: University of Exeter Press, 2002), line 631.

24. The most common title for the work is *St. Patrick's Purgatory*, as, e.g., in *St. Patrick's Purgatory*, ed. Robert Easting, Early English Text Society, O.S. 298 (Oxford, 1991). *Owayne Miles* was a title more in use in the nineteenth century, borrowed from the heading to the couplet version in Cotton Caligula A.ii. Edward E. Foster calls the poem *Sir Owain* in his edition for the TEAMS volume: *Three Purgatory Poems* (Kalamazoo: Western Michigan University, Medieval Institute Publications, 2004).

25. For the history of the pilgrimage and the various writings associated with it, see Michael Haren and Yolande de Pontfarcy, *The Medieval Pilgrimage to St Patrick's Purgatory: Lough Derg and the European Tradition* (Enniskillen: Clogher Historical Society, 1988).

26. *Three Purgatory Poems*, xvii. Foster never makes this goal explicit, however, simply calling *Sir Owain* a "more precise" title than *Saint Patrick's Purgatory*.

signed to inspire others to comparable acts of devotion. The generic shift that Foster proposes does, however, correspond to the one traced by Auchinleck more broadly, and there are also narrative echoes between *Sir Owain* and other parts of the manuscript, for this is one of three texts in Auchinleck that focus on the penitential process of a romance hero after he has concluded his chivalric exploits: we also have *The Legend of Pope Gregory* (text 1, which I will discuss later in conjunction with booklet 3's *Sir Degaré*) and the *Speculum Gy de Warewyke* (text 10). *Speculum Gy*, in turn, looks forward to the three later poems that narrate precisely those chivalric achievements of Guy and his son Reinbrun (texts 22–24).

Auchinleck's religious overture thus displays a marked interest in romance heroes who subsequently become imitable models of devotion and penitence. How this happens in *Speculum Gy* is particularly relevant since that poem concerns the hero who is central to so much of the manuscript's subsequent material. In the most sustained consideration of the *Speculum Gy*'s Auchinleck context, Jean Harpham Burrows argues that the poem represents an attempt to make the doctrinal matter that it largely comprises palatable to an audience that apparently also enjoyed tales of chivalric derring-do; depicting a figure like Guy eager to lead a more virtuous life would encourage an audience enamored of his heroism to see themselves "in the same position [as Guy] with regard to Alcuin," his spiritual mentor in the poem.[27] Guy's chivalric renown thus furthers the *Speculum*'s homiletic purpose: like a contemporary celebrity spokesman for volunteerism, Guy uses his exemplarity in one sphere to spur adoring fans to emulate his activities in another, less glamorous but more virtuous one.[28] This gambit implicitly narrows the social gap between Auchinleck's mercantile audience and the aristocratic Guy since the hero's devotions (being kind to the poor, giving alms, and so on) are far more relatable than his chivalric exploits. The exemplum that closes the *Speculum Gy*, more-

27. Jean Harpham Burrows, "The Auchinleck Manuscript: Contexts, Texts and Audience" (Ph.D. diss., Washington University in St. Louis, 1984), 40.

28. Burrows argues along these lines that Auchinleck had "an audience especially interested in this great English hero [Guy of Warwick], who saw him as an example of proper behavior, whom they could emulate" (ibid., 9).

over, reinforces the morality of the doctrine that has preceded it in ways particularly gratifying to a mercantile temper. It tells of Elijah's request to the woman of Zarephath that she give him some of her meager store of meal and oil; when she does so willingly, he blesses her and promises that she will not suffer for her generosity. Alcuin subsequently repeats the moral, lest we missed it: "gret plente had þe widewe þo."[29] As glossed by the text, generosity becomes, not simply a means to heaven (line 1008), but almost a kind of financial planning here on earth:

> And þi god shal multiplie,
> So seiþ þe bok, þat nyl nauȝt lie.
> Þe godspel seiþe to þe and me:
> "Ȝif and men shal ȝefe þe."
> (lines 1009–12)

Four lines describe how almsgiving offers tangible rewards, twice the number describing its heavenly payoff, a literal doubling of emphasis from spiritual to earthly benefit. Even as it encourages its mercantile audience to engage in the spiritually ennobling penance and almsgiving of its hero, then, the Auchinleck *Speculum Gy* takes care to emphasize that this imitation makes sense in earthly as well as heavenly terms. The imitation of Guy that the *Speculum Gy* encourages here is perfectly conventional and orthodox, and the need for repentance in the face of certain death and judgment does indeed act as a social leveler in Christian thought. In the context of the manuscript as a whole, however, the *Speculum Gy* begins to sketch out an issue that will recur in booklet 3: whether, and how, imitative models can withstand the transition from a spiritual to a secular context and how such models might be particularly applicable to the manuscript's mercantile audience.

With this broader context in place, we can now turn to booklet 3, which opens with two short religious works, "On þe seuen dedly

---

29. *Speculum Gy de Warewyke*, ed. Georgiana Lee Merrill, Early English Text Society, E.S. 75 (London: K. Paul, Trench, Trubner, 1898), line 1003. Subsequent citations are given parenthetically in the text.

sinnes" and "Þe pater noster undo on englisch" (texts 14 and 15).[30]
These represent, of course, an antimodel and model, respectively, for
the good Christian. In that sense, they continue a broader theme of
spiritual imitation. They also hint that they should be read as a pair; in
this, it may be significant that both poems are unique to Auchinleck.
"Dedly sinnes," for example, emphasizes the following as one key
means of avoiding the eponymous temptations:

> And þe Pater noster and þe Crede,
> Þeroffe ȝe sscholden taken hede,
> On Englissch to segge what hit were.[31]

This is of course precisely the instruction that the following
"Pater noster" provides. That poem, meanwhile, looks back to "Dedly
sinnes" by emphasizing the same number 7; the Lord's Prayer, it informs us, is itself made up of seven discrete prayers, all joined together
to make up the Paternoster:

> Seuen oreisouns þer beȝ inne
> Þat helpeȝ men out of dedli sinne
> And ȝif ȝe willeȝ a while dwelle,
> Al on Englissch ich wille ȝou telle
> Þe skile of hem alle seuene,
> Wiȝ help of Godes miȝ t of heuene.[32]

These lines emphasize the number 7 by placing it first line initial
(line 21) and then line final (line 25); their mention of "dedli sinne"
(line 22) also looks back to the previous text, where we find the same
"seuene/heuene" rhyme pair (lines 10–11). Taken in the context of
booklet 3 more broadly, both texts' emphasis on the number 7 establishes them as a reference point for readers to recall when the number
recurs prominently later, in *Seven Sages of Rome* and *Floris and Blauncheflur*. These two short texts are already somewhat strange in that they
look and feel like filler, but appear at the beginning rather than the end

---

30. All but the word *sinnes* has been lost from the first of these titles; its current title is the
plausible reconstruction offered in the facsimile edition (*The Auchinleck Manuscript*, xxi).

31. Lines 17–19. "On þe seuen dedly sinnes" is included in E. Kölbing, "Kleine Publicationen aus der Auchinleck-hs," *Englische Studien* 9 (1886): 35–52, 42–46.

32. Lines 21–26. "Þe pater noster undo on englisch" is included in ibid., 47–49.

of their booklet. This suggestion that they may be more important than we might at first suppose is complemented by the significance that they gain only in retrospect, when they are evoked by more substantial texts later in the booklet.[33]

Auchinleck's next poem, "The Assumption of Our Lady" (text 16), merits particular consideration because it is the last religious text in booklet 3 and the last substantial one in the manuscript as a whole.[34] It is actually the second Marian text in the manuscript; the first, "Anna our leuedis moder" (text 13), narrates Mary's birth and early life, focusing especially on the Immaculate Conception, while the "Assumption" describes her last days. By narrating her conception free from sin and her bodily assumption into heaven, these texts emphasize miraculous demonstrations of Mary's holiness that are modeled on and in that sense imitate Christ's own pure conception and ultimate ascension. The Auchinleck "Assumption," moreover, highlights and adds to the elements of spiritual imitation already implicit in the basic narrative.[35] Describing the fear of death that keeps Mary awake after she learns of her impending death, Jesus sends an angel to reassure her, remembering that he too feared death:

> Drede of deȝ was in here þout,
> Þerfore ȝhe ne slep nowt,

33. For a perceptive account of the importance of comparable seeming filler in reaching both historical and literary-critical conclusions, see Susanna Fein, "*Somer Soneday*: Kingship, Sainthood, and Fortune in Oxford, Bodleian Library, MS Laud Misc. 108," in *The Texts and Contexts of Oxford, Bodleian Library, MS Laud Misc. 108: The Shaping of English Vernacular Narrative*, ed. Kimberly K. Bell and Julie Nelson Couch (Leiden: Brill, 2011), 275–97.

34. "The Assumption of Our Lady" begins imperfectly and has 756 surviving lines. Auchinleck's remaining clearly religious texts are substantially shorter: "Hou our leuedi saute was ferst founde" (text 29) is 258 lines long, while "David þe kyng," an expanded, glossed translation of the Vulgate Psalm 50 (text 36), is about 100 lines (depending on whether one includes the Latin text that is intercalated into the English). The Auchinleck "Assumption" has been edited only in M. Schwarz, "Kleine Publicationen aus der Auchinleck-MS," *Englische Studien* 8 (1885): 427–64. Subsequent citations are given parenthetically in the text.

35. Noel J. Ryan makes a similar assertion in the paragraph that he devotes to the poem in his wide-ranging consideration of medieval English narrations of the Assumption. See "The Assumption in the Early English Pulpit," *Theological Studies* 11 (1950): 477–524, 495. He bases his claim on comparison with other versions of the Assumption narrative circulating in England at the time but offers no specific examples.

And no wonder hit nas.
Of deʒ ʒhe moste ben adrad:
God, þat on þe rode was sprad,
Als telleʒ þe profecie,
Aʒens deʒ, þat was to come,
Er he was wiʒ Jues nome,
He was afered to die.
(lines 256–64)

Mary's emotional state is thus explicitly linked to Jesus', and other echoes of his last hours follow. The "erthe quok for dred" of Mary's death (line 290), reminiscent of the earthquake that attends the Crucifixion in Matthew's version of the Passion (Matt. 27:51), and Mary chides the apostles for falling asleep during her melancholy vigil (lines 298–300), recalling Jesus' rebuke of them for sleeping during his prayers in Gethsemane (Matt. 26:40–46). In an echo of Jesus' prayer to the Father that, "if it is possible, let this cup pass from me" (Matt. 26:39), she prays to Jesus that he allow her not to die:

Þanne seide our leuedi Marie:
"Leue sone, let me nowt die,
Ich beseche þe!
Leue sone, for mi loue
Let mi deʒ be forʒoue,
Ʒif hit mai so be!"
(lines 331–36)

When that proves impossible, like Jesus she bends her will to that of another; her "As þou wult, ich wille also" (line 344) is a close paraphrase of Jesus's "yet not what I want but what you want" (Matt. 26:39).

Mary's prayer is unique to Auchinleck's version of the poem,[36] which means that the Auchinleck poet has emphasized beyond his already emphatic source how Mary's attitude surrounding her assumption is patterned on Christ's crucifixion and ascension. Moreover, her imitation of Jesus is at once literal (as a person, she imitates his actions) and

---

36. Ibid. Auchinleck's version is a uniquely surviving stanzaic poem that appears to have been based on a couplet version extant in multiple manuscripts.

literary (her words are close paraphrases of his). The text's play with these two modes of imitation extends, not just from "The Assumption" to the text of the Gospels, but back to earlier texts in Auchinleck: in both "The Clerk who would see the Virgin" (text 9) and "Anna our leuedis moder," other characters (the Clerk and Saint Anne) receive angelic greetings that parallel Gabriel's to Mary at the Annunciation (Luke 1:30). As she laments her childlessness, for example, Anne is greeted by an angel who tells her not to fear ("Doute þe noþing" [line 67]) and congratulates her for bearing the child through whom the world will be saved. The textual imitation is even more striking in "The Clerk who would see the Virgin."[37] There, a clerk who prays for a vision of Mary is informed by an angel that his desire will be granted:

> "Mi clerk, drede þe noþing,
> Grace of God be ous bitven.
> Tidandes now y þe bring
> Fram Marie our heuen-quen."
> (lines 11–14)

This text evokes two passages from the Annunciation: the "gratia plena" ("Grace of God") with which Gabriel greets Mary and the "Fear not" ("drede þe noþing") with which he subsequently reassures her; the Clerk's fear ("He þouȝt his hert schuld tospring" [line 9]) also recalls Mary's initial reaction to Gabriel. Although the similarities between Mary and the Clerk diverge dramatically as the tale progresses,[38] such moments imply a transitivity to spiritual imitation that we have seen adumbrated in other religious texts, like *Sir Owain*, the

---

37. The only full edition of the poem is *Altenglische Legenden*, ed. Carl Horstmann (Heilbronn: Henninger, 1881), 499–502. Subsequent citations are given parenthetically in the text. Most of the Auchinleck text is included in *The Middle English Miracles of the Virgin*, ed. Beverly Boyd (San Marino, CA: Huntingdon Library, 1964), but the first forty or so lines, which have been damaged in the manuscript, have been omitted.

38. The angel informs the Clerk that the price of his vision of the Virgin will be either his eyesight or his life. He chooses to give up his eyesight but then tries to cheat by keeping one eye closed during his vision. Repentant, he laments his foolishness and prays to Mary for forgiveness, which she readily grants, and he offers ecstatic thanks and praise. Though it dissociates the tale from the Virgin's unvarnished holiness, this plot does align it with the opening booklets' interest in the efficacy of penitence for reformed sinners.

Auchinleck "Life of Adam and Eve," and *Speculum Gy*; ordinary and sinful people can imitate the spiritually effective imitations of others. Throughout, these texts take care to make such imitative models relatable: Owain makes his pilgrimage to an already popular shrine (though his activities once there are rather less accessible); the *Speculum Gy* demystifies and domesticates the great hero Guy of Warwick by having him renounce self-aggrandizing chivalric exploits; the Virgin's imitation of Jesus in the Auchinleck "Assumption" is principally of human, affective experiences.

All this means that, when we come to *Sir Degaré* (text 17), arguably the first "clear-cut" romance in Auchinleck,[39] we have been primed to look for approachable imitative models. In fact, the apparent generic clarity of *Sir Degaré*—it includes such classic tropes of romance as the foundling protagonist, the fairy knight, and the talismanic weapon—is deceptive, for its plot echoes with uncanny precision the first text in the manuscript as it now stands, *The Legend of Pope Gregory*. Both works tell of a mother who conceives a son under shameful circumstances and so sends him away. A holy man raises the foundling for a time; when the boy is old enough, he receives the tokens left with him as a baby by his mother. The boy, eager to become a knight, sets off to claim his birthright. Arrived in his mother's lands, but unaware of her true identity, he bests the man who stands between them; mother and son decide to wed. At this point, the plots of the two texts diverge,[40] but only because of a small and arbitrary chance: in *Sir Degaré*, the hero's mother recognizes the gloves that she left with him

---

39. My scare quotes hint at the near futility of such designations. Of the other two possible candidates, however, *King of Tars* has the insistently religious focus one would expect from a story of "hou wer bigan / Bitvene a trewe Cristen king / And an hethen heye lording" (lines 3–5), while *Amis and Amiloun* includes the strongly homiletic influence that we have seen noted by Crane (*Insular Romance*), Kratins ("Middle English *Amis and Amiloun*"), and others.

40. There are, of course, slight differences within this synopsis. In the *Legend*, the shameful circumstance surrounding the mother's conception is incest with her brother; in *Sir Degaré*, it is rape by a fairy knight. Even here, however, *Sir Degaré* maintains the hint of incest by suggesting that the woman's father (Degaré's grandfather) keeps his daughter single out of lustful jealousy. On this theme, see Cheryl Colopy, "*Sir Degaré*: A Fairy Tale Oedipus," *Pacific Coast Philology* 17 (1982): 31–39. Accordingly, the man whom Degaré defeats to win his mother's hand is his own grandfather, whereas in the *Legend* it is an unnamed duke of Rome whose attempts to woo Gregory's mother she had earlier rebuffed.

as a foundling, which prevents the incestuous marriage that proceeds unimpeded in the *Legend*. There, a parallel scene nearly occurs when Gregory's mother thinks that she recognizes the clothes in which she wrapped him as a baby; reasoning inethat "o cloþ was oþer y liche,"[41] however, she considers the matter no further, and her marriage to her son takes place.

The fact that Gregory nearly avoided his incestuous marriage in precisely the same way that Degaré actually did emphasizes the two texts' remarkable similarities in plot. Through the first two thirds of the *Legend*, Gregory gives every indication of becoming a romance hero like Degaré; to his abbot mentor's promise that "Þou schalt ben abot after me" (line 420), his response is emphatic:

> Nay for soþe quaþ he sone
> Þi þouȝt is now fro min riȝt
> Ac ȝif þou wilt ouȝt for me don
> Ȝif me order to be kniȝt.
> (lines 421–24)

These suggestions—that Gregory might just as easily have continued to resemble the romance hero Degaré and that had Degaré, like Gregory, married his mother he would have needed a comparable form of spiritual cleansing—highlight the interpenetration of romance and religious texts within the first third of the Auchinleck manuscript more broadly. In a paradoxically opposed move, however, these similarities also draw attention to the dramatic divergence that eventually takes place in the poems' respective denouements and the ever after that they imagine for their protagonists. In this respect, *Sir Degaré* evokes the generic movement of the manuscript as a whole: while the manuscript does contain a few subsequent brief religious texts, its emphasis over the next two hundred folios is resolutely on romance. Through its initial similarities to and ultimate divergence from the *Legend*, *Sir*

---

41. *Die Mittelenglische Gregoriuslegende*, ed. Carl Keller (Heidelberg: Carl Winters, 1914), line 558. Subsequent citations are given parenthetically in the text. Keller's edition includes all surviving versions of the poem.

Degaré effectively restarts the manuscript in the romance mode, both evoking and marking closure with the preceding homiletic overture.

How one experiences the similarities between *Sir Degaré* and *The Legend of Pope Gregory* thus depends on when and how one reads them. Read sequentially, *Sir Degaré* looks backward to *The Legend of Pope Gregory*, and its secular content would not immediately mark it as distinct from Auchinleck's religious opening since both the *Legend* and *Amis and Amiloun* also begin like straightforward romances. Read in the context of Auchinleck as a whole, however, it marks a break with that opening's religious concerns and announces the manuscript's far greater emphasis, proportionally, on romance-world heroism of precisely the sort that earlier texts depicted characters renouncing. The contrast between these two meanings that emerges when we apprehend them together—*Sir Degaré* as both continuity and disjunction with what has come before—raises the question of whether and how the idea of salutary imitation that permeated Auchinleck's religious overture can be translated into this other, secular world of romance. *Sir Degaré*'s *literary* imitation of an earlier text's plot, in other words, evokes the role of *literal* imitation in the preceding texts more broadly. It thus questions how a comparable motif of imitation might or might not make the generic transition that Auchinleck itself is in the process of effecting.

Grasping the full import of all this depends on our willingness to read *Sir Degaré* across multiple temporalities: the linear historicity of a first reading of the manuscript, on which *Sir Degaré* initially seems like a continuation of what has come before, and the retrospective historicity of the reader returning to the poem now fully aware of the proportions of Auchinleck's contents. (To these we might add the prospective historicity of the patron, perhaps waiting impatiently for the manuscript to get going with the romances that he seems principally to have desired by his commission.) Ultimately, this question of time and historicity becomes a question of form, for *Sir Degaré*'s meaning changes depending on whether it is part of a relatively local codicological form (the religious overture), a much larger one (the manuscript as a whole), or yet another, booklet 3, whose contours are visible only before (i.e., in the production phase) and after (i.e., now) the manuscript's presentation to its original audience.

Thus, the particular textual position of *Sir Degaré* within Auchinleck and that position's relation to how the manuscript itself was and is constructed—all elements of codicological form, mediated through historical forces planned and accidental—give complex interpretive possibilities to a poem that can seem somewhat lifeless when read in isolation. By looking back so precisely to a text earlier in the manuscript but then diverging so dramatically from it, the Auchinleck *Sir Degaré* encourages contemplation of other contexts that might bring meaning to the poem and to which the poem might itself give meaning. This is one way in which the evolution of Degaré's character can make itself significant to Auchinleck's mercantile audience. Raised by the sister of the hermit who found him, whose husband is a "riche marchaunt,"[42] Degaré initially self-identifies as bourgeois; on setting off on his own, he declines to take up the aristocratic trappings that his hermit mentor recommends, using a rough oaken staff rather than a sword, and refusing the proffered horse and armor. In fact, the letter that his mother left with him specifies clearly that he "is comen of gentil blod" (line 209), but it is only after he has performed his first heroic deed, saving an earl from a dragon, that he accepts the sword, horse, and armor that the hermit earlier proposed, this time from the rescued earl. Degaré's initial reluctance to take up the outward manifestations of his station thus implies that such nobility must be earned: the earl reinforces this hint by asserting that Degaré "was better worhti / To usen hors and armes also / Than with his bat aboute to go" (lines 418–20). Worthiness and deeds must legitimize noble birth.

In isolation, this sounds like a conventional "true gentility comes from within" moral akin to those of the *Wife of Bath's Tale* or the *Franklin's Tale*, but within its Auchinleck context it becomes rather more. By proposing that unearned nobility is no nobility at all, *Sir*

---

42. *Sir Degaré*, in *The Middle English Breton Lays*, ed. Anne Laskaya and Eve Salisbury (Kalamazoo, MI: Medieval Institute Publications, 1995), line 260. Subsequent citations are given parenthetically in the text.

Degaré subtly raises the tantalizing possibility of the converse: that true nobility is in fact open to those who are not born with it—if, like Degaré, they perform the right kinds of actions. The poem reinforces this possibility with its gloss on the name that the hermit gives the foundling, which evokes French *égaré* (lost):

> He hit nemnede Degarre,
> Degarre nowt elles ne is
> But thing that not never what hit is,
> Other thing that is neggh forlorn also;
> Forthi the schild he nemnede thous tho.
> (lines 254–58)

Of course, Degaré does eventually discover who he is, but the text's presentation of him as lost and unknown suggests that nonnoble birth is really just a blank folio on which can be inscribed the romance of any real-life protagonist's acquisition of courtly trappings and, from there, of aristocratic reality. It does so only as a form of fantastic wish fulfillment, to be sure, since the manuscript's mercantile readers were unlikely to find any dragons to kill or earls to rescue, but such fantasies are not the less significant for that. Indeed, they are central to the appeal of romance—and, in the provocatively blank pages that conclude booklet 3, we will see a literal, physical evocation of this fantasy.

Sir Degaré offers one mercantile-inflected narrative arc, in which an apparently unaristocratic hero (on foot, wielding a staff) first performs and only then acknowledges his own nobility. *Floris and Blauncheflur* (text 19) offers a contrasting take on mercantile performance, one in which an acknowledged prince must disguise himself as a traveling merchant in order to achieve the classic romance goal of winning his true love. The poem tells the story of its eponymous characters, a pagan prince of Spain and his family's Christian slave, respectively. Born on the same day and raised together, they develop such a childhood devotion that Floris's father sells Blauncheflur to visiting Babylonian merchants so that his son will not disgrace the family with his passion for her. When Floris appears likely to die of grief at her loss, his parents relent and give him the ornately decorated cup that they received for her so that he can find her and buy her back. His mother also gives him a magic ring that will preserve the life of whoever wears it. Floris disguises himself as a merchant, and by skillfully questioning other merchants, paying for information with a series of luxury goods, he eventually finds Blauncheflur in the harem of the emir of Babylon. When they are discovered in bed together, their mutual spirit of self-sacrifice as they await the emir's death sentence—each insists that the other wear Floris's life-preserving ring—so impresses the assembled court that the emir has mercy and releases them. Floris converts to Christianity, he and Blauncheflur marry, and they become king and queen of Spain.

Kathleen Coyne Kelly has usefully complicated the text's long-standing reception as a "charming" narrative of naively intense love by emphasizing Blauncheflur's status as a slave, literally a piece of property exchanged among various parties.[43] These mercantile transactions, which are described in considerable detail, make her an ideal heroine for what in the Auchinleck manuscript becomes a mercantile romance.[44] As Floris travels, he is not just physically disguised; he performs the part of a merchant as well, paying his various hosts for news of Blauncheflur with precious objects: gold and silver cups, a mantle of scarlet and miniver.[45] Kelly notes that the poem's many dramatizations of such exchanges "are apparently original with the Middle

43. Kathleen Coyne Kelly, "The Bartering of Blauncheflur in the Middle English *Floris and Blauncheflur*," *Studies in Philology* 91 (1994): 101–10. Kelly cites *charming* as the tale's adjective of critical choice and then announces her intention "to offer a darker reading" (ibid., 102). She cites many of the same passages I do, although from a more explicitly feminist perspective that does not link the poem's interest in commerce to its audience or its situation in the Auchinleck manuscript. Like my interpretation, however, hers also argues that the romance "highlight[s] the commercial nature of the activity in which Floris is . . . engaged" (ibid., 107).

44. Karen Cherewatuk offers a similar characterization of the poem in "The Middle English *Floris and Blauncheflur*, Another Merchant's Tale," *New Comparison* 12 (1991): 54–70. She discusses contrasts with the poem's French source that heighten the mercantile flavor of the English poem but does not address its manuscript contexts.

45. For these exchanges, see *Floris and Blauncheflur*, ed. A. B. Taylor (Oxford: Clarendon, 1927), lines 444ff., 517, and 518, respectively. Subsequent citations will be given parenthetically in the text.

English poet, for they are not found in his French source."[46] One of the romance's few ekphrastic set pieces is that of the cup that the king receives from the Babylonian merchants in return for Blauncheflur (lines 161–84), and the text later describes, not just the lavish gifts that Floris gives his various hosts to pay for news of her, but also precisely how and for how much the emir bought her: seven times her weight in gold (at both lines 527–36 and lines 1099–1106). This emphasis on the number 7 further knits the poem to the first two texts of booklet 3 and the immediately preceding *Seven Sages of Rome*—on which more momentarily.

In playing the merchant, moreover, Floris sharply differentiates himself from the romance's negative royal figures: his parents, who in sacrificing love to propriety make a nearly fatal miscalculation about how their son will react to Blauncheflur's supposed death, and the emir, who is readily cuckolded by Floris, tricked by Blauncheflur's confidante, and betrayed by his own porter. Floris's actions, by contrast, are explicitly not those of his royal station. In warning him how dangerous it will be to free Blancheflur, Daris notes:

> Þameral haþ to his iustening
> Oþer half hondred of riche kinge;
> Þat alþerrichest kyng
> Ne dorste biginne swich a þing,
> Þilke maide to awinne. . . .
> (lines 609–13)

The "alþerrichest kyng" might not dare attempt such a rescue, but merchants like Floris, the text implies, are more effective because they know how to accomplish their goals with stealth and gold when force is impossible.[47] The scene between Floris and the porter offers a similar contrast between aristocratic expectations and Floris's actions. Floris plays the porter in chess but deliberately loses, giving

---

46. Kelly, "The Bartering of Blauncheflur," 104.

47. Geraldine Barnes addresses this contrast in "Cunning and Ingenuity in the Middle English *Floris and Blauncheflur*," *Medium Ævum* 53 (1984): 10–25.

him more and more gold with every loss until "þourgh his gold and his garsome / Þe porter is his man bicome" (lines 821–22). The conclusion to this scene—Floris's triumphant claim of victory, the porter's rueful acknowledgment that he has been bested and now must serve the victor—echoes other romances in which the protagonist extracts feudal service from an enemy bested in combat. Floris uses this feudal language but has acquired his mastery over the porter by losing rather than winning, paying rather than fighting. His ingenuity in using mercantile tactics to triumph over two different sets of royal adversaries makes him an attractive model for Auchinleck's audience, which, as we have seen, was obliged to rely on comparable forms of clever resourcefulness in dealings with the Crown.

While it is true, however, that the challenges that Floris faces are not the typical romance-hero ones of "hostile knights, giants, or dragons" and that he "simply has to trade wisely,"[48] the very similarity of these actions to the everyday business of Auchinleck's audience serves ultimately to reinforce the distance between them and the hero when the conclusion of the romance reestablishes aristocratic norms and the happy couple assumes their royal duties as king and queen of Spain. *Floris and Blauncheflur* depicts an aristocratic hero who must accomplish his goals with mercantile prowess, but it finally suggests that this imitative model is strictly one-way: a prince like Floris can slum it by playing the merchant when he needs to, but it is not at all apparent how the poem's merchants—or Auchinleck's audience—could do the reverse. In this respect, *Floris and Blauncheflur* contrasts pointedly with *Sir Degaré*. The earlier text did not present mercantile behavior in the same positive light as *Floris and Blauncheflur*; Degaré's childhood with the "riche marchaunt" and his wife is unnarrated, and, after earning his proper, aristocratic status, the hero adopts it without question and never looks back. But by taking someone who "not never what hit is, / . . . that is neggh forlorn also" (lines 256–57) and showing him how to earn his rightful inestatus by deeds rather than claim it by blood, *Sir Degaré* suggests the ideal of a self-made hero. *Floris and Blaunche-*

---

48. Kelly, "The Bartering of Blauncheflur," 107.

flur, by contrast, carefully brackets its hero's mercantile exploits with a frame narrative that makes his royal status both the impetus behind the central adventure (princes shouldn't fall for slave girls) and the evidence of that adventure's successful conclusion (princes should, by contrast, become king and ensure an orderly succession). Apprehended together, these poems implicitly ask whether the fantasy of *Sir Degaré* can ever come true or whether, as in *Floris and Blauncheflur*, social norms will reassert themselves regardless of how much they may have been blurred. In the ambivalence that this dual perspective suggests, both aspirational and realistic, these poems recall portions of the Horn corpus that we considered earlier, like the juxtaposed *puy* statutes or the adaptations from Latini's *Livres dou Tresor*.

I do not claim that either *Sir Degaré* or *Floris and Blaunchefleur* is simplistically *about* the question of whether and how mercantile social aspirations could be realized. I do, however, suggest that their codicological situation gives additional force and complexity to the way in which each subtly evokes this issue: force because of their proximity to one another and to the spiritually imitative set of texts that preceded them and complexity because they evoke the issue in contrasting, even opposed ways. The "Battle Abbey Roll," which concludes booklet 3, will offer yet another perspective on this same question, but the two poems' more immediate context is the romance that they bracket, *The Seven Sages of Rome* (text 18), booklet 3's longest and central work. *Seven Sages* evokes royal rather than civic politics and culture, heightening the tension between the two spheres that is at the heart of the conversation between *Sir Degaré* and *Floris and Blauncheflur* on the question of imitative social aspiration. Literally inserted into that conversation, *Seven Sages* raises its stakes by implicitly questioning whether fictional discourse—like the poems on either side of it or, indeed, the Auchinleck manuscript itself—can or should have any concrete effects in the real world. Its physical centrality to booklet 3 makes *Seven Sages'* interrogation of the texts around it likewise central to the booklet as a whole. Like the tension between *Floris and Blaunchefur* and *Sir Degaré*, however, the questions it poses will be fully addressed only at the end of the booklet, by the riddling union of codicological form and social history that is the "Battle Abbey Roll."

Seven Sages and the Conclusion of Booklet 3:
Fragmentation and Construction, Stasis and Movement

The Seven Sages of Rome tells of the emperor Dioclesian, a widower who after sending his son Florentine to be educated by seven sages marries a wicked woman who hates the boy. When an unlucky constellation prevents Florentine from speaking for an entire week, the empress sees her chance and accuses him of attempting to rape her. Enraged, Dioclesian orders him executed, and the seven sages must intervene to save his life. The bulk of the poem consists of the ensuing storytelling duel between the sages and the empress: she tells Dioclesian stories, usually about the iniquity of sons and counselors, from which she extrapolates the moral that he should kill Florentine; the sages counter with stories establishing that women's advice leads to ruin, thereby blunting Dioclesian's fury and saving the son from execution that day. This process continues for the entire week, whereupon Florentine (now able to speak) uses a story of his own to convince his father of his innocence, and the wicked empress is executed.

By staging a storytelling contest in which the succession of the kingdom itself is at stake, *Seven Sages* suggests that even fictive discourse can have real consequences on vital social and political questions. This is hardly a radical proposition, as the vast literature of exempla suggests, but *Seven Sages* plays with this notion in a number of interesting ways. First, the empress draws from a number of her stories morals that seem quite at odds with the stories themselves but that Dioclesian uncritically accepts.[49] Such episodes serve partly to

---

49. One such dubious moral involves the story of a thief who raided a treasury with his son, then got caught in the trap set the next night. At the thief's request, the son cut off his head so he couldn't be identified, then threw the head down a privy. The king had the headless corpse paraded through the streets: whoever cried would be seized as a relation of the dead thief. The son could not help crying and so stabbed himself to provide cover for his grief, thereby fooling the king's officer. The empress's moral, however, is that the son should be condemned for throwing his father's head down a privy; Dioclesian agrees to kill Florentine. This seems a strangely inappropriate moral to draw: the son was clever and loyal and even in his grisliest actions was following his father's commands.

characterize the empress (women with twisted motives likewise twist their stories' morals), but the readiness, the inevitability even, with which Dioclesian accepts these dubious morals also discredits him, suggesting that failures of literary interpretation can become failures of practical authority. Yet neither these improperly adduced morals nor indeed any others, from the empress or the sages, lead to any forward movement in the frame tale; the empress always convinces her husband to kill Florentine, and the sages just as surely convince him not to. In part, this stasis is simply a device that allows the stories to continue, but it is striking for a poem premised on the relevance of fictive discourse to public policy to present such discourse as unable to bring about any narrative progress at all.

Seven Sages includes other hints of meta-awareness, too, for the characters themselves recognize the growing absurdity of the stalemate that the emperor's infinite malleability has produced. When Dioclesian professes eagerness to hear yet another story from the empress, for example, she initially refuses, pointing out that her exempla have not helped her in the past:

> Nai, sire, ȝe saide, hit his nowt worþ,
> Mi tale ne mot nowt forþ
> Telle ich þe ensaumple neuer so god,
> Þou me haldest of wit wod.
> Þerfore ich wille holde me still,
> And suffri wel þat man þe spille.
> (lines 1539–44)

Ultimately, of course, she relents and tells a story with the moral that Dioclesian should kill his son; he agrees (of course), only to change his mind (of course) when the next of the sages presents his own story of wicked wives. This narrative stasis, moreover, occurs in spite of increasingly pointed attempts by both sides to link their fictive stories to the real world of the frame tale. In the most dramatic such example, the empress tells the story of Herod, like Dioclesian "an emperour . . . in Rome" (line 2329), who seeks a cure for his mysterious blindness. You can almost see the empress winking and nudging as she describes his seven sages' promise to help him and the subsequent discovery that the sages themselves are to blame; only after all seven are executed does the emperor regain his sight. Dioclesian agrees with his wife that sages are clearly not to be trusted but fails to apply his supposed understanding of the story's message by taking the logical next step and having his own sages executed. This episode has complex literary effects, for, even as we laugh at Dioclesian's inability to understand the blindingly obvious analogues between the fiction he has heard and the situation he inhabits, this failure ironically leads to the correct result within the poem's moral structure: Florentine survives another day of the tale-telling duel.

Such contrasts and disjunctions pointedly raise the issue of fiction's relevance to external contexts and how it might be illumined by them. For the Auchinleck *Seven Sages*, those contexts include both texts within the manuscript and recent external political events. Within booklet 3, for example, the poem's obsessive emphasis on the number 7 recalls the first two texts in the booklet, "On the seuen dedli sinnes" and "Þe pater noster undo on englisch," which used that number to establish themselves as a linked pair. Florentine is seven years old when his mother dies and Dioclesian sends him to be educated by the seven sages, and it is after seven years with them that his ordeal begins. (He is thus fourteen years old during the main action of the frame tale, perhaps not coincidentally the same age as Edward III when he was crowned in 1327.) He must remain silent for seven days and, in the Egerton manuscript (Auchinleck has lost the quire that contained the end of the poem), names seven monks to pray for his father's soul. *Seven Sages* thus represents yet another translation of the number that prominently opened the booklet and that then recurs in *Floris and Blauncheflur*, where Blauncheflur's price is twice specified as seven times her weight in gold. *Seven Sages'* numerical evocation of booklet 3's linked opening pair, and its anticipation of the number's prominence in the following romance, might be remarked on only in passing, if at all, by Auchinleck's original audience. For contemporary readers with access to booklet 3's codicological identity, however, it gives us a point of connection with the booklet's original maker(s), drawing as it were another line in the emerging constellation.

While this internal, numerical resonance might not have registered with the manuscript's contemporary audience, however, the poem's evocation of recent political events doubtless would have since *Seven Sages'* family drama—a simultaneously ineffectual and headstrong king, a conniving queen, and an idealized young prince—offers hints of the main players of Edward II's final years: the weak king, impervious to the well-meaning advice of his loyal advisers; his subtle and iniquitous queen, Isabella; and the young Edward III, hope of a weary nation. The parallels are inexact,[50] and my point is not that the Auchinleck *Seven Sages* is purely or simply *about* the external political situation, any more than *Floris and Blauncheflur* was *about* the social aspirations of London merchants. Rather, I suggest that the poem raises the stakes on one central question—the relevance of literary interpretation to political leadership and external reality more broadly—by teasingly encouraging its audience to engage in precisely such interpretation of the text itself. It is significant, therefore, that Florentine is the only character in the entire poem who is depicted effectively translating literary content into practical action by convincing his father of his innocence. He tells of a son who can understand the speech of birds. When he reveals to his father some birds' prediction that he will far exceed his father in greatness, his father furiously throws him into the sea to drown. The son is rescued and in due course becomes steward of a king who is being bothered by the incessant crowing of three ravens. The son's

---

50. This is particularly so in the case of the empress and Isabella, who obviously championed her son's cause rather than seeking to have him executed. The young king did effectively imprison his mother (and execute her lover, Mortimer) not long after ascending the throne, however, and Londoners too soured notably on her and Mortimer once their autocratic tendencies became clear (which they had, in any event, by the time of the poem's inclusion in Auchinleck). For a succinct account of these events, see Roy Martin Haines, *King Edward II: Edward of Caernarfon, His Life, His Reign, and Its Aftermath, 1284–1330* (Montreal: McGill-Queens University Press, 2003), esp. 177–218. Isabella and Mortimer do, moreover, make another allusive cameo in Auchinleck; Turville-Petre points out that, by describing Lancelot as holding Guenevere in Nottingham Castle, the *Liber Regum Anglie* "merg[es] a recollection of the French *Mort Artu*, in which Lancelot protects Guenevere in Joyeuse Garde, with a much more recent memory of Roger Mortimer and Queen Isabella in 1330 barricading themselves into Nottingham Castle, from which Mortimer was ignominiously dragged and sent to London to be hanged" (*England the Nation*, 111–12).

gift allows him to diagnose the cause, an avian love triangle that the king must settle by deciding which of two suitors deserves the formel's love: the elder raven, who abandoned her in hard times, or the younger raven, who has cared for her since. The king awards the formel's love to the younger, loyal bird, and the three fly off, while the son is rewarded with the hand of the king's daughter. When he becomes king himself, he summons his now poverty-stricken parents to a feast, where his original prophecy comes true, as his father humbly holds the basin of water as he washes and his mother offers him a towel. The son reveals his identity to his father, who is fearful of being punished.

At this point, fragmentation ensues. Since Auchinleck has lost the gathering that contained the last thousand or so lines of *Seven Sages*, we cannot know how the story ended in this manuscript. In some, the son graciously forgives his father; in others, Florentine abruptly ends his tale before the son can respond to his father's fear, leaving the audience in suspense as to whether and how the son punished his treacherous father.[51] All versions agree, however, that Florentine compares his own father's behavior to that of the wicked father in his story and blames the empress for his troubles. After meekly admitting her guilt (in some manuscripts begging for forgiveness, which is refused), she is burned for her crime, and the story ends with Florentine assuming the throne after his father's death from natural causes. Whichever conclusion Auchinleck contained, the story sits oddly with its most immediate outcome within the frame tale. Dioclesian never acknowledges the justice of Florentine's charge against him, instead turning immediately on the empress, whose psychologically implau-

---

51. Since Auchinleck, which formed the base text of Brunner's edition, has lost the last thousand lines of the poem, Brunner provides in parallel-text format the conclusions from the three other manuscripts whose versions are closest to Auchinleck's: British Library MS Egerton 1995, Oxford Balliol College MS 354, and Cambridge University Library MS Ff.2.38. Of these, the first two lack the conclusion in which the son forgives his father, while the last includes four concluding lines in which he does. In this instance, codicological lack has led to plenitude of information and consequent interpretive potential: if Auchinleck had not been damaged, Brunner would have presented its text and the existence of the alternate possibilities offered by these other manuscripts consigned to the textual notes, if there.

sible admission of guilt only imperfectly distracts us from Dioclesian's complicity in the affair. The strangeness of her sudden confession is magnified by the fact that the preceding tale has not, like most of the sages' tales that came before, focused on the iniquity of women. Instead, it has concentrated on the need for older male figures to yield to younger ones. This male-male generational tension underlies the original conflict between father and son and is evoked later too: the older raven must cede the formel to the younger, and the king whom the son aids is in due course succeeded by him. As with the empress's earlier story of the emperor deluded by his sages, then, the correct moral result within the frame tale does not flow naturally from the logical exemplary power of Florentine's story itself. It is therefore impossible to determine whether the empress's feeble admission of guilt is a mechanical imposition of the frame tale (i.e., all seven sages have told their stories, so it's time to wrap up) or a demonstration of the rhetorical power of the idealized prince, which induces wicked stepmothers to admit their guilt—even when offering stories that do not seem particularly addressed to them. In this sense, the poem itself presents an interpretive crux comparable to other moments of fragmentation that we considered in the introduction. Are mechanical or aesthetic causes behind a given textual codicological feature, and how can we know? The literal fragmentation that concludes the Auchinleck *Seven Sages* thus parallels the interpretive aporia that obtains at the end of even complete versions of the poem.

However its Auchinleck version once ended, *Seven Sages* is forcefully recalled two texts later in booklet 3, with the macaronic introduction to "The Sayings of the Four Philosophers" (text 20):

L'en puet fere & defere, ceo fait-il trop souent;
It nis nouþer wel ne faire, þerfore engelond is shent.
Nostre prince de engleterre per le consail de sa gent,
At Westminster after þe feire maden a gret perlement.
La chartre fet de cyre ieo l'enteink & bien le crey
It was holde to neih þe fire and is molten al awey.
Ore ne say mes que dire, tout i va a tripolay,
Hundred, chapitle, court & shire, al hit goþ a deuel wey.

Des plu sages de la tere, ore escoteʒ vn sarmoun,
Of iiij wise men, þat þer were, whi engelond is brought adoun.[52]

If *Seven Sages* recalled contemporary English politics only allusively, these lines are insistently specific, twice repeating "engelond" (lines 2, 10) as they refer to "nostre prince de engleterre" (line 3), the parliament at Westminster (line 4), and the Ordinances of 1311, whose provisions Edward repeatedly disregarded (line 5). The French *sages* of line 9 likewise evoke the sages of the earlier poem, while the next line continues the theme of (numbered) "wise men" offering advice. Two other moments from the text of that advice also seem to echo *Seven Sages*: the first sage's insistence that "may no king wel ben in londe . . . / But he kunne him-self rede" (lines 22–24) and the concluding exhortation to be "gode & stedefast" (line 87). The first of these recalls Dioclesian's inability to take any appropriate counsel, while the latter echoes the praise of Florentine ("most he louyde stedefastenys" [line 3566])[53] that concludes the poem and implicitly condemns Dioclesian's indecisiveness. Every reader of the manuscript would know, moreover, that Edward II listened to his sages no more effectively than Dioclesian did.

In its references to specific kings and documents as opposed to the distant romance world of ancient Rome, however, the macaronic introduction does mark a generic transition of sorts from the romance materials that precede "Four Philosophers" in booklet 3; within the *mise-en-abyme* structure of booklet 3 that I sketched out earlier, "Four Philosophers" marks its movement out of romance and into history, corresponding to booklets 10–12 of Auchinleck's overall structure (see table 1 above). The echoes of *Seven Sages* here thus function akin to the similarities of plot between *The Legend of Pope Gregory* and *Sir Degaré*: the resemblances prompt association, even as the differences suggest

52. Robbins, ed., *Historical Poems*, 140–43. While using Robbins's text, I have reproduced the long-line format in which the lines are written in Auchinleck, so these ten lines correspond to Robbins's lines 1–20. Subsequent citations are given in the text.

53. Quoted from the closely related Egerton version (British Library, MS Egerton 1995) since, as we have seen, the gathering that included the end of *Seven Sages* has been lost in Auchinleck. This statement concludes a long list of Florentine's virtues; the poet has apparently saved the most important for last.

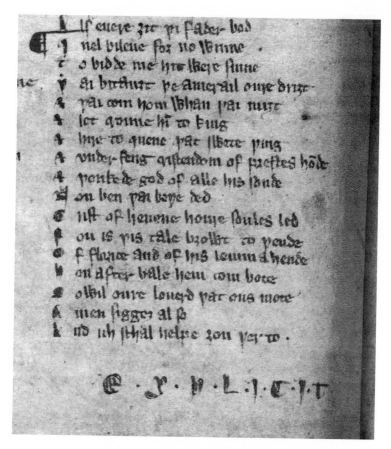

FIGURE 3. National Library of Scotland, Advocates MS 19.2.1 (Auchinleck), fol. 104v (detail). Courtesy the Trustees of the National Library of Scotland.

a generic break between the two texts. The manuscript suggests this break visually as well, for the poem that immediately precedes "Four Philosophers," *Floris and Blauncheflur*, ends with an unusually florid and conspicuous explicit (see fig. 3). Our loss of so many miniatures, which usually open texts, has meant that a great many of Auchinleck's texts also end imperfectly, so we have no way of knowing precisely how unusual this explicit might once have been. Comparison with those that do remain, however, suggests that it was more eye-catching than most[54] and could thus have inclined a reader to mark visually the generic transition that I have proposed takes place between *Floris and Blauncheflur* and "Four Philosophers."

In sharp contrast with *Floris and Blauncheflur*, "Four Philosophers" has no visually marked explicit; the "am*en*" that concludes the poem is spatially part of its last line (see fig. 4). On turning the page and seeing the verso, however, we are confronted by the arresting wall of names that is the "Battle Abbey Roll" (see fig. 5). This work is untitled, and its imposing *mise-en-page* performs codicologically the same function as booklet 3's many other textual allusions and echoes, namely, raising the question of what outside contexts might profitably inform the text at hand. Here, there is no narrative to contextualize, just a list of names continuing inexorably from folio 105v to folio 107r. Only a sixth or so of that last page was initially filled; the rest of that recto and the entirety of its verso were left blank save for the catchphrase "here ginneþ Sir Gij" at the bottom of folio 107v, which looks forward to booklet 4's opening text, the romance *Guy of Warwick*. Over the centuries, however, other hands have added to this white space, and these later interventions both constitute a key way in which this enigmatic text achieves meaning today and suggest ways in which it might have meant to its original audience. The Auchinleck "Battle Abbey Roll" manages paradoxically both to halt forward motion (what else can one do, initially at least, with folio 105v and the facing 106r but stop and stare?) and to suggest, in its evolving codicological form and the comparably evolving social histories recorded by its names, that movement into the future is both inevitable and salutary.

The daunting appearance of the "Roll" and its total lack of both narrative and context help explain why it was the last text from the manuscript to be published, in the 1948 essay by H. M. Smyser that remains the only modern study of the work of which I am aware. I quote his readable account at some length:

---

54. The explicits for the texts *Seint Katherine*, *Reinbrun*, and the "Alphabetical Praise of Women," e.g., are all considerably less florid than that of *Floris and Blauncheflur*.

In the *Chronicon Monasterii de Bello*, presumably written towards the end of the twelfth century, we read that William [the Conqueror] made a vow when the battle of Hastings was about to be joined to erect an abbey for the salvation of his followers and especially of those who should fall in the battle. We need not go into the vexed question of whether or not Battle Abbey was supplied with an actual bede-roll at its dedication, or not until much later, or even not at all; the fact is that in any case by the end of the Middle Ages there were in existence a number of lists of Norman names which, though not so headed, were accepted by early modern scholars as the Battle Abbey Roll.

Working from the nineteenth-century study by the admirably named Catherine L. W. Stanhope Powlett, Duchess of Cleveland, Smyser argues that the list found in John Leland's *De Rebus Britannicis Collectanea* is the oldest, predating the version from Raphael Holinshed's *Chronicles of England, Scotland, and Ireland*, though of course the text in Auchinleck is "diplomatically by far the oldest known copy." Again, I quote Smyser: "Leland's list is made up of pairs of alliterating names, and nearly every pair rhymes with one or more pairs immediately preceding or following. Thus: *Aumarill et Deyncourt*; *Bertrem et Buttencourt*; *Biard et Biford* (probably for *Brehus et Byset*); *Bardolf et Basset*;

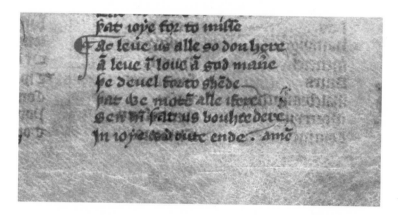

Aumarle	Samt denys	Merke	Malour
Bertram	Otuel	fiz felyp	payfer
Brehufe	Gorgis	Takel	Bretoun
Bardolf	Gorges	le mare	Mourhermer
Deayuile	Wyne	Delamare	Bayrnfe
Pygot	limefy	Tourkuyle	Beke
Vurnay	Boys	Samz auer	Deffe
Tregoz	fenes	Mountagu	Gangi
Canoys	fiz Roger	fourneus	Raum
Hautayn	Mufe	Valence	payner
Warayne	Quincy	Cternaus	fiz anger
Chauuent	Longulers	Dodingzeley	Dakeny
Loueny	Criketot	Mautalent	Meneuple
Trehuitone	poucr	Chpis	Mauconenant
Bigot	Toudrt	Chauntclew	pykard
Mohuut	perhe	Sayntes	Grey
Maruulon	Daubny	Bande	Dilneny
Marroys	Samt amand	fiz otes	Maune
Ballyik	Ryuers	Maule	Banafter
Vepuut	louetay	Sulay	Baloun
Estrange	Deupas	Bruis	Louenor
Monbray	Munt bretchr	Neuple	Baudyn
Veer	fiz marmeduk	fiz Willam	Saluayn
Auele	Rous	Delamere	Rye
Waltraays	Cruffebut	Sorel	fiz Rauf
Soudy	Maleuile	Samt Johm	pygart
Couetay	Hermarthe	Warruyle	Damari
ferrers	Corbyn	Dela pole	Vanazour
ferre	Mountemy	Mortuaus	perpoum
Braunccon	Gaunte	Cruffy	Oybny
Rouwers	Maleherbe	Samt leo	Hermute
Chumberlayn	Geneuile	Bauent	Vilers
fiz Wauter	Someruile	Lascls	Cimmpenays
Argenteym	pyuot	Taps	Malebyfe
Roffe	Chuudoys	haureel	Clouny
Ros	Dela hay	longebile	Samt Gorge
Hastangey	Mufegros	longeule	Wafe
Menerel	Moynly	De la ware	fenlk
Butes	fauecourt	Chtloufe	Wake
Maldraundly	Vescy	Conestable	pungeys
Monteyne	Braiufoun	poynce	Scaleo
Comine	Chlons	Couke	Efturs

5A

FIGURE 5. National Library of Scotland, Advocates MS 19.2.1 (Auchinleck), fols. 105v–107r (fig. 5A–5D, respectively; shown here on consecutive pages). Courtesy the Trustees of the National Library of Scotland.

5B

Deyville et Darcy; *Pygot et Percy* (etc.). Holinshed's list is alphabetical in the old fashion, in which each name is merely classified according to its first letter without regard to the following letters. It begins: *Aumarle*; *Aincourt*; *Audeley*; *Adgillam*; *Argentoune* (etc.)."[55] The Auchinleck version looks like neither of these; although using an alliterating copy like

55. Smyser, "The List of Norman Names," 262, 261, 263.

5C

Leland's, Scribe 4 has split up the alliterating pairs.[56] Besides rearranging the order of the names, the Auchinleck "Battle Abbey Roll" includes some forty-eight names that are not found in Leland and omits two pairs of names that are.

56. Smyser helpfully summarizes the complicated details: "The Auchinleck scribe copies out Leland's 1a–186a; 1b–190b; 187a–248a; 191b–248b" (ibid., 265).

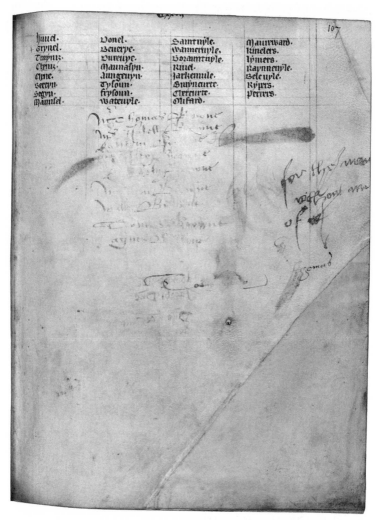

5D

The most immediate question that this "text" poses both to us and to Auchinleck's first readers is of course who these people are. Smyser endorses Stanhope Powlett's conclusion that most of these names do indeed date to the eleventh or twelfth century and that the problem lies rather in determining absolutely which ones do not.[57] Just as the

---

57. "Nothing is more likely than that the list contains numerous interpolations, but detecting those interpolations is no easy matter. . . . All we have to judge by is the bare name—no

Latin lines that precede *Mirror of Justices* in the Horn corpus offered a test of their audience's compilational acuity, so too the "Battle Abbey Roll" becomes a test of historical memory, which its appearance in Auchinleck, untitled and uncontextualized, flatteringly presupposes that the manuscript's audience will pass. It does not just challenge its readers to make sense of it as a whole, however, to recognize it as the "Battle Abbey Roll" rather than a random set of names. It also offers a second, still more hidden test: that of discerning in this imposing wall of text which individual names do not in fact date back to the Norman Conquest, for Smyser argues that "the Roll was at least expanded (if not invented) some time near the close of the thirteenth and beginning of the fourteenth centuries."[58]

This expansion matters because it demonstrates that history is not static. For the savvy reader of the manuscript, perhaps the patron himself (patrons themselves?), the nature of these later additions might have offered still deeper relevance, for a number of these more recent names are likewise of less than ancient social pedigree. Smyser identifies "Mounthermer" (which corresponds to Leland's 121a) with Ralph de Monthermer, the second husband of Edward I's daughter Joan, Countess of Gloucester and Hertford. Before becoming an earl *jure uxoris*, Monthermer was a steward of Joan's first husband, and Edward was initially enraged at this socially unsuitable marriage. Monthermer eventually gained the king's trust, however, and "remained a figure of prominence in warfare and statecraft." Comparably, Smyser identifies "Chauvent" (Leland 12a) with Peter de Chauvent, enrolled in the bar-

---

characterization of rank, or paternity, or domicile, or coat of arms—and the name itself may have been corrupted in the copying" (ibid., 269).

58. Ibid. Compare, from a very different historical moment, the game periodically played by the main characters of Douglas Coupland's *JPod* (Toronto: Random House of Canada, 2005), whereby the first hundred or so digits of π are inserted somewhere into a massive wall of numbers; whichever character finds them first wins. In the book, this game is not just described narratively but performed by having ten to twenty pages of numbers interrupt the novel each time the game is played. The effect is uncannily like that produced by the "Battle Abbey Roll," though in *JPod* we are given the context before hitting our first visual wall. I never hunted for the digits of π, the novel's equivalent of the more recent names in the "Battle Abbey Roll," so I cannot say whether Coupland was playing fair.

onage only in 1299, and "De la Pole" (Leland 104a) with Sir William de la Pole, a Hull merchant knighted in 1296.[59] The "Battle Abbey Roll" thus convenes in a single list both the elite of the distant past and worthies of more recent and approachable vintage; such a collection of names across history encourages Auchinleck's audience to imagine themselves a part of their company.

In its concluding textual gesture, then, booklet 3 offers a third take on the question explored by *Sir Degaré* and *Floris and Blauncheflur*: how can a merchant become a knight? *Sir Degaré* presented a hero whose determination to earn rather than merely claim his noble heritage raised the tantalizing image of the self-made noble, while *Floris and Blauncheflur* seemed to close the door to that possibility by reestablishing absolutely at its conclusion the boundaries of class that its main narrative had blurred. Some of the names in the "Battle Abbey Roll," however, demonstrate that such a fantastic transformation was in fact possible for the lucky, rich, and well connected. That demonstration, however, gains its force only when completed by the textual and historical acumen that the reader himself brings to the list. Booklet 3's final and most concrete offering of an imitative fantasy to its mercantile audience, then, is also the one that places the most direct and daunting interpretive burden on them, and it enables a more optimistic reading of the romances that precede it only if we interpret this sequence of texts as a whole in compilational terms.

Still more broadly, the "Battle Abbey Roll" asserts that a mercantile-owned textual collection is the proper repository for the memorial history of the nation as a whole. The immediately preceding "Sayings of the Four Philosophers" lamented that "ffor niht is liht, þe lond is lore-les; / ffor fiht is fliht, þe lond is nameles" (lines 31–32). The "Battle Abbey Roll" ensures that, for Auchinleck's London audience at least, the "lore" and the "names" of England's foundational history will not be lost. In so doing, it implies a broader, more expansive sense of textual conservatorship than just the discrete manifestations of parochial self-interest that one might be inclined to see in much

---

59. Smyser, "The List of Norman Names," 270 (quotation), 270–72.

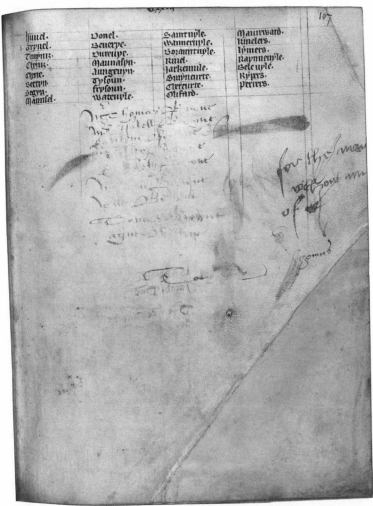

FIGURE 6. National Library of Scotland, Advocates MS 19.2.1 (Auchinleck), fols. 107r and 107v (fig. 6A and 6B, respectively; shown here on consecutive pages). Courtesy the Trustees of the National Library of Scotland.

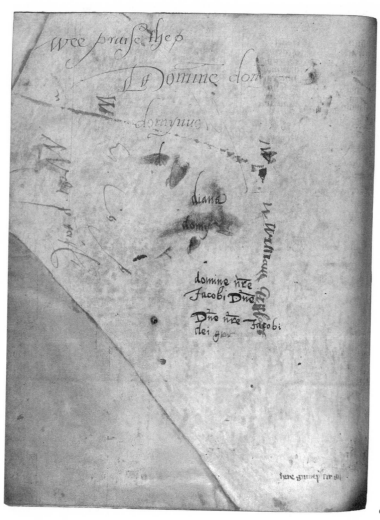

6B

of the Horn corpus. And by asserting the manuscript's audience as knowledgeable textual consumers, convening them with each other and with national heroes from the distant and recent past whose names it inscribes, the "Battle Abbey Roll" reverses the destructive image of the melted charter and dispersed political units from the macaronic introduction to "Four Philosophers." The "Roll," in other words, is compilational both codicologically and temporally, gaining meaning from its relation, not just to a larger structure of texts as sequenced within a specific manuscript, but also to other historical moments. Implicitly looking to the future, it thus imagines itself growing in length as lucky members of the audience convened by its convocational gesture metaphorically inscribe ethemselves in its listing of the nation's good and great.

Whatever its underlying motivation, the white space offered by most of folio 107r and all of folio 107v gave Auchinleck's readers literal room to do so. That white space proved an irresistible invitation to readers from later centuries, whose giant, expansive scrawls make the hand of Scribe 4 seem tightly compressed in comparison; the way in which the ruling structure encloses each name of the "Battle Abbey Roll" enhances this contrast (see fig. 6). That visual contrast should not obscure the fact, however, that the "Battle Abbey Roll," those later additions, and the white space itself are all congruent in highlighting the impossibility of pinning history down; the text whose form stopped us in our tracks back on folio 105v here demonstrates that such stasis is just one aspect of a broader historical movement.[60] The shape of that movement, however, is no more straightforward or linear than the later scrawls that are evidence of it.

There is space for one more name within the ruled structure of the "Battle Abbey Roll" (see fol. 107r), whose now permanent incompleteness signifies differently to its medieval and its modern readers. To the most astute members of its medieval audience, it is an actualization of the promise implied by the presence, earlier in the list, of names like Monthermer and Chauvent and de la Pole: you too can appear here. It is an absence, in other words, that offers the potential of presence. To the modern reader, this lack can assume very different significance: a reminder of what we do not, cannot, and will never know about many

---

60. See further on this topic John Dagenais, "Decolonizing the Medieval Page," in *The Future of the Page*, ed. Peter Stoicheff and Andrew Taylor (Toronto: University of Toronto Press, 2004), 37–70. Dagenais considers a range of pages that are blank or nearly so in ways comparable to Auchinleck's fol. 107r and reaches the conclusion that "in these blank pages we can perceive, perhaps even more readily than in those more full of writing, the potential for movement, the essential incompleteness of the medieval page" (ibid., 54).

of these names, Auchinleck's lost texts, and so much else in our period of study. The melancholy to which such reflections might incline, however, should be balanced by the exuberance that the later hands offer: evidence, however unrelated or inane their literal intentions, that the physical characteristics of manuscripts invite us to write, by offering puzzles and delights and new spurs to interpretation. Like the long romances that it most famously contains, Auchinleck frustrates even wily efforts to impose closure. In that sense, it is both perfectly appropriate and even poetic that the final words of booklet 3 are, not a name from the distant past, or a seventeenth-century scribble, but a statement of narrative and literary promise: the catchphrase at the bottom right of folio 107v that looks forward to the romance that starts the next gathering, "here ginneþ Sir Gij" (see fig. 7).[61]

FIGURE 7. National Library of Scotland, Advocates MS 19.2.1 (Auchinleck), fol. 107v (detail). Courtesy the Trustees of the National Library of Scotland.

61. This catchphrase further frustrates attempts to impose linear historicity on the manuscript since Guy's history has, by one metric, already been concluded in the preceding *Speculum Gy* that narrated his conversion to a life of penance and devotion.

Appendix: The Contents of the Auchinleck Manuscript

Text Number and Title	First Folio	Scribe	Booklet
1. *The Legend of Pope Gregory*	1r	1	1
2. *The King of Tars*[a]	7r	1	1
3. "The Life of Adam and Eve"	14r[b]	1	1
4. "Seynt Mergrete"[a]	16r	1	1
5. "Seynt Katerine"[a]	21r	1	1
6. *Sir Owain* (St. Patrick's Purgatory)	25r	1	1
7. "Þe desputisoun bitvuen þe bodi & þe soule"[a]	31v	1	1
8. "The Harrowing of Hell"	35r	1	1
9. "The Clerk who would see the Virgin"	37r	1	1
10. *Speculum Gy de Warewyke*	39r	2	2
11. *Amis and Amiloun*	48r	1	2
12. "Life of Mary Magdalene"	61a[c]	1	2
13. "[Anna our] leuedis moder"[a]	65v	1	2
14. "[On þe seuen dedly] sinnes"[a]	70r	3	3
15. "Þe pater noster vndo on englissch"[a]	72r	3	3
16. "The Assumption of Our Lady"	72a	3	3
17. *Sir Degaré*	78r	3	3
18. *The Seven Sages of Rome*	84a	3	3
19. *Floris and Blauncheflur*	100r	3	3
20. "The Sayings of the Four Philosophers"	105r	2	3
21. The so-called "Battle Abbey Roll"	105v	4	3
22. *Guy of Warwick* (couplet)	107a	1	4
23. *Guy of Warwick* (stanzaic)	146v	1	4
24. *Reinbrun Gij Sone of Warwike*[a]	167r	5	4
25. *Sir Beues of Hamptoun*[a]	176r	5	5
26. *Of Arthour and of Merlin*[a]	201r	1	5
27. "The wench that [lou]ed [a ki]ng"[a]	256v	1	5
28. "[A penni]worth [of wi]tte"[a]	256a	1	5
29. "Hou our leuedi sauté was ferst founde"[a]	259r	1	5

Text Number and Title	First Folio	Scribe	Booklet
30. "Lay le Freine"[a]	261r	1	6
31. *Roland and Vernagu*	262a	1	6
32. *Otuel a Kniȝt*[a]	268r	6/1(?)[d]	7
33. *Kyng Alisaunder*	278r[e]	1	8
34. "The Thrush and the Nightingale"	279v	1	8
35. "The Sayings of St. Bernard"	280r	1	8
36. "David þe kyng"[a]	280r	1	8
37. *Sir Tristrem*	281r	1	9
38. *Sir Orfeo*	299a	1	9
39. "The Four Foes of Mankind"	303r	1	9
40. *Liber Regum Anglie*[a,f]	304r	1	10
41. *Horn childe & maiden rimnild*[a]	317v	1	10
42. "Alphabetical Praise of Women"	324r	1	11
43. *King Richard*[a,g] (*Richard Coer de Lyon*)	326r	1	11
44. *Þe Simonie*[a]	328r	2	12

Sources: *The Auchinleck Manuscript: National Library of Scotland Advocates' MS. 19.2.1*, ed. Derek Pearsall and I. C. Cunningham (1977; reprint, London: Scolar, 1979); *The Auchinleck Manuscript*, ed. David Burnley and Alison Wiggins, Version 1.1, July 5, 2003, http://auchinleck.nls.uk.

a. The title is supplied in the manuscript.

b. The first 352 lines of this text are preserved in two bifolia of Edinburgh University Library MS 218 that were removed from the Auchinleck manuscript at some point after its completion. One further bifolium is missing; the current Auchinleck fol. 14 contains lines 353–780.

c. This text begins imperfectly on what is now numbered fol. 62r, and there is a stub between it and fol. 61; apparently, the text originally began on what is now the stub (fol. 61a). This foliation is used in *The Auchinleck Manuscript: National Library of Scotland Advocates' MS. 19.2.1* (1977; reprint, London: Scolar, 1979), Derek Pearsall and I.C. Cunningham's facsimile of the manuscript, and it is what I mean by the *a* both here and in texts 16, 18, 22, 28, 31, and 38.

d. Although conceding the "superficial resemblance" between the hands of Scribes 1 and 6, A. J. Bliss ("Notes on the Auchinleck Manuscript," *Speculum* 26 [1951]: 653) argues that they may nevertheless be distinguished by eight distinct differences, which he describes in detail. Pamela Robinson ("Some Aspects of the Transmission of English Verse Texts in Late Mediaeval Manuscripts" [B.Litt. thesis, Oxford University, 1972], 128–31)

Notes to Appendix (continued)

and Ralph Hanna ("Reconsidering the Auchinleck Manuscript," in *New Directions in Later Medieval Manuscript Studies*, ed. Derek Pearsall [York: York Medieval Press, 2000], 92–93) disagree, arguing that Bliss's Scribes 1 and 6 are in fact one and the same.

e. A great deal of the manuscript between *Otuel a Kniȝt* and *Kyng Alisaunder* has been lost. The contemporary numeration identifies the former as the thirty-seventh text in the manuscript and the latter as the forty-fourth. Only lines 7760–8021 of *Kyng Alisaunder* (as recorded in Bodleian MS Laud misc. 622) are preserved in the Auchinleck manuscript itself, but fragments that were once part of the text are now the bifolia shelved as Saint Andrews University Library, MS PR.2065 A.15, and London University Library, MS 593.

f. This text is a considerably expanded and reworked version, unique to the Auchinleck manuscript, of the work known and edited as *An Anonymous Short English Metrical Chronicle*, ed. E. Zettl, Early English Text Society, O.S. 196 (London: Oxford University Press, 1935).

g. The Auchinleck version is highly fragmentary, lacking all of lines 2958–7136. Fragments once part of the manuscript that contain lines of this text are shelved now as Edinburgh University Library, MS 218, and Saint Andrews University Library, MS PR.2065.R.4.

Chapter Three

CONSTRUCTING
COMPILATIONS OF CHAUCER'S
CANTERBURY TALES

The previous two chapters have argued that the codicological forms of the Horn corpus and the Auchinleck manuscript are fragmentary, shifting, and allusive in ways that complement and complicate their textual content, and that they therefore become receptive to the kinds of close readings that have generally been reserved for texts, self-consciously literary or otherwise. In turning now to the *Canterbury Tales*, I begin by acknowledging that, despite its considerable and complex investment in textual self-representation, "it" is not a physical object like the subjects of my other chapters. In the first section of this chapter, I address the theoretical and practical complications that this fact poses, using some of the Benjaminian terms from my introduction (particularly the distinction between construction and reconstruction) to analyze Chaucer's decision to use one of his earlier, self-standing poems as the *Knight's Tale*. By opening up his own past textual productions to the compilational play that the *Tales* offers, Chaucer encourages his readers to do the same, making the *Tales'* invitations to compilational construction, a kind of ever-evolving and interactive poetics of assemblage, integral to its medieval self-conception and contemporary form alike.

That premise established, in the second section I will argue that, even as Fragment I uses the *quyting* drama of its headlinks to ensure its codicological integrity (it retains its structure across all surviving manuscripts of the *Tales*), it invites us to contemplate the construction of alternate tale orderings, which I will call *threads*, that would radiate outward from the *Knight's Tale* if and when the storytelling contest runs aground. That happens, of course, with the spectacular implosion of the *Cook's Tale*, whose contemporary London setting contrasts sharply with the Knight's ancient and distant Athens. I argue that the trajectory traced by Fragment I suggests disillusionment with the notion that the idealized, socially reinforcing courtly performances central to the *Knight's Tale* could be effectively translated into "oure citee" of Chaucer's London. This skepticism suggests how powerfully Richard II's adoption of courtly pomp into his arsenal of weapons to wield against a recalcitrant City had soured Londoners on the notion, still available (if only as ideals) in parts of the Horn corpus and Auchinleck, that courtly imitation and chivalric performance offered models for or even means to civic unity, pride, and autonomy.

The *Cook's Tale* produces not just narrative silence but also the first substantially conflicting evidence from manuscript witnesses as to what this abrupt conclusion means and where to go from there. Yet this highly fragmentary and critically neglected text is integral to Chaucer's complex role as Continentally inflected London poet, for the London-centered *Cook's Tale* anticipates a wide range of figures associated with the Franco-Flemish Low Countries: the Squire, the Pardoner's *riotoures*, and Sir Thopas. Their associations with the Cook return to London the significance of a compilational thread extending, I propose, from the always-initiating tale of the Knight, through that of his son the Squire, to Geffrey's own *Tale of Sir Thopas*, like the *Squire's Tale* a romance interrupted by the teller's fellow pilgrims. Partly because of these interruptions, this Franco-Flemish Knight–Squire–Sir Thopas thread complements the skeptical attitude toward courtly performance and imitation recorded by Fragment I.

By looking back to the *Knight's Tale* in both his interruption of the Squire and his own tale, however, the Franklin proposes himself as a worthier continuation of the ideals initiated by the Knight. In my reading, this idealistic gesture does not fully counterbalance the pessimism of the other structures I examine, but the Franklin's invitation to construct such a rival Knight-Franklin thread is yet another reminder of the multiple, fragmentary, and even subjective forms of the *Tales*, which, by frustrating efforts to establish conclusively their correct sociocultural content, ensure Chaucer's continuing aesthetic resonance and historical vitality.

Forming the *Canterbury Tales*: Fragments, Manuscripts, Editions

One striking aspect of the *Canterbury Tales* is that its most devoted commentators cannot seem finally to agree on how best to describe or represent it. If we take its initiating storytelling program literally, it is massively incomplete, a tiny fragment of the announced project. In critical discourse, however, it is not one fragmentary poem but a poem of fragments whose conventional capitalization (e.g., Fragment I or VII) implies a secure, stable integrity at odds with the meaning of the word *fragment* itself. Comparably, the canonical status (monumentalized by physical heft) attained by the third edition of *The Riverside Chaucer* for scholarly purposes contrasts sharply with continued scholarly uncertainty over how Chaucer envisioned his work taking shape and whether Hengwrt, Ellesmere, or some other formula should settle questions of authenticity, tale and fragment orderings, and individual readings. Linne Mooney's establishment of Adam Pinkhurst as the scribe of Ellesmere and Hengwrt lent reassuring concreteness to her argument that, as a consequence, they "offer the closest we can come in the surviving materials to Chaucer's own authorial version of the *Tales*."[1] Even conceding this point, however, does not resolve the substantial differences between those two manuscripts, and Simon Horobin has in any event recently demonstrated that Pinkhurst's association with Chaucer does not appear to have given him inside knowledge as to the prospective shape of the *Tales*, such that we should not "accord his extant copies . . . privileged status over the many other important copies that survive."[2]

Such questions exist alongside growing debate as to whether our continued, nearly universal reliance on an object like *The Riverside*

1. Mooney, "Chaucer's Scribe," 105.
2. Horobin, "Adam Pinkhurst," 367.

Chaucer can still be theoretically justified. As Robert Meyer-Lee has elegantly demonstrated, this reliance exposes an uncomfortable contradiction: having supposedly dispensed with New Critical veneration of the transcendent verbal icon, we continue to cite and teach a version of Chaucer that runs the risk of becoming that icon—and, for most of our students, almost inevitably does so.[3] One way forward would be to create a new, more historically and codicologically sensitive kind of edition. Proposals go back at least to 1985, with Derek Pearsall's famous characterization of the *Tales* as "a partly assembled kit with no directions" and his daring suggestion that the work be disseminated as such, "partly as a bound book (with first and last fragments fixed) and partly as a set of fragments in folders, with the incomplete information as to their nature and placement fully displayed," thus leaving the reader responsible for arranging all fragments save I and X on her own.[4] This proposal risks misrepresenting the codicological evidence somewhat since the fragments themselves are neither wholly nor equivalently stable structures, but it would have the very great benefit of thwarting what Pearsall describes elsewhere as our pervasive "desire to see in the *Canterbury Tales* the lineaments of a grand design, unfinished but not incomplete," which with characteristic verve and candor he designates a "kind of antiscientific, even antirational creationism."[5] In a review that same year of Helen Cooper's *The Structure of the Canterbury Tales*,[6] Alastair Minnis demonstrated the appeal such an edition might have when, skeptical as to whether "we [can] justifiably speak of *the* structure of *The Canterbury Tales*," he went on to ask: "Why not develop an 'aesthetic of the unfinished,' an approach which would focus directly on the alternative patterns both between

3. Robert Meyer-Lee, "Manuscript Studies, Literary Value, and the Object of Chaucer Studies," *Studies in the Age of Chaucer* 30 (2008): 1–37.

4. Derek Pearsall, *The Canterbury Tales* (London: George Allen & Unwin, 1985), 23.

5. Derek Pearsall, "Authorial Revision in Some Late-Medieval English Texts," in *Crux and Controversy*, ed. A. J. Minnis and Charlotte Brewer (Cambridge: D. S. Brewer, 1992), 39–48 (quotation 42).

6. Helen Cooper, *The Structure of the Canterbury Tales* (Athens: University of Georgia Press, 1983).

and within the groups of tales, and celebrate these phenomena rather than minimizing or ignoring them?"[7]

Twenty-first-century technology has made it easier to imagine such a radical edition of the *Tales*, which "might be achieved by a representation of various interlaced manuscript matrices, in which manuscript reproductions are linked rhyzomically to each other and hypertextually embedded in myriad informing contexts."[8] By enabling a "more interesting free-play of discourse" across tales, as Phyllis Portnoy puts it,[9] such an edition would seem to respond to the desires of poststructuralists while also satisfying codicologically inclined critics with a practical interest in, and an ideological commitment to, making manuscript evidence central to literary interpretation. I am not sure that such an edition would prove quite so attractive in practice as it sounds in theory,[10] but both it and Pearsall's lower-tech kit idea have the benefit of respecting the strongly textual self-representation of the *Tales* that I considered in the introduction: its decoupling of textual arrangement from textual authorship through its initiating allusions to *compilatio*; the evocation of estates satire such that the pilgrims become both social and textual beings; its self-presentation as a collection of genres that we are invited physically to manipulate; and its vastly conflicting codicological afterlife, which offers vibrant evidence of just how variously later readers and scribes took up this invitation.[11]

7. A. J. Minnis, "Ordering Chaucer," *Essays in Criticism* 35 (1985): 265–69 (quotation 266–67).

8. Meyer-Lee, "Manuscript Studies," 26. I should make clear that Meyer-Lee does not in fact endorse (though neither does he dismiss) such an edition.

9. Phyllis Portnoy, "The Best-Text/Best-Book of Canterbury: The Dialogic of the Fragments," *Florilegium* 13 (1994): 161–72 (quotation 167).

10. In part, my doubts stem from how long such an edition has been technically possible yet how far we remain as a body of teachers and scholars from adopting one. Our collective reluctance to do so, I think, stems largely from how overwhelming such a mass of data could easily become, for scholars and students alike. Certain kinds of scholarly and pedagogical projects would clearly be empowered by such an edition, but I would be surprised if in the foreseeable future it became the dominant means of engagement with the *Tales*.

11. On this last, see Seth Lerer, *Chaucer and His Readers: Imagining the Author in Late-Medieval England* (Princeton, NJ: Princeton University Press, 1993); and Thomas A. Prendergast

The impossibility of decisively *reconstructing* the *Tales'* various manuscripts into the stable, unified work on which old formalism depended now offers new-formalist, *constructive* interpretive possibilities akin to those we saw in the previous chapter's examination of the Auchinleck manuscript. Such a pursuit of form can draw on the theoretical model of Ralph Hanna's *Pursuing History*, which argues that editions like the *Riverside* are valuable because they provide a kind of collective control group against which the interesting behavior of codicological outliers can be perceived; since "history is not to be found initially in 'the genuinely authorial' but only through what is 'inauthentic,' 'not genuine,'" these outliers allow Hanna and like-minded scholars to achieve "a more pervasive historicization, that of medieval literary communities."[12] Even for studies like mine with a somewhat different object of value, a comparable approach is quite attractive. The responsibly constructed *Riverside* (Hanna himself produced the textual notes for the *Tales*) can be used as a base for literary-critical interpretation, much as a generally reliable manuscript might be selected as the base text for an edition. Codicological variations from that base can then be noted, analyzed, and interpreted—not just for what they reveal as literary-historical data, but also for the particularly literary-aesthetic effects that they create when considered as variants within a larger whole. Such an approach could give us greater access to the always multiple and shifting nature of the *Tales*, making it more fully open to interpretive assembly of the sort that Chaucer's canonicity has too often discouraged.

Such a hybrid critical practice can draw support from both the Benjaminian terms of my introduction and elements of the *Tales* itself. For, while the *Riverside* is clearly a collaborative endeavor that we can encounter only at considerable distance from the time and mind of Geoffrey Chaucer, this is also (though not equivalently) true for all

---

and Barbara Kline, eds., *Rewriting Chaucer: Culture, Authority, and the Idea of the Authentic Text, 1400–1602* (Columbus: Ohio State University Press, 1999).

12. Ralph Hanna, *Pursuing History: Middle English Manuscripts and Their Texts* (Stanford, CA: Stanford University Press, 1996), 11. See also the fuller account of this argument in Meyer-Lee, "Manuscript Studies."

surviving manuscripts of the *Tales*; as Meyer-Lee and Theresa Tinkle suggest, the difference between Hengwrt and *Riverside* is more of degree than of kind.[13] If we regard Hengwrt, *Riverside*, and everything in between properly as constructions and not reconstructions of something collectively called the *Canterbury Tales*, then our critical practice can appreciate less hierarchically the distinct interpretive potential that any one of them offers, individually or in conjunction with others. Constructing an interpretive practice that combines medieval manuscripts and modern editions would be one way of making that "tiger's leap into the past" that Benjamin argues is necessary for "the object of history to be blasted out of the continuum of historical succession," potentially liberating Chaucer from the suspended animation of reverential canonicity.[14] Or, as he puts it elsewhere: "Historical materialism must renounce the epic element in history. It blasts the epoch out of the reified 'continuity of history.' But it also explodes the homogeneity of the epoch, interspersing it with ruins—that is, with the present."[15] The *Canterbury Tales* is the quintessential and too often distorting "epic element" in the literary history of medieval England, but the work's very nature—fragmentary, internally contradictory, composed across decades and recorded across centuries—gives us all the tools we need to do this salutary blasting. Ruins and the present become one as, from the various formulations of Fragments I–X, assembled across our often fragmentary sources, we construct an interpretive practice that is itself compilational: subjective but not arbitrary, assembling difficult but worthwhile materials into something greater than the sum of their parts.

---

13. Meyer-Lee writes: "In Tinkle's apt phrasing, the pages of any manuscript reflect a 'hybrid, cumulative authorship.' Hence, even what is arguably the most historically authentic version of the *Tales*, the Hengwrt, is already a historical composite—as indeed is any material literary object in any era" ("Manuscript Studies," 32). His citation is of Theresa Tinkle, "The Wife of Bath's Textual/Sexual Lives," in *The Iconic Page in Manuscript, Print, and Digital Culture*, ed. George Bornstein and Theresa Tinkle (Ann Arbor: University of Michigan Press, 1998), 55–88 (quotation 76).

14. Benjamin, "On the Concept of History," 395, and *The Arcades Project*, 475 (N10,3).

15. Benjamin, *The Arcades Project*, 474 (N9a,6).

This model—what we might call *compilational construction* as a form
of literary interpretation—is one way of working with the fact of
medieval and postmedieval variance across the *Tales'* textual iterations.
Such creative compilational construction is in fact anticipated, invited,
and even performed by Chaucer within the *Tales*, such that this practice becomes integral to the form of the work itself. His suggestion in
the "Miller's Prologue" that we turn the leaf and skip ahead (I.3176–
80) is the most obvious and famous of these moments. As I argued in
the introduction, however, it is far from a straightforward joke. Such
a derailment of announced narrative ordering has in fact just taken
place, with the Miller's interruption of the Host and self-substitution
for the Monk. So, while we laugh at that class-based humor (drunken
millers don't respect social decorum), as we do at the invitation to turn
the page (our appetite has been whetted such that we surely don't, at
least not on a first reading), the idea that we too might create a different extension out from the *Knight's Tale* has nevertheless been planted.
The pilgrim portraits of the *General Prologue* have already created a
kaleidoscopic set of possible links among them as tale tellers, any of
which could be used to engage in such imaginative constructions ourselves. The *Knight's Tale* establishes another such set of associations by
initiating plot motifs, thematic nodes, and key words that subsequent
tales variously spin out: a very partial list of these would include the
love triangle that is taken up in too many tales to name; the blurry
line between autocracy and benevolent dictatorship (*Clerk's Tale*), the
treatment of pagan deities (*Manciple's Tale*); repeated key words like
trouthe and *gentilesse*; even the assertion that "pitee renneth soone in
gentil herte" (I.1761), which is repeated exactly, though to very different effect, by the Merchant (IV.1986) and the Squire (V.479).[16]

The invitation of the "Miller's Prologue" thus looks back to the
General Prologue and the *Knight's Tale* and forward to the many resonant ways (both literary-formally and socioculturally) of extending a
structure out from the *Knight's Tale* if we reject the Miller as he did

16. Compare Cooper's observation that the *Knight's Tale* "leads in many directions and
opens out on to many of the problems and perspectives explored later" (*The Structure of the
Canterbury Tales*, 91).

the Monk. Of course, doing so requires rereading, so already Chaucer is encouraging us to play with a version of the multiple temporalities that I have emphasized throughout this study. Another embedding of such temporalities, and a subtler invitation to conceive of the *Tales* as a manipulable and variable object, can be found in the concrete and remembered existence that the *Knight's Tale* of the (mostly) 1390s *Tales* project has as a self-standing narrative from the previous decade, when, according to the *Prologue* to the *Legend of Good Women* (ca. 1386–88), Chaucer had written "al the love of Palamon and Arcite" (F.420).[17] No copy of this version survives, but there is little evidence that it was revised substantially for inclusion in the *Tales*: four easily extractable lines about the tale-telling competition near the beginning (I.889–92) and an even briefer reference to "this faire compaignye" of pilgrims at the very end (I.3108). Nor does the tale itself give us a particular sense of the Knight's voice as distinct in tone or perspective. Alone of Fragment I's poems, his tale has no prologue, so only three quick lines at the end of the *General Prologue* are incontrovertibly in the Knight's voice, and, as Lee Patterson notes, the tale's "celebration of the ostentatious inessentials of the chivalric life-style seems dramatically at odds with what the *General Prologue* has suggested of the Knight's personal austerity."[18] Not only has Chaucer thus declined to create any particularly strong links between the Knight of the *General Prologue* and his

17. John Bowers has pointed out that Sir John Clanvowe's *Boke of Cupide* uses as its opening lines an excerpt from Chaucer's poem and that, since Clanvowe died abroad in 1391, he must have known the poem from its 1380s incarnation as *Palamon and Arcite*. See "Three Readings of *The Knight's Tale*: Sir John Clanvowe, Geoffrey Chaucer, and James I of Scotland," *Journal of Medieval and Early Modern Studies* 34 (2004): 279–307. The verse form of the *Knight's Tale*, rhymed pentameter couplets, also links it to the *Legend of Good Women* while distinguishing it from Chaucer's preceding pentameter compositions in rhyme royal (*Troilus, Parlement of Foules*), further marking it as a transitional production for Chaucer from his manner of the 1380s to that of the 1390s.

18. Lee Patterson, *Chaucer and the Subject of History* (Madison: University of Wisconsin Press, 1991), 179. See also the comparable comments of C. David Benson: "[While] nothing in the *Knight's Tale* absolutely conflicts with the pilgrim Knight of the *General Prologue*, neither are the similarities especially striking. . . . [W]e might have expected something more specifically Christian from one who is described less as a courtly hero than as the model of a crusader" (*Chaucer's Drama of Style: Poetic Variety and Contrast in the Canterbury Tales* [Chapel Hill: University of North Carolina Press, 1986], 65).

tale; he also leaves untouched the reference to "Palamon and Arcite" in the G version of the *Prologue* to the *Legend of Good Women*, which is generally dated to 1394 at the earliest. Well after work on the *Tales* must have begun in earnest, then, the *Knight's Tale* had an alternate (if only remembered) existence as the self-standing *Palamon and Arcite*, and the *Tales* project as a whole seems at no pains to mark its version of this poem as distinct from the earlier one.

Despite such noninvitations to regard the *Knight's Tale* as particularly inflected by its pilgrim narrator, however, a wide range of critics have attributed detailed and complex attitudes to the Knight himself.[19] I find such arguments largely unconvincing since most of the narrative devices cited as evidence of the Knight's perspectives are simply Chaucerian, well attested throughout the *Tales* and beyond.[20] This critical

---

19. Minnis, e.g., argues that, "while Chaucer's Knight dislikes and distrusts the pagan gods, he considerable respect and sympathy for the noble paganism of his characters, especially that of Theseus" (A. J. Minnis, *Chaucer and Pagan Antiquity* [Cambridge: D. S. Brewer, 1982], 141), and Patterson contends that "it is clear that the Knight himself intends it [his tale] to celebrate both Theseus as a model of rational governance and chivalry as a force for civilization" (*Chaucer and the Subject of History*, 198). Staley makes the opposition even more explicit: "The Knight . . . seems determined to offer a narrative structure that also contains and explains. Chaucer, on the other hand, hints at the political implications of literary form and prepares us for the spectacle of characters who explode the provisions he has made for them" (*Languages of Power*, 15).

20. Patterson argues, e.g., that one of the ways in which the Knight attempts to control the events of his tale "is, literally, to build containers. . . . Each narrative event is carefully sealed off from the others with a statement of finality." He cites examples like "there is namoore to telle" (I.974), "what nedeth wordes mo?" (I.1029), and "this is th'effect; ther is namoore to seye" (I.2366) (*Chaucer and the Subject of History*, 210). Yet nearly identical examples can be found throughout and beyond the *Canterbury Tales*: "What nedeth gretter dilatacioun?" (*Man of Law's Tale* II.232); "It nedeth nat reherce it yow namoore" (*Franklin's Tale* V.1466); "What nedeth it to sermone of it moore?" (*Pardoner's Tale* VI.879); "This is th'effect; ther is namoore to seyn" (*Manciple's Tale* IX.266); "Hyt nedeth noght yow more to tellen" (*House of Fame*, line 1299); "This is th'effect; what sholde I more seye?" (*Legend of Good Women*, line 1180).

Similarly Chaucerian, rather than Knightly, is the Knight's habit of announcing that he is speaking "shortly," a gambit that Patterson argues "expresses the uncertainty of the Knight's relation both to temporality and to the historical life in time" (*Chaucer and the Subject of History*, 213). But again, a sampling from Chaucer's corpus shows how widespread the technique is: "For shortly for to tellen, at o word" (*Man of Law's Tale* II.428); "But shortly if this storie I tellen shal" (*Clerk's Tale* IV.760); "But shortly myn entente I wol devyse" (*Pardoner's Tale* [prologue] VI.423); "And shortly of this story for to trete" (*Monk's Tale* VII.2311); "To telle shortly al my speche" (*Book of the Duchess*, line 1223); "But in effect, and shortly for to seye" (*Troilus*

eagerness to hear a Knightly voice in his tale is understandable, how-ever, since both it (in Fragment I) and he (in subsequent fragments) be-come so extensively implicated in disputes among other pilgrims and their tales; he becomes after the fact much more of a "character" than he is as pilgrim-narrator of his own tale. After the Host's insult of the Pardoner threatens to turn violent, for example, it is the Knight who restores some semblance of peace; he also interrupts a *Monk's Tale* that has consisted of one tragedy too many. In both episodes, he valorizes social harmony and literary delight, urging the Pardoner and the Host to be "glad and myrie of cheere . . . / And, as we diden, lat us laughe and pleye" (VI.963–67), and likewise encouraging the Monk to speak of "joye and greet solas" (VII.2774).[21] Each case sees the Knight put an end to social and literary distress with a "Namoore of this" (VI.962, VII.2767), contending along the way with a party's stated refusal to "pleye" (the Host at VI.958, the Monk at VII.2806).

While the Knight himself is not similarly present in the headlinks between tales in Fragment I, these poems are presented as the liter-ary and social aftereffects of his tale. The Miller, of course, follows the *Knight's Tale* with his famous *quyting*, an enterprise that the Reeve also identifies as the basis of his own tale; while the Miller promises to "quite the Knyghtes tale" (I.3127), however, the Reeve insists that he "shal *hym* [the Miller himself] quite anoon" (I.3916; emphasis added). In the hands of the Reeve, then, personal and professional rivalry rather than imitative literary play becomes the basis of tale genera-tion. This shift subtly suggests, not just the *Tales'* interest in the social ramifications of literary production, but also the fact that the *Knight's Tale* initiates an interlocked series of tale *quytings* that fails markedly

---

and Criseyde 5.1009); "And shortly to the poynt ryght for to go" (*Legend of Good Women*, line 1634). Given the universality of such phrases throughout Chaucer's work, it is hard to attach any individuating, characterizing weight to their appearance in the *Knight's Tale*.

21. As Benson points out (*Chaucer's Drama of Style*, 65), the kind of tale the Knight appears to prefer here sounds quite unlike his own *Knight's Tale* in its explicit rejection of sudden mis-fortunes that call for Boethian reserves of emotional fortitude; he asks the Monk for a tale of "whan a man hath been in povre estaat, / And clymbeth up and wexeth fortunate, / And there abideth in prosperitee" (VII.2775–77). This episode further weakens the proposition that, as a social being effectively constructed over the course of the *Tales*, the pilgrim-Knight should be substantially identified with the narrative voice or indeed the themes of the *Knight's Tale*.

to produce the social harmony that elsewhere the Knight values and tries to foster. Given the Knight's later emphasis on the literature of delight and smooth social relations, his silence here as the tale-telling game fails on both levels to sustain harmonious play is retroactively surprising.

This idea of retroactivity is as crucial to my interpretation of the Knight specifically as it is to the compilational practice—of rereading and then either imaginatively or physically assembling tales in newly significant orders—that the *Tales* as a whole extends. On a first reading, the Knight's lack of involvement with the tales of Fragment I is unsurprising precisely because he himself is so uncharacterized, either by the narrative voice of his tale or by his portrait in the *General Prologue*, which is more an idealized curruiculum vitae than a description of anything we would call a *character*. As the *Tales* continues, however, the Knight's involvement with the pilgrims and the Host increasingly allows us to say things like, "The Knight values social harmony," in a way that his presentation in Fragment I does not. We have seen in the preceding chapters that compilational meaning demands and rewards engaged rereading, an ability to reimagine the import of earlier texts in light of those that follow; the same is true here of the Knight's relation with Fragment I. His initial undercharacterization is further important because it allows us to hear more acutely other indications that we should understand his tale as a textual rather than an oral production; the fact that the *Knight's Tale* would presumably have been recognizable as the preexisting *Palamon and Arcite* would only strengthen this suggestion for the many readers familiar with Chaucer's earlier corpus. Both the textuality that I have argued is key to the *Canterbury Tales* and the multiple temporalities that I have emphasized throughout this book now have another facet: the very opening of the tale-telling project is in effect simultaneously the preexisting text *Palamon and Arcite*, with a quintessentially Chaucerian rather than Knightly narrator, and the *Knight's Tale*, whose images, themes, and pilgrim-narrator will come to exert a defining influence on the *Tales* as a whole.

In its role as one key element of a much larger, ongoing compilational project, the *Knight's Tale* complements the concern for textual construction visible in the *General Prologue* and the "Miller's Prologue" with its own interest in the interrelation of physical, social, and literary construction. Alastair Minnis, Anne Middleton, and Lawrence Clopper have all noted that Theseus's physical construction of the theater and temples, one of Chaucer's additions to the *Teseida*, parallels and enables his social construction of a more civilized means for Arcite and Palamon to settle their love feud: tourneying rather than brawling.[22] This theme extends to literary construction as well, with Helen Cooper emphasizing the centrality of juxtaposition and parallelism as formal devices whose resultant "architectonic form" is essential to understanding the tale's exploration of its Boethian themes.[23] Lee Patterson uses the same word to describe the tale's narration, arguing that it should be conceived of "as construction, as *architectonics* . . . [that leave] traces in the large number of transitional passages that staple the narrative together."[24] By so regularly drawing attention to its narration of Arcite, for example, and contrasting that with a subsequent description of Theseus's or Palamon's actions, then finally bringing all these narrative strands together in its denouement, the *Knight's Tale* becomes a single poem made up of discrete narrative units that attains a literary power greater than any of those constituent parts: in short, a compilation. By having this compilation initiate the tale-telling competition, Chaucer foregrounds for the entire story collection this theme of literary assemblage, prompting attention to the effects of subsequent tales' various juxtapositions.

Still more significantly, Chaucer initiates his literary project of the 1390s with a prewritten text of his own, taking no apparent pains to distinguish it from its earlier incarnation, but rather enabling his audience to appreciate how its new literary and codicological contexts

---

22. See Minnis, *Chaucer and Pagan Antiquity*, 108–50; Anne Middleton, "War by Other Means: Marriage and Chivalry in Chaucer," *Studies in the Age of Chaucer: Proceedings* 1 (1984): 119–33; and Lawrence M. Clopper, "The Engaged Spectator: Langland and Chaucer on Civic Spectacle," *Studies in the Age of Chaucer* 22 (2000): 115–39.

23. See the discussion of the *Knight's Tale* in Cooper, *The Structure of the Canterbury Tales*, 91–107.

24. Patterson (*Chaucer and the Subject of History*, 210–11 [emphasis added]) cites ten examples, of which this one is typical: "But stynte I wole of Theseus a lite, / And speke of Palamon and Arcite" (1.2093–94). Such rhetorical moves are markedly less common elsewhere in Chaucer's work, though they certainly exist.

might likewise alter its significance. He thus makes his own textual productions part of the compilational game that the *Canterbury Tales* offers its readers, strengthening his other invitations to manipulate its forms both conceptually and physically.[25] If the Horn corpus tested our ability to be creatively, compilationally minded readers of the particular manuscripts he bequeathed us, then Chaucer builds radically on the social and literary implications of that gesture by creating a work whose evocations of textuality (generally) and *compilatio* (specifically) embed within it the invitation, not just to compilational interpretation of texts already written, but also to compilational construction of those texts into a still evolving set of forms, both medieval and modern. We are not simply tiger leaping into the past, in other words, with the strategic anachronism of juxtaposing modern editions and medieval manuscripts, or Walter Benjamin and Geoffrey Chaucer. Rather, by projecting the continuing construction of his work into a range of shapes that he could not himself anticipate or control, Chaucer makes a still more radical leap into the future, becoming partner in that disruption of linear historicity on which the productive explosion of his canonicity depends.

From Southwark to Athens to London: Fragment I

The arguments offered above do not entail regarding the *Canterbury Tales* as a site of wholly deconstructive free play, or supposing that Chaucer's serious invitation of future compilational activity by his readers means that his texts are unconcerned with or unillumined by

---

25. Such invitations might seem to fly in the face of the attitude implied by the famous "Adam Scriveyn," with its threats of harsh punishment for even the slightest copying error. This contrast seems unproblematic to me for at least two reasons. First, that poem seems concerned principally with the accuracy of copying, not with the potential rearrangement of an (accurately copied) text into a different form—a version of Bonaventure's distinction between scribe and compiler that we considered in the introduction. Second, "Adam Scriveyn" alludes to *Troilus* and *Boece*, both works from the 1380s, and it seems perfectly possible that Chaucer might have had different attitudes toward those works and his more sprawling, open-ended Canterbury project of the 1390s.

his own present and recent past. In fact, the creative approach to questions of form that I have just proposed can shed light on whether and how Chaucer imagined that the ancient ideals of the *Knight's Tale* could be translated into the contemporary English context that dominates the rest of Fragment I, the subject to which I now turn. The contrast between the *Knight's Tale*'s ancient Athens and the otherwise firmly English settings of Fragment I is conspicuous enough to raise questions about the literary and social effects of such a juxtaposition, particularly given Fragment I's interest in how literary, social, and physical constructions—like Fragment I and, indeed, the *Knight's Tale* itself—interrelate and either cohere or collapse. Fragment I's exploration of this question is grounded in issues of historical and geographic distance like those at work in Horn's *Liber regum*: not just the difference between mythical Athens and "oure citee" of London, but also between the 1380s, when something called *Palamon and Arcite* was first written, and the 1390s, when it was reconceived as the first tale of a new literary project for a very different sociocultural moment.

The sharp contrast between Theseus's management of the amatory rivalry between Palamon and Arcite and the Host's handling of analogous competitive tensions in Fragment I's headlinks can shed some initial light on how the Knight's courtly imagination of ancient Athens makes the journey into contemporary England. Dueling to the death for Emelye's love in a forest outside Athens, Palamon and Arcite are depicted as more beasts than men. Arcite is "as fiers as leon" (I.1598) and "a crueel tigre" (I.1657), while Palamon fights like a "wood leon" (I.1656), and together "as wilde bores gonne they to smyte" (I.1658). Theseus is comparably enraged on discovering them, but he allows himself to be mollified by the pleas of his queen and her ladies, ordering the quarrel settled in a tournament to be held in lists whose construction he will personally oversee. Theseus's role as judge is emphasized throughout: his speech is larded with legal language like *conclusioun*, *recorde*, and *repplicacioun*, and Palamon goes on to ask for his *juwise* (I.1739). Indeed, Minnis notes that part of Theseus's anger stems from the fact that Palamon and Arcite are fighting "withouten juge or oother officere" (I.1712), a situation that he rectifies by naming himself as "evene juge . . . and trewe" (I.1864).[26] By bringing Palamon and Arcite into the civilizing bounds of society's laws, turning their destructive fighting into an occasion for royal construction, and submitting to good advice by controlling his initial anger, Theseus embodies a model king.[27] Though Palamon had been fighting like a mad lion, for example, Theseus recognizes that such behavior cannot be condoned in a ruler: "Fy / upon a lord that wol have no mercy, / But been a *leon*, both in word and dede" (I.1773–75; emphasis added). By using chivalric display to effect social reconciliation, the *Knight's Tale* presents a model of courtly production and performance that unifies its polity's warring factions.

Like Theseus, the Host is called *governour* and *juge* (I.813–14) of the tale-telling competition and thus by extension of the polity that competition initiates. This parallel only highlights the precariousness of his control, however, for as soon as he invites the Monk to *quite* the *Knight's Tale* the Miller interrupts and barges ahead with his own tale, which the Reeve then fundamentally misinterprets, understanding it not as literary play but as professional and personal attack.[28] This episode shows how readily the order, balance, and symmetry initiated by the *Knight's Tale* disintegrate as Fragment I unfolds. It also prepares us to interpret as a social failure the literary short-circuiting that terminates the fragment, for it is precisely as the focus of its head-links shifts from literary play to personal competition that the social arena in which stories are told and appreciated gradually narrows. The Miller builds on the unanimous approval that greeted the *Knight's Tale* by addressing "alle and some" (I.3136), periphrastically emphasizing the expansiveness of his gesture, which the Reeve condenses to "yow alle" (I.3910) even as it becomes clear that his tale really addresses, and

---

26. Minnis, *Chaucer and Pagan Antiquity*, 122.

27. Even Wallace, who takes a considerably darker view than I do of what he calls "Thesian polity," contends that "Chaucer goes to some lengths to argue that Theseus is an un-tyrant, a ruler who is offered temptations to follow his emotions into tyranny but reins himself back for the *bonum commune*" (*Chaucerian Polity*, 108).

28. On the Host's consistent inability to control the tale-telling proceedings, see also Turner, *Chaucerian Conflict*, 152, part of a broader discussion of "conflicted *compaignyes*" (ibid., 127–66).

attacks, the Miller alone: "for leveful is with force force of-showve" (I.3912).

The "Cook's Prologue" narrows this ambit still more sharply, for, although initially presented as a promise to "yow telle . . . / A litel jape that fil in oure citee" (I.4342–43), the plural *yow* shifts to *thou* as the Cook vows to *quyte* Harry in a later tale:

> "And therfore, Herry Bailly, by thy feith,
> Be *thou* nat wrooth, er we departen heer,
> Though that my tale be of an hostileer.
> But nathelees I wol nat telle it yit;
> But er we parte, ywis, *thou* shalt be quit."
> (I.4358–62; emphasis added)

This familiarity of address complements both characters' frequent use of each other's personal names—the Cook is called Roger three times—such that, when the phrase "in oure citee" recurs in the first line of the *Cook's Tale* (I.4365), it is easy to hear just Roger talking to Harry, the other pilgrims thoroughly on the sidelines. And, although the Cook tells of an apprentice in the same victualing craft that had been associated with London's elite citizens since the day of Andrew Horn, fishmonger and City chamberlain, this version of London literary production contrasts sharply with the expansive moves we saw throughout the Horn corpus and the Auchinleck manuscript: the impressive 1312 pageant of the fishmongers, *omnibus intuentibus*; *Liber regum*'s assertion of London's place on the world stage in Fitz Stephen and the *puy* statutes; Auchinleck's implication in the "Battle Abbey Roll" that the grand literary artifacts of London merchants offer an appropriate repository for England's heroic and living history. The "Cook's Prologue" promises nothing of the sort, merely a "litel jape" (I.4343). The impressive literary and idealistic social gestures initiated by the *Knight's Tale* have ended here in a London that is emphatically not an international metropolis, just a small, fractious neighborhood.

This physical smallness is emphasized, of course, by the fact that the *Cook's Tale* runs aground after just fifty-eight lines. Chaucer's emphasis on the compiled nature of the *Tales* project generally, and of this fragment in particular, encourages us to seek an explanation for this conspicuously anticlimactic ending in the preceding narratives. E. G. Stanley does just this in a compelling argument that "in order to understand *The Cook's Prologue and Tale* we must read the three tales that precede his as if through the Cook's eyes." Focusing on the Cook's use of the word *herbergage* in his response to the *Reeve's Tale*, Stanley theorizes as follows: "The Cook connects with putting up young men for the night, i.e. with *herbergage*, the disturbance, or destruction even, of seeming domestic felicity; for on the one hand they are likely to rob the master of the house of whatever he cherishes most, and on the other hand they stand in danger of being robbed by him."[29] Stanley reads the *Cook's Tale* as a cynical answer to this practical problem, whereby self-preservation lies in embracing the essential griminess of human nature:

> The last few lines of *The Cook's Tale* give the recipe for carefree *herbergage*: though the lodger be a thief, no loss if a thief in cahoots with him puts him up; though the lodger be a swiver, no danger if the landlady is a whore, and no honor to lose if the pimping landlord is her husband. The three tales of the First Fragment, if seen by the Cook as consequences of incautious *herbergage*, are answered by the formula of the situation described at the end of *The Cook's Tale*. There is no more for him to say on that subject: *Of this Cokes Tale maked Chaucer na moore*.[30]

I rehearse Stanley's argument at such length because of its imaginative yet textually grounded attempt to engage with the *Cook's Tale* in the compilational terms that I believe Fragment I encourages and because of its boldly interpretive use of codicological detail (Pinkhurst's note from Hengwrt) as equal partner with literary text. I am less con-

---

29. E. G. Stanley, "'Of This Cokes Tale Maked Chaucer Na Moore,'" *Poetica: An International Journal of Linguistic-Literary Studies* 5 (1976): 36–59 (quotation 56). The dangers of *herbergage* for John the Carpenter and Symkyn the Miller are evident; in the *Knight's Tale*, Stanley points to the Knight's *demande d'amour* as to which lover is worse off, Palamon for his imprisoned proximity to the beloved or Arcite for his ladyless liberty (I.1347–52): "The right answer in terms of chivalric love . . . lies in the lover's proximity to the beloved, but at the Cook's level the solution lies in *herbergage*; a mind lacking innocence and quiet will still be able to seize the center of the argument, though more coarsely: lodging nearby brings opportunity" ("'Of This Cokes Tale Maked Chaucer Na Moore,'" 57). And, sure enough, Theseus does lose his sister-in-law, albeit honorably, to a "lodger" who he thought was well under his control.

30. Stanley, "'Of This Cokes Tale Maked Chaucer Na Moore,'" 59.

vinced than Stanley that the Cook is the central object of Chaucer's criticism,[31] though his experience of the *Reeve's Tale* as a viscerally delightful "claw[ing] . . . on the bak" (I.4326) is undeniably disquieting, forcing us into "itchy proximity" with a figure heretofore most dermatologically notable for his disgustingly oozing *mormal*;[32] that this physically noisome enjoyment is at so mean-spirited "a jape of malice in the derk" (I.4338), as the Cook approvingly calls it, suggests a similarly distasteful personality. But the parallels between his performance and those of the Miller and the Reeve—the emphasis on professional rivalry as the basis of a literary *quyting* and a comparably bawdy subject—suggest that the *Cook's Tale* passes judgment on more than just its pilgrim-narrator.

It is therefore significant that the *Cook's Tale* takes place in London, rather than in the comparatively tiny university towns of Oxford and Cambridge at issue in the previous two tales. The selection of victualing, a trade fraught with memories of the contested mayoral elections of the 1380s, for both the tale's teller and its protagonist, makes the London setting even more pointed, as does the sheer vitality of City life as described in the tale's opening lines, that vitality finding metonymic expression in the untrammeled energy of the protagonist, Perkyn Revelour:

> At every bridale wolde he synge and hoppe;
> He loved bet the taverne than the shoppe.
> For whan ther any ridyng was in Chepe,
> Out of the shoppe thider wolde he lepe—
> Til that he hadde al the sighte yseyn,
> And daunced wel, he wolde nat come ayeyn—
> And gadered hym a meynee of his sort
> To hoppe and synge and maken swich disport;
> And ther they setten stevene for to meete,
> To pleyen at the dys in swich a streete.
> (I.4375–84)

31. Stanley writes that the tale represents "a shrinking of all humanity to its lowest essentials. . . . [T]he Cook's range of sight shrinks rather than enlarges what he sees" (ibid., 48–49).

32. Ibid., 46.

This, the Cook twice repeats, is "oure citee," a London of movement, instability, and (ex)change, its streets and taverns clogged with leaping *meynees* of like-minded Perkyns in literal pursuit of the next wedding party to crash or equestrian display to take in. This exciting but destabilizing sense of perpetual motion transfers to such plot as the tale offers: money disappears (leaping, no doubt) from strongboxes; Perkyn's master fears that his apprentice's bad qualities will attach themselves equally energetically to his other servants; the dismissed Perkyn hops off cheerfully to live with a similarly thieving friend and his wife, a prostitute whose clients presumably also come and go with regularity. Such frenetic energy makes the tale's abrupt cessation undeniably striking; far from manifesting absence,[33] however, the City's exuberant, uncontrollable presence establishes itself all the more dramatically for its sudden and anticlimactic collapse.

This collapse makes most sense as that of the compilation initiated by the *Knight's Tale*, whose concluding jousts and marriage represent precisely the diversions in search of which Perkyn bounds so enthusiastically about London. In the *Knight's Tale*, such activities take place in elaborately constructed spaces and are narrated in an equally well-wrought poem. The temples built on Theseus's orders are most famous, but the amphitheater constructed for the tournament is equally imposing:

> The circuit a myle was aboute,
> Walled of stoon, and dyched al withoute.
> Round was the shap, in manere of compas,
> Ful of degrees, the heighte of sixty pas,
> That whan a man was set on o degree,
> He letted nat his felawe for to see.
> Estward ther stood a gate of marbul whit,
> Westward right swich another in the opposit.
> (I.1887–94)

33. Wallace (*Chaucerian Polity*, chap. 6)—who, as we have seen, characterizes London as an "absent city"—discusses the *Cook's Tale* at some length. This characterization of London cannot, however, be sustained in light of Turner's *Chaucerian Conflict* and Butterfield's collection *Chaucer and the City*.

This is a structure built to endure, to reflect in its architectural perfection the "faire cheyne of love" (I.2991) and harmony of the spheres celebrated at the end of the tale; not for nothing does Theseus consult every "crafty man / That geometrie or ars-metrike kan" (I.1897–98). The stable expanse of this tournament site contrasts with the narrow crush of streets through which Perkyn pursues his *ridynges*, and this contrast is part of the broader one between the *Knight's Tale*'s emphasis on permanence, here figured architecturally but also raised metaphorically by the tale's Boethian conclusion, and the *Cook's Tale*'s energetic pursuit of diverting ephemera. Formally and thematically, the trajectory of Fragment I enacts the universal descent described by Theseus:

> For nature hath nat taken his bigynnyng
> Of no partie or cantel of a thyng,
> But of a thyng that parfit is and stable,
> Descendynge so til it be corrumpable.
> (I.3007–10)

As we have seen, the Cook's body is literally and nastily *corrumpable*, and his tale first thematizes and then succumbs to a similar instability.

This disintegration gains added resonance by taking place in London, for, as the Horn corpus amply showed, the City was desperate to imagine itself comparable to the great urban spaces of the Continent, both contemporary (the Arras of the *puy*; Latini's Florence) and antique (*urbe Roma satis antiquior est*, as Fitz Stephen would have it). Londoners' long-standing preoccupation with their supposed Trojan origins became especially intense in the Ricardian period, culminating in one overenthusiastic mayor's purported plan to rename the City Troia Nova,[34] so it is especially significant that the Cook's *jape* of "oure citee" should fail so conspicuously to match the Knight's

---

34. Thomas of Walsingham writes that one of the crimes for which Nicholas Brembre was executed in 1388 was that "he had planned to destroy the name of the Londoners, and to apply a new name, namely Little Troy; of which city and name he intended to make and name himself Duke" (*Historia Anglicana*, ed. Henry Thomas Riley, 2 vols., Rolls Series, vol. 28 [London: Longmans, 1863], 2:174). Henry Knighton agreed, suggesting that Brembre "would have had himself made duke of Troy by the king, for in ancient times London was called the second Troy, and so he would have been the duke of London, the name of London being

initiating narrative of similarly ancient and storied Athens. Imitative literary models, which were crucial to the compilational potential of the Auchinleck manuscript, recur here in the form of *quyting*; but contemporary English imitation of the Knight's chivalric romance does not grandly establish London's rightful place in the register of great cities, *renomee de touz biens en tuz lieus*, as the *puy* statutes optimistically imagined. Instead of sweetly sung *chants royaux*, it produces a cacophony of increasingly bitter professional rivalries and a gradually descending sequence of literary productions that collapses into nothingness on reaching precisely the place, London, where it might reasonably be expected to flourish. The play of such a place neither envisions nor creates harmony; rather, it is as riven by disorder and ungovernable energy as its factionally fraught pursuit of diverse trades, crafts, and livelihoods.[35]

In this context, we should recall that the *Knight's Tale* of the (mostly) 1390s Canterbury project is a resituation, though so far as we can tell not a substantial rewriting, of the self-standing poem that the *Prologue* to the *Legend of Good Women* referred to as "al the love of Palamon and Arcite" (F.420). Lynn Staley has argued that Richard II's declaration of his majority in January 1390 "had a pronounced effect on the language of courtly speech" and that works like the *Legend* "seem not to speak to the world of the 1390s; they seem to belong to an earlier courtly community."[36] Taken on its own, the text now surviving as the *Knight's Tale* but first composed in that earlier period presents courtly construction and performance as equal to the task of meaningfully addressing, if not resolving, fundamental problems of human existence. When it becomes part of the later Canterbury project, however, it is placed on equal footing with the far less exalted (if comparably accomplished) narratives of far less savory individuals; and, as Staley and others have plausibly reconstructed it, the

---

changed to Troy" (*Knighton's Chronicle, 1337–1396*, ed. and trans. G. H. Martin [Oxford: Clarendon, 1995], 500–501).

35. See further the discussion in Turner, *Chaucerian Conflict*, 136–40.

36. Lynn Staley, "Gower, Richard II, Henry of Derby, and the Business of Making Culture," *Speculum* 75 (2000): 68–96 (quotation 69).

decade in which this literary and codicological recontextualization took place saw Richard adopt a far more formal royal persona, one in which courtly performance became one aggressive tactic of an increasingly absolutist reign.[37] The disintegration of the grand civic and internationalizing literary gestures of the *Knight's Tale* when they are *quyted* in the contemporary, urban English settings of Fragment I thus suggests disillusionment with the modes of courtly performance that the *Knight's Tale* celebrates but that for the London of the 1390s had become just another weapon in the Crown's arsenal.

Evidence of just how devastatingly that weapon could be deployed survives in the form of detailed accounts of several royal processions provided by the City. By 1390, Richard had already received two processions in imitation of the *joyeuses entrées* with which Franco-Flemish cities welcomed their feudal rulers, one at his coronation and another for the 1382 arrival of his bride, Queen Anne of Bohemia. These, however, could at least theoretically be construed as genuinely happy occasions, akin to the fishmongers' joyful procession at the birth of the future Edward III that we considered in chapter 1. The same could hardly be said of the festivities prepared for Richard in August 1392.[38] Having unwisely withheld loans from the impecunious monarch, London found itself the target of a royal campaign to punish and humiliate

---

37. In addition to Staley's article (ibid.), see Nigel Saul's "Richard II and the Vocabulary of Kingship" (*English Historical Review* 110 [1995]: 854–78), which argues that the 1390s saw Richard associate himself with an increasingly princely lexicon atypical of English monarchs to that point and probably borrowed from Continental terms of address, and Sheila Lindenbaum's "The Smithfield Tournament of 1390" (*Journal of Medieval and Renaissance Studies* 20 [1990]: 1–20), which argues that the tournament in question was precisely constructed so as to exclude the City and mark the division between aristocratic and mercantile citizens. It is worth noting that Chaucer himself was clerk of the king's works at the time of the Smithfield tournament and thus had ample opportunity to see for himself how impressive courtly constructions could be assembled—and, likewise, be prone to collapse.

38. This pageant is described in Knighton, *Knighton's Chronicle*, 547–49; Walsingham, *Historia Anglicana*, 2:207–11; *The Westminster Chronicle, 1381–94*, ed. and trans. L. C. Hector and Barbara Harvey (Oxford: Clarendon, 1982), 503–9; and a Latin poem by Richard Maidstone, "Concordia Facta inter Regem Riccardum II et Civitatem Londonie," ed. and trans. Charles Roger Smith (Ph.D. diss., Princeton University, 1972). Helen Suggett discovered another narration of the events in a French letter of an anonymous member of Richard's company that she includes in "A Letter Describing Richard II's Reconciliation with the City of London in 1392," *English Historical Review* 62 (1947): 209–13.

it, and in due course Richard had taken over the City: all elected officials had been replaced by royal appointees, all liberties were forfeit
to the king, and a corporate fine of £100,000 was levied.[39] Aware of
their monarch's passion for pomp and flattery, the desperate citizens
put on a two-day spectacle in which the king and queen were paraded
through the city, welcomed and cheered by costumed representatives
of the trades and crafts, while lavish tableaux were enacted for the
king's pleasure. Only after thoroughly taking in this pageant of praise
and penitence (and being more pragmatically plied with many expensive gifts) did Richard forgive his erring city. Courtly spectacle, which
in Horn's London had offered at least the image (if not the reality) of
civic pride and autonomy, became under Richard the means by which
London was forced to play the role of servile supplicant.

By leaving the Knight undercharacterized as a pilgrim until long
after his own tale has finished, its ceremoniously antique narrative
replayed in the dissonant registers of the *Cook's Tale*'s contemporary
London, Chaucer makes a first reading of the *Knight's Tale* hauntingly
like a reading of the text's original, self-standing version from the
1380s, allowing his audience of the following decade a taste of the
idealism, by now nostalgic, with which the poem was first infused.
Comparison with the Horn corpus is instructive here. Just as the
straightforward legal text *Britton* could have fundamentally opposed
effects depending on whether it had a comparably straightforward
codicological context (as in *Liber Horn*) or one that implicitly satirized
its performative theory of the law (as in the *Mirror* codex), so too the
Knight's Tale–cum–Palamon and Arcite functions radically differently
depending on the broader context of its form and history. In this way,
Chaucer's decision to resituate the earlier work as the *Knight's Tale*
becomes a gesture not unlike Horn's inclusion of the similarly obsolete *puy* statutes or Fitz Stephen's *Description of London*: all allude to a
pleasing yet ultimately irrecoverable ideal. The similarities between

39. The fullest description of the events is Caroline M. Barron, "The Quarrel of Richard II
with London, 1392–7," in *The Reign of Richard II: Essays in Honor of May McKisack*, ed. F. R. H.
Du Boulay and Caroline M. Barron (London: Athlone, 1971), 173–201.

the *Knight's Tale* and Fitz Stephen's text are particularly strong, for in each case a text whose idealism was to some degree counterfactual even when first composed becomes even more so when it takes part in a later compilational structure: just as the *Description* emphasized the City's virtues and minimized its vices, so too the *Knight's Tale* as originally written glossed over the many conflicts of the 1380s, with its emphasis on the productive potential of the kind of courtly play identified by Staley as typical of that decade.[40]

I have argued to this point that the construction of Fragment I suggests that the kind of courtly performance that the Knight initiates in his tale could not produce comparably coherent social and literary results when imitated in the Cook's London of the 1390s. In the following section, I will argue that the *Cook's Tale*'s London context does more than inform the (de)construction of the fragment it concludes; it also crucially inflects a range of pilgrims and tales from later in the project, especially those associated with the Franco-Flemish Low Countries: the Squire, the Pardoner and his *riotoures*, and Sir Thopas. These Franco-Flemish associations with the Cook's London make relevant to the City the relation among the *Knight's Tale*, the *Squire's Tale*, and the *Tale of Sir Thopas*. This incipient compilational thread is motivated both generically (all three poems are romances) and by pilgrim identity (Knight and Squire are father and son, while the Squire and Geffrey are the only pilgrims with literary avocations) as well as by the fact that its last two tales are both interrupted by fellow pilgrims. Because various forms of courtly imitation and performance remained relevant in the cities of the Low Countries into the late fourteenth century, the disintegration of a Franco-Flemish tale thread like Knight–Squire–Sir Thopas, when confected in the English context of the Canterbury pilgrimage, recalls and deepens Fragment I's skepticism about the potential of such modes to have socially reinforcing effects in English urban spaces.

---

40. For an argument that Chaucer reflects aspects of these conflicts in the very different *House of Fame*, see Turner, *Chaucerian Conflict*, 8–30.

The Squire and the Cook, London and the Low Countries

If as I have argued Chaucer implicitly encourages the construction of alternate tale threads extending out from the *Knight's Tale*, then the Squire is one of the most logical figures to turn to, both as the Knight's son and as the pilgrim depicted second in the *General Prologue*, immediately after his father. Each is defined in terms of overseas travel, although the Knight's expansive theater of action ("therto had he riden, no man ferre" [I.48]) makes the Squire's own expeditions ("in Flaundres, in Artoys, and Picardie" [I.86]) seem diminutively close to home, their smallness reinforced by their occupying a single line, as against fifteen for the Knight's travels (I.51–66). The Squire's purpose in the Low Countries is *chyvachie* (I.85), which David Wallace and Lee Patterson have identified as the Despenser Crusade of 1383;[41] if they are correct, then the Squire's expedition targeted fellow Christians, yet another contrast with the Knight's righteous crusading and his portrait's opening statement that "he loved chivalrie, / Trouthe and honour, fredom and curteisie" (I.45–46). Whereas the Knight is described in terms of these ideals that he loves, the Squire is characterized in terms of the activities that he practices (singing, jousting, dancing, poetic composition), which read like a résumé of the *festes* celebrated in precisely the territories to which his *chyvachie* took him: Flanders, Artois, Picardy.[42] This concatenation of geography and pastime gives the Squire a complex set of literary and sociocultural associations with a wide range of figures in the *Tales* and beyond, particularly since many

---

41. Patterson characterizes this expedition as "shameful . . . an inconclusive if brutal *chevauchée* that had brought discredit to everyone involved" (*Chaucer and the Subject of History*, 189), while Wallace writes that "the aim of the *chevauchee* was *not* to engage the enemy in battle, but rather to cut a wide swathe of havoc, damage, and destruction" ("In Flaundres," 72). I am not convinced that the word here refers solely to this specific historical occurrence since it often means simply a cavalry expedition or even just horseback riding, without any implication of especially wanton mayhem. Such a neutral meaning appears, e.g., in Chaucer's *Complaint of Mars*, which describes Cilenius "rydinge in his chevache" (line 144). And, while the Despenser Crusade took place in Flanders, it did not extend into Picardy or Artois, also named as sites of the Squire's *chyvachie*.

42. On these *festes*, see the discussions in Vale, *Edward III and Chivalry*; van den Neste, *Tournois*; and Vale, *The Princely Court*.

of them turn out to be instanced as well by the Cook's protagonist, Perkyn Revelour.

Although the Squire's portrait offers only subtle implications of vice, it closely resembles the incarnation of vainglory described by Genius in *Confessio Amantis*:

> Mor jolif than *the brid in Maii*
> He makth him evere freissh and gay,
> And doth al his array desguise,
> So that of him *the newe guise*
> Of lusti folk alle othre take;
> And ek he can carolles make,
> *Rondeal, balade and virelai.*
> And with al this, if that he may
> Of love gete him *avantage*,
> Anon he wext of his corage
> So overglad, that of his ende
> Him thenkth ther is no deth comende.
> For he hath thane at alle tide
> Of love such a maner pride,
> Him thenkth his joie is endeles.[43]
> (I.2703–17; emphasis added)

Like Vainglory, the Squire is also "as fressh as is the month of May" (I.92) and birdlike (compared to the nightingale at I.98), dressed in the latest fashions (I.93) and intent on using his various courtly and chivalric pursuits in order to secure amorous *avantage* (I.87–88). The concluding emphasis on Vainglory's blithe confidence in the permanence of youth and gaiety recalls a passage earlier in the description:

> Hise worldes joyes ben so grete,
> Him thenkth of hevene no beyete;
> This lives Pompe is al his pes:
> Yit schal he deie natheles.
> (I.2683–86)

---

43. Quotations of the *Confessio Amantis* are taken from vols. 2–3 of Gower's *Complete Works* and are cited by book and line number parenthetically in the text.

This foolish nonchalance evokes the *riotoures* of the *Pardoner's Tale*, likewise wedded to transient joys and heedless of Death's stalking footsteps. Though the tone of their description is very different from that of the Squire in the *General Prologue*, aspects of their pastimes are not dissimilar, and their setting is of course the same:

> In Flaundres whilom was a compaignye
> Of yonge folk that haunteden folye,
> As riot, hasard, stywes, and tavernes,
> Where as with harpes, lutes, and gyternes,
> They daunce and pleyen at dees bothe day and nyght.
> . . . .
> And right anon thanne comen tombesteres
> Fetys and smale, and yonge frutesteres,
> Syngeres with harpes, baudes, wafereres
> Whiche been the verray develes officeres
> To kyndle and blowe the fyr of lecherye,
> That is annexed unto glotonye.
> (VI.463–67, 477–82)

As imagined here, folly is an almost physical, urban location that can be "haunted" like the stews and taverns.

The Squire and the Pardoner's *riotoures* are associated with the geography of *Flaundres*, but aspects of both are evoked by the London-based protagonist of the *Cook's Tale*, Perkyn Revelour, and his teller, Roger of Ware. David Wallace has noted that both Perkyn and the Squire are "young men of comparable age and of comparable sexual energy living in the shadow of powerful masters,"[44] and the parallels are in fact considerably more acute. "So hoote" the Squire loves, we are told, that he sleeps no more than a nightingale (I.97–98); Perkyn, meanwhile, is compared to a goldfinch that is "ful of love and paramour" (I.4372). The Squire's exhausting list of activities suggests a state of perpetual motion, an impression furthered by his light sleeping and his singing or fluting "al the day" (I.91); he moves equally quickly in amatory matters, managing his exploits "weel, as of so litel space, / In hope to stonden in his lady grace" (I.87–88). Both his activities

---

44. Wallace, *Chaucerian Polity*, 168.

themselves and his eagerness in pursuing them accord with what we have seen of Perkyn's preferred pastimes and boundless energy. Our image of the Squire, then, is of a literally dashing young man whose wide range of pleasurable pursuits is nevertheless restricted to "so litel space," a geographic compression of his father's expansive theater. In this too he is like Perkyn, whose bounding and leaping occur within the geographic confines of London's narrow streets and the even narrower literary ones of the Cook's implosive tale.

Perkyn shares characteristics with other Canterbury characters, too. V. J. Scattergood, for example, has traced Perkyn's literary associations to the stereotype of "fashionable, dissipated urban wastrels" to which the Pardoner's *riotoures* also bear strong similarities.[45] Like them, Perkyn is addicted to gambling and the tavern: the *Cook's Tale* manages to work three separate references to dicing into its incredibly brief span (I.4384, 4386, 4420). Perkyn is also localized "in Chepe" (I.4377), which the Pardoner references twice (VI.564, 569). The *Pardoner's Tale*, meanwhile, thematizes food in its masterful apostrophes ("O wombe! O bely! O stynkyng cod, / Fulfilled of dong and of corrupcioun!" [VI.534–35]), which also attack the cooks who pander to such appetites:

> Thise cookes, how they stampe, and streyne, and grynde,
> And turnen substaunce into accident
> To fulfille al thy likerous talent!
> (VI.538–40)

This reference, part of the Pardoner's larger project of linking gluttony and lechery, further connects his tale to the Cook's, as a bawdy narrative told by a professional purveyor of foodstuffs. The Pardoner's excoriation of drunkenness (VI.549–88) also evokes the Cook, who in the "Manciple's Prologue" reacts apoplectically when the Manciple taunts him for his drinking:

> And with this speche the Cook wax wrooth and wraw,
> And on the Manciple he gan nodde faste

45. V. J. Scattergood, "Perkyn Revelour and the *Cook's Tale*," *Chaucer Review* 19 (1985): 14–23 (quotation 16).

For lakke of speche, and doun the hors him caste,
Where as he lay, til that men hym up took.
This was a fair chyvachee of a cook!
(IX.46–50)

The Cook's fall and speechlessness recall the Pardoner's apostrophe to
the drunken man ("Thou fallest as it were a styked swyn, / Thy tonge
is lost" [VI.556–67]), and his *chyvachee*—the word's only other appearance in the *Tales*—looks back to the Squire's of the *General Prologue*.
Whatever its possible military associations, however, that *chyvachee* was
presented within a larger battery of courtly activities that included
poetic production and left the Squire "in hope to stonden in his lady
grace" (I.88); this one, by contrast, leaves the Cook silent, drunk, and
"foul . . . to embrace" (VI.552). The *chyvachee* of the "Manciple's Prologue" thus offers a tragic coda to the disintegration of Fragment I, a
final, literal *descendynge* of the word, the Cook, and all that the *Knight's
Tale* optimistically promised. Fallen, helpless, speechless, this Cook is
not even the noisomely mormalicious figure of Fragment I, content-
edly chortling at nasty doings in the dark, but something far more pa-
thetic: an "unweeldy . . . sory palled goost" (IX.55). These *Flaundrish*
associations of the *Cook's Tale* and its figures return to London the
relevance of any Franco-Flemish-tinged Knight-Squire compilational
thread that we might construct across the *Canterbury Tales*.

Indeed, the shared interest in construction of the *Knight's Tale* and
the *Squire's Tale* is one crucial factor, beyond their tellers' associations
as pilgrims, that prompts us to associate these tales in the first place.
Frequent denigrations of its artistry notwithstanding, the *Squire's Tale*
in fact demonstrates a lyric power appropriate to its narrator's pastimes
as described by the *General Prologue* and his associations with *forme-
fixe*-affiliated Vainglory from Gower's *Confessio Amantis* (1.2709). The
Squire's difficulty in assembling coherently the many disparate elements of interest and beauty that his tale offers, however, marks his
failure adequately to imitate the structurally sophisticated literary production of his father, the Knight. This *quyting* is neither explicit nor,
like the tales of Fragment I, concerned with plot motifs. Rather, it is
generic, with the Squire aiming to outdo his father by telling an even

longer romance with even more characters and subplots and the occasional direct textual echo to sharpen the comparison. Yet, whereas the *Knight's Tale* successfully draws together its own narrative threads into a conclusion as structurally strong as the "faire cheyne of love" praised by Theseus, the *Squire's Tale* becomes progressively more diffuse, the *knotte* alluded to in one key *occupatio* fraying into the multiple narrative threads that the Squire previews just before being interrupted. The *Squire's Tale* thus becomes an "anticompilation" that adds up to less than the sum of its often attractive parts; unlike the *Tale of Sir Thopas*, that other interrupted chivalric romance with a Franco-Flemish flavor, it fails not because it is gloriously bad poetry throughout but because it cannot synthesize its attractions into a coherent whole. Like *Sir Thopas*, however, the *Squire's Tale* performs a gradual poetic disintegration, offering a literary version of the *descendynge* alluded to by the *Knight's Tale* that is reinforced by the Squire's literal descent from the Knight.[46]

That the *Squire's Tale* offers delights all the same can be seen in the fact that Spenser and Milton, hardly unsophisticated readers, wished it had continued.[47] The tale contains many arresting images: the "strange knyght" mounted on a steed of brass that will travel anywhere in the world; the magical sword with the power both to harm and to heal; the swooning falcon, betrayed in love but comforted by Canacee "in signe of trouthe that is in wommen sene" (V.645). Nor is the appeal limited to prospective plot motif; the falcon's lament is beautifully constructed, as in the description of her false lover's hypocritical wooing.[48] Recalling the "every sondri hewe" in which Gower's

---

46. Compare the argument by Lerer that "the Squire fails both the requests of Harry Bailly and his own ambitions as a literary son," which is part of a broader argument on the subject of "reading like the Squire." This Lerer describes as "reading like a lover, attending to the worlds of dream and vision, to the courtly patterns of rhetorical behavior, and to the structures of disputation that frame the *débats d'amour* of the vernacular literature" (*Chaucer and His Readers*, 57, 61 [see generally 57–84]).

47. Spenser developed one of the threads started in the *Squire's Tale* as the basis of bk. 4 of *The Faerie Queene*, and Milton writes in *Il Penseroso* of his desire to "call up him that left half told / The story of *Cambuskan* bold" (lines 109–10).

48. While recognizing that this and other, comparable expressions of aesthetic judgment are both individually subjective and culturally contingent, I do not think that they should be

vainglorious youth clothed himself (*Confessio Amantis* 1.2699), the falcon uses the complex multiple meanings of *hewe* and *coloures* to link colors of rhetoric like those later alluded to by the Franklin (V.723–26), the metaphoric *hewe* of whatever new *semblaunt* will get the lover what he wants, and the ever-changing literal colors of the latest fashion:

> Al were he ful of treson and falsnesse,
> It was so wrapped under humble cheere,
> And under hewe of trouthe in swich manere,
> Under pleasance, and under bisy peyne,
> That no wight koude han wend he koude feyne,
> So depe in greyn he dyed his coloures.
> Right as a serpent hit hym under floures
> Til he may seen his tyme for to byte,
> Right so this god of loves ypocryte
> Dooth so his cerymonyes and obseisaunces,
> And kepeth in semblaunt alle his observaunces
> That sownen into gentillesse of love.
> As in a toumbe is al the faire above,
> And under is the corps, swich as ye woot,
> Swich was this ypocrite, bothe coold and hoot.
> (V.506–20)

The similes here are well managed, the connection between flowers and the hypocrite's *semblaunt* recalling the *Roman de la Rose*'s Faux Sem-

---

as wholly suppressed from scholarly discourse as they have recently tended to be. The desire to perform our now-normalized recognition that medieval and contemporary aesthetic judgments cannot fully coincide, e.g., has caused many of us to attempt to divorce our aesthetic experience of medieval literature from our analysis of it. Such a thoroughgoing separation is of course impossible actually to maintain and may even be less historically responsible than we might suppose. As Mary Carruthers has shown, e.g., there is considerable overlap between contemporary and medieval taste. Taking up the concept of *sweetness* (*dulcedo* or *suavitas*), a term ubiquitous in medieval aesthetics, Carruthers argues that "the most interestingly medieval aspect of 'sweetness'—as with many other medieval aesthetic terms—is that it is not just one thing, but has a contrarian nature that includes within itself its opposites: bitter, salt, and sour." It is likewise "profoundly ambivalent and morally difficult" but "worth risking for the sake of some greater expressive good" ("Sweetness," *Speculum* 81 [2006]: 999–1013 [quotations 1000, 1003]). Adjectives like *contrarian*, *ambivalent*, and *difficult* recall the terms of praise associated with New Critical–type close reading, long dismissed as wrongheadedly ahistorical. While recognizing the need to anchor them in more than purely subjective contemporary taste, then, perhaps we can trust our aesthetic judgments a bit more than we have tended to lately.

blant and perhaps also Satan's seduction of a trusting Eve in the Garden of Eden. The elaborate polysyllables of the tercelet's *cerymonyes* and *obeisaunces* and *observaunces* combine to suggest the suaveness with which he concealed his true intentions "til he may seen his tyme for to byte"—a set of bitterly contrasting monosyllables.[49]

If it is poetically powerful at isolated moments, the *Squire's Tale* nevertheless gradually comes unglued, and contrasts between comparable structural moments within the tale help us see how that happens. I restrict myself here to a consideration of two *occupatios*, from the beginning and the middle of the tale, and the conclusions of the two narrative *partes* into which nearly all manuscripts divide the tale.[50] The first *occupatio*, in which the Squire declines to describe Cambyuskan's feast, is quite sophisticated:

> And eek it nedeth nat for to devyse
> At every *cours* the ordre of hire servyse.
> I wol nat tellen of hir strange *sewes*,
> Ne of hir swannes, ne of hire *heronsewes*.
> Eek in that lond, as tellen knyghtes olde,
> Ther is som *mete* that is ful deynte holde
> That in this lond men recche of it but smal;
> Ther nys no man that may reporten al.
> I wol nat taryen yow, for it is pryme
> And for it is no *fruyt* but los of tyme;
> Unto my firste I wole have my *recours*.
> (V.67–75; emphasis added)

The opulently bisyllabic *rime riche* of *sewes/heronsewes* suggests poetically the lavishness of the feast, reinforced by the assonance of the *s* and *h* sounds that accumulate in that couplet. The concluding reference to *fruyt*, meanwhile, punningly picks up on the *mete* just a few lines previous, and the final *recours* plays with line 68's allusion to the feast's

---

49. The meter, of course, suggests that the final *-e* of *tyme* would be pronounced in this line, but the word could elsewhere be a monosyllable, so I think that the power of the contrast holds.

50. Partridge ("Minding the Gaps," 61–62) writes that while a number of manuscripts omit the *Incipit tercia pars* between lines 670 and 671—doubtless because this *tercia pars* advances only two lines before being interrupted—Hengwrt, Ellesmere, and the *Riverside* all maintain it.

multiple courses. Coming just over sixty lines into the tale, these lines are structurally paralleled by another major *occupatio* sixty lines into the *secunda pars*, however, which is handled much less adroitly:

> The *knotte* why that every tale is toold,
> If it be taried til that lust be coold
> Of hem that han it after herkned yoore,
> The savour passeth ever lenger the moore,
> For fulsomnesse of his prolixitee;
> And by the same resoun thynketh me,
> I sholde to the *knotte condescende*,
> And maken of hir walkyng soone an ende.
> (V.401–8; emphasis added)

The reference to cooling and lost savor subtly recalls the earlier *occupatio*. Whereas that figure oozed plenitude, however, its swans and herons offering a metonymic glimpse into a world of exotic food left tantalizingly undescribed, this one is strangely abstract, its vocabulary of abundance (*savour*, *fulsomnesse*) only emphasizing the lack that it records. The repetition of the relatively rare word *knotte* (it appears only one other time in the *Tales*) within these few lines reminds us of our lack of narrative progress, a stumbling paralleled by the knotty consonant clusters of "knotte condescende." The whole concludes on a note of slight absurdity, meanwhile, by deploying the high style of words like *fulsomnesse*, *prolixitee*, and *condescende* in order to (refuse to) describe something as quotidian as walking.

The fact that this oddly unsatisfying episode precedes the most impressive poetry of the tale, the falcon's lament, forces us to distinguish between aesthetically satisfying poetry and its increasingly insufficient packaging. A comparable sense of structural disintegration can be found in the contrast between the end of the tale's two *partes*. The first concludes its description of the feast and the knight's arrival with formal efficiency:

> But thus I lete in lust and jolitee
> This Cambyuskan his lordes festeiynge
> Til wel ny the day bigan to sprynge.
> (V.344–46)

The end of the *pars secunda*, on the other hand, dispenses with such straightforward gestures and promises instead a more complicated structure and narrative. After announcing that he will take his leave of Canacee and the falcon before returning to them later (along the way suggesting how that drama will ultimately conclude), the Squire says:

> But hennesforth I wol my proces holde
> To speken of aventures and of batailles
> That nevere yet was herd so grete mervailles.
> First wol I telle yow of Cambyuskan,
> That in his tyme many a citee wan;
> And after wol I speke of Algarsif,
> How that he wan Theodora to his wif,
> For whom ful ofte in greet peril he was,
> Ne hadde he ben holpen by the steede of bras;
> And after wol I speke of Cambalo,
> That faught in lystes with the bretheren two
> For Canacee er that he myghte hire wynne.
> And ther I lefte I wol ayeyn bigynne.
> (V.658–70)

What is frustrating here is not these lines' projection of an infinite narrative[51] but the juxtaposition of narrative and poetic promise (just how *did* the brass horse help Algarsif win Theodora?) with suspect organizational skills. The twice-repeated image of the knot from the *occupatio* of V.401–8 encourages us to evaluate the *Squire's Tale* in terms of its ability to unite its multiple narrative threads, and here they fray into wild ribbons of narrative potential, spinning outward so

---

51. It is something of a commonplace to assert that the vast narrative projected here could never have "fit" into the Canterbury scheme; typical is William Kamowski's assertion that "no one has satisfactorily explained how so massive a narrative . . . could have been embedded in its entirety into the *Canterbury Tales*" ("Trading the 'Knotte' for Loose Ends: The *Squire's Tale* and the Poetics of Chaucerian Fragments," *Style* 31 [1997]: 391–412 [quotation 391]). So long a tale would obviously have changed the nature of the *Canterbury Tales* as a whole, but so too would any substantial change to the work as it now stands. It therefore strikes me that the principle of critical modesty should make us reluctant to claim that Chaucer would necessarily have failed at any given poetic endeavor, even the completion of the *Squire's Tale* as described here.

overenthusiastically (we might recall the impression of perpetual motion given by the Squire's *General Prologue* portrait) as to violate the image of rhetorical success suggested by the tale itself.

The fact that the failure of the *Squire's Tale* is primarily structural takes on added urgency because the Squire is imitating his father's literary production, which was defined in large part by its interest in grand, coherent structures, physical, literary, and social. This imitation extends not just to genre (large-scale courtly romance) but also to image and phrase. We are told, for example, that any tiger or cruel beast "that dwelleth outher in wode or in forest" (V.420) would have wept at the falcon's grief, a line that punningly recalls both the forest setting and the two antagonists (*wood leon* and *crueel tigre* [I.1656–67]) of Palamon and Arcite's duel. And the falcon herself opines that "pitee renneth soone in gentil herte" (V.479), later admitting to having "made vertu of necessite" (V.593) in accepting the male falcon's suit. These exact repetitions of two of the *Knight's Tale*'s most prominent phrases—together with the connections between the pilgrim figures of Knight and Squire that we saw in the *General Prologue*—make the *Squire's Tale* one of the most compelling ways of extending a tale thread out from the Knight's story. Both sets of narrative outgrowths of the *Knight's Tale*, moreover, are figured as forms of imitation: the explicit *quyting* of the tales of Fragment I and the subtler but still audible evocation of the Knight's thematic interests and concern for literary structure that we see in the *Squire's Tale*.

A rare moment of linguistic specificity that further links the *Knight's Tale* and the *Squire's Tale* may therefore be particularly significant. Of Canacee's beauty the Squire says:

> It lyth nat in my tonge, n'yn my konnyng;
> I dar nat undertake so heigh a thyng.
> Myn Englissh eek is insufficient.
> (V.35–37)

Only two other such instances of a linguistically specific modesty topos exist in the *Canterbury Tales*, and one is the Knight's, who speaking of Palamon wonders: "Who koude ryme in Englyssh proprely / His

martirdom? For soth it am nat I" (I.1459–60).[52] While this echo further links the *Squire's Tale* to the *Knight's Tale*, however, the Knight's
confession comes some six hundred lines into the poem, and it lacks
any other resonances that would cause it particularly to stand out in
the reader's mind. The Squire's confession, by contrast, comes at the
beginning of his narrative and gains added heft from his own associations with poetic composition and with the Franco-Flemish Low
Countries, where unlike in London the *puys* and other poetry-infused
festes continued to flourish. His suggestion of linguistic incompetence
thus recalls the fact that although he is imitating his father's genre of
epic romance, the literary mode suggested by the Squire's portrait is in
fact francophone lyric like the "rondeal, balade, and virelai" mentioned
in the Squire-like portrait of Vainglory in Gower's *Confessio Amantis*
(1.2709) and practiced at the *festes* of the geographic ambit specified
by the Squire's *General Prologue* portrait. The *Squire's Tale* is at its most
aesthetically effective when it enters the lyric mode, as in the falcon's
lament; its failure stems from the Squire's inability to assemble these
moments of lyric power into sustained narrative motion.[53] Together
with his linguistically specific admission of insufficiency, all this suggests that, while his version of literary production might have worked
"in Flaundres, in Artoys, and Picardye," it will not in England. The
lyric expressions of Franco-Flemish literary culture, in other words,
prove unsuitable materials for the construction of narrative in English.
As it extends outward thematically from the *Knight's Tale*, the *Squire's
Tale* thus implicitly complements Fragment I's skepticism about the

52. Marie Neville noted this connection long ago in a pioneering article on the relation
between the *Knight's Tale* and the *Squire's Tale*, but she sees the echo as purely parallel, arguing
that both figures are more at home in French and that their distaste for English is aristocratic:
"Too great linguistic and rhetorical facility is the mark of the professional bourgeois, not of
the military gentleman" ("The Function of the *Squire's Tale* in the Canterbury Scheme," *Journal
of English and Germanic Philology* 50 [1951]: 167–79 [quotation 172]).

53. A wide range of studies address the kinds of distinctions I am drawing between lyric
stasis and narrative movement; particularly valuable to me has been Sylvia Huot's *From Song to
Book: The Poetics of Writing in Old French Lyric and Lyrical Narrative Poetry* (Ithaca, NY: Cornell
University Press, 1987).

viability of translating courtly display (geographically, linguistically, generically) into late Ricardian England.

That message gains power from the fact that any Knight-Squire connection is inflected by the London-centered *Cook's Tale*, not just because of Perkyn's literary associations with the Squire, but also because, to this point in the Canterbury project, theirs are the only unfinished tales. This fact makes our Cook-inflected Knight-Squire thread implicitly codicological as well as thematic. This is because the contrasting ways in which the *Cook's Tale* and the *Squire's Tale* are fragmentary, and their fragmentariness represented in manuscripts and editions, blur the boundary between literary text and codicological data, not unlike Stanley's interpretive use of Pinkhurst's line at the end of the *Cook's Tale*. In the *Riverside*, and therefore in most readers' minds, the *Cook's Tale* is a *fragment*, with all that word's associations of physical loss, while the *Squire's Tale* is gently interrupted by the Franklin and thus itself incomplete but a coherent part of a larger narrative arc. With the *Cook's Tale*, the *Riverside* makes one of its rare acknowledgments of the manuscript(s) behind Chaucer's work by including Pinkhurst's note from Hengwrt; its presentation of the *Squire's Tale*'s interruption by the Franklin, by contrast, emphasizes the naturalism of the pilgrimage frame tale, making the *Tales* as a whole feel more like a novel and less like a manuscript. My point is not that these editorial decisions are illegitimate, either as a matter of principle or as representations of the codicological evidence; rather, I suggest that the *Squire's Tale* is linked to Fragment I not just by its thematic affiliations with the *Knight's Tale* and the *Cook's Tale* but also by the fragmentariness that it shares with the latter. The various ways in which that fragmentariness is represented in both manuscripts and editions in turn offer yet another reminder that the *Canterbury Tales* is a text both inherently multiple and implicitly physical.

The *Tale of Sir Thopas* and the Return to London

I will return to the Franklin's interruption of the Squire at the end of this chapter; here, I would like to turn to another *Flaundrish* narrative of chivalric exploits interrupted before its conclusion: Geffrey's own

Tale of Sir Thopas.[54] Thematically, this poem continues associations from the Knight-Squire compilational thread that we have considered to this point. Like the *Squire's Tale*, it is interrupted by a fellow pilgrim; like both the *Knight's Tale* and the *Squire's Tale*, it shows considerable interest in literary structure: both the fitts into which it is divided and the multiple stock motifs and literary gestures out of which Geffrey tries, haplessly, to construct a proper and pleasing poem.[55] In his failure to do so, analogous to Thopas's own chivalric failures within the narrative, he implicitly asks what kind of chivalric literary production is worth our time. Or, put another way, how much and what kinds of distance (historical, linguistic, generic) make a given piece of literature inaccessible to the kind of compilational game that the *Canterbury Tales* presents as literary and social practice? As with the *Squire's Tale*, the relevance of those questions will return to England, but with *Sir Thopas* it is more a matter of the poem itself and less the associations of its teller. The tail-rhyme stanza form (complemented in a number of manuscripts by that form's visual representation) and explicit appeals to romances of homegrown heroes like *Beues of Hamptoun* and *Guy of Warwick* make these English resonances clear enough.

Indeed, the conspicuous conjunction of Flemish setting and English form has fueled much of the debate as to just what the delightful doggerel of *Sir Thopas* is satirizing.[56] The famous catalog of Middle

54. Throughout this discussion, I follow the critical convention of distinguishing between Chaucer, the author of *Sir Thopas* and the *Canterbury Tales* as a whole, and Geffrey, the comically inept narrator of *Sir Thopas* and Chaucer's fictional alter ego on the pilgrimage.

55. As Joanne Charbonneau puts it: "*Sir Thopas* is not really a tale at all, but is instead a hodgepodge of common rhetorical devices and popular plot motifs" ("*Sir Thopas*," in *Sources and Analogues of the Canterbury Tales* [2 vols.], ed. Robert M. Correale and Mary Hamel [Cambridge: D. S. Brewer, 2002–5], 2:649–714 [quotation 649]).

56. For a list and bibliography of possibilities, the most popular of which are tail-rhyme romance, the bourgeoisie, and the Flemish (or some combination thereof), see ibid., 649–51. Particularly acute is the reading in V. J. Scattergood, "Chaucer and the French War: *Sir Thopas* and *Melibee*," in *Court and Poet*, ed. Glyn S. Burgess (Liverpool: Francis Cairns, 1981), 287–96. Scattergood argues that, "by making his hero the product of an urban, bourgeois, mercantile and essentially contemporary culture, Chaucer is emphasizing the irrelevance in the late fourteenth century of the values romances traditionally celebrate" (ibid., 290). Aspects of his interpretation are congruent with my broader arguments in this chapter. While he astutely identifies Thopas's many bourgeois traits, however, Scattergood argues that the real object of

English romances over all of whose heroes Thopas "bereth the flour /
Of roial chivalry" (VII.901–2) makes it clear that imitation is key to
the humor: not only is the poem an inept imitation of romances like
Beues and *Guy* that are themselves generally Middle English translations of French originals; Thopas himself is also inexpertly imitating
the chivalric practices of such romance heroes.[57] This recognition in
turn makes Thopas's Flemish provenance and apparently bourgeois
social status more obviously relevant since Franco-Flemish towns
abounded in *festes* at which bourgeois participants performed precisely
the kind of chivalric and aristocratic imitation that appears to come
in for mockery in *Sir Thopas*. This context helps answer the sartorial
question posed by Glen Wright: "If Thopas's Flemish stockings are
laughably bourgeois, why does he also sport an exotic robe of syklatoun?"[58] John H. Munro has documented the obsession of Flemish
aldermen with wearing scarlet, the vastly expensive cloth otherwise
reserved for princes, emperors, and popes; the joke is therefore that,
while Flemish Thopas has remembered to put on his flashy robe, he's
forgotten that he's still wearing his embarrassingly déclassé stockings
underneath.[59] F. Blockmans has shown that Flemish merchants imitated the francophone aristocracy by assiduously cultivating French

---

Chaucer's satire is "the warrior ethos and . . . those sorts of literature that served to sustain"
it; Chaucer is thus "unmistakably implying that the upper classes might reasonably listen to
what he has to say" (ibid., 289–91). The weakness of this argument is that Thopas's bourgeois
affiliations and Flemish birth reassuringly distance his inadequacies from those that an audience
of English nobles might see in themselves.

57. Wallace has also argued that *Sir Thopas*'s Flemish setting "suggests, to Chaucer's audience, the vigorous imitation of nobility in the land of the non-noble," but he sees a less complex set of imitative resonances than I propose and, additionally, relies on the outdated characterization of Middle English romance as "offer[ing] lower to middling audiences economic
accounts of great Anglo-Norman ancestral heroes" ("In Flaundres," 74). On the aesthetic sub-
tlety of popular romances like *Beues*, *Guy*, and comparable romances to which Geffrey alludes,
see Siobhan Bly Calkin's important *Saracens and the Making of English Identity: The Auchinleck
Manuscript* (New York: Routledge, 2005); as well as the brief but trenchant discussion of *Guy
of Warwick* in Hanna, *London Literature*, 109–16.

58. Glen Wright, "Modern Inconveniences: Rethinking Parody in *The Tale of Sir Thopas*,"
Genre 30 (1997): 167–94 (quotation 180).

59. John H. Munro, "The Medieval Scarlet and the Economics of Sartorial Splendor,"
in *Textiles, Town, and Trade: Essays in the History of Late-Medieval England and the Low Countries*
(Aldershot: Ashgate, 1996), 17–70.

even in principally Flemish-speaking cities like Bruges and Ghent,[60] and this context allows us to hear the humor of the *par ma fay* with which Thopas swears to kill the giant Olifaunt after fetching his armor (VII.820): though a Fleming, Thopas is careful to swear in French when playing at chivalric romance.

Yet the civic *festes* of the Low Countries created great social prestige for their urban patriciates, whose imitation of aristocratic cultural practices, far from arousing scorn or derision, often incorporated the nobility itself.[61] The satire of *Sir Thopas* therefore relies on specific literary-formal associations rather than simply the sociocultural cue of Franco-Flemish chivalry. Chaucer's choice of a quintessentially English literary form, and of such native heroes as Beues, Guy, and Horn for comparison with Thopas, suggests that, rather than mocking Flanders or its imitative courtly *festes*, he is really talking about England and English town dwellers in particular; it is *their* imitative practices, rather than those of their Continental brethren, that *Sir Thopas* pokes fun at. The poem thus forms part of a broader skepticism that I have argued Chaucer records at the continued viability of courtly performance and imitation in 1390s London. Importantly, this skepticism marks a shift from earlier in the century. During the 1359 London tournament celebrating the marriage of John of Gaunt and Blanche of Lancaster, for example, "the king, his four sons, and nineteen other knights jousted disguised as the mayor and aldermen of London . . .

---

60. F. Blockmans, *Het Gentsche Stadspatriciaat tot omstreeks 1302* (Antwerp: De Sikkel, 1938), 341–52.

61. We have already considered the example of the 1263 *puy* of Arras where figures like the future Edward I of England and Charles d'Anjou participated alongside local merchants and bankers. Vale (*Edward III and Chivalry*, 31ff.), meanwhile, cites an episode at the *fieste dou Rosier* held in Douai in 1284 where two bourgeois jousters from Lille were rudely refused local combatants by their Douaisien hosts, a serious breach of chivalric etiquette that the Count of Flanders and his son took the trouble to rectify by providing jousters for the aggrieved Lillois from among their personal retinue. Caroline Barron suggests that this easy mixing of disparate social classes continued into the civic *festes* of the fourteenth-century Low Countries, writing that there is "nothing to suggest that there was antipathy between the nobility and the urban elite" ("Chivalry, Pageantry and Merchant Culture in Medieval London," in *Heraldry, Pageantry and Social Display in Medieval England*, ed. Peter Coss and Maurice Keen [Woodbridge: Boydell & Brewer, 2002], 219–41 [quotation 220]).

as a mark of respect and as a compliment."[62] Even as recently as the 1381 Rising, the scribe of *London Letter-Book H* could begin by relating the humiliations to which king and citizen alike were subject, only to introduce their savior in heroically martial terms:

> God sent remedy . . . by the hand of the most renowned man, Sir William Walworthe, the then Mayor; who in Smethefelde [Smithfield], in presence of our Lord the King . . . most manfully, by himself, rushed upon the captain [of the rebels] and, as he was altercating with the King and the nobles, first wounded him in the neck with his sword, and then hurled him from his horse, mortally pierced in the breast; and further, by favor of the divine grace, so defended himself . . . that he departed from thence unhurt. . . . The Mayor himself, who had gone into the City at the instance of our Lord the King, in the space of half an hour led forth therefrom so great a force of citizen warriors, that the whole multitude of madmen [i.e., rebels] was surrounded and hemmed in. . . . For this same deed our Lord the King, beneath his standard, in the said field, with his own hands decorated with the order of knighthood the said Mayor.[63]

When the king finds himself helpless, it is not the lords of the realm but the citizens of London who come to the rescue; having led his "citizen warriors" to victory, their mayor becomes a knight. (Auchinleck's "Battle Abbey Roll" would be proud.) In discussing this passage, David Wallace concurs that "the letter-book scribe . . . sounds more like a chivalric chronicler than a mercantile one" but asserts that this represents an "uncertainty of style."[64] In fact, it demonstrates mercantile *imitation* of chivalric style.

It remains to explore how this sociocultural context makes itself visible through *Sir Thopas*'s famously awful literary form. One of the funniest aspects of *Sir Thopas* is how perfectly both Geffrey and Thopas understand all the concrete accoutrements that chivalric heroes need—*love-longynge* (VII.772), an exchange of insults with one's foe (VII.810–26), a formal arming ceremony (VII.847)—even as each

---

62. Barron, "Chivalry, Pageantry and Merchant Culture," 221.
63. Cited and translated in *Memorials of London and London Life*, 450–51.
64. Wallace, *Chaucerian Polity*, 163.

proves completely unable to use them correctly. Even supernatural lovers become simply another item to check off the list; after dreaming that "an elf-queene shal my lemman be" (VII.788), Thopas realizes that he wants one ("an elf-queene wol I love, ywys" [VII.790]) and declares his intention of finding one, even though encounters with fairies and fairy lands invariably take place on their terms, not human terms.[65] The desired elf queen, then, is one way in which Thopas tries to dress the part he is playing even as his generic awareness goes awry; he knows a fairy mistress is required but does not understand the literary context, that you cannot just go out and get one. He thus proves analogous to Geffrey, who is familiar with the components of a good metrical romance (the fairy mistress, the arming of the knight, the horrible giant, commands of *Listeth* to the audience) but cannot make the pieces add up right. The long catalogs that dominate the poem— of flowers, birds, pieces of Thopas's armor, appeals for quiet—thus become a thematic as well as a structural motif; these lists only draw attention to the fact that *Sir Thopas* itself adds up to less than the sum of its rapidly diminishing parts. Indeed, in laughing at Thopas for forgetting to arm himself until after meeting the giant Olifaunt, one almost questions whether Geffrey instead is to blame, for putting the stock elements of tail-rhyme romances that he knows he needs (arming of knight, fierce battle with giant) in the wrong order. Geffrey's and Thopas's French oaths further reinforce their comparable inadequacies: the *par ma fay* of Thopas to the giant and the *par charitee* with which Geffrey tries to quiet his increasingly restive audience at the beginning of the final fitt (VII.891).

English Geffrey's (inadvertent) imitation of Thopas the Fleming, who is himself poorly imitating forms of courtly display and chivalric performance, pointedly returns the tale's relevance to England, for these two are not the only characters in the *Canterbury Tales* who

---

65. To take two examples from romances in the Auchinleck manuscript, Degaré's mother in *Sir Degaré* meets her fairy assailant by getting lost in the woods, and Orfeo's wife in *Sir Orfeo* is abducted by the fairy king after falling asleep under an *ympe-tre* (a grafted tree). In *Sir Launfal* and *Thomas of Erceldoune*, two romances often proposed as sources for the elf queen in *Sir Thopas*, the hero stumbles on his fairy mistress rather than seeking her out.

self-consciously use French and show interest in trappings "that been roiales" (VII.848; Geffrey references "roial chivalry" at VII.902):

> It is ful fair to been ycleped "*madame*,"
> And goon to vigilies al bifore,
> And have a mantel *roialliche* ybore.
> (I.376–78; emphasis added)

Such is the considered opinion of the wives of the five guildsmen described in the *General Prologue*, whose sartorial splendor recalls Thopas's robe of *syklatoun* (VII.44). Of their husbands the guildsmen Chaucer writes:

> Wel semed ech of hem a fair burgeys,
> To sitten in a yeldehalle on a deys.
> Everich, for the wisdom that he kan,
> Was shaply for to been an alderman.
> (I.371–74)

In this context, it is worth remembering Thopas's multiple associations with town (VII.793, 838), which further link his inadequacies to those of the urban English. This evocation of an English context for *Sir Thopas*'s satire is important, for it encourages us to understand the tale's comic failure as literature in the context of the assembled social grouping of the Canterbury pilgrims. The more telling denunciation of the poem is therefore not the Host's characterization of it as literature ("drasty speche," "rym dogerel," and so on [VII.923, 925]), but his assessment of the activity it represents when he tells Geffrey, "Thou doost noght elles but despendest tyme" (VII.931).

This accusation of time wasting brings to *Sir Thopas* and its interruption the complex and generally solemn associations of time in the *Tales* as a whole.[66] The Host, for example, sounds quite unlike his usual boisterous self in the introduction to the *Man of Law's Tale*:

---

66. Study of this topic has often focused on the contrast between mortal time and divine timelessness, as, e.g., in E. D. Blodgett, "Chaucerian *Pryvetee* and the Opposition to Time," *Speculum* 51, no. 3 (1976): 477–93. See also Paul Beekman Taylor, "Time in the *Canterbury Tales*," *Exemplaria* 7 (1995): 371–93, which addresses the same contrast without reaching the same Robertsonian conclusions.

> "Lordynges," quod he, "I warne yow, al this route,
> The fourthe party of this day is gon.
> Now for the love of God and of Seint John,
> Leseth no tyme, as ferforth as ye may.
> Lordynges, the tyme wasteth nyght and day,
> And steleth from us, what pryvely slepynge,
> And what thurgh neclligence in our wakynge,
> As dooth the streem that turneth nevere agayn,
> Descendynge fro the montaigne into playn."
> (II.16–24)

The vocabulary of warning, the repeated direct address to his audience, and the invocation of God and Saint John all indicate that wasting time, Geffrey's alleged sin in offering up *Sir Thopas*, is no mere cliché. This religious dimension is stronger still in the "Parson's Prologue," which links the setting sun, the conclusion of the tale-telling contest, and what the Parson calls "thilke parfit glorious pilgrymage / That highte Jerusalem celestial" (X.50–51). These associations, together with a reference to Libra and its scales of justice (X.11),[67] give the Host's insistence that the Parson hurry up with his tale an almost apocalyptic tone: "But hasteth yow; the sonne wole adoun; / Beth fructuous, and that in litel space" (X.70–71). Condemning *Sir Thopas* as a waste of time is thus more than just aesthetic criticism of a specific poem: it questions the personal and social value of a whole mode of literary production. Indeed, it is a temporal reference—"Til on a day" (VII.918)—that finally shatters the Host's patience with the tale and prompts his interruption, suggesting that *Sir Thopas*'s reduction of time to formulaic, interchangeable expressions is a critical part of its triviality: in not taking time seriously, the poem loses its claim to the time it takes to read or listen to it.

We have already seen how critically structure informs apprehension of compilational meaning, so the parallels among Fragment I, the

---

67. Chaucer actually makes an error here: the *exaltacioun* of the moon (the zodiacal sign in which a planet exerts its greatest influence) referred to at 10 is Taurus, not Libra, as Chaucer writes. Chauncey Wood has plausibly argued on this basis that the reference to Libra here represents an attempt to lend the imagery of divine justice to the Parson's penitential tale. See *Chaucer and the Stars* (Princeton, NJ: Princeton University Press, 1970), 272–97.

TABLE 2. The Gradual Disintegration of
Three *Canterbury Tale* Structures

Fragment I	Knight–Squire–Sir Thopas Thread	*Tale of Sir Thopas*
Knight's Tale: 2,250 lines	*Knight's Tale*: 2,250 lines	Fitt 1: 18 stanzas
"Miller's Prologue" + *Miller's Tale*: 746 lines	*Squire's Tale*: 672 lines	Fitt 2: 9 stanzas
"Reeve's Prologue" + *Reeve's Tale*: 470 lines	*Tale of Sir Thopas*: 206 lines	Fitt 3: 4.5 stanzas (interrupted by the Host midway through)
"Cook's Prologue" + *Cook's Tale*: 98 lines	. . .	. . .

Knight–Squire–Sir Thopas thread that I am proposing, and *Sir Thopas* itself are likewise crucial. J. A. Burrow noticed some decades ago that each of *Sir Thopas*'s fitts is half the length of the preceding one, leading the tale finally to collapse in on itself.[68] The graphic tail-rhyme format in which both Hengwrt and Ellesmere present *Sir Thopas*, moreover, evokes this diminution visually. Table 2 confirms that a similar dwindling into nothingness is at work across the structures I have been analyzing.[69] Fragment I and the Knight–Squire–Sir Thopas thread

68. J. A. Burrow, "'Sir Thopas': An Agony in Three Fits," *Review of English Studies* 22 (1971): 54–58. See further E. A. Jones, "'Loo, Lordes Myne, Heere is a Fit!': The Structure of Chaucer's *Sir Thopas*," *Review of English Studies* 51 (2000): 248–52. Jones supports Burrow's argument about the progressive halving of fitt length by analyzing the number of lines within those fitts (as opposed to the number of stanzas) and finding a broadly similar degenerative movement.

69. See further the important Rhiannon Purdie, "The Implications of Manuscript Layout in Chaucer's *Tale of Sir Thopas*," *Forum for Modern Language Studies* 41 (2005): 263–74. There, Purdie demonstrates that "graphic tail-rhyme is a relatively rare, if traditional, layout: readers would not only recall seeing it in some manuscripts of tail-rhyme romances, but the additional hurdles Chaucer throws in their path would keep them constantly aware of the process of navigating through it" (ibid., 268). For an example of the visual chaos that results once Chaucer starts including bob lines, see ibid., 267. I agree with Purdie's contention that "this use of bob-lines demonstrates fairly conclusively that both they and the graphic tail-rhyme layout of which they make a nonsense were part of Chaucer's original *Sir Thopas*" (ibid.). This reading is particularly convincing in light of Purdie's subsequent reminder that such bob lines, familiar

lack the mathematical precision of *Sir Thopas*, but the structure as well as the themes of all three suggest that, when imitated in the contemporary English polity of the Canterbury pilgrimage, the grand courtly gestures of the *Knight's Tale*—impressive as they were in the 1380s as a self-standing *Palamon and Arcite*—disintegrate into nothingness, with social discord and literary silence alike the end result.

The Franklin's Challenge: Co-Opting the Squire, Redeeming Courtly Imitation

The conclusion to *Sir Thopas*, whose fraught references to time imply the ultimate need for repentance,[70] hauntingly recalls the *Pardoner's Tale*, also a *Flaundrish* narrative whose concluding call to repentance ends in angry silence and the temporary suspension of the game: "I wol no lenger pleye" (VI.958), says the same Host who initiated the tale-telling competition in the first place. There, however, the Knight intervenes and effects a social reconciliation, however grudging, so that literary production can continue. Throughout the *Canterbury Tales*, in other words, one serious structural exploration is what kinds of convocational interactions (or failures to interact) effectively silence literary negotiation. The slight, optimistic grace note that this evocation suggests—there is still, sometimes, a Knight to rescue us from awkward silences, literary and social—reminds us that, because the tales invite compilational reformulations of themselves, embedding such prospective construction into their very form, we are not bound to so pessimistic a concatenation of tales as I have outlined here. I would like to conclude this chapter by considering how, if as in many

---

from alliterative poems like *Sir Gawain*, were "unknown to the Middle English tail-rhyme romances themselves, so their appearance in *Sir Thopas* is best explained as a joke inspired by the graphic tail-rhyme layout itself." See further the discussion in Rhiannon Purdie, *Anglicising Romance: Tail-Rhyme and Genre in Medieval English Literature* (Cambridge: D. S. Brewer, 2008), 78–82 (quotation 80).

70. Compounding this association is the thick cluster of references to God (VII.919, 922, 929, 936), followed by Geoffrey's discussion of the four Evangelists' complementary narrations of "the peyne of Jhesu Crist" (VII.944) and "his pitous passioun" (VII.950).

manuscripts (though not, significantly, Hengwrt) we read the *Franklin's Tale* after the *Squire's Tale*, we can see in their respective relations with the *Knight's Tale* the outlines of a more optimistic compilational thread to follow if we choose.

While the Franklin's interruption of the Squire might be read as simply dismissing a literary gambit that seems to have been lost in translation on the way back to England from *Flaundres*, I read it slightly differently: as an acknowledgment of the weakness of the *Squire's Tale*, to be sure, but one nervously defensive rather than patronizingly dismissive. The Franklin's interruption of the *Squire's Tale* recognizes that its incipient failures threaten to taint the enterprise of courtly imitation that the *Franklin's Tale* proposes as central to the ideal functioning of society. By silencing the *Squire's Tale* even as he looks back to the *Knight's Tale*, imitating its key words and phrases and exploring its themes, the Franklin attempts to construct his own tale as a rival compilation extending out from the *Knight's Tale* and cutting off the Knight–Squire–Sir Thopas thread that we have just considered. If successful, the Franklin's rhetorical gesture would reestablish the links among courtly performance, social harmony, and marital happiness first proposed by the *Knight's Tale* but undermined by the two broader tale threads that I have considered to this point.

The *Franklin's Tale* tells of a marriage founded on *gentillesse* and *trouthe* (V.754, 759; these are the two virtues, we recall, betrayed by the courtly male falcon in the *Squire's Tale*) that is shaken to its core by Dorigen's willingness to humor the young squire Aurelius's pretensions to *fin'amor* and engage in the kind of love banter favored by both the Squire and the falcon of his tale. Implored to have mercy on Aurelius's *peynes smerte* (V.974), Dorigen responds *in pley* (V.988) with a condition that she intends, and Aurelius understands, to be *an impossible* (V.1009). When Aurelius pays for an illusion and Arveragus insists that Dorigen hold her *trouthe*, the tale looks to be headed for the conclusion that courtly love play like Dorigen's with Aurelius is incompatible with marital virtue. In fact, the whole conflict resolves itself perfectly because marital *trouthe* and courtly imitation are shown to be mutually reinforcing gestures, Arveragus's concern for *trouthe* (V.1519, 1530) and *gentillesse* (V.1524, 1527) inspiring Aurelius to an explicitly imitative gesture:

> My trouthe I plighte, I shal yow never repreve
> Of no biheste, and heere I take my leve,
> As of the treweste and the beste wyf
> That evere yet I knew in al my lyf.
> ....
> Thus kan a squier doon a gentil dede
> As wel as kan a knyght, withouten drede.
> (V.1537–39, 1543–44)

By depicting a Squire whose imitation of a Knight's courtly perfection leads to a perfect happily ever after, the Franklin here in a single gesture redeems both the *Squire's Tale*'s failed imitation of the *Knight's Tale* and the courtly vocabulary (*trouthe, gentillesse, routhe*) there deployed by the duplicitous tercelet, which threatened to turn similarly destructive in the hands of Aurelius.

This redemptive power of courtly imitation becomes still more radical when it transfers from Aurelius to the unnamed clerk of Orléans. Part of a squire's job is to imitate knightly grandeur, after all, and the similarity between Aurelius's and Arveragus's names, together with their shared love for Dorigen, all prepare us for Aurelius's noble forbearance. The clerk's decision to imitate this *gentillesse* is far more striking, however, since he inhabits a completely different social sphere and has to this point in the tale been characterized in terms of "his japes and his wrecchednesse / Of swich a supersticious cursednesse" (V.1271–72). But like Aurelius he is impressed by *gentillesse*:

> "Everich of yow dide gentilly til oother.
> Thou art a squier, and he is a kynght;
> But God forbede, for his blisful myght,
> But if a clerk koude doon a gentil dede
> As wel as any of yow, it is no drede!"
> (V.1607–12)

This conclusion optimistically supposes that the courtly performance of *gentillesse* need not function to demarcate class boundaries, defining one social class in opposition to another (as did, say, the Smithfield tournament of 1390);[71] rather, it offers a model whereby courtly

---

71. On the Smithfield tournament, see n. 37 above.

imitation harmoniously unites disparate social groups. We are not given much time either to appreciate the clerk's noble deed or to question his motives, however, for he quickly disappears from the narrative, and the Franklin concludes with his famous *demande d'amour*—"Which was the mooste fre, as thynketh yow?" (V.1622)—which evokes the Knight's own *demande d'amour* of I.1347–54. The Franklin thus ends his tale much as he introduced it: with an effort to play father to the Squire and so establish his own tale as the one that would most properly continue the compilational thread initiated by the Knight. This, I think, is how we should interpret the "wordes of the Frankeleyn to the Squier" with which (in some manuscripts) he interrupts the *Squire's Tale*. There, he contrasts the noble Squire with his own son, whose dicing and vice drive him to distraction. The Franklin's stated desire to be the father of a son like the Squire establishes him as structurally analogous to the Knight and thus encourages us to read his tale as a continuation of the *Knight's Tale*'s compilational thread.

The precise diction of the Franklin's *demande* is worth examining in more detail, however, for while evoking that of the *Knight's Tale* it also offers significant contrasts; I quote them side by side for easier comparison:

Yow loveres axe I now this questioun:	Lordynges, this question, thanne, wol I aske now,
Who hath the worse, Arcite or Palamoun?	Which was the mooste fre, as thynketh yow?
That oon may seen his lady day by day,	Now telleth me, er that ye ferther wende.
But in prison he moot dwelle alway;	I kan namoore; my tale is at an ende.
That oother wher hym list may ride or go,	(V.1621–24)
But seen his lady shal he nevere mo.	
Now demeth as yow liste, ye that kan,	
For I wol telle forth as I bigan.	
(I.1347–54)	

The most obvious contrasts are of addressee (lovers vs. *lordynges*, though this last may be conventional, as in *Sir Thopas* [VII.712, 832]) and subject matter (love pains suffered vs. nobility of action performed), but the follow-up to the question itself is equally important. The Knight's last two lines decouple his audience's consideration of the question from his own narrative progress, but the Franklin urges the pilgrims to discuss this issue of *fredom* among themselves "er that ye ferther wende" (V.1623). He thus insists on the applicability of his depiction of courtly imitation to the pilgrims' contemporary polity; this is a teachable moment rather than simply an admirable anecdote or, like the Knight's *demande*, an abstract exercise. Unlike the *Tale of Sir Thopas* (explicitly) and the *Squire's Tale* (implicitly), the *Franklin's Tale* ends by asserting the social relevance not just of courtly imitation but also of something very like literary interpretation. Here and in his tale, the Franklin's rhetorical gambit takes up Fragment I's invitation to construct alternate, imaginative tale threads and thus proposes that, while the particulars of history may rob specific sociocultural forms of their appeal, the broader impulse to textual and literary engagement will endure: not just as an abstract exercise like the Knight's *demande*, but as one vital way of engaging with precisely those complex and shifting historical forces.

Like many a well-meaning pedagogical gambit, the Franklin's exhortation yields no immediate response from his audience. Just as silence in the classroom need not always be the vacuum we abhor, so too the *Tales'* silence here is salutary, for it means that not just the pilgrims' response to the *Franklin's Tale* but also Chaucer's own attitude toward the project that the tale represents remains characteristically, provocatively, and happily open to interpretation. My sense is that the cumulative pessimistic weight of the threads that I have analyzed outbalances the noble gesture embodied by the *Franklin's Tale*, in part because the socially inflected terms in which the Franklin frames his *demande (lordynges, fredom)* threaten to highlight precisely those social insecurities that his tale optimistically supposes collapsable by the social project of courtly imitation. Moreover, evoking the *Knight's Tale* puts the Franklin at risk likewise of recalling the deconstructive ending to Fragment I, specifically in his rueful reflections on his son's addiction to dicing (V.688–91), Perkyn Revelour's favorite activity. The Squire himself does not appear to be a gambler, but he shares enough other traits with Perkyn that this slight echo of the *Cook's Tale*, though ostensibly part of a sharp contrast between the noble Squire and the Franklin's dissipated son, may function rather differently. The Franklin's disingenuousness has already been suggested by his fulsome praise of the Squire's performance, which may further incline us to hear secondary or even opposed meanings from his speeches. Nevertheless, while I have argued strongly for one way of interpreting the *Tales'* involvement with the sociocultural nexus of London and Continental models of courtly performance, I would suggest that the larger goal, here and elsewhere, should not be somehow to reconstruct the past so as to assign the historically correct sociopolitical content to Chaucer's verse; rather, it should be to both enjoy and take seriously the invitation to compilational activity, aesthetic and historical, that the *Tales* presents. After all, it is impossible fully to separate out the historically contextualized arguments that I have presented here from my own historical moment's (and, perhaps, my generation's especial) passion for ironizing or dismissing as callow any seriously presented suggestions of true idealism.

It therefore seems fitting to conclude by recognizing that, whatever the precise terms of the Franklin's *demande* may suggest, his tale's imagination of courtly imitation as a socially potent gesture recalls aspects of Auchinleck's booklet 3, particularly *Sir Degaré* and the "Battle Abbey Roll." In this context, we should recall that, like *Sir Degaré* and two other poems in Auchinleck ("Lai le Freine" and *Sir Orfeo*), the *Franklin's Tale* introduces itself as a Breton lay; indeed, it is this generic association that led Laura Hibbard Loomis to propose that Chaucer knew the Auchinleck manuscript itself.[72] Whether he did or not, it is worth remembering that the delightful absurdity of *Sir Thopas* was not Chaucer's only inheritance from the literature that compilation contains. "Auchinleck romance," which Ralph Hanna argues "Chaucer made every effort to laugh out of the canon," includes not just *Beues* and *Guy* but also *Sir Degaré* and *Sir Orfeo*, so his contention thus seems something of an overstatement.[73] If, as I have argued, a

---

72. See Loomis, "Chaucer and the Breton Lays of the Auchinleck MS." I find Loomis's arguments for the *Franklin's Tale*'s debt to *Sir Orfeo* especially potent.

73. Hanna, *London Literature*, 305.

Knight–Squire–Sir Thopas construction suggests that the "rym I lerned longe agoon" (as Geffrey introduces *Sir Thopas* [VII.709]) is ill equipped to respond productively to contemporary Ricardian culture, then the *Franklin's Tale* offers an alternate tradition, likewise held "in remembraunce" (V.714), to take up and follow. The fairy-tale beauty of that world suggests that Chaucer retained some allegiance to its ideals, however unlikely they were to be realized in the here and now of the *Tales* project as a whole.

Chapter Four

REWRITING THE PAST,
REASSEMBLING THE REALM

The Trentham Manuscript of John Gower

Of all the objects I take up in this book, the Trentham manuscript of works by John Gower most resembles a compilation as traditionally understood: an entire, nearly complete manuscript, rather than (as in the previous chapters) a corpus of manuscripts, a fragmentary subset of a larger manuscript, or a literary text whose self-presentation encourages evolving compilational construction.[1] This conventional appearance is deceptive, however, for Trentham's seemingly straightforward presentation of its author (it is a single-author codex that consistently refers to Gower in detailed and personal terms) and audience (it is universally supposed to have been either presented to or imagined for Henry IV) is substantially complicated by the architectural complexity of the manuscript's codicological form and its texts' evocation of past history. That past is both authorial, since many of Trentham's texts are rewritings or recontextualizations of works from earlier in Gower's career, and political, since its frequent references to the newness of Henry IV's reign cannot help but recall his recently deposed predecessor, Richard II. Like the subjects of my previous three chapters, then, Trentham insists on the relevance of the past to both the present of its construction and the future of its reception. This range of temporalities both encourages and models the retrospective mode of apprehension that will be required most fully to grasp its complex formal blend of the aesthetic and the historical.

---

1. The manuscript is now London, British Library Add. MS 59495, but it retains the sobriquet that it acquired during its long sojourn in aristocratic hands at Trentham Hall.

Another reason to conclude this study with Trentham, and to juxtapose it with the previous chapter's consideration of the *Canterbury Tales*, is that it so thoroughly upends some of the more reductive literary histories that Chaucer has been made to serve: of the triumph of English and genial, secular irony and of the narrowing of medieval England's literature into "Ricardian poetry," with Chaucer typically dominating the other three poets of J. A. Burrow's elegantly realized study (though not, it should be noted, in Burrow's own admirably evenhanded treatment of them).[2] The most extreme versions of these literary histories have now been rejected, but the trilingual mode of Trentham's counterexemplarity deserves particular attention since the linguistic trajectory of Gower's three long poems (from the French *Mirour de l'Omme* to the Latin *Vox Clamantis* to the English *Confessio Amantis*) might be used to support an anglo-triumphalist literary history of England. In fact, Trentham contains just one English text, which takes up only about 20 percent of the manuscript; instead, it makes courtly French literature—*forme-fixe* lyrics like those of the Squire, Franco-Flemish urban *festes*, and the London *puy*—literally central to its broader hopes for social harmony and political renewal, thus revivifying a literary tradition that Chaucer conspicuously declined to extend. By embodying some of the many non-Chaucerian ways in which England's post-Chaucerian literary forms developed

2. J. A. Burrow, *Ricardian Poetry: Chaucer, Gower, Langland, and the "Gawain" Poet* (New Haven, CT: Yale University Press, 1971). I do not mean to suggest either that this narrowing remains widely accepted—it does not—or that our now immensely broader conceptualization of medieval English literature has had universally salutary effects. For evidence of both these propositions, one need but turn to David Wallace, ed., *The New Cambridge History of Medieval English Literature* (Cambridge: Cambridge University Press, 1999). This massive volume includes deserved chapters on such broader topics as writing in Scotland (and Wales and Ireland), Middle English mystics, and post-1400 romance. What it does not include in its more than one thousand pages is a chapter on the *Pearl* poet or, indeed, more than two incidental mentions of *Pearl* itself, one of Middle English literature's most dazzling poetic achievements. This oversight suggests the extent to which the welcome expansion of a scholarly field can inadvertently lead to neglect of some of its most worthy objects of study. This is one reason why the new formalism, which calls for renewed attention to the question of form and the reality of beauty, has the potential to be such an energizing force in medieval studies—as long as it works with and not against the historical consciousness and inclusive spirit so profitably on display throughout Wallace's collection.

and looking back to elements of literary culture from the 1320s and 1330s that we examined in chapters 1 and 2, Trentham valuably reminds us that Chaucer himself need be neither end point nor center of the literary histories we see in medieval England.

Trentham's Forms:
Architectural Symmetry, Ambivalent Design

We can arrive at these broader conclusions, however, only after giving Trentham the detailed attention that it deserves on its own terms, as a collection of works from throughout Gower's career, in all three of his literary languages, that includes the only surviving copy of both *In Praise of Peace* and the *Cinkante Balades*.[3] It directly addresses a newly crowned Henry IV, and the remarkable symmetry of its arrangement of texts and the literary and codicological connections among them give the impression of quite sophisticated design. This impression, coupled with Gower's well-known and much-discussed shift to the Lancastrian cause, encourages us to interpret the manuscript as a celebration of Henry's coronation; and indeed, from as early as the seventeenth century, the only real debate among commentators has been whether Trentham itself was given to Henry or whether it was the plainer draft copy for a now-lost presentation manuscript.[4] Close

---

3. This attention, sadly, it has not generally received, although Siân Echard has recently written a fine account of the manuscript's postmedieval transcription and editorial history in *Printing the Middle Ages* (Philadelphia: University of Pennsylvania Press, 2008), 97–125. She there identifies one key aspect of modern editorial practice that has marginalized Trentham: our tendency to collect shorter texts on linguistic rather than codicological grounds (ibid., 124). Trentham's texts are thus dispersed throughout three of the four volumes of Macaulay's edition of Gower's *Complete Works*, and the fascinating multilingualism of the whole can be apprehended by the modern reader only by using Macaulay's textual notes and introductions (or, of course, by study of the original artifact).

4. The first blank leaf of the manuscript contains a note in the hand of Sir Thomas Fairfax, its owner in the seventeenth century, identifying the compendium as "Sr. John Gower's learned Poems the same booke by himself presented to kinge Edward ye fourth att his Coronation," with *Edward* subsequently corrected to *Henry* and *or before* added above *att*, after which the words *att* and *or* were struck through. G. C. Macaulay points out that Fairfax was unlikely to have trustworthy authority for his claim that Trentham itself was presented to Henry; he thinks it more likely "that this was not the actual presentation copy, but another written

examination of Trentham's overarching structure will establish this strong appearance of design but also the interpretive challenges that arise when we try to pin down that design's precise nature. The contents of the manuscript are listed below.

1. 7 lines of Latin verse addressed to Henry IV ("Electus Christi pie Rex Henrice")
2. 385 lines of English decasyllabic rhyme royal (*In Praise of Peace*)
3. Latin prose link identifying the preceding work as *carmen de pacis commendacione* and naming Gower as author of both it and the following *epistola*
4. 56 lines of Latin verse ("Rex celi deus")
5. 1 3-stanza dedicatory *balade* in French addressing the king by name, followed by Latin (12 lines of verse, 2 lines of prose) and a second, 4-stanza French dedicatory *balade*, also addressing Henry by name
6. 52 French *balades* totaling 1,390 lines, with French incipit and Latin explicit (the *Cinkante Balades*)
7. 36 lines of Latin verse ("Ecce patet tensus," possibly incomplete owing to the loss of 1 folio)
8. The *Traitié pour essampler les amantz marietz*, here missing the first *balade* and a half owing to the loss of 1 folio, but in all other manuscripts consisting of 18 *balades* totaling 385 lines of decasyllabic rhyme royal
9. 17 lines of Latin verse on love and marriage, drawn from lines that follow the *Traitié* in all 10 of its extant manuscripts
10. 12 lines of Latin verse referring to Henry IV ("Henrici quarti primus")

The first point to emerge from this brief résumé is the extent to which the manuscript concerns the newly crowned Henry IV, whom the opening Latin verses directly address. Of the three longest works, *In Praise of Peace* also addresses him by name, and the *Cinkante Balades* is dedicated to him. "Rex celi deus" is a prayer to God on Henry's behalf and fulsomely praises the monarch, who then recurs in the first line of the manuscript's final poem. Given their explicit links to Henry, the

---

about the same time and left in the hands of the author," largely on the grounds of its not being ornate enough. For his entire description of the manuscript, see Gower, *Complete Works*, 1:lxxix–lxxxiii (quotation lxxxi). John H. Fisher argues by contrast that "both the script and initials appear to be up to the standard of the best Gower manuscripts" but does not actually dispute Macaulay's conclusion. See *John Gower: Moral Philosopher and Friend of Chaucer* (New York: New York University Press, 1964), 72. R. F. Yeager likewise concurs with Macaulay, noting that "the manuscript is plain, unlike most royal presentation copies." See further "John Gower's French," in Echard, ed., *A Companion to Gower*, 137–51 (quotation 145).

fact that *In Praise of Peace* and the *Cinkante Balades* are unique to Trentham heightens the sense that this particular object, or one modeled on it, was designed for him.

This impression of design is strengthened by the remarkable symmetry with which the manuscript's texts have been arranged, a pattern that the streamlined list here makes clear.

A. Brief Latin verses addressing Henry
B. 385 lines of vernacular rhyme-royal stanzas, followed by Latin matter (prose explicit and incipit to following text)
C. 56-line Latin poem
D. *Cinkante Balades*, preceded by dedicatory and introductory material in French and Latin, followed by Latin explicit
C'. 36-line Latin poem (possibly incomplete)
B'. 385 lines of vernacular rhyme-royal stanzas (assuming missing material identical to all other manuscript witnesses), followed by Latin matter (17 lines of verse)
A'. Brief Latin verses referring to Henry

The identical length of *In Praise of Peace* and the *Traitié* is remarkable, particularly since they are codicological mirror images of one another, and, while the broader symmetry of the manuscript as a whole is not perfect, it is marked enough to suggest definite effort. So too is the way in which the Latin is woven throughout Trentham, framing it at the beginning and the end (A and A'), and recurring after each major vernacular work as a kind of literary palate cleanser (C and C'). Four of the five main poems, in turn, are further linked by textual matter ranging from simple incipits and explicits to sets of dedicatory verses,[5]

---

5. As we saw in the introduction, the folio that contained the first balade and a half of the *Traitié* has been lost, so we cannot be certain that there was ever a link between it and the preceding "Ecce patet tensus," though the evidence of the rest of the texts in the manuscript would make it surprising if there was not. The *Cinkante Balades* is preceded by two dedicatory balades with Latin verses and prose in between; these verses are themselves a combination of the first eight lines of the "O recolende, bone, pie Rex Henrice" and the brief, four-line "H. aquile pullus." The link between the *Cinkante Balades* and "Ecce patet tensus," by contrast, is a brief explicit: "Expliciunt carmina Iohannis Gower, que Gallice composita Balades dicuntur." *In Praise of Peace*, "Rex celi deus," the Latin prose that links the two poems, and the manuscript's opening "Electus Christi, pie Rex Henrie" are all included in the order in which they appear in Trentham in Gower, *Complete Works*, 3:481–94 (vol. 3 is the second of the two volumes of English works). Similarly, the Latin verses that connect the *Traitié* and "Henrici

suggesting an attempt to unite the manuscript's disparate languages and genres into a coherent whole. Given Gower's history as Lancastrian supporter and Trentham's insistent address to Henry in its opening texts, we can imagine interpreting its multilingual codicological symmetry as an elaborate compliment to the new king: just as Trentham uses Gower's poetry to unite the multiple languages set loose on the world by human pride at Babel, so too will the manuscript's royal recipient reunite his fractious kingdom, undoing the political chaos that Gower so strongly associated with linguistic *divisioun*.[6]

Yet Trentham's codicological form resists such a tidy summary of its propositional content, for other texts and contexts in the manuscript work against a Henrician reading of both parts and whole. "Ecce patet tensus" takes blind Cupid to task for the destructive effects of love—Henry is not mentioned—and the *Traitié* likewise offers no explicit connection with the king. The *Traitié*'s various exempla demonstrate a pointed interest in royal misbehavior that might suggest admonitory content for the newly crowned Henry, but this interpretation seems hard to square with the manuscript's earlier praise of him. We should note, too, that references to the king become thinner and more oblique as the manuscript progresses: its three longest texts go from embedding an address to Henry in the poem itself (*In Praise of Peace*), to sequestering this address outside the text proper in dedicatory matter (*Cinkante Balades*), to finally just offering up historically distant royal figures for moral assessment (*Traitié*). The considerable length of the *Cinkante Balades* means, moreover, that nearly all the numerous direct addresses to the king take place in the first quarter or so of the manuscript. When he recurs at the very end, in "Henrici quarti primus," it is only to measure time: "It was in the first year of the reign of King Henry IV" that Gower went blind, he tells us.[7] Instead

---

quarti primus" are printed immediately following the *Traitié* in ibid., 1:391–92 (vol. 1 contains the French works). These orderings represent two of Macaulay's relatively rare nods to codicological rather than linguistic unity.

6. On this connection, see introduction, n. 55, above.

7. See the edition and translation in John Gower, *John Gower: The Minor Latin Works*, ed. and trans. R. F. Yeager (Kalamazoo, MI: TEAMS and Medieval Institute Publications, 2005),

of the monarch that its early texts addressed, Trentham concludes by emphasizing the author who composed them all: "Henrici quarti primus" includes seven first-person pronouns and six first-person verbs in its just twelve lines, which offer an intimate farewell to writing, and the preceding *Traitié* ends with a dedication that grandiloquently puts Gower in conversation with the entire world rather than just his king.[8] All these facts make it difficult to sustain fully Trentham's initial invitation to read its texts in Henrician terms, and no external confirmation of the manuscript's provenance or recipient exists that would conclusively resolve the matter.[9]

The material state of the manuscript further complicates the situation since, as we briefly considered in the introduction, Trentham has been damaged in two key places. The end of the dedication to the *Cinkante Balades* and the first poem of the sequence proper have been mangled, leaving about one and a half stanzas of each illegible, while the loss of an entire page later in the manuscript has deprived us of the

where it is included as a unique version of "Quicquid homo scribat," the first line of the poem as it appears in Oxford, All Souls College MS 98.

8. "Al universiteé de tout le monde, / Johan Gower ceste Balade envoie" (18.22–23). My citations of both the *Traitié* and the *Cinkante Balades* are from John Gower, *John Gower: The French Balades*, ed. and trans. R. F. Yeager (Kalamazoo, MI: TEAMS and Medieval Institute Publications, 2009), which Yeager was gracious enough to allow me to consult before it went to press. Subsequent citations are given parenthetically in the text. My translations tend closely to track his but are my own throughout unless otherwise noted. I take *universiteé* as even more all inclusive than Yeager's *community*, and so: "To the entirety of all the world / John Gower sends this balade."

9. The contrast with another poetic compilation that has been described as a royal presentation copy is instructive. Bibliothèque Nationale fr. 831 is a collection of works by Froissart, arranged in roughly chronological order, and including introductory and concluding rubrics that identify Froissart as having "made, versified, and ordered" ("fais, dittés et ordonnés") the poems it contains. Since Froissart claims in his *Chronicles* to have presented a compilation of his poetry to Richard II, the manuscript is known to have been in England by the early fifteenth century, and it omits poems included in a largely parallel collection, Bibliothèque Nationale fr. 830, that might have proved politically distasteful to England generally or Richard specifically, Sylvia Huot suggests that "it is possible" that MS 831 could be the volume referred to by Froissart. She nevertheless acknowledges that even this preponderance of evidence, which is collectively stronger than anything in Trentham, "does not prove [the point] conclusively." See *From Song to Book*, 238–41. This example suggests how much more evidence we might want before concluding definitively on the intended or actual audience of the Trentham manuscript.

end of "Ecce patet tensus" (if that poem is in fact incomplete),[10] the first balade and a half of the subsequent *Traitié*, and whatever linking material might once have joined them. The evidence of the scribal hands deepens the ambiguity created by this codicological fragmentation. With two exceptions, all of Trentham's texts were written by Scribe 5 (identified by Malcolm Parkes), who also worked extensively on a number of other Gower compilations.[11] The exceptions are "Ecce patet tensus" and "Henrici quarti primus," which were copied by Parkes's Scribe 10, who wrote two of the final poems in Cotton Tiberius A.iv but otherwise appears in no other Gower manuscripts.[12] Both scribes added various revisions and corrections, but Parkes argues that Scribe 10 added his texts after Scribe 5 had finished his work. This somewhat confounding fact gives Trentham ambiguities reminiscent of those we saw in booklet 3 of the Auchinleck manuscript. Because of his work with other Gower manuscripts, Scribe 5 might seem a plausible candidate for Trentham's architectural mastermind, not unlike Auchinleck's Scribe 1. Despite their relative brevity, however, the two texts copied by Scribe 10 are crucial to the manuscript's symmetrical form, which is one of the main inducements to seek such a mastermind in the first place; if Scribe 5 was uninvolved in their copying, then the manuscript's originating principle presumably lies elsewhere. Scribe 10, however, is sufficiently peripheral to this manuscript in particular and other Gower manuscripts in general that he does not seem a particularly likely candidate either.

We are reminded, in short, that our wealth of data about the Horn corpus of chapter 1 makes it very much the exception that proves the rule; far more usually, as with Trentham, large manuscript compilations offer no such securely identifiable source of author-like meaning.

---

10. Macaulay argues that it is, on the basis of this missing page (Gower, *Complete Works*, 1:lxxx), but this is impossible to know since the poem is unique to Trentham and ends grammatically, if a bit abruptly.

11. Malcolm B. Parkes, "Patterns of Scribal Activity and Revisions of the Text in Early Copies of Works by John Gower," in *New Science out of Old Books: Studies in Manuscripts and Early Printed Books in Honour of A. I. Doyle*, ed. Richard Beadle and A. J. Piper (Aldershot: Ashgate, 1995), 81–121.

12. Ibid., 94.

Trentham becomes a compelling puzzle, however, because its suggestions of purpose (its addresses to Henry IV, its symmetrical arrangement of texts) are too numerous and fundamental to ignore or dismiss as the result of mere chance, but they are sufficiently complicated by literary ambiguity and material uncertainty that we cannot extract from the manuscript a single goal, audience, or agent. Maura Nolan has argued that in situations like these we should not insist on provable authorial or scribal intention but instead "locate intention in the *manuscript*, where it is lodged in the interstices of the various sequences of poems that structure it."[13] This gambit does not simply transfer the author function intact to an inanimate object, for both the inherently collaborative nature of manuscript production and the historical uncertainties surrounding nearly every medieval manuscript ensure that its "intentions," as Nolan puts it, cannot be totalizing or unitary. As it has throughout this book, history of various sorts has a vital role to play here, both in grounding potentially fanciful interpretations and in preventing this approach as a whole from turning into a codicological kind of New Criticism, devoted to beautiful close readings of the interplay of texts in manuscripts without reference to the historical circumstances of either. The histories that will most directly inform my analysis of Trentham are Gower's own authorial history, which the manuscript's texts revise and reimagine at several key points, and his history of shifting, complex relations with royal power.

These histories intersect with particular force in Trentham, for once we abandon a chimerical search for the manuscript's all-knowing architect its overriding concern emerges more clearly: the nature and performance of kingship. This includes but is not limited to Henry's, for the three major texts not addressed to him explicitly—"Rex celi deus," "Ecce patet tensus," and the *Traitié*—all concern royal behavior and misbehavior. "Rex celi deus" prays to the king of its opening words, God, on behalf of the king identified in its incipit as Henry, while its text draws on a section of *Vox Clamantis* that addressed Richard II, Henry's predecessor on the throne; "Ecce patet tensus" depicts

13. Nolan, "Lydgate's Worst Poem," 80.

Cupid as a crowned king (*coronatus*) defined by chaotic and destructive misrule;[14] and the *Traitié* cites a host of misbehaving kings to insist on self-control in love. Underlying this pervasive theme of kingship is the suggestive, chiastic structure created by Trentham's symmetrical codicological form, by which the poems that follow the central *Cinkante Balades* recall their structural counterparts from the first half of the manuscript, but in darker or more ambivalent terms. *In Praise of Peace* is largely laudatory, its hints of disquiet kept mostly below the surface, while its chiastic neother, the *Traitié*, uses the same rhyme-royal stanza to take a darker tone, emphasizing the dire consequences of royal malfeasance. The fulsome praise of King Henry contained in "Rex celi deus," meanwhile, contrasts sharply with the comprehensive denunciation of King Cupid's rule in its codicological mirror image, "Ecce patet tensus." Even the brief initial and concluding Latin verses take part in this pattern. The opening "Electus pie rex Henrice" implies that Henry has inspired the poetry that follows, a suggestion that the next three texts confirm. In "Henrici quarti primus," by contrast, the first year of his reign also marks Gower's farewell to writing. At the beginning of Trentham, Henry inspires poetic production; by its conclusion, his accession is swiftly followed by its permanent cessation.

Even before we engage closely with its any of its individual texts, then, the Trentham manuscript itself offers a version of that excess, a refusal to submit to the denotative, that in the introduction we saw Derek Pearsall, Maura Nolan, and Samuel Otter all persuasively describe as one key aspect of the literary. By celebrating Henry with its early texts, Trentham strongly suggests one kind of purpose; other texts later undercut the impression of that *specific* design, even as the continuing theme of kingship and sophisticated codicological form continue to support the impression of *some sort* of design(s) whose originating source)sources?(nevertheless remains elusive. The pleasurable challenge of sorting through this shifting, complex relation between content, form, and history makes Trentham more than just the material medium of its texts; it becomes an aesthetically compelling work

---

14. For the text and translation, see Gower, *Minor Latin Works*, 40–41. Cupid is described as *ipse coronatus* at line 13.

in its own right. The question then becomes how, in the absence of provable audience or agent, to ground our interpretations of it, and here Gower's authorial history complements Trentham's codicological form. Specifically, I will argue that Trentham's first two texts, those that most explicitly celebrate Henry's accession, rewrite poems from earlier in Gower's career in ways that raise cautionary doubts about that accession. These doubts become most fully legible, however, only when reconsidered in the context of the manuscript as a whole, after a reading of "Ecce patet tensus" and the *Traitié*, which are far more obviously cautionary but also far less explicitly connected with Henry. The manuscript thus crafts at least two different meanings for its first two poems: the largely celebratory explicit content that they would have on a first reading and the darker resonance they acquire only gradually and retrospectively, in conjunction with other texts and other aspects of Gower's career. We are thus reminded once again that compilational meaning emerges only with and across time.

Constructing a New King: Rewriting the Ricardian Past

Gower's revision and rededication of the *Confessio Amantis* to Henry, *comes Derbiae*, is only the most famous instance of the poet's lifelong penchant for rewriting earlier works.[15] A subtler form of rewriting also characterizes Trentham's first two main texts, *In Praise of Peace* and "Rex celi deus." Frank Grady has demonstrated that the first of these

---

15. For a revisionist argument concerning the standard "three recension" narrative of the *Confessio*'s composition, see Wim Lindeboom, "Rethinking the Recensions of the *Confessio Amantis,*" *Viator* 40 (2009): 319–48. For an acute (and slyly humorous) reading of how Gower manipulates and rewrites images of kings in boats in *Vox Clamantis* and *Confessio Amantis*, see Frank Grady, "Gower's Boat, Richard's Barge, and the True Story of the *Confessio Amantis*: Text and Gloss," *Texas Studies in Language and Literature* 44 (2002): 1–15. Other poets also inspired Gower to recast past works; on his use of *cento*, the originally classical practice of constructing a poem out of lines written by earlier famous poets, see Eve Salisbury, "Remembering Origins: Gower's Monstrous Body Poetic," in *Re-Visioning Gower*, ed. R. F. Yeager (Asheville, NC: Pegasus, 1998), 159–84; and R. F. Yeager, *John Gower's Poetic: The Search for a New Arion* (Woodbridge: D. S. Brewer, 1990), 52–60, and "Did Gower Write Cento?" in *John Gower: Recent Readings*, ed. R. F. Yeager (Kalamazoo, MI: Medieval Institute Publications, 1989), 113–32.

returns to and reverses the opposition between Solomon and Alexander found in book 7 of the *Confessio*, where Alexander was presented as a model of philosophically enlightened governance and Solomon condemned for lustful idolatry. *In Praise of Peace*, by contrast, distinguishes between Solomon, who "ches wisdom unto the governynge / Of goddis folk" and thereby "gat him pees" (lines 31–32, 35), and Alexander, who is introduced in the next stanza with the adversative *Bot* (line 36) and achieves his mythic status by war and conquest. Grady argues that Gower steps back at the last moment and, rather than "condemning Alexander, choos[es] instead to indict the world in which he existed, as if it deserved to be subdued and conquered."[16] Yet so stark a reversal of the roles that they played in the *Confessio* (likewise a poem ultimately dedicated to Henry of Lancaster) nevertheless forces the reader of Trentham to think long and hard about the ramifications both of Gower's cautionary use of Alexander here and of the fact that the hero of one poem could so abruptly become the villain of the other.

Indeed, Gower's suggestion that Alexander's pagan world deserved conquest, in contrast with the "pite and grace" that Christians deserve from their princes (line 52), somewhat exculpates Alexander but even more deeply condemns Henry, should he follow such an example in his own Christian era. The *bot* that opened the stanza introducing Alexander is the first word of the next two stanzas as well, grammatically establishing the adversative as a central thematic in the poem as a whole, by which any affirmative statement can be instantly qualified, withdrawn, rewritten. The stanzas following those that introduce Alexander offer a wealth of examples:

> It sit hem [Christian princes] wel to do pite and grace;
> *Bot* yit it mot be tempred in manere.
>
> So mai a kyng of werre the viage
> Ordeigne and take . . .
> *Bot* other wise if god himsilve wolde . . .
> Pes is the beste above alle erthely thinges.

---

16. Frank Grady, "The Lancastrian Gower and the Limits of Exemplarity," *Speculum* 70 (1995): 552–75 (quotation 563).

> Thus stant the lawe, that a worthi knyght
> Uppon his trouthe may go to the fight;
> *Bot* if so were that he myghte chese,
> Betre is the pees, of which may no man lese.
> (lines 52–53, 57–63, 67–70)

These passages all allude to the fact that political idealism is subject to revision by practical realities. Grady notes the adversatives that here enact that revision but argues that Gower forestalls the "implicit and dangerous analogy between Macedonian conquest and Lancastrian usurpation . . . by plunging ahead on the theme of peace" and delaying the next adversative *bot* for some ten stanzas, by which time "the poem has safely established some momentum away from the vortex of this stanza [lines 64–70]."[17] Gower cannot, however, so readily elide the larger and more daunting reality that his early use of the word *bot* suggests: just as any clear-cut statement can be undone by a simple adversative construction, so too the contrasting examples of Solomon and Alexander in the *Confessio* and *In Praise of Peace* demonstrate that a once idealized ruler can be textually deposed by subsequent rewriting.

In this context, the poem's generally simplistic "praise of peace" (e.g., "The werre is modir of the wronges alle" [line 106]) cannot be taken at face value because, as we saw in the *bot*-infused passages cited above, Gower has begun the poem as a meditation on the tension between moral idealism and political reality, giving neither a chance to triumph completely; a similar *bot* therefore lurks behind the clear-cut statements of lines 71–133, waiting to undo them. And, sure enough, the word returns later to qualify similarly straightforward principles:

> Aboute a kyng good counseil is to preise
> Above alle othre thinges most vailable;
> *Bot yit* a kyng withinne himself schal peise,
> And se the thinges that ben resonable. . . .
>
> Ha, wel is him that schedde nevere blod,
> *Bot* if it were in cause of rihtwisnesse.
> (lines 141–44, 148–49)

17. Ibid., 565.

Later in the poem the word clusters so thickly that it threatens to undermine the explicit meaning of the text, as in the following passage:

> *Bot* if the men withinne hemself be veine,
> The substance of the pes may noght be trewe,
> *Bot* every dai it chaungeth uppon newe.
>
> *Bot* who that is of charite parfit. . . .
> (lines 313–16)

The *bot*'s of lines 313 and 315 enclose and thus highlight the pessimistic statement of line 314, and, while line 316 attempts to start a new stanza with a contrast that leaves this pessimism behind, its initial *bot* connects it both to the preceding stanza and to that word's thematization of abrupt reversals and subtle qualifications of seemingly straightforward commonplaces about good governance. The cumulative effect of this repetition is that, when *bot* shows up twice in close proximity to Henry near the end of the poem,[18] it is tinged with the ambivalence it has acquired over the course of the work as a whole.

This ambivalence is hardly overpowering. *Bot* is a sufficiently common word that it would be easy to ignore hints of deeper significance in it; the reversal of the Alexander/Solomon dichotomy, while striking, relies for its effect on the reader's familiarity with the antecedent in *Confessio Amantis*, and these elements could be easily drowned out by the generally laudatory tone of the whole, set by the introductory Latin verses and straightforwardly celebratory opening stanzas. The cautionary undertones of *In Praise of Peace* are therefore sufficiently subtle that they require a substantial level of active apprehension from the reader. They thus begin the Trentham manuscript's gradual construction of ambivalent patterns whose initial outlines—a fraught conjunction, a rewritten comparison—seem significant, and potentially threatening, only in retrospect. Here, those outlines suggest a recognition that, whatever our idealistic wishes, the possibility re-

---

18. "*Bot* evere y hope of King Henries grace / That he it is which schal the pes embrace" (lines 272–73); "Noght only to my king of pes y write, / *Bot* to these othre princes cristne alle" (lines 379–80).

mains that Henry's reign will slide off in the other direction: not peace but war; not ancestry or acclamation or any of the other Lancastrian claims alluded to in the poem's opening stanzas,[19] but conquest like Alexander's, pure and simple.

The role of "Rex celi deus" in this process of gradually ambivalent rewriting is suggested by the explicit and incipit that link it with *In Praise of Peace*:

> Explicit carmen de pacis commendacione, quod ad laudem et memoriam serenissimi principis domini Regis Henrici quarti suus humilis orator Iohannes Gower composuit. Et nunc sequitur epistola, in qua idem Iohannes pro statu et salute dicti domini sui apud altissimum devocius exorat.

> Here ends the poem about the excellence of peace, which in praise and memory of the most serene prince of God, King Henry IV, his humble orator John Gower composed. And now follows an epistle, in which with the highest devotion the same John entreats for the health and well-being of his said lord.[20]

The incipit to "Rex celi deus" in other manuscripts fails to identify Gower as author,[21] whereas Trentham not only does so but also emphasizes the identity of the John who writes (*idem Iohannes*) and the Henry being written of (*dicti domini sui*) in the two linked texts. These identifications of Gower and Henry, moreover, depend on the first sentence, the explicit to *In Praise of Peace* that initially identifies them. These two sentences thus present the two poems as parallel efforts, implying that their strategic rewritings are likewise parallel. "Rex celi deus," moreover, suggests a significantly more threatening binary than

19. For an overview both of the various claims put forth by Lancastrians in favor of Henry's accession and of how those claims find expression in literary texts, including *In Praise of Peace*, see Paul Strohm, "Saving the Appearances: Chaucer's *Purse* and the Fabrication of the Lancastrian Claim," in *Chaucer's England: Literature in Its Historical Context*, ed. Barbara Hanawalt (Minneapolis: University of Minnesota Press, 1992), 21–40.

20. Gower, *Complete Works*, 2:492.

21. See, e.g., the All Souls manuscript, which reads: "Here follows a poem by which our magnificent King Henry, singled out by God and men with every blessing, will be glorified" ("Sequitur carmen unde magnificus rex noster Henricus prenotatus apud Deum et homines cum omni benediccione glorificetur"). See further Gower, *Minor Latin Works*, 42–43.

the Solomon/Alexander one of *In Praise of Peace*: Henry/Richard.[22]
The technique here is different, however, for "Rex celi deus" gains its
initial force precisely by declining to rewrite: its first eight lines are
exactly the same as those that open 6.xviii of the earliest version of
Vox Clamantis, the one most kindly disposed to Richard. The praise
of Henry in Trentham thus recalls the fact that Gower once prayed,
for example, that "it be granted to you, O king [Richard], always to
hold the honored scepter firmly in your hand during our lifetime"
or that "He Who gave you [Richard] your first realms [should] give
you assurance of your future realms."[23] That these lines appear almost
unchanged in "Rex celi deus" suggests the contingent nature of the
poem's praise of Henry,[24] particularly since Gower substantially re-
wrote this entire chapter in subsequent versions of the *Vox*, replacing
them with much sterner admonitions to wise rulership. What happened to Richard could, in theory, happen to Henry.

Indeed, the epistle in the *Vox* from which "Rex celi deus" derives
addresses Richard merely as "our king now reigning at present" (head-
note to 6.viii), and "Rex celi deus," too, nowhere explicitly names
Henry as the king being praised; we have to read the incipit to discover his identity. This fact emphasizes the importance of Trentham's
codicological links between texts by making the manuscript itself, no
less than its "main texts," key to those texts' meanings. More broadly,
the refusal of "Rex celi deus" to name the new king explicitly and the
decision to recycle praise of an earlier, now deposed monarch emphasize both the transience of royal power and the ultimate instability of
subjects' loyalty. The revised *Vox* states explicitly that, "if you turn
yourself strictly to your own affairs, then the people which should be

---

22. For a fascinating exploration of how this binary works in the repeated letters, *R* and
H, by which the two kings are known at the end of the *Cronica Tripertita*, see Robert Epstein,
"Literal Opposition: Deconstruction, History, and Lancaster," *Texas Studies in Literature and
Language* 44 (2002): 16–33.

23. "O tibi, Rex, euo detur, fortissime, nostro / Semper honorata ceptra tenere manu"
(6.1175–76); "Qui tibi prima dedit, confirmet Regna futuri" (6.1187). Quotations of the *Vox
Clamantis* are taken from vol. 4 of Gower's *Complete Works* and are cited by book and line number parenthetically in the text.

24. *Vox Clamantis* 6.1159–98. R. F. Yeager makes a suggestion similar to my argument here.
See Gower, *Minor Latin Works*, 72.

yours will turn itself away."[25] Far from condemning such behavior as disloyal fickleness, as we might expect, Gower implies that kings who cannot maintain the people's loyalty have only themselves to blame. By transferring praise of Richard to Henry, moreover, he suggests that similar shifts are possible in the future as well—but in that case Henry would be the dispossessed party. As with *In Praise of Peace*, this ambivalence is subtle and relies on knowledge of the text being alluded to and its then addressee, so I do not claim that "Rex celi deus" demands or even encourages this interpretation on a first reading. It gains cumulative force by being juxtaposed with *In Praise of Peace*, however, and through its links to that poem in the explicit/incipit that we considered above.

The *Cinkante Balades*, which follows "Rex celi deus," is Trentham's central and longest text, and it immediately presents interpretive challenges, not least because *forme-fixe* love poetry is a genre of highly conventional themes and images, making broader sociocultural significance hard to establish.[26] Fortunately, Trentham's first two texts' subtle evocations of Gower's authorial past offer a key way of grappling with the *Cinkante Balades*, for the French lyrics likewise rewrite the poet's authorial history as Gower himself has twice represented it. As early as the *Mirour de l'Omme*, he describes such "fols ditz d'amours" as the product of a misspent youth:

> Jadis trestout m'abandonoie
> Au foldelit et veine joye,
> Dont ma vesture desguisay
> Et les fols ditz d'amours fesoie,
> Dont en chantant je carolloie
> Mais ore je m'aviseray
> En tout cela je changeray,
> Envers dieu je supplieray

25. "Si tamen econtra rigidus tua verteris acta, / Vertet se populous qui solet esse tuus" (6.1197–98).

26. Ardis Butterfield discovers in such lyrics' penchant for citation, translation, and intertextuality a powerful way of reading key moments in the *Cinkante Balades* that draws on English, Anglo-French, and French texts. See *The Familiar Enemy: Chaucer, Language, and Nation in the Hundred Years War* (Oxford: Oxford University Press, 2009), 238–68.

> Q'il de sa grace me convoie;
> Ma conscience accuseray,
> Un autre chançon chanteray,
> Que jadys chanter ne soloie.[27]

This passage precedes the life of the Virgin that concludes the *Mirour*, so it is possible to interpret its many future-tense verbs as referring only to the current poem. But, combined with Gower's later and far more famous leave-taking from love in the *Confessio* (8.3138–72), it suggests that, whenever it was originally written, the *Balades* as presented in Trentham represents a return to the literary and personal past. In the dedication to the *Cinkante Balades*, however, Gower emphasizes the newness and nowness of this gesture. After two stanzas praising the king, he writes:

> Vostre oratour et vostre humble vassal,
> Vostre Gower, q'est trestout vos soubgitz,
> Puisq'ore avetz receu le coronal,
> Vous frai service autre que je ne fis,
> Ore en balade, u sont les ditz floriz,
> Ore en vertu, u l'alme ad son corage:
> Q'en dieu se fie, il ad bel avantage.[28]

The first two *ore*'s suggest an equivalence between the newness of Henry's kingship and that of Gower's poetic effort. The allusion to present service recalls Gower's earlier dedication of the *Confessio* to Henry, so at its most literal this anaphoric *ore* simply analogizes the difference between King Henry and Henry *comes Derbiae* and the literary works addressed to each. While it may be literally true that Gower has never before written love poetry for Henry, however, line 18's

---

27. *Mirour de l'Omme*, lines 27337–49: "Once I entirely abandoned myself to foolish pleasure and vain joy, with which I adorned my appearance, and I made foolish poems of love to which I danced while singing. But now I will take counsel and change in all this; I will pray to God that He send me his grace; I will rebuke my conscience and sing a different song, which I have not in the past tended to sing."

28. Dedicatory balade 1.15–21: "He who prays for you and is your humble vassal, / Your Gower, who is entirely your subject, / Since now you have received the crown, / I do you a service different from what I have done before, / Now in *balade*, where poetry's flower resides, / Now in virtue, where the soul has its heart: / Whoever trusts in God has the best of it."

insistence that the forthcoming offering marks a break with the past ignores the fact that, within Gower's own authorial history, love poetry is the very genre that the poet has twice foresworn. The *Cinkante Balades* is a return to the past that presents itself as wholly new.

Each of Trentham's first three texts thus has an important antecedent in Gower's authorial history: reversed exempla (*In Praise of Peace*), readdressed political praise ("Rex celi deus"), or renewed generic activity (the love poetry of the *Cinkante Balades*). Moreover, Gower draws attention to this contrast between past and present elsewhere in the dedicatory balades:

> Noz coers dolentz par vous sont *rejois*;
> Par vous, bons Roys, nous susmes enfranchis,
> Q'ainçois sanz cause fuismes en servage. . . .
>
> Ensi le bon amour q'estre soloit
> El temps jadis de nostre ancesserie,
> Ore entre nous *recomencer* om doit
> Sanz mal pensier d'ascune vileinie.[29]

The repeated *re-* words (*rejois*, *recomencer*) emphasize that Henry is merely and properly restoring the good things his subjects have recently (i.e., under Richard) been denied. Inasmuch as Gower's choice of genre recalls his own earlier depictions of his authorial history, we can see the outlines of a still more elaborate compliment: that, in addition to returning his kingdom to an idealized past of freedom and "bon amour," Henry's accession has reversed the inexorable process of age that left Gower an absurd *senex amans* at the end of the *Confessio*, enabling the poet at the dawn of the fifteenth century to take up once more the poetry of his youth in order to "desporter vo noble Court roia[l]."[30]

---

29. Dedicatory balade 1.5–6: "Our grieving hearts are *rejoiced* by you; / By you, good King, we are freed, / Who before, without cause, were in servitude." Dedicatory balade 2.21–24: "And so we should *begin again*, between us, the good love that used to exist in the former time of our ancestors—without a wicked thought of any villainy" (emphasis added).

30. Dedicatory balade 2.27: "To entertain your noble roya[l] Court." After receiving his letter in the *Confessio*, Venus tells Gower that he must "remembre wel hou thou art old" (8.2439). It is, however, only her later production of a mirror, which leads to a devastatingly

Nor are these allusions to and revisions of Gower's authorial history the only connections among Trentham's first three texts; the dedicatory material to the *Balades* creates others. Gower's characterization of himself as the king's *oratour* in the passage we considered earlier (dedicatory balade 1.15) echoes *suus humilis orator*, the term used for him in the explicit/incipit between *In Praise of Peace* and "Rex celi deus." Even Trentham's brief, opening "Electus Christi, pie Rex Henrice" is echoed by later works; its initial characterization of the king as "pie Rex" is taken up repeatedly by "Rex celi deus," where the epithet describes Henry five times in the poem's fifty-five lines.[31] These Latin poems are also thick with the *re-* verbs of renewal and rejoicing that we saw in the passages from the *Cinkante Balades* cited above.[32] Collectively, these instances draw attention to how "minor" introductory and dedicatory texts inform the larger works that they surround and link; their subtle poetics of assemblage further encourages reading Trentham as a meaningfully constructed object.

What remains is to consider how, as constructed to this point, Trentham associates the seemingly dissimilar themes it treats: of politics and a Henrician restoration in *In Praise of Peace* and "Rex celi deus" and of love and *desport* in the *Cinkante Balades*. The echoes of phrasing and vocabulary that we considered above offer a generalized invitation to connect these two realms, but the anaphoric passage that we have already briefly considered constitutes a more pointed one:

> Puisq'ore avetz receu le coronal,
> Vous frai service autre que je ne fis,
> Ore en balade, u sont les ditz floriz,
> Ore en vertu, u l'alme ad son corage:
> Q'en dieu se fie, il ad bel avantage.

---

exhaustive antiblason of the poet's decrepitude (8.2820–33), that finally convinces Gower to abandon the posture and the poetry of courtly love.

31. Lines 10, 21, 33, 51, 55. By contrast, Henry is described as "rex ... fortissime" (line 41) and plain "rex" (line 30) just once each, which makes "pie Rex" by far the poem's favorite term for the king, whom, as we saw above, the poem never addresses by name.

32. Two of the seven lines of "Electus Christi, pie Rex Henrice" end with *re-* verbs: *restituisti* (line 3) and *renovata* (line 5). Such verbs occur six times in just the first twenty-eight lines of "Rex celi deus" (lines 13, 15, 18, 19, 22, 28).

O gentil Rois, ce que je vous escris
Ci ensuant ert de perfit langage,
Dont en latin ma sentence ai compris:
Q'en dieu se fie, il ad bel avantage.[33]

The third *ore* links Henry's coronation, Gower's offering of love poetry, and a concern for virtue that echoes the themes of *In Praise of
Peace* and "Rex celi deus." This connection then leads into the envoy,
which draws attention to the multilingualism of the dedicatory material, encouraging us to read the entirety of that material—French
poems, Latin verses, and Latin prose—as a single authorial gesture
("ce que *je* vous escris . . . en latin *ma* sentence *ai* compris"). These
connections are significant because the intercalated Latin material is
emphatically political and thus connects the amatory *Cinkante Balades*
that it introduces with the preceding poems in the manuscript.[34] Like
"Electus Christi, pie Rex Henrice" and "Rex celi deus," these lines
address Henry as "pie Rex" (line 1); like *In Praise of Peace*, they urge
him to seek peace ("pacem compone" [line 5]). These lines allude to
the deliverance from Egypt, the sacred anointing oil of Saint Thomas
Becket, and prayers drawn from the Psalms that the people will "live
under the rule of reason" and that Henry will "moderate the powers
of the crown."[35]

None of this Latin in the least suggests the elegant love poetry
that follows, yet its presence in the manuscript is obtrusive, abruptly
changing the language, verse form, images, and tone of the first dedicatory balade, which has nevertheless presented this Latin as Gower's

---

33. Dedicatory balade 1.15–25: "He who prays for you and your humble vassal, / Your
Gower, who is entirely your subject, / Since now you have received the crown, / I do you a
service different from what I have done before, / Now in *balade*, where poetry's flower resides, /
Now in virtue, where the soul has its heart: / Whoever trusts in God has the best of it. / Oh
gentle king, this which I write for you— / What follows here uses polished language, / Whose
message I have written in Latin: / Whoever trusts in God has the best of it."

34. The Latin is an odd mixture: the first eight lines of "O recolende, bone, pie Rex
Henrice," followed by the four-line "H. aquile pullus" and a two-sentence prayer, in prose,
offering a further prayer for Henry's health and success. The whole is included in Gower,
French Balades, 56–59.

35. These references are at lines 2, 11, 4 ("vivant sub racione"), and 5 ("vires moderare
corone"), respectively. The quotations are from the Vulgate, Psalms 88:23 and 40:3.

own speech. We then shift, equally abruptly, back to the French balade form and the vocabulary of "bon amour" of the following, second dedicatory poem. Like the Trentham manuscript as a whole, then, the codicological form of the *Cinkante Balades* and its dedication offers a strong initial impression of design while presenting discontinuities that make that design hard to pin down. Here, however, the lexicon of virtue shared by both courtly love speech and political discourse offers an interpretively helpful tangent point. The Latin praised Henry, "than whom no one is more gracious" ("quo nunquam gracior ullus" [line 9]), and the French likewise identifies God as having imbued "Henri le quarte . . . de grace especial" (dedicatory balade 2.2–3). The Latin's general emphasis on moral and political rectitude, combined with this sort of direct echo, enables us to read the dedicatory balades' explicit and insistent focus on virtue (long lists open the first poem and close the second)[36] as suggesting a greater relevance for the following *Cinkante Balades* than mere *desport*.

   This suggestion is significant because we will see that, even taking into account the generic expectation of intense erotic lament over the instability of love and sudden shifts of fortune, the balades themselves present striking discontinuities of tone, narrative, and persona. I suggested earlier that we might read Gower's representation of his return to love poetry as a complimentary gesture to Henry on the personally rejuvenating effects of the king's *renovatio imperii*. The discontinuities in the *Cinkante Balades* proper, however, suggest another possible interpretation. If we read these fissures in the context of the dedication's concern with virtue, its normally distinct courtly and political associations blurred by that material's juxtaposition of the two discourses, their effects are reminiscent of the ambivalent authorial revisions that we saw earlier with *In Praise of Peace* and "Rex celi deus"; that is, they subtly call into doubt the most purely celebratory attitude toward Henry's accession. As with Trentham's first two texts, there are plenty

---

36. "Pité, prouesse, humblesse, honour roial" (dedicatory balade 1.1: "Mercy, prowess, humility, regal honor"). "Honour, valour, victoire et bon esploit, / Joie et saunté, puissance et seignurie" (dedicatory balade 2.33–34: "Honor, valor, victory, and good success, / Joy and health, power and lordship").

of reasons not to take up this darker interpretation: here, the conventionality of the genre and subject matter, which makes the interpretation of any larger significance, including the political, difficult to substantiate. My argument therefore is not that this is the only or the correct way, then or now, of reading the balades themselves. Rather, it is that Trentham's codicological form, its juxtaposition of poems and intervening material and the echoes among them, is gradually offering an alternate, more cautionary way of understanding poems of both political praise and courtly *desport*.

Narrative Structure in the *Cinkante Balades*: Juxtaposition and Reversal

I have space here to discuss only a few of the many delights and complexities offered by the *Cinkante Balades*, but even this truncated analysis requires a brief résumé of the narrative arc that the sequence suggests.[37] The male lover laments his lady's inaccessibility and attacks the scandalmakers who are damaging her reputation. He eventually absents himself from her in order to preserve her honor but then reproaches her for infidelity. She makes the same charge against him, but they are reconciled at the end of the sequence, which concludes with generalized thoughts on love and an address to the Virgin. Many of these plot elements are conventional, yet the whole adds up to something considerably stranger and more interesting than this brief summary would suggest. The sequence is marked by odd silences and discontinuities, the most striking of which is the shift in the lady's tone between balades 43 and 44. Balade 43 concludes a set of three poems excoriating the lover's faithlessness, which she denounces as worse even than Jason's to Medea or Aeneas's to Dido. Yet the very next poem, also written in a female voice, praises him (or some male

---

37. Yeager has argued that the *Cinkante Balades* has "a narrative unity, even a chronology, traceable through references to feast days and seasonal changes over the course of two or three years" ("John Gower's French," 146). I find this metanarrative both less consistently apparent and less coherent than does Yeager, but he is nevertheless right to emphasize its general contours.

figure, at least) as "vailant, courtois, gentil et renomée / Loyal, verrai, certain de vo promesse."[38] The shift is striking and sudden enough to prompt wry, antifeminist commentary by Macaulay (we are informed that the "startling abruptness" with which she changes her mind represents "the prerogative of her sex"),[39] while R. F. Yeager feels it necessary to propose that a second, worthier lover has here taken the place of the first.[40]

How significant we judge this and other, comparable discontinuities to be to the Henrician context that Trentham's opening texts have established will depend largely on how inclined we are to read the *Cinkante Balades'* representations of erotic virtue and constancy, deceit and treachery, in social or political terms. One of the text's only substantive codicological features, which occurs early in the sequence, encourages us to ponder precisely this issue of the balades' deeper significance; two marginal glosses to balades 5 and 6, respectively, read:

> Les balades d'amont jesques enci sont fait especialement pour ceaux q'attendont lours amours par droite mariage.

> Les balades d'ici jesqes au fin du livere sont universeles a tout le monde, selonc les propretés et les condicions des Amantz, qui sont diversement travailez en la fortune d'amour.[41]

Written in the same hand and with the same decoration as the balades themselves, these glosses are presented by the manuscript as integral to the poems that they comment on.[42] What they suggest, however,

---

38. Balade 44.1–2: "valiant, courteous, honorable and renowned, / Loyal, true, unwavering in your promise."

39. Gower, *Complete Works*, 1:lxvii.

40. Gower, *French Balades*, 49.

41. "The balades from the beginning up to this point are made especially for those who wait on their loves in expectation of rightful marriage; the balades from here until the end of the book are universal, for everyone, according to the properties and conditions of Lovers who are diversely suffering the fortunes of Love" (Gower, *French Balades*, 134).

42. The initial letter of the first margin note is gold, that of the second blue; this is the same pattern that predominates for the balades, all of which have an initial gold letter that usually (though not always, e.g., balades 12 and 21) alternates with blue. On the importance of marginal glosses to Gower's work and the *Confessio* in particular, see Siân Echard, "Gower's 'bokes

is distinctly odd. Only the first six poems,[43] we are told, celebrate the kind of love that looks forward to marriage for its ultimate fulfillment; the remaining, far greater number address the many vicissitudes endured by those under *la fortune d'amour*. This trajectory—away from the legally permanent and divinely sanctioned love of marriage and into the fortune-tossed seas of courtly wooing—contrasts sharply with the emphasis on stability, law, and virtue that we saw in the dedicatory material preceding the *Cinkante Balades*. It also runs counter to the trajectory of the manuscript as a whole, in which the courtly wooing of the *Cinkante Balades* is followed by the condemnation, in "Ecce patet tensus," of the destructiveness of blind Cupid and then by the *Traitié*'s defense of that very marital love that the *Balades* begins by briefly exploring, then casts aside. Of course, for this very reason it is possible to read the trajectory as a whole as rationalizing and minimizing the disjunction provided by these two margin notes. Nonetheless, in the course of reading the balades sequentially (which their metanarrative and their numbering in the manuscript encourage us to do), we experience the strangeness of a movement from marriage to courtly love.

Still odder, the reference to *droite mariage* grafts onto the first six balades a significance that they themselves nowhere make explicit or even particularly suggest. To be sure, in them the narrator promises his lady constancy and loyal love, which could in theory be taken as describing the permanent and holy bonds of marriage. But these terms are even more characteristic of courtly love discourse, and the first six poems also feature plenty of the pain-as-sweetness/sweetness-as-pain language that typifies such *forme-fixe* expression and emphatically resists association with marriage:

---

of Latin': Language, Politics, and Poetry," *Studies in the Age of Chaucer* 25 (2003): 123–56, and "With Carmen's Help: Latin Authorities in the *Confessio Amantis*," *Studies in Philology* 95 (1998): 1–40; Ardis Butterfield, "Articulating the Author: Gower and the French Vernacular Codex," *Yearbook of English Studies* 33 (2003): 80–96; and Pearsall, "Gower's Latin."

43. The manuscript marks two adjacent balades *4*, so "balade *5*" is actually the sixth in the sequence.

D'ardant desire celle amorouse peigne
Mellé d'espoir me fait languir en joie;
Dont par dolçour sovent jeo me compleigne
Pour vous, ma dame, ensi com jeo soloie.[44]

Although this poem's refrain, "en attendant que jeo me reconforte,"
does pick up the lexicon of waiting from the first marginal gloss,[45]
the vocabulary of this passage and the poem as a whole is such that
only the most stubbornly ascetic reader would conclude that it's marriage for which the narrator is burning. The codicological form of
the *Cinkante Balades'* opening thus implausibly claims that very different interpretive contexts apply to these poems that look initially like
straightforward representatives of their genre.

The second marginal gloss attempts to shut down that disconnect
between apparent and deeper significance by reassuring us that the remaining, substantial majority of the balades are, in fact, just what they
appear: poems about the travails of lovers and the fortunes of love. But
the first gloss's introduction of extratextual meaning is not so easily
forgotten since the supposed marriage balades do not sound markedly
different from those that follow. The effect of these glosses, I think, is
to make us read the *Cinkante Balades* as a whole more actively and more
skeptically than the conventionality of its theme and expression might
otherwise encourage. After all, if we are told that the opening poems of courtly *desport* actually signify something quite different, even
though they seem broadly similar to those that the manuscript insists
are, in fact, just what they appear, then the arbitrariness of that distinction and the initial encouragement to read for more than outward content are likely to make us suspect the later poems, too, of containing
some other or deeper meaning. In this spirit, I read three of the most
arresting moments in the sequence: the reappearance of one line from
the dedicatory balades as the refrain to balade 21; the bizarre about-face

---

44. Balade 3.1–4: "This loving punishment of burning desire / Mingled with hope sickens
me with joy: / Thus from sweetness often I complain / On your account, my lady—just so
am I accustomed."

45. "Awaiting the time when I shall be comforted." Compare the vocabulary of the first
marginal gloss: "Les balades d'amont jesques enci sont fait especialement pour ceaux *q'attendont*
lours amours par droite mariage" (emphasis added).

of the lady toward her courtly lover alluded to earlier; and the final five poems' attempts to define love, which raise again the glosses' contrast between "amours par droite mariage" and "la fortune d'amour."

The first of these moments offers us yet another instance of Gower's penchant for self-echoing: "sanz mal pens(i)er d'ascune vileinie" is both the refrain of balade 21 and the twenty-fourth line of the second dedicatory balade.[46] Gower's lover persona is thus making the same address to his courtly lady that earlier, as poet, he made to his newly crowned sovereign. In itself, the echo is not so surprising since, as we have seen, the discourses of politics and courtly love share a lexicon of virtue (e.g., *mal pensier, vileinie*). It does, however, constitute a further invitation to link the balades themselves to their dedicatory material, whose French-Latin-French structure conjoined political with amatory discourse, and which also linked the *Cinkante Balades* to the explicitly political *In Praise of Peace* and "Rex celi deus." If we take up this invitation to look outward for the *Balades'* significance, an invitation first made by the marginal glosses we just considered, then we find other similarities between the dedicatory material and balade 21, as this comparison suggests:

Vostre oratour et vostre humble vassal,	Au solail, **qe les herbes eslumine**
Vostre Gower, q'est *trestout vos soubgitz*,	**Et fait florir**, jeo fai comparisoun
Puisq'ore avetz receu le coronal,	De celle q'ad dessoutz sa discipline
<u>Vous frai service</u> autre que je ne fis,	Mon coer, mon corps, mes sens, et ma resoun

46. Dedicatory balade 2.24 and balade 21, refrain: "Without a wicked thought of any villainy." Yeager adds variation to the refrain in his translation by rendering *vileinie* variously as *vulgarity, wickedness, deceit,* and *degradation,* but the word remains the same throughout in the original (as of course it must, being part of a refrain). He also translates *penser* in balade 21 as a noun ("without wicked thought of any *vileinie*"), and *pensier* in the dedicatory poem as a verb ("without thinking *vileinie* of any"). But *pensier* can just as easily be a noun (the orthographic difference between *penser* and *pensier* is not lexically significant), and it works better understood as such. For one thing, this allows *ascune* to be an adjective modifying *vileinie* (as in balade 21), instead of a substantive that *vileinie* must look backward to—a considerably more awkward option. It is also thoroughly typical of Gower's career-long penchant for strategic revising and self-echoing, which we have already seen Trentham exploit in its first two texts.

Ore en balade, **u sont les ditz**
   floriz,
Ore en vertu, u l'alme ad son
   corage:
Q'en dieu se fie, il ad bel avantage.

Par fin amour *trestout a sa bandoun*:
Et servirai de bon entencioun,
Sanz mal penser d'ascune vileinie.[47]

These and other, comparable similarities of phrasing and image that I
could quote are sufficiently conventional that individually they do not
support much interpretive weight. Collectively, however, and in the
contexts of the repeated "Sanz mal penser" line, of Trentham's insistent focus on politics generally and Henry specifically to this point, and
of the marginal glosses' initial invitation to read the balades in terms
of other, essentially extratextual interpretive programs, they suggest
that the "bon amour" promised by the *Cinkante Balades* in some way
reflects the political harmony that Lancastrian partisans hoped would
result from Henry's accession.

    Balade 21 particularly engages the reader's attention, moreover, be-
cause it reverses with striking suddenness the images and tenor of the
preceding balade. That poem laments Fortune's unceasing hostility to
the narrator, which he claims belies the adage that her wheel is always
turning (20.1–4). This perverse constancy defies the natural processes
of change that he observes elsewhere:

> Apres la guerre om voit venir la pes,
> Apres l'ivern est l'estée beal flori,
> Mais mon estat ne voi changer jammes.[48]

---

47. Dedicatory balade 1.15–21: "He who prays for you and is your humble vassal, / Your
Gower, who is entirely your subject, / Since now you have received the crown, / I do you a
service different from what I have done before, / Now in *balade*, where poetry's flower resides, /
Now in virtue, where the soul has its heart: / Whoever trusts in God has the best of it." Balade
21.1–7: "To the sunshine that shines on the plants / And makes them flower, I compare / The
one who has under her control / My heart, my body, my sense and my reason. / Because of
the pure love entirely in her power— / By that I shall live a joyful life. / And serve with good
intention, / Without wicked thought of any villainy."

48. Balade 20.9–11: "After war one sees peace arrive, / After winter the beautiful foliage of
summer; / But never do I see my situation change."

This image of flowers following winter looks forward to the opening lines of the next balade, quoted above, in which the narrator's constant torment has abruptly eased. The parallel, juxtaposed war-peace/winter-summer comparisons, meanwhile, further suggest a political resonance for these amatory poems since both *In Praise of Peace* and the Latin dedication to the *Cinkante Balades* exhorted Henry to choose peace rather than war and balade 20 has itself just made several references to figures from the Trojan War.[49] That conflict conjoined the political and the amatory, not just in the celebrated judgment and abduction that precipitated it, but also in its aftermath (philandering Agamemnon murdered by an adulterous Clytemnestra) and in the way in which Troilus's erotic fortune and ultimate fall paralleled those of his city. Gower was intimately familiar with this theme, having earlier used London's associations with Troy in *Vox Clamantis* to inveigh against the rebels of the 1381 Rising and, with increasing harshness, Richard II as well.[50] As we have seen, Gower's use of material from the *Vox* for Trentham's "Rex celi deus" implied that similar rewritings could occur to Henry, and balade 20's Trojan references likewise allude to sudden and unforeseen reversals, though here in the realm of love: Fortune saw to Diomedes' happiness by changing Criseyde's affections (20.19–21), for example, and though Gower does not allude to it here we know what sort of welcome Agamemnon was to receive from Clytemnestra on returning home from Troy. (If by chance we *are* ignorant of that episode, we will be educated by balade 6 of the *Traitié* at the end of Trentham.)

To this point, the *Cinkante Balades* has given only brief hints of the metanarrative that makes the sequence more than a loosely juxtaposed set of *forme-fixe* lyrics, and this minimizes the importance of psychological plausibility as a way of accounting for the narrator's sudden shift from abject despair to reverent joy in balades 20–21. But this larger question of what such abrupt shifts in tone suggest returns dramatically when the lovers address one another in balades 40–46,

49. See balade 20.17–24, where Diomedes, Agamemnon, Troilus, and Calchas are all referenced.

50. On Gower's use of Troy in *Vox Clamantis* and his career more broadly, see Federico, *New Troy*, 1–28.

by which time the initially fitful metanarrative has been much more firmly established. The preceding balade is one of the most ecstatic in the set, its envoy sending many thousands of greetings ("Mil et Mil et Mil et Mil salutz" [39.27]) to one the lover hails as full of goodness (39.3). In the next poem, however, he abruptly accuses his lady of inconstancy, calling her a Helen to his forsaken Menelaus (40.5–6). This charge prompts her to respond in three increasingly furious balades (41–43) that lob back both the accusation of faithlessness and the classical references: the lover is "au matin un et autre au soir" ("one person in the morning and another at night" [41.25]); a serial traitor of women (42.5) worse even than Jason or Aeneas (43.1–5); and a lecher who beds his victims with greater haste than Hector displayed in arming himself at Troy (43.9–11). Yet balade 44, also in the lady's voice, fulsomely praises the lover with long lists of his virtues and the refrain that "au tiel ami jeo vuil bien estre amie."[51]

What on earth has happened? Even if the lover who graciously answers her in balade 45 and whose love she happily accepts in balade 46 is, as Yeager suggests, a different person from the lover of balades 1–40, the effect is exceptionally disorienting. Moreover, while positing a love triangle may restore some semblance of psychological plausibility, it does so at the expense of narrative coherence: if the lover of balades 44–45 is *not* the same as that of balades 1–40, then much the greatest part of the *Cinkante Balades* as a whole has been devoted to his predecessor in the lady's good graces; if he *is* one and the same, then he stands accused of vile conduct that the lady's subsequent about-face does not resolve and, indeed, in its abruptness manages to highlight. In any event, no interpretation can remove either the initial, highly destabilizing effect of these multiple quick shifts in tone or the suspicion that something more is at issue than a lover's quarrel. The allusions to Paris and Helen, Menelaus and Hector, return us to the Trojan context initiated in balade 20 and to that conflict's melding of the political and the erotic. The lady's most elaborate classical reference is also the most striking:

> Unqes Ector, q'ama Pantasilée,
> En tiele haste a Troie ne s'armoit,
> Qe tu tout nud n'es deinz le lit couché.[52]

The counterintuitive nature of this comparison—Hector's presumably laudable eagerness to defend Troy is similar to but exceeded by the lover's despicably quick-acting lust—emphasizes by its strangeness the link between erotic vice and a great city's ultimate downfall and, by extension, the vocabulary of love and politics.

Balade 46 suggests a context for interpreting both these wild shifts in tone and the Trojan references that underlie them. Its opening stanza reads:

> En resemblance d'aigle, qui surmonte
> Toute autre oisel pour voler au dessure,
> Tresdouls amis, vostre amour tant amonte
> Sur toutz amantz, par quoi jeo vous assure
> De bien amer, sauf toutdis la mesure
> De mon honour, le quell jeo guarderai:
> Si parler n'ose, ades jeo penserai.[53]

This is the final poem in the *Cinkante Balades'* narrative sequence—balades 47–50 offer general thoughts on love, and balade 51 is a concluding address to the Virgin—so its opening image of a noble eagle soaring above deserves special consideration, particularly since it echoes the four-line poem "H. aquile pullus," which concludes the poetic part of the Latin dedication to the *Cinkante Balades* and is included in a number of other Gower manuscripts as a self-standing poem:

---

52. Balade 43.9–11: "Never did Hector, whom Penthesilea loved, / Arm himself in such haste at Troy, / As you fully naked have lain down in bed." The reference to Penthesilea also suggests the connection between love and battle: she is the queen of the Amazons who for love of Hector fights on the Trojan side, only to be slain by the son of Achilles. Gower tells her story in *Confessio Amantis* 4.2135–82.

53. Balade 46.1–7: "Just like the eagle, which surpasses / All other birds for flying up above, / Very sweet friend, your love ascends so / Above all lovers, for which I assure you / Of true love, saving always the measure / Of my honor, which I shall protect: / If I dare not speak, I shall think unceasingly."

H. aquile pullus, quo nunquam gracior ullus,
Hostes confregit, que tirannica colla subegit.
H. aquile cepit oleum, quo regna recepit;
Sic veteri iuncta stipiti nova stirps redit uncta.

H. son of the eagle, than whom no one is ever more graceful,
Has broken his enemies, and subjugated tyrannical necks.
H. the eagle has captured the oil, by which he has received the
    rule of the realm;
Thus the new stock returns, anointed and joined to the old stem.[54]

Prompted by this imagistic echo to look back to the dedication, we
find further connections: the lady repeatedly praises this lover's *prouesce*
(line 9), *valour* (lines 11, 23), and *honour* (lines 12, 22)—all virtues attributed to Henry by the dedicatory balades that frame the Latin verses
cited above.[55]

What are we to do, interpretively, with the abrupt tonal shifts, narrative discontinuities, and outward-looking allusions and references
displayed by this sequence of poems? By this point, we have received
a wide range of invitations from both the *Cinkante Balades* and the
manuscript as a whole to read them as more than merely conventional
reverses. The narrative sequence ends with the joy and devotion expressed in balades 44–46, and, given the last poem's reference to the
lover as a soaring eagle, we might interpret this happy ending as an
optimistic comment on the prospects for "bon amour," and the hosts
of virtues associated with it by the dedication, under the ascendance of
"H. aquile pullus." But balade 46's emphasis on silence, discretion, and
thoughtfulness likewise encourages the reader to reflect on the broader

---

54. See Gower, *Minor Latin Works*, 46–47. In addition to Trentham, the poem survives in
five other manuscripts; in three of these, it follows the *Cronica Tripertita*, which narrates the
downfall of Richard II. Yeager writes further: "The reference is to the 'Prophecy of the Eagle,'
a thirteenth-century offshoot of the Merlin prophecies . . . which among Lancastrian supporters associated Henry IV with an eaglet (*pullus aquilae*) who comes from across the sea to depose
a white king (*rex albus*—i.e., Richard, whose badge was a white hart). Henry was supposed the
eagle because the symbol of John the Evangelist, namesake of his father, John of Gaunt, was
an eagle, and because the badge of Edward III, his grandfather, was an eagle also—little notice
was given to Edward's status as Richard's grandfather also" (ibid., 78).

55. See dedicatory balades 1.1 and 2.33.

arc of the lovers' dialogue,[56] which includes a range of disquieting and
largely unresolved elements: the abrupt revelation of amatory discord
in balade 40, its equally sudden disappearance just four poems later,
and the politically charged allusions to classical and especially Trojan
history. Even leaving aside the potential for disruptive love triangles,
this sequence that concludes the *Balades'* narrative portion scarcely
performs that seamless continuity emphasized by the last line of "H.
aquile pullus." Instead, the juxtaposed performance of irreconcilable
extremes of emotion presses us to consider more critically what these
poems might suggest or represent.

Any hope that the last poems in the sequence might resolve these
contradictions quickly evaporates, for the more gnomic tone of balades
47–50 raises its own set of problems. Each poem's refrain makes a claim
about love:

> N'est pas oiceus sil qui bien amera.

> En toutz errours amour se justifie.

> Lors est amour d'onour la droite meire.

> Amour s'acorde a nature et resoun.[57]

The autonomous, amoral, self-justifying love described in balade 48
is antithetical both to the love of the following two poems (where she
is the mother of Honor and the handmaid of Reason) and to the "bon
amour" promised in the dedication. Yet by using the same word in
each case—we cannot instantly distinguish between *caritas* and *cupi-
ditas*—these poems collectively recall the early marginal glosses' challenge to distinguish between celebrations of courtly as opposed to
marital love. Indeed, balade 48 takes the impossibility of defining love

---

56. The refrain line quoted above emphasizes silence and thoughtfulness; other verbs of
protection (*guarderai* [line 6]) and discretion (*m'aviserai* [line 13]) pepper the poem.

57. Balades 47–50, refrains: "He who will love well is not lazy"; "In all errors love justifies itself"; "Then love is the rightful mother to honor"; and "Love accords itself with nature
and reason."

as its opening theme: "Amour est une chose merveilouse, / Dont nulls porra savoir le droit certain."[58] The rest of this poem consists largely of oxymora, which characterize love itself ("odible et graciouse" [line 17], serf and sovereign [line 24]) and which love in turn creates in whatever it touches: under its influence, "le riche est povere et le courtois vilein, / L'espine est molle et la rose est urtie," and so on.[59] This is a radically destabilizing poem to include at this point, after Gower has so self-consciously and heavy-handedly resolved the lover's spat of balades 40–45. In their exuberantly contradictory definitions of love, balades 47–50 perform as a sequence a version of the oxymora that, according to balade 48, constitute love's chief characteristic. In this sense, that sole dissenting poem has the last word, effectively trumping the other balades' individually performed insistence on love's socially and ethically reinforcing power.

The sequence's final poem acknowledges these contradictions and attempts simply to define them away:

> Amour de soi est bon en toute guise,
> Si resoun le governe et justifie;
> Mais autrement, s'il naist de fole emprise,
> N'est pas amour, ainz serra dit sotie.[60]

And so we are told, finally, that the socially disruptive contradictions of balade 48 were not love at all but rather madness. Yet the echoes between the two balades make it hard to forget the assertion of love's disruptive qualities made by the earlier poem, which included the same "amour de soi" formula we see above (48.3) and similar language of justification in its refrain ("en toutz errours amour se justifie"). Its envoy, moreover, defined love in terms of that very sotie that this later balade insists is wholly different from it: "N'est qui d'amour poet dire la sotie."[61] Balade 51's earnest protestations thus draw attention to pre-

---

58. Balade 48.1–2: "Love is a marvelous thing / Of which no one is able to know the true certainty."

59. Balade 48.5–6: "the rich man is poor and the courteous man a knave, / The thorn is soft and the rose is a nettle."

60. Balade 51.1–4: "Love in itself is good in every guise, / If reason governs and justifies it; / But otherwise, it is but a foolish enterprise, / It is not love, but will be called madness."

61. Balade 48.23: "There is no one who is able to describe the folly of love."

cisely the poem whose unsettling assertions it is attempting to shut down. This gambit is comparable to others we have seen in the *Cinkante Balades*: the early marginal glosses' initial demand that we read for more than the poems' apparent *desport*, only then to insist on the fundamental difference of later poems that look very much the same, and the abrupt, forced resolution of a lovers' quarrel that was itself an abrupt shift from the narrator's tone to that point. This final instance of the pattern, however, is especially striking because its very existence, *after* Gower has supposedly shut the lid on troublesome kinds of love by imposing a happy ending to the lovers' spat, suggests the ultimate futility of all such moves. Whatever their intention, all these moments elicit a more careful, skeptical mode of reading than either the poems' genre or the dedication's emphasis on *desport* might otherwise suggest.

Earlier, I raised but did not answer the question of what a Henrician context might suggest about how to interpret these discontinuities and the manuscript's efforts to resolve them. The *Cinkante Balades'* final stanza gives new urgency to this issue by naming Henry explicitly, recalling and rewriting elements of the dedication as it does so:

> O gentile Engleterre, a toi j'escrits,
> Pour *remembrer* ta joie q'est novelle,
> Qe te survient du noble Roi Henri,
> Par qui dieus ad *redrescé* ta querele:
> A dieu purceo prient et cil et celle,
> Q'il de sa grace au fort Roi coroné
> Doignt peas, honour, joie et prosperité.[62]

The final list of virtues echoes those that open the first dedicatory balade and close the second;[63] the *re-* verbs italicized above

---

62. Balade 51.25–31: "Oh gentle England, I write to you, / In *remembrance* of your new joy, / Which comes to you from the noble King Henry, / By whom God has *redressed* your quarrel: / Let one and all therefore pray to God, / That He may graciously give to the strong, crowned King / Peace, honor, joy, and prosperity" (emphasis added).

63. "Pité, prouesse, humblesse, honour roial" (dedicatory balade 1.1: "Mercy, prowess, humility, regal honor") and "Honour, valour, victoire et bon esploit, / Joie et sauнеté, puissance et seignurie" (dedicatory balade 2.33–34: "Honor, valor, victory, and good success, / Joy and health, power and lordship").

recall the profusion of such verbs in the dedication and earlier in the manuscript; and the reference to Henry as "Roi coroné" evokes the "ore avetz receu le coronal" line discussed earlier (dedicatory balade 1.17). Gower's claim to be writing to England (*a toi j'escrits*) recalls the phrase with which he addressed Henry earlier (*ce que je vous escris* [dedicatory balade 1.22]), although this echo reinforces the fact that Henry is only being referred to here, not addressed. The most striking thing about this stanza, however, is its explicit reference to discord—the *querele* of line 28—that the dedication would allude to only obliquely.[64] Within this stanza, the most obvious referent for such conflict would seem to be that which led to Richard II's deposition and Henry's elevation as king. In the context of the *Cinkante Balades*, however, it would surely recall the quarrel between the lovers in balades 40–44 and thus continue the subtle connection of the political and amatory realms that the sequence as a whole has gradually suggested.

In so doing, this *querele* suggests a cautious perspective on Henry's accession, for, although this final stanza in isolation is straightforwardly laudatory, the idea of redressed quarrels reminds readers that earlier instances of narrative discord (between the lovers) and thematic discontinuity (on just what love really is) were more papered over than resolved. This ambivalence is thoroughly consonant with what we have seen in *In Praise of Peace* and "Rex celi deus," where authorial revisions suggested ambiguity at odds with those poems' outwardly celebratory tone and content. These suggestions gather force cumulatively, reinforcing the fact that all these poems are most compellingly complex when analyzed in the context of form and history alike: the codicological form of the Trentham manuscript, which includes multiple invitations to read its poems as building on and linked to one another and its intervening material (incipits, explicits, dedications) as significant, and the authorial history of Gower himself, which makes many of these invitations legible and significant in the context of a broader history of Lancastrian power.

---

64. For example, the references to "our former servitude" (dedicatory balade 1.6) or to beginning again the "bon amour" that used to exist in former times (dedicatory balade 2.21–24).

Blind Cupid, Libidinous Kings, and an Author's Farewell

The next work in the manuscript, the Latin poem "Ecce patet tensus," amply demonstrates the impossibility of simply defining away the dangerous, disruptive side of love as mere *sotie*, as the concluding balade 51 has just attempted to do. This poem, which is unique to Trentham, opens with the declaration that "love conquers all" (line 3 ["omnia vincit amor"]) and depicts a lord Cupid whose reign is terrifyingly absolute in its destructive chaos.[65] The blind god "knows not whither his trail will lead" (line 4 ["quo sibi directum carpere nescit iter"]), and his blindness is matched only by his power: "everyone obeys his precepts" (line 12 ["sua precepta quisquis ubique facit"]), for "he is the crowned king" (line 13 ["ipse coronatus"]) who "subdues everything that Nature has created" (line 15 ["amor omne domat, quicquid natura creavit"]). Because the crown is not a universal attribute for Cupid, his depiction as *coronatus* gains added force and thus recalls the *Cinkante Balades'* initial address to Henry and concluding reference to him as likewise crowned.[66] It is hard to read this resemblance as other than admonitory, given the amatory subject matter of the *Cinkante Balades* and the fact that several moments in "Ecce patet tensus" look even further back in the manuscript, to *In Praise of Peace*:

> Vulnerat omne genus, nec sibi vulnus habet.
> Non manet in terris qui prelia vincit amoris,
>   Nec sibi quis firme federa pacis habet.

> He [Cupid] wounds every nation, but receives no wound himself.
> In the wars of Love there is no victor on earth,
>   Nor has anyone concluded with him a firm treaty of peace.
> (lines 18–20)

---

65. Elliot Kendall has recently proposed that Cupid in the *Confessio Amantis* embodies a "magnificent lordship" that alienates and objectifies the servitor, as contrasted with the more productive "reciprocalist lordship" offered by Venus; this interpretation is consonant with my reading of Cupid in "Ecce patet tensus." See *Lordship and Literature: John Gower and the Politics of the Great Household* (Oxford: Oxford University Press, 2008), 109–131.

66. Compare "ore avetz receu *le coronal*" (dedicatory balade 1.17 [emphasis added]: "you who have now received *the crown*") with "fort Roi *coroné*" (balade 51.30 [emphasis added]: "strong *crowned* king").

Trentham's first long poem admonished Henry to be a peacemaker, so at its most basic "Ecce patet tensus" presents Cupid as an antimodel for the new king. But a set of four couplets apostrophizing human nature hints at the difficulty of avoiding completely the competing model of kingship that Cupid embodies:

> O natura viri, poterit quam tollere nemo,
>> Nec tamen excusat quod facit ipsa malum!
> O natura viri, que naturatur eodem
>> Quod vitare nequit nec licet illud agi!
> O natura viri, duo que contraria mixta
>> Continet, amborum nec licet acta sequi!
> O natura viri, que semper habet sibi bellum
>> Corporis ac anime, que sua iura petunt!

> O human nature, which no one can abolish,
>> Nor yet excuse the evils it does!
> O human nature, irresistibly disposed
>> To that unlawful thing which it cannot shun!
> O human nature, that contains two mixed contraries
>> But is not allowed to follow the deeds of both!
> O human nature, which always has war within itself
>> Of body and soul, both seeking the same authority!

(lines 23–30)

This passage emphasizes that every person must somehow cope with two antithetical and competing impulses, the "two mixed contraries" of human nature: "body and soul," each seeking to be ruler of the self. The couplets' anaphora distances this message from Henry by universalizing its relevance. But Trentham has been full of competing dualities that threaten to morph into one another: the Alexander/Solomon and Alexander/Henry binaries of *In Praise of Peace*, the Henry praised by "Rex celi deus" competing with the spectral presence of Richard from the lines' earlier existence in *Vox Clamantis*, and the "bon amour" to which the *Cinkante Baldes* exhorts the king, which dissolved into charges of treachery only hastily and artificially resolved by the end of the sequence. "Ecce patet tensus" offers yet another such binary: a lord who competes with Henry and whose *amor* differs radically from the "bon amour" that Henry was earlier imagined promoting.

These broad, structural, and thematic connections between "Ecce patet tensus" and other works in Trentham are reinforced by more local echoes, too. A reference to Solomon in "Ecce patet tensus," for example, recalls his role in *In Praise of Peace*, where he served as an exemplary figure for Henry, the one who (unlike Alexander) "ches wisdom unto the governynge / Of goddis folk" and thereby "gat him pees" (lines 31–32, 35). As the later Latin poem would have it, however, even "the intelligence of Solomon" offers "nothing of praise" when faced with the all-consuming destructiveness of Love (lines 21–22).[67] These lines not only cast retrospective doubt on the exemplary status he enjoyed earlier in the manuscript; they also recall the fact that in the *Confessio* precisely this voracious sexual appetite prompted his descent into idolatry (7.4469–4573). But the Alexandrine model, exemplary in the *Confessio* and abruptly reversed in *In Praise of Peace*, is no more acceptable here than that of Solomon. Not just Solomon's wisdom but also Samson's strength and David's sword are powerless in the face of love (line 21), and the image of Cupid as an indiscriminate conqueror who refuses to make peace takes the negative depiction of the conquering Alexander initiated in Trentham's first long poem to an almost nightmarish extreme.

All this broader significance, however, is intelligible only in the context of Trentham as a whole, and in that sense "Ecce patet tensus" offers its own form of duality: interpreted as I have suggested, it is the most cautionary of any of Trentham's texts about Henry's accession, but it also includes the fewest explicit indications—none, in fact—that it should be read in this way; such an interpretation depends on our willingness to read Trentham's cross-textual echoes as meaningful. "Ecce patet tensus" thus allows itself to be read as a conventionally homiletic text whose universally applicable admonitions neither threaten nor particularly speak to Henry or as a serious warning to right behavior that has gained cumulative force by building on the images and associations of the manuscript as a whole. This creation of a dual meaning that depends on broader codicological context recalls

---

67. "Sampsonis vires, gladius neque David—in istis / Quid laudis—sensus aut Salomonis habent."

the Horn corpus's varied deployment of *Britton*, which could function
either as a straightforward and practical legal treatise (when appearing
in the comparably straightforward and practical compendium *Liber
Horn*) or as half of a bitterly satiric attack on the notion that the king's
pleasure rather than documents or rights determines the law (as I argued it functioned in the *Mirror* codex). My larger point here is that,
by repeatedly prompting us to ponder these sorts of issues, Trentham's
codicological form gives its texts deeper aesthetic and historical resonance than they have if analyzed in isolation.

Trentham's final major text, the *Traitié pour essampler les amantz marietz*, begins by continuing the project of distinguishing the love-as-*sotie*
of balade 48 and "Ecce patet tensus" from a more wholesome love, re-
strained by the body's recognition that reason must be its constable.[68]
Balades 1–4 hail marriage as God's instrument for promoting this second, nobler love, and in that sense the "Ecce patet tensus"/*Traitié* pairing appears to be playing a similar role to the *Confessio/Traitié* pairing
in the Fairfax manuscript that gives the poem its modern title.[69] Together, these two poems finally subdivide the category of love, whose
dangerous slipperiness the *Cinkante Balades* had performed, into the
bad ("Ecce patet tensus") and the good (*Traitié*). Indeed, the Trentham
copy of the *Traitié* appears particularly eager to avoid love's contradic-

---

68. As noted earlier, the folio that contained the end of "Ecce patet tensus" (if it is actually
incomplete) and the first balade and a half of the *Traitié* has been cut away. Since the textual
witnesses to the *Traitié* are quite consistent, I have assumed for the purposes of my argument
that the *Traitié* as it originally appeared in Trentham was essentially equivalent to the versions
in Fairfax 3, Glasgow Hunterian T.2.17, and Bodley 294, our three surviving witnesses to
Traitié's first balade and a half. (The All Souls manuscript also includes the *Traitié*, but it lacks
the first two poems and the first three lines of the third.)

69. Oxford, Bodleian Library, MS Fairfax 3 includes the following link between *Confessio
Amantis* and the *Traitié*: "Puisqu'il ad dit ci devant en Englois par voie d'essample la sotie de
cellui qui par amours aime par especial, dirra ore apres en François a tout le monde en general
un traitié selonc les auctour pour essampler les amantz marietz, au fin q'ils la foi de lour seintes
espousailes pourront par fine loialté guarder, et al honour de dieu salvement tenir" ("Because
the preceding poem in English was by way of example of the foolishness of those in particular
who love in a courtly manner, now the subsequent treatise will be in French, for all the world
generally, following the authorities, as an example for married lovers, in order that they might
be able to protect the promise of their sacred spousal through perfect loyalty, and truly hold
fast to the honor of God"). Quoted in Gower, *French Balades*, 34.

tions, for it omits the Latin poem "Est amor," which follows the *Traitié* in all other manuscripts and consists of oxymoronic definitions of love akin to those of balade 48 in the *Cinkante Balades*.[70] Reading the *Traitié* in this way, we could see it as attempting to shut down both these definitional ambiguities and others that we have considered in Trentham: those of *In Praise of Peace* and "Rex celi deus," where authorial rewriting hinted at warnings for their royal addressee, or of the *Cinkante Balades*, whose dedication implied a larger relevance for the "bon amour" that it imagined Henry promoting but that the sequence's metanarrative only imperfectly displayed. Indeed, the *Traitié* declines clear opportunities to emphasize the Henrician context that the manuscript's early texts established. It nowhere addresses or even refers to the king, and the poem's final moves instead highlight Gower: the envoy that concludes the *Traitié* (the only one in the sequence) puts him in direct address with the entire world,[71] while the Latin verses adjoined to the sequence's conclusion first universalize the audience of the *Traitié* as all who have undertaken "the sacred order of marriage," then retreat into another mention of Gower and the fact that he himself, "old in years . . . / Safely approach[es] the marriage bed in the order of husbands."[72]

Yet the *Traitié* is still crucially informed by other poems in the manuscript, particularly in its choice of verse form and exempla. Like the *Cinkante Balades*, of course, it is a balade sequence. But its uniformly rhyme-royal stanzas, as opposed to the *Cinkante Balades'* varied stanza structures, look back to *In Praise of Peace*, which, aside from the letter to Venus at the end of the *Confessio* (8.2217–2300), is Gower's only use of rhyme royal in English. These two poems have exactly the same number of total lines (385) and are thematically linked as well. *In Praise of Peace* considered how the examples of two celebrated antecedents,

---

70. For "Est Amor," see Gower, *Minor Latin Works*, 32–33, 67–69. Claims that love is "warlike peace" (*pax bellica* [line 1]), "a peaceful fight" (*pugna quietosa* [line 3]), and "a joyful death" (*mors leta* [line 7]) typify the poem.

71. Balade 18.22ff.: "Al université de tout le monde / Johan Gower ceste Balade envoie. . . ."

72. "vetus annorum Gower, sub spe meritorum / Ordine sponsorum tutus adhibo thorum." See Gower, *Minor Latin Works*, 33.

Alexander and Solomon, might inform the reign of the newly crowned Henry IV. The *Traitié*, meanwhile, uses kings for most of its exempla on the dire consequences that await adulterers: Nectanabus and Ulysses, Jason and Agamemnon, Tarquin and Albinus, Tereus and Pharaoh, are all duly punished for their adulterous behavior.[73] This adultery, moreover, is typically framed as violence or conquest, from Nectanabus's rape of Olimpeas (6.4) or Hercules' conquest of Deianira (7.5–6: "en armes *conquestoit* / La belle Deianire par *bataile*" [emphasis added]) to Albinus's marriage of his defeated enemy's daughter (11.3–45) or Pharaoh's *ravine* of Abraham's wife, Sarrai (13.9). This association of love and war recalls the depiction of Cupid as a rapacious warlord in "Ecce patet tensus" as well as the Trojan references in the *Cinkante Balades* and *In Praise of Peace*'s more general admonition to avoid conquest. Moreover, the emphasis on royal figures in these exempla means that, while Trentham ends by moving away from the specifically Henrician context that its initial texts suggested, it continues and even strengthens the focus on kingship more generally that we have seen in each of the main texts so far: the first three dedicated to or addressing Henry directly, the final two presenting countermodels of royal misbehavior, from Cupid's in "Ecce patet tensus" to that of legendary adulterous kings in the *Traitié*.

This context makes the *Traitié*'s final exemplum, the only positive one in the sequence, particularly important. Balade 16 tells of how the Roman emperor Valentinian lived to a miraculously old age by maintaining his chastity. He denied meriting any praise for "the kinges and the londes / To his subjeccion put under,"[74] however, accepting accolades only for his victory over fleshly desire. He thus not only becomes the antithesis of Cupid as presented in "Ecce patet tensus" but also presents a model of spiritual might that could redeem the negative associations of earthly conquest from *In Praise of Peace*. The only prob-

---

73. On what this fact might suggest about the dating and intended audience of the *Traitié*, see Cathy Hume, "Why Did Gower Write the *Traitié*?" in Dutton, Hines, and Yeager, eds., *John Gower, Trilingual Poet*, 263–75.

74. *Confessio Amantis* 5.6408–9. Gower also tells the story of Valentinian in both the *Confessio* (5.6395–6417) and the *Mirour de l'Omme* (lines 17089–17100).

lem with this positive interpretation of Valentinian is that his example runs oddly counter to the *Traitié*'s focus on marriage since he achieved his heroic conquest of the flesh without the help of matrimony. The strangeness of this exemplum would be most apparent to readers of Trentham with a detailed knowledge of Gowerian antecedents, since Gower's other two treatments of him are more explicit about the fact that Valentinian never married.[75] Even here, however, the *Traitié* cites him as an example of one of those few who "guarderont chaste lour condicion,"[76] before pivoting to assert near the end of the poem that "en mariage est la perfeccioun."[77] The *Traitié*'s only positively depicted figure thus turns out actually to have rejected the institution that the sequence as a whole supposedly praises. We should recognize here a gambit that we have seen throughout Trentham: a laudatory moment or a positive exemplum reveals darker significance when apprehended in the context of the manuscript, and Gower's career, as a whole.

Trentham's final text, "Henrici quarti primus," puts this issue of Gower's career squarely before us; it is brief enough to quote in its entirety:

> Henrici quarti primus regni fuit annus
> > Quo michi defecit visus ad acta mea.
> Omnia tempus habent; finem natura ministrat,
> > Quem virtute sua frangere nemo potest.
> Ultra posse nichil, quamvis michi velle remansit;
> > Amplius ut scribam non michi posse manet.
> Dum potui scripsi, set nunc quia curua senectus
> > Turbavit sensus, scripta relinquo scolis.
> Scribat qui veniet post me discrecior alter,
> > Ammodo namque manus et mea penna silent.
> Hoc tamen, in fine verborum queso meorum,
> > Prospera quod statuat regna futura Deus. Amen.

---

75. Valentinian comes up in *Mirrour de l'Omme* in the encomium of virginity (lines 16825–17136), not the subsequent discussion of matrimony (lines 17137–748), and in the *Confessio* is introduced as "withoute Mariage" (5.6401).

76. Balade 16.4: "Guard their chaste condition."

77. Balade 16.19: "In marriage is perfection."

It was in the first year of the reign of King Henry IV
>   When my sight failed for my deeds.
All things have their time; nature applies a limit,
>   Which no man can break by his own power.
I can do nothing beyond what is possible, though my will has remained;
>   My ability to write more has not stayed.
While I was able I wrote, but now because stooped old age
>   Has troubled my senses, I leave writing to the schools.
Let someone else more discreet who comes after me write,
>   For from this time forth my hand and pen will be silent.
Nevertheless I ask this one final thing, the last of my words:
>   That God make our kingdoms prosperous in the future. Amen.[78]

Two other, apparently later versions of this poem assert a simple physical causation ("I stopped writing, because I am blind"; "I am unable
to write any longer, because I am blind")[79] for the poet's farewell to
writing, instead of the circumlocutions used here: "my sight failed for
my deeds" (line 2) and "stooped old age has troubled my senses" (lines
7–8).[80] Compared to the later two versions, these are curiously allusive formulations.[81] This contrast makes another line in the Trentham
version stand out: Gower's desire, expressed in line 9, that "someone

---

78. Gower, *Minor Latin Works*, 47.

79. The first reading survives in three manuscripts and reads: "Scribere . . . cesso, sum
quia cecus ego" (line 2). The three manuscripts are Glasgow, Hunterian Museum, MS T.2.17;
London, British Library, MS Cotton Tiberius A.iv; and London, British Library, MS Harleian
6291. The second is from the All Souls manuscript and reads: "scribere quicquam / Ulterius
nequio, sum quia cecus ego" (lines 3–4).

80. "Henrici quarti primus" is unique to Trentham. A slightly longer, fifteen-line version,
"Henrici regis annus," appears in the Cotton, Harley, and Glasgow manuscripts, while the All
Souls manuscript version opens "Quicquid homo scribat" and consists of seventeen lines. For
all three, see Gower, *Minor Latin Works*, 47–50. The parenthetical quotations about blindness
are from lines 2 and 4 of "Henrici regis annus" and "Quicquid homo scribat," respectively.

81. I should acknowledge that "Henrici quarti primus" appears to be the earliest of the
three versions since it references the first year of Henry's reign while "Henrici regis annus"
mentions the second; "Quicquid homo scribat" incorporates phrases from both versions and
thus appears to be the latest. We can therefore, if we wish, embrace the simplest explanation
for the different vocabularies of blindness: that, when Trentham was being compiled, Gower
merely suffered from failing eyesight and that it was not until a year later that he actually went
blind and felt compelled to describe himself as such. The possibility of this explanation does
not, however, preclude the metaphoric interpretation of the poem that I suggest above.

else more discreet who comes after me" should write in his stead, a prayer that the final All Souls version omits.[82] What deeds has Gower failed at in Trentham that a more discreet, more prudent, wiser man will have to take up? The poem is legible in completely conventional and therefore nonthreatening terms by a Lancastrian audience, but I wonder whether it might also represent a private acknowledgment that the Gower compilation it rounds out is not as fully laudatory as discretion and prudence might dictate and that the safest course, not just the one prompted by physical disability, might be to retire from writing altogether?

This is a biographically inflected reading of Trentham's final poem. The poem itself, with its insistent deployment of first-person verbs and pronouns, encourages such interpretations even as the manuscript as a whole makes itself difficult to pin down, historically or paleographically, as precisely intended by anyone, scribe(s) and/or author. This kind of paradox, resurgent at the end of Trentham and this chapter alike, reminds us once more that the manuscript's codicological form collaborates with its individual texts and their multiple evocations of Gower's authorial history to create that excess, that refusal to submit to clear messages or single meanings, that has emerged throughout this book as one key component of the literary. Thus far, I have emphasized the ways in which Trentham creates meaning through juxtaposition and accretion, but it is worth remembering in conclusion that fragmentariness is the necessary corollary of such assemblage; every collection, examined closely, reveals destabilizing fissures, evidence of its status as a constructed object that is imperfect like every other. I have suggested that Trentham thematizes those fissures, allowing us to see disjunctions between the most obvious, explicit content of its texts and the significance that they might have if examined in the context of other (codicological) forms and (authorial and political) histories. Much of that significance seems to me cautionary: Trentham's early texts, laudatory and Henrician, seem more ambivalent when read in the context of Gower's authorial history and the manuscript's later,

---

82. "Scribat qui veniet post me discrecior alter."

darker poems. Those texts' relevance to the king, however, emerges only when we read them compilationally, in the context of the manuscript as a whole.

That manuscript is, among other things, an artfully constructed meditation on the multiple natures and implications of kingship. The very complexity of its construction, however, highlights both the visceral pleasure of using literary and aesthetic modes to grapple with such vitally important social and political questions and, equally, the impossibility of creating clear-cut "propositional content" as answers to them. In this sense, we can understand Trentham's literal, physical fragmentariness, considered briefly in the introduction, as complementing key elements of its texts' meanings even as it occludes others. Any of the manuscript's missing pieces—the fragmentary stanzas of the second dedicatory balade and the first poem of the *Cinkante Balades* proper, the end (perhaps) of the (perhaps) incomplete "Ecce patet tensus," and whatever linking material might once have joined it to the *Traitié*—might have provided the key to a certain kind of understanding of the manuscript that we now will never have. But the tidy meaning such a key might have made available to us might in turn have compromised the manuscript's aesthetic power by pinning down the range of shifting meanings offered by Trentham's texts and form. Trentham's physical lacunae are as much a part of its texts' meaning as are its many attempts to stitch those texts together into a coherent and unified whole. The manuscript thus becomes much more than a gift to Henry IV, or a warning to him, or a book of poems neabout kingship, or a collection of Gower's verse. It is a reminder of why we grapple with literary texts in the first place: the fact that their delights and their frustrations, their significances and their silences, are all—literally—bound up together.

AFTERWORD

Throughout this book, I have argued that compilations are assemblages in at least two main senses: that they are, literally, collections of disparate textual pieces into a larger whole and that the precise disposition of those pieces invites readers metaphorically to assemble, out of their relation to one another and their surrounding structures, some broader set of meanings or perspectives that would not be legible if those pieces were read in isolation. I have also argued, however, that neither literary texts nor physical manuscripts are inherently compilations in the sense outlined above. Rather, each reader must determine whether the particular constellation of formal and historical vectors offered by a given object makes such compilational interpretation illuminating, that is, whether such an object adds up to more than the sum of its parts. Such a determination must be subjective, for reasons both historical and formal: the vast temporal distance between the now of our analysis and the many thens of a given object's often gradual construction, and the frequently fragmentary contemporary state of that object and its constituent parts. That fragmentation, various forms of which we have seen in each of this study's compilations, requires us to acknowledge and even embrace the limits of what we can know about objects from the distant past. The literal fragmentation of these compilations, in other words, valuably reminds us of the impossibility of fully reconstructing either the intentions that created them or the histories in which they have participated.

Such lacunae, whether physical or metaphoric, enable a wider range of interpretive modes than the conclusively historicizing one that has long dominated manuscript studies. Conclusive work of that sort has been and remains immensely valuable; this book could not have been written without it, and indeed I have used this book to present some comparably conclusive findings of my own.[1] The time that I have spent with these compilations, however, has convinced me that they are at heart implicative: in their strange juxtapositions, suggestive fragmentation, and complex literary effects, they press us to reread, to continue rather than conclude. This quality is in fact that which distinguishes what I have called *compilations* from the *compilatio* with which I began this study: instances of the latter seek to streamline, clarify, and make things easier for the reader, while the former force, encourage, or beguile us into a more complex and evolving relation with them and their texts. Just as compilations are at once fragments and assemblages, however, so too implicative and conclusive modes of scholarship cannot be neatly separated out. What follow therefore are some of the conclusions that I have reached in this book, along with my own sense of where those conclusions and the investigations that underwrite them remain fragmentary—implicative spurs, I hope, to continuing scholarly research, debate, and all the pleasure those activities can yield.

The conclusion to which I am most committed, and that I hope will prove the most broadly generative for others, is that delight in what

---

1. For my use of the terms *conclusive* and *implicative* to describe two poles of scholarly endeavor, see Andrew H. Miller, *The Burdens of Perfection: On Ethics and Reading in Nineteenth-Century British Literature* (Ithaca, NY: Cornell University Press, 2008), 26–32, 219–22. As Miller characterizes it, conclusive scholarship "aims, reasonably enough, to establish facts, convey information, and make judgments" and is conclusive in that "ending is its end, its goal: conclusions are what its exposition or argument drives forward" (ibid., 221). Miller himself aspires to a different, more "suggestive" mode of criticism that is implicative in that the critic asks the reader "to elaborate on his writing," extending this invitation "by himself interpreting his prose, unfolding the implications of his claims, thus tacitly allowing and encouraging me [Miller] to continue them" (ibid., 30). As a result, he regards his study as "less a sequence of claims concerning nineteenth-century literature, or new knowledge about it, than an implicative style and experimental method" (ibid., 32). This formulation strikingly evokes another scholarly model for my own work, Dillon's *Medieval Music-Making and the Roman de Fauvel*. Dillon writes: "[Her project] does not offer new 'hard' evidence to repaint the scholarly scenery. More modestly, it attempts to open up new interpretive possibilities in a manuscript that offers just one brief glimpse of a fabulously inventive and imaginative musical culture" (ibid., 10). Although Dillon does in fact offer a wealth of "conclusive" findings about her manuscript, she does so with an implicative spirit that I found inspiring and have tried to bring to my own work.

I have called the *literary* can be found, and care for it nurtured, in the many ways in which codicological form and textual content create and complicate one another in particular medieval manuscripts. All definitions of the *literary* must of course be partial, in both senses of the word, but characterizations by Derek Pearsall (of poetic meaning) and Maura Nolan (of aesthetic excess) especially have helped me articulate what I take to be some of its key components: shifting and allusive meaning, ambiguity and ambivalence, resistance to paraphrase, and openness to rereading. These are of course culturally constructed and historically contingent values. As Mary Carruthers has demonstrated in her analysis of medieval aesthetic terms like *dulcedo* and *suavitas*, however, they were far from unappreciated in the Middle Ages.[2] They likewise represent a newly energized object of value to many readers today; discovering them in unexpected places and ways is therefore exciting and worth sharing on that basis alone.

The implicative nature of these compilations, meanwhile, their sustained refusal to mean in straightforwardly conclusive ways, somewhat paradoxically allows us to reach a second conclusion: that the ability to engage in such active, restless, creative forms of reading was one element of a broader textual acuity cultivated by key members of London's merchant elite in the fourteenth century. More immediately practical forms of textual mastery were clearly important too, as evinced by both *Liber Horn* and the many anecdotes from civic life that we have seen recorded by Gwyn Williams, Ralph Hanna, Caroline Barron, and others. But the *inaestimabilis* quality of this study's compilations, to quote Horn's *Annales Londonienses*, their construction of literary resonance out of even the least propitious of materials (the by-laws of a defunct bourgeois poetic society, a pages-long list of historically distant names without context or narrative), suggests that, when we read their forms for what we might find in them rather than for what we cannot know about them, they and their disparate parts can be assembled into a surprisingly powerful set of arguments, not just about medieval histories, but about how those histories continue to

2. For a fuller discussion of Carruthers's "Sweetness," see n. 47, chapter 3, above.

mean in the present. Put another way: because medieval manuscripts offer a tangible performance of history's complex vectors, analysis of their aesthetic potential reminds us that engagement with history and concern for form can be mutually supportive rather than antagonistic. (That this proposition is not the cliché it may sound can be seen from the harshness of rhetoric too often used by partisans of both sides in recent scholarly debates.)

The very complexity of the histories that create manuscript compilations, meanwhile, makes them an ideal way of complicating the literary histories of the texts that they contain. Chaucer has long been subjected to literary histories that risk enshrouding him in a deadening form of canonicity, a kind of suspended animation that can obscure both his relation to other English literary traditions and the value of those traditions independent of him. Taking his evocation of *compilatio* as my starting point, I have argued that he understood and embraced the notion that later readers would imaginatively construct their own versions of the *Canterbury Tales*. This radical openness to continuing compilational performance embeds within the *Tales* both his and his work's explosion out of a limiting, linear historicity. The compilations that I have studied here sketch the outlines of an alternate literary history, one in which Chaucer's debts to a tradition of urban, mercantile compilational construction and interpretation, as embodied by the Horn corpus and the Auchinleck manuscript, can help us understand both the complex, evolving form of the tales and their engagement with the sociocultural history of their composition. Gower's Trentham manuscript, meanwhile, also evokes aspects of those earlier civic compilations, such as multilingual production and Continental literary models. It thereby suggests that Chaucer's dismissive attitude toward courtly literary modes and his apparent disinclination to embrace medieval England's multilingualism in his own work[3] were not the only sophisticated ways for England's literary forms to continue into the early fifteenth century or to build on the early fourteenth.

---

3. For the possibility that Chaucer may in fact be the author of surviving French lyrics, see James I. Wimsatt, *Chaucer and the Poems of "Ch" in University of Pennsylvania MS French 15* (Cambridge: Boydell & Brewer, 1982).

The literary history that I have uncovered here is not tidily linear, as suggested by its wide range of not-always-contiguous historical nodes: tensions between Crown and City; the evolving appeal of
Franco-Flemish cultural models; the nature and practice of royal and
civic government; whether and how literary production might have
real-life consequences. The gaps and outgrowths created by these disparate objects of value are likewise implicative, for both the literary
histories that they (fragmentarily) embody and the many others that
they might be assembled into depend on my readers' continuing investigations. Fortunately, all the compilations that I have taken up invite
more sustained attention than I have been able to give them here. I will
draw attention in closing to a few specific lines of inquiry that seem
particularly fruitful.

My most nearly complete analysis has been of Gower's Trentham
manuscript (likewise and perhaps not coincidentally my most nearly
complete compilation), but the *Cinkante Balades* in particular deserve
fuller treatment. Quite apart from their often extraordinary depth
and lushness (read balade 34 out loud to hear what I mean), their possible links to contemporary French balade sequences by the likes of
Christine de Pizan offer one avenue for further exploration.[4] They
also valuably remind us that French had a far longer shelf life in England than has too often been implied, suggesting that we should take
up more seriously as "literature of England" works by Jean Froissart and Charles d'Orléans, sometime residents who boast either English patrons (Froissart) or English poetry (Charles). The Hainaulter
Froissart, meanwhile, offers yet another link to Franco-Flemish *festes*
since manuscripts record over twenty-five of his lyrics as having been
crowned at various festivals of the *puy*.[5]

Such civic, mercantile-inflected festivals return us to the Horn corpus of chapter 1, and here the most immediately enticing possibility

4. On Christine's *Livre des Cent Balades*, its popularity in France, and its possible dissemination in England, see R. F. Yeager, "John Gower's Audience: The Ballades," *Chaucer Review*
40 (2005): 81–104.

5. See James I. Wimsatt, *Chaucer and His French Contemporaries* (Toronto: University of
Toronto Press, 1991), 274–76.

for further investigation seems to me the so-called London Collection that once preceded *Mirror of Justices* and *Britton*. Its massively complicated construction and content made it impossible for me to treat here, but like *Mirror* it contains a great deal of untruth, its reputable legal statements having been "depraved . . . by many mythical interpolations," as Maitland inimitably puts it.[6] Ralph Hanna, however, argues that its misstatements of legal practice should instead be conceived of as "'visionary legislation,' a gesture recurrent in English legal literature and law itself . . . an account of what the king should have promulgated (but didn't)."[7] The congruence of this characterization with my own arguments about *Mirror* in this book suggests that the London Collection merits more detailed analysis alongside and in terms of *Mirror* and *Britton*—particularly since, as we have seen, Horn himself conceived of these texts in conjunction with one another.

Chapter 2 argued that Auchinleck's third booklet rewards attention, not just as a codicological feature, but also as a literary form that gains new depths of aesthetic resonance from its evolution across time. I would be excited to see a comparable kind of analysis brought to the manuscript's fifth booklet and especially to the relation between the two long romances with which it begins and its final three, very brief texts. The opening romances demand attention: *Beues of Hamptoun* is one of Auchinleck's most famous texts, cited in the catalog that comes near the end of *Sir Thopas*, while *Of Arthour and of Merlin* is the manuscript's longest text of all. The three final texts, by contrast, seem like the kind of filler long assumed to be aesthetically pitiful and codicologically interchangeable—whatever a scribe had at hand to fill up the space. My investigations of booklet 3 have shown that seemingly insignificant texts and odd juxtapositions can yield surprising resonance, however, which means that a flexible interpretive spirit might likewise find more of interest in the David-and-Goliath-style matchup of booklet 5's enormous initial texts with the tiny, critically neglected concluding ones that they dwarf.

6. For a full description of the London Collection, see n. 4, chapter 1, above. For Maitland's critique, see *The Mirror of Justices*, xv–xvi.

7. Hanna, *London Literature*, 70.

In chapter 3, I argued for a hybrid critical practice of freely using the modern *Riverside* in conjunction with particularly interesting or anomalous manuscript evidence, not just as codicological data points for the sketching of local literary histories, but as resonant sites of literary-aesthetic analysis. That argument was largely theoretical, part of my broader goal of showing that the *Tales'* literary form anticipated and implicitly welcomed its readers' participation in its evolving construction, and that both participatory compilationalism and fragmentariness are embedded into the Canterbury project in ways that help shatter any monolithic form of Chaucerian canonicity. As a practical matter, however, I was unable to use this promising critical practice as fully there as I would like to in the future; the sociocultural and intertextual arguments of the rest of that chapter proved too complicated to sustain the addition of significant amounts of variant codicological data. The Franklin's interruption of the Squire with which I ended that chapter, however, offers an ideal site for this mode of literary-critical investigation since, as I have argued, the Squire's attempts to frame himself and his tale as an outgrowth of the pilgrimage-initiating *Knight's Tale* make the nature of its success or failure particularly significant and since, as Robert Meyer-Lee has shown, the codicological evidence does not in fact support the conventional Fragment IV/V distinction.[8]

In fact, the most common follow-up to the *Squire's Tale* apart from the *Franklin's Tale* is the *Merchant's Tale*, which includes a repetition of that same line from the *Knight's Tale* about pity's effect on gentle hearts (I.1761, IV.1986, V.479). Read in the normative Ellesmere and *Riverside* ordering, the Squire's later use of the line takes some of the edge off its brutally misogynistic deployment by the Merchant. Read the other way, however, as we would both in Hengwrt and in a host of Hengwrt-derived manuscripts, the movement is precisely the opposite, with the Squire's naively intense encomium of feminine *pitee* for the

---

8. See Meyer-Lee, "Fragments IV and V of the *Canterbury Tales* Do Not Exist." That distinction, Meyer-Lee persuasively suggests, is one reason for the "tentativeness" displayed by "even those critics most famous for their intricate account of the relationships among tales" when it comes to crossing this supposed 4–5 barrier (ibid., 27).

smertes of others (Canacee comforts and nurses the female falcon "in signe of trouthe that is in wommen sene" [V.645]) metamorphosing into the Merchant's sneering, "Heere may ye se how excellent franchise / In wommen is," as he announces May's decision to show *pitee* to the hardly analogous Damian (IV.1987–88). That this Squire-Merchant ordering does not appear to be Chaucerian is relevant (for that reason, it does not structure the *Riverside*, which looks set to remain a kind of base text for literary-critical endeavor) but not absolutely determinant, both because this variant ordering structured a great many readers' experience of the *Tales* and because its radical otherness to the version of Chaucer recorded in both Ellesmere and the *Riverside* (i.e., the apparently authorial Merchant-Squire ordering) and in canonizing literary histories of him (i.e., with his surprisingly nuanced, sympathetic take on female agency and autonomy) may offer new ways of rereading and reseeing his always complex and shifting work.

These lines of inquiry extend rhyzomically from my individual chapters and thus highlight the wide-ranging nature of the compilations I have taken up. Other opportunities for further inquiry, however, would be more purely manuscript driven. What might a historically and materially grounded new formalism tell us about other large collections like the Vernon, Simeon, or Thornton manuscripts or Harley 2253? What might those investigations tell us in turn about the very different, non-London contexts of their production and reception? Just as crucially, how should the fruits of those historical investigations affect contemporary literary-critical appreciation? Many of these objects are now receiving versions of the attention that I am encouraging, and such interest is continuing to grow. These and other comparable compendia are so large and complex, however, that not just more work but more *kinds* of work, more modes of inquiry, and different objects of critical value trained on the same physical and textual artifacts, will always be profitable. Such a range of critical approaches can itself become compilational, yielding through sometimes counterintuitive juxtapositions new insights and refreshed perspectives.

My own contribution, here, to such counterintuitive juxtapositions has been of the aesthetic and the codicological and of Benjamin and the medieval. From the latter pair, *The Arcades Project* in particular deserves fuller analysis through the lens of compilationalism, both medieval and contemporary.[9] In the introduction, I discussed some of the structural similarities between Benjamin's project and the compilations I have taken up in this book. The thematic similarities are also worth investigating, for his subject, like mine, was an urban, mercantile landscape in the throes of lasting social, political, and economic change. More broadly, the juxtapositional model that informs so much medieval literature, in both manuscript compilations and individual works (consider the episodic structure of so many medieval romances or the asyndetic parataxis that gives Old English poetry so much of its power), likewise structures not just *The Arcades Project* but also Theodor Adorno's *Minima Moralia*.[10] This curious formal resonance between the medieval and two iconic productions of the Frankfurt school, visible across vast reaches of time and ideology, suggests that further investigation might yield other fruitful points of contiguity between them.

By now I have laid out enough invitations to further research that I risk becoming the overenthusiastic Squire, whose breathless announcement of coming attractions led to his interruption by the Franklin. Some elements of that resemblance would not be unwelcome, but there is at least one important difference. One irritating aspect of the Squire's final speech (V.651-70) is that he seems oblivious to the narcissistic effect of his sprawling promise, which includes no fewer than six iterations of the "I wol/wol I" construction. Even as he attempts to whet our appetite for the exciting adventures of his characters, in other words, the Squire implies that the focus should really be on him and his own storytelling powers. By contrast, I finish this book fully aware that I will not be able to follow up on all or even most of the scholarly threads that I have set loose in this after-

9. See the trenchant discussion of *The Arcades Project* in the context of Chaucer and the medieval city, which is congruent with my own efforts to connect Benjamin's text and the concept of compilation, in Butterfield, "Introduction: Chaucer and the Detritus of the City," in Butterfield, ed., *Chaucer and the City*, 3-22.

10. Theodor Adorno, *Minima Moralia: Reflections from Damaged Life* (London: Verso, 2005).

word. My hope therefore is that some of what I've written here will inspire other people to do so, both individually and collaboratively. After all, if compilations consist of disparate pieces that can add up to something larger and more meaningful, the same too can be said of the range of methodological approaches and objects of value that constitute scholarship itself. And so I do not conclude, but rather close, with that call to continuation.

BIBLIOGRAPHY

Primary Texts and Editions

Altenglische Legenden. Edited by Carl Horstmann. Heilbronn: Henninger, 1881.

An Anonymous Short English Metrical Chronicle. Edited by Ewald Zettl. Early English Text Society, O.S. 196. London: Oxford University Press, 1935.

The Apocryphal Lives of Adam and Eve. Edited by Brian Murdoch and J. A. Tasioulas. Exeter: University of Exeter Press, 2002.

The Auchinleck Manuscript. Edited by David Burnley and Alison Wiggins. Version 1.1, July 5, 2003. http://auchinleck.nls.uk.

The Auchinleck Manuscript: National Library of Scotland Advocates' MS. 19.2.1. Edited by Derek Pearsall and I. C. Cunningham. 1977; reprint, London: Scolar, 1979.

Britton. Edited and translated by Francis Morgan Nichols. Oxford: Clarendon, 1865; reprint, Holmes Beach, FL: W. W. Gaunt, 1983.

Calendar of the Letter Books of the City of London, E. Edited by R. R. Sharpe. London: Corporation of the City of London, 1903.

Chaucer, Geoffrey. *The Riverside Chaucer*. Edited by Larry D. Benson et al. 3rd ed. Boston: Houghton Mifflin, 1987.

Floris and Blauncheflur. Edited by A. B. Taylor. Oxford: Clarendon, 1927.

Gower, John. *The Complete Works of John Gower*. Edited by G. C. Macaulay. 4 vols. Oxford: Clarendon, 1899–1902.

———. *John Gower: The French Balades*. Edited and translated by R. F. Yeager. Kalamazoo, MI: TEAMS and Medieval Institute Publications, 2009.

———. *John Gower: The Minor Latin Works*. Edited and translated by R. F. Yeager. Kalamazoo, MI: TEAMS and Medieval Institute Publications, 2005.

———. *The Major Latin Works of John Gower*. Translated by Eric Stockton. Seattle: University of Washington Press, 1962.

Historical Poems of the XIVth and XVth Centuries. Edited by Rossell Hope Robbins. New York: Columbia University Press, 1959.

Knighton, Henry. *Knighton's Chronicle, 1337–1396*. Edited and translated by G. H. Martin. Oxford: Clarendon, 1995.

Latini, Brunetto. *Li livres dou tresor*. Edited by Spurgeon Baldwin and Paul Barrette. Tempe: Arizona Center for Medieval and Renaissance Studies, 2003.

Liber custumarum. Edited by Henry Thomas Riley. Vols. 2–3 of *Munimenta Gildhallae Londoniensis: Liber albus, Liber custumarum, et Liber Horn*. Rolls Series, vol. 12. London: Longmans, 1859–62.

Maidstone, Richard. "Concordia Facta inter Regem Riccardum II et Civitatem Londonie." Edited and translated by Charles Roger Smith. Ph.D. diss., Princeton Univeristy, 1972.

Memorials of London and London Life in the XIIIth, XIVth, and XVth Centuries, 1276–1419. Edited by Henry Thomas Riley. London: Longmans, Green, 1868.

The Middle English Breton Lays. Edited by Anne Laskaya and Eve Salisbury. Kalamazoo, MI: Medieval Institute Publications, 1995.

Middle English Dictionary. Edited by Hans Kurath et al. Ann Arbor: University of Michigan Press, 1952–2000.

The Middle English Miracles of the Virgin. Edited by Beverly Boyd. San Marino, CA: Huntingdon Library, 1964.

The Mirror of Justices. Edited by William Joseph Whittaker, with an introduction by F. W. Maitland. London: Selden Society, 1895.

Die Mittelenglische Gregoriuslegende. Edited by Carl Keller. Heidelberg: Carl Winters, 1914.

Recueil général des jeux-partis français. Edited by Arthur Långfors. Paris: Edouard Champion, 1926.

St. Patrick's Purgatory. Edited by Robert Easting. Early English Text Society, O.S. 298. Oxford, 1991.

The Seven Sages of Rome. Edited by Karl Brunner. Early English Text Society, O.S. 191. London: Oxford University Press, 1933; reprint, Oxford, 1971.

The Seven Sages of Rome (Midland Version). Edited by Jill Whitelock. Early English Text Society, O.S. 324. Oxford: Oxford University Press, 2005.

The South English Nativity of Mary and Christ. Edited by O. S. Pickering. Heidelberg: Carl Winter Universitätsverlag, 1975.

Speculum Gy de Warewyke. Edited by Georgiana Lee Merrill. Early English Text Society, E.S. 75. London: K. Paul, Trench, Trubner, 1898.

Three Purgatory Poems. Edited by Edward E. Foster. Kalamazoo: Western Michigan University, Medieval Institute Publications, 2004.

Über die Leges Anglorum saeculo XIII ineunte Londoniis collectae. Edited by Felix Liebermann. Halle, 1894.

Walsingham, Thomas. *Historia Anglicana*. Edited by Henry Thomas Riley. 2 vols. Rolls Series, vol. 28. London: Longmans, 1863.

The Westminster Chronicle, 1381–94. Edited and translated by L. C. Hector and Barbara Harvey. Oxford: Clarendon, 1982.

Secondary Literature

Adorno, Theodor. *Minima Moralia: Reflections from Damaged Life*. London: Verso, 2005.

Anderson, Benedict. *Imagined Communities: Reflections on the Origin and Spread of Nationalism*. London: Verso, 1983.

Barnes, Geraldine. "Cunning and Ingenuity in the Middle English *Floris and Blauncheflur*." *Medium Ævum* 53 (1984): 10–25.

Barron, Caroline. "Chivalry, Pageantry and Merchant Culture in Medieval London." In *Heraldry, Pageantry and Social Display in Medieval England*, ed. Peter Coss and Maurice Keen, 219–41. Woodbridge: Boydell & Brewer, 2002.

———. *London in the Later Middle Ages: Government and People, 1200–1500*. Oxford: Oxford University Press, 2004.

———. "The Quarrel of Richard II with London, 1392–7." In *The Reign of Richard II: Essays in Honor of May McKisack*, ed. F. R. H. Du Boulay and Caroline M. Barron, 173–201. London: Athlone, 1971.

———. "Richard II and London." In *Richard II: The Art of Kingship*, ed. Anthony Goodman and James Gillespie, 129–54. Oxford: Clarendon, 1999.

Barron, Caroline, and Nigel Saul, eds. *England and the Low Countries in the Late Middle Ages*. Bodmin: Sutton, 1995.

Benjamin, Walter. *The Arcades Project*. Translated by Howard Eiland and Kevin McLaughlin. Cambridge, MA: Belknap Press of Harvard University Press, 1999.

———. "On the Concept of History." In *Selected Writings* (4 vols.), trans. Edmund Jephcott et al., ed. Howard Eiland and Michael W. Jennings, 4:389–400. Cambridge, MA: Belknap Press of Harvard University Press, 2003.

———. "Paralipomena to 'On the Concept of History.'" In *Selected Writings* (4 vols.), trans. Edmund Jephcott et al., ed. Howard Eiland and Michael W. Jennings, 4:401–11. Cambridge, MA: Belknap Press of Harvard University Press, 2003.

Benson, C. David. *Chaucer's Drama of Style: Poetic Variety and Contrast in the Canterbury Tales*. Chapel Hill: University of North Carolina Press, 1986.

———. "Some Poets' Tours of Medieval London: Varieties of Literary Urban Experience." *Essays in Medieval Studies* 24 (2007): 1–20.

Berger, Roger. *Littérature et société arrageoises au XIIIème siècle*. Arras: Editions Université de Paris, 1981.

Bhabha, Homi, ed. *Nation and Narration*. London: Routledge, 1990.

Biddick, Kathleen. *The Shock of Medievalism*. Durham, NC: Duke University Press, 1998.

Bird, Ruth. *The Turbulent London of Richard II*. New York: Longmans, Green, 1948.

Black, Anthony. *Guilds and Civic Society in European Political Thought from the Twelfth Century to the Present*. Ithaca, NY: Cornell University Press, 1984.

Bliss, A. J. "Notes on the Auchinleck Manuscript." *Speculum* 26 (1951): 652–58.

Blockmans, F. *Het Gentsche Stadspatriciaat tot omstreeks 1302.* Antwerp: De Sikkel, 1938.

Blodgett, E. D. "Chaucerian *Pryvetee* and the Opposition to Time." *Speculum* 51 (1976): 477–93.

Bowers, John. "Three Readings of *The Knight's Tale*: Sir John Clanvowe, Geoffrey Chaucer, and James I of Scotland." *Journal of Medieval and Early Modern Studies* 34 (2004): 279–307.

Brand, Paul A. "Edward I and the Judges: The 'State Trials' of 1289–93." In *Thirteenth Century England I*, ed. P. R. Cross and S. D. Lloyd, 31–40. Woodbridge: D. S. Brewer, 1986. Reprinted in Paul A. Brand, *The Making of the Common Law* (London: Hambledon, 1992), 103–12.

Bryan, Elizabeth J. *Collaborative Meaning in Scribal Culture: The Otho Laȝamon.* Ann Arbor: University of Michigan Press, 1999.

Burrow, J. A. *Ricardian Poetry: Chaucer, Gower, Langland, and the "Gawain" Poet.* New Haven, CT: Yale University Press, 1971.

———. "'Sir Thopas': An Agony in Three Fits." *Review of English Studies* 22 (1971): 54–58.

Burrows, Jean Harpham. "The Auchinleck Manuscript: Contexts, Texts and Audience." Ph.D. diss., Washington University in St. Louis, 1984.

Bush, Jonathan A., and Alain Wijffels, eds. *Learning the Law: Teaching and the Transmission of Law in England, 1150–1900.* London: Hambledon, 1999.

Butterfield, Ardis. "Articulating the Author: Gower and the French Vernacular Codex." *Yearbook of English Studies* 33 (2003): 80–96.

———, ed. *Chaucer and the City.* Cambridge: D. S. Brewer, 2006.

———. *The Familiar Enemy: Chancer, Language, and Nation in the Hundred Years War.* Oxford: Oxford University Press, 2009.

———. "French Culture and the Ricardian Court." In *Essays on Ricardian Literature in Honor of J. A. Burrow*, ed. A. J. Minnis, Charlotte C. Morse, and Thorlac Turville-Petre, 82–120. Oxford: Clarendon, 1997.

———. "Introduction: Chaucer and the Detritus of the City." In *Chaucer and the City*, ed Ardis Butterfield, 3–22. Cambridge: D. S. Brewer, 2006.

———. *Poetry and Music in Medieval France.* Cambridge: Cambridge University Press, 2002.

Calkin, Siobhan Bly. *Saracens and the Making of English Identity: The Auchinleck Manuscript.* New York: Routledge, 2005.

Cannon, Christopher. "Chaucer and the Auchinleck Manuscript Revisited." *Chaucer Review* 46 (2011): 131–46.

———. "Form." In *Middle English* (Oxford Twenty-First Century Approaches to Literature), ed. Paul Strohm, 175–90. Oxford: Oxford University Press, 2007.

Cannon, Debbie. "London Pride: Citizenship and the Fourteenth-Century Custumals of the City of London." In *Learning and Literacy in Medieval England and Abroad*, ed. Sarah Rees Jones, 179–98. Turnhout: Brepols, 2003.

Carlin, Martha. *Medieval Southwark*. London: Hambledon, 1996.

Carruthers, Mary J. "Sweetness." *Speculum* 81 (2006): 999–1013.

Casey, Jim. "Unfinished Business: The Termination of Chaucer's *Cook's Tale*." *Chaucer Review* 41 (2006): 185–96.

Catto, Jeremy. "Andrew Horn: Law and History in Fourteenth-Century England." In *The Writing of History in the Middle Ages: Essays Presented to Richard William Southern*, ed. R. H. C. Davis and J. M. Wallace-Hadrill, 367–91. Oxford: Clarendon, 1981.

Charbonneau, Joanne. "*Sir Thopas*." In *Sources and Analogues of the Canterbury Tales* (2 vols.), ed. Robert M. Correale and Mary Hamel, 2:649–714. Cambridge: D. S. Brewer, 2002–5.

Cherewatuk, Karen. "The Middle English *Floris and Blauncheflur*, Another Merchant's Tale." *New Comparison* 12 (1991): 54–70.

Chickering, Howell D. "Poetic Exuberance in *Judith*." *Studies in Philology* 106 (2009): 119–36.

Clanchy, M. T. *From Memory to Written Record: England, 1066–1307*. Cambridge, MA: Harvard University Press, 1979, 2nd ed., Oxford: Blackwell, 1993.

Clopper, Lawrence M. "The Engaged Spectator: Langland and Chaucer on Civic Spectacle." *Studies in the Age of Chaucer* 22 (2000): 115–39.

Colopy, Cheryl. "*Sir Degaré*: A Fairy Tale Oedipus." *Pacific Coast Philology* 17 (1982): 31–39.

Cooper, Helen. "London and Southwark Poetic Companies: 'Si tost c'amis' and the *Canterbury Tales*." In *Chaucer and the City*, ed. Ardis Butterfield, 109–25. Cambridge: D. S. Brewer, 2006.

———. *The Structure of the Canterbury Tales*. Athens: University of Georgia Press, 1983.

Cooper, Lisa H. "The Poetics of Practicality." In *Middle English* (Oxford Twenty-First Century Approaches to Literature), ed. Paul Strohm, 491–505. Oxford: Oxford University Press, 2007.

Copeland, Rita. *Rhetoric, Hermeneutics, and Translation in the Middle Ages*. Cambridge: Cambridge University Press, 1991.

Coupland, Douglas. *Jpod*. Toronto: Random House of Canada, 2005.

Crane, Susan. *Insular Romance: Politics, Faith, and Culture in Anglo-Norman and Middle English Literature*. Berkeley and Los Angeles: University of California Press, 1986.

Cunningham, I. C., and J. E. C. Cunningham. "New Light on the Signatures of the Auchinleck Manuscript." *Scriptorium* 36 (1982): 280–92.

Dagenais, John. "Decolonizing the Medieval Page." In *The Future of the Page*, ed. Peter Stoicheff and Andrew Taylor, 37–70. Toronto: University of Toronto Press, 2004.

Davidson, Mary Catherine. *Medievalism, Multilingualism, and Chaucer*. New York: Palgrave Macmillan, 2009.

Deleuze, Gilles, and Félix Guattari. *A Thousand Plateaus: Capitalism and Schizophrenia*. Translated by Brian Massumi. Minneapolis: University of Minnesota Press, 1987.

Dennison, Lynda. "'Liber Horn,' 'Liber Custumarum,' and Other Manuscripts of the Queen Mary Psalter Workshops." In *Medieval Art, Architecture, and Archaeology in London* (Conference Transactions, no. 10), ed. Lindy Grant, 118–34. London: British Archaeological Association, 1990.

Dillon, Emma. *Medieval Music-Making and the Roman de Fauvel*. Cambridge: Cambridge University Press, 2002.

Doyle, A. I. "English Books in and out of Court from Edward III to Henry IV." In *English Court Culture in the Later Middle Ages*, ed. V. J. Scattergood and J. W. Sherborne, 163–82. London: Duckworth, 1983.

Dutton, Elizabeth, John Hines, and R. F. Yeager, eds. *John Gower, Trilingual Poet: Language, Translation, and Tradition*. Woodbridge: D. S. Brewer, 2010.

Echard, Siân. "Gower's 'bokes of Latin': Language, Politics, and Poetry." *Studies in the Age of Chaucer* 25 (2003): 123–56.

———. *Printing the Middle Ages*. Philadelphia: University of Pennsylvania Press, 2008.

———. "With Carmen's Help: Latin Authorities in the *Confessio Amantis*." *Studies in Philology* 45 (1998): 1–40.

Epstein, Robert. "Literal Opposition: Deconstruction, History, and Lancaster." *Texas Studies in Literature and Language* 44 (2002): 16–33.

———. "London, Southwark, Westminster: Gower's Urban Contexts." In *A Companion to Gower*, ed. Siân Echard, 43–60. Woodbridge: Boydell & Brewer, 2004.

Evans, Murray J. *Rereading Middle English Romance: Manuscript Layout, Decoration, and the Rhetoric of Composite Structure*. Montreal: McGill-Queens University Press, 1995.

Federico, Sylvia. *New Troy: Fantasies of Empire in the Late Middle Ages*. Minneapolis: University of Minnesota Press, 2003.

Fein, Susanna. "*Somer Soneday*: Kingship, Sainthood, and Fortune in Oxford, Bodleian Library, MS Laud Misc. 108." In *The Texts and Contexts of Oxford, Bodleian Library, MS Laud Misc. 108: The Shaping of English Vernacular Narrative*, ed. Kimberly K. Bell and Julie Nelson Couch, 275–97. Leiden: Brill, 2011.

———, ed. *Studies in the Harley Manuscript: The Scribes, Contents, and Social Contexts of British Library MS Harley 2253*. Kalamazoo, MI: Medieval Institute Publications, 2000.

Finlayson, John. "*Richard, Coer de Lyon*: Romance, History, or Something in Between?" *Studies in Philology* 87 (1990): 156–80.

Fisher, John H. *John Gower: Moral Philosopher and Friend of Chaucer*. New York: New York University Press, 1964.

Gillespie, Alexandra. "Analytical Survey 9: The History of the Book." *New Medieval Literatures* 9 (2007): 245–86.

Grady, Frank. "Gower's Boat, Richard's Barge, and the True Story of the *Confessio Amantis*: Text and Gloss." *Texas Studies in Language and Literature* 44 (2002): 1–15.

———. "The Lancastrian Gower and the Limits of Exemplarity." *Speculum* 70 (1995): 552–75.

Grandsen, Antonia. *Historical Writing in England, c. 1307 to the Early Sixteenth Century.* Ithaca, NY: Cornell University Press, 1982.

———. "Realistic Observation in Twelfth-Century England." *Speculum* 46 (1972): 29–51.

Haines, Roy Martin. *King Edward II: Edward of Caernarfon, His Life, His Reign, and Its Aftermath, 1284–1330.* Montreal: McGill-Queens University Press, 2003.

Hanna, Ralph. "*Compilatio* and the Wife of Bath: Latin Backgrounds, Ricardian Texts." In *Latin and Vernacular: Studies in Late Medieval Texts*, ed. A. J. Minnis, 1–11. Woodbridge: D. S. Brewer, 1989.

———. *London Literature, 1300–1380.* Cambridge: Cambridge University Press, 2005.

———. "Miscellaneity and Vernacularity: Conditions of Literary Production in Late Medieval England." In *The Whole Book: Cultural Perspectives on the Medieval Miscellany*, ed. Stephen G. Nichols and Siegfried Wenzel, 37–51. Ann Arbor: University of Michigan Press, 1993.

———. *Pursuing History: Middle English Manuscripts and Their Texts.* Stanford, CA: Stanford University Press, 1996.

———. "Reconsidering the Auchinleck Manuscript." In *New Directions in Later Medieval Manuscript Studies*, ed. Derek Pearsall, 91–102. York: York Medieval Press, 2000.

Hanssen, Beatrice. *Walter Benjamin's Other History: Of Stones, Animals, Human Beings, and Angels.* Berkeley and Los Angeles: University of California Press, 1998.

Harding, Vanessa. "Cross-Channel Trade and Cultural Contacts: London and the Low Countries in the Later Fourteenth Century." In *England and the Low Countries in the Late Middle Ages*, ed. Caroline Barron and Nigel Saul, 153–68. Stroud: Sutton, 1998.

———. "Medieval Documentary Sources for London and Paris: A Comparison." In *London and Europe in the Later Middle Ages*, ed. Julia Boffey and Pamela King, 85–110. London: Centre for Medieval and Renaissance Studies at Queen Mary and Westfield College, University of London, 1995.

Haren, Michael, and Yolande de Pontfarcy. *The Medieval Pilgrimage to St Patrick's Purgatory: Lough Derg and the European Tradition.* Enniskillen: Clogher Historical Society, 1988.

Hathaway, Neil. "*Compilatio*: From Plagiarism to Compiling." *Viator: Medieval and Renaissance Studies* 20 (1989): 19–44.

Heffernan, Carol. "Chaucer's *Squire's Tale*: The Poetics of Interlace or the 'Well of English Undefiled.'" *Chaucer Review* 31 (1997): 32–45.

Hinton, Norman. "*The Canterbury Tales* as Compilatio." *Proceedings of the Illinois Medieval Association* 1 (1984): 28–47.

Holloway, Julia Bolton. *Brunetto Latini: An Analytic Bibliography.* London: Grant & Cutler, 1986.

Horobin, Simon. "Adam Pinkhurst, Geoffrey Chaucer, and the Hengwrt Manuscript of the *Canterbury Tales.*" *Chaucer Review* 44 (2010): 351–67.

Hume, Cathy. "Why Did Gower Write the *Traitié*?" In *John Gower: Trilingual Poet: Language, Translation, and Tradition,* ed. Elizabeth Dutton, John Hines, and R. F. Yeager, 263–75. Woodbridge: D. S. Brewer, 2010.

Huot, Sylvia. *From Song to Book: The Poetics of Writing in Old French Lyric and Lyrical Narrative Poetry.* Ithaca, NY: Cornell University Press, 1987.

Jones, E. A. "'Loo, Lordes Myne, Heere is a Fit!': The Structure of Chaucer's *Sir Thopas.*" *Review of English Studies* 51 (2000): 248–52.

Joughin, John J., and Simon Malpas. Introduction to *The New Aestheticism,* ed. John J. Joughin and Simon Malpas, 1–20. Manchester: Manchester University Press, 2003.

Justice, Steven, and Kathryn Kerby-Fulton. "Scribe D and the Marketing of Ricardian Literature." In *The Medieval Professional Reader at Work: Evidence from Manuscripts of Chaucer, Langland, Kempe, and Gower,* ed. Kathryn Kerby-Fulton and Madie Hilmo, 217–37. Victoria, BC: University of Victoria, 2001.

Kamowski, William. "Trading the 'Knotte' for Loose Ends: The *Squire's Tale* and the Poetics of Chaucerian Fragments." *Style* 31 (1997): 391–412.

Kelly, Kathleen Coyne. "The Bartering of Blauncheflur in the Middle English *Floris and Blauncheflur.*" *Studies in Philology* 91 (1994): 101–10.

Kendall, Elliot. *Lordship and Literature: John Gower and the Politics of the Great Household.* Oxford: Oxford University Press, 2008.

Ker, Neil. "Liber Custumarum, and Other Manuscripts Formerly at the Guildhall." In *Books, Collectors, and Libraries: Studies in the Medieval Heritage,* ed. Andrew G. Watson, 135–42. London: Hambledon, 1985. The essay originally appeared in *Guildhall Miscellany* 3 (1954): 37–45. *Books, Collectors, and Libraries* is a collection of Ker's essays.

Knapp, Peggy. *Chaucerian Aesthetics.* New York: Palgrave Macmillan, 2008.

Kölbing, E. "Kleine Publicationen aus der Auchinleck-hs." *Englische Studien* 9 (1886): 35–52.

Kratins, Ojars. "Middle English *Amis and Amiloun*: Chivalric Romance or Secular Hagiography." *PMLA* 81 (1966): 347–54.

Lerer, Seth. *Chaucer and His Readers: Imagining the Author in Late-Medieval England.* Princeton, NJ: Princeton University Press, 1993.

Levinson, Marjorie. "What Is New Formalism?" *PMLA* 122 (2007): 558–69.

Liebermann, Felix. "A Contemporary Manuscript of the 'Leges Anglorum Londoniis collectae.'" *English Historical Review* 28 (1913): 732–45.

Lindeboom, Wim. "Rethinking the Recensions of the *Confessio Amantis*." *Viator* 40 (2009): 319–48.

Lindenbaum, Sheila. "The Smithfield Tournament of 1390." *Journal of Medieval and Renaissance Studies* 20 (1990): 1–20.

Lloyd, T. H. *Alien Merchants in England in the High Middle Ages*. New York: St. Martin's, 1982.

Loesberg, Jonathan. *A Return to Aesthetics: Autonomy, Indifference, and Postmodernism*. Stanford, CA: Stanford University Press, 2005.

Loomis, Laura Hibbard. "The Auchinleck Manuscript and a Possible London Bookshop of 1330–1340." *PMLA* 57 (1942): 595–627.

———. "Chaucer and the Breton Lays of the Auchinleck MS." *Studies in Philology* 38 (1941): 14–33.

Lyle, E. B. "*Sir Orfeo* and the Recovery of Amis from the Otherworld in *Guy of Warwick*." *Neuphilologische Mitteilungen* 80 (1979): 65–68.

Machan, Tim William. "Medieval Multilingualism and Gower's Literary Practice." *Studies in Philology* 103 (2006): 1–25.

Mann, Jill. *Chaucer and Medieval Estates Satire*. Cambridge: Cambridge University Press, 1973.

McDonnell, Kevin. *Medieval London Suburbs*. London: Phillimore, 1978.

McGrady, Deborah. *Controlling Readers: Guillaume de Machaut and His Late Medieval Readers*. Toronto: University of Toronto Press, 2006.

Meyer-Lee, Robert. "Fragments IV and V of the *Canterbury Tales* Do Not Exist." *Chaucer Review* 45 (2010): 1–31.

———. "Manuscript Studies, Literary Value, and the Object of Chaucer Studies." *Studies in the Age of Chaucer* 30 (2008): 1–37.

Middleton, Anne. "War by Other Means: Marriage and Chivalry in Chaucer." *Studies in the Age of Chaucer: Proceedings* 1 (1984): 119–33.

Miller, Andrew H. *The Burdens of Perfection: On Ethics and Reading in Nineteenth-Century Literature*. Ithaca, NY: Cornell University Press, 2008.

Minnis, A. J. *Chaucer and Pagan Antiquity*. Cambridge: D. S. Brewer, 1982.

———. "*De Vulgari Auctoritate*: Chaucer, Gower, and the Men of Great Authority." In *Chaucer and Gower: Difference, Mutuality, Exchange*, ed. R. F. Yeager, 36–74. Victoria, BC: University of Victoria, Department of English, 1991.

———, ed. *Latin and Vernacular: Studies in Late-Medieval Texts and Manuscripts*. Wolfeboro, NH: D. S. Brewer, 1989.

———. *Medieval Theory of Authorship: Scholastic Literary Attitudes in the Later Middle Ages*. London: Scolar, 1984.

———. "*Nolens Auctor Sed Compilator Reputari*: The Late-Medieval Discourse of Compilation." In *La méthode critique au Moyen Âge*, ed. Mireille Chazan and Gilbert Dahan, 47–63. Turnhout: Brepols, 2008.

———. "Ordering Chaucer." *Essays in Criticism* 35 (1985): 265–69.

Mooney, Linne. "Chaucer's Scribe." *Speculum* 81 (2006): 97–138.

Munro, John H. "The Medieval Scarlet and the Economics of Sartorial Splendor."
    In *Textiles, Town, and Trade: Essays in the History of Late-Medieval England and the
    Low Countries*, 17–70. Aldershot: Ashgate, 1996.

Neville, Marie. "The Function of the *Squire's Tale* in the Canterbury Scheme." *Jour-
    nal of English and Germanic Philology* 50 (1951): 167–79.

Nichols, Stephen. "Introduction: Philology in a Manuscript Culture." *Speculum* 65
    (1990): 1–10.

Nightingale, Pamela. *A Medieval Mercantile Community: The Grocers' Company and the
    Politics and Trade of London*. New Haven, CT: Yale University Press, 1995.

Nolan, Maura. "Lydgate's Worst Poem." In *Lydgate Matters: Poetry and Material Cul-
    ture in the Fifteenth Century*, ed. Lisa H. Cooper and Andrea Denny-Brown, 71–87.
    New York: Palgrave Macmillan, 2007.

———. "Making the Aesthetic Turn: Adorno, the Medieval, and the Future of the
    Past." *Journal of Medieval and Early Modern Studies* 34 (2004): 549–75.

Olson, Glending. *Literature as Recreation in the Later Middle Ages*. Ithaca, NY: Cornell
    University Press, 1982.

Otter, Samuel. "An Aesthetic in All Things." *Representations* 104 (2008): 116–25.

Parkes, Malcolm B. "The Influence of the Concepts of *Ordinatio* and *Compilatio*
    on the Development of the Book." In *Scribes, Scripts, and Readers: Studies in the
    Communication, Presentation, and Dissemination of Medieval Texts*, by Malcolm B.
    Parkes, 35–70. The essay originally appeared in *Medieval Learning and Literature:
    Essays Presented to Richard William Hunt*, ed. J. J. G. Alexander and M. T. Gibson
    (Oxford: Clarendon, 1976), 115–41.

———. "Patterns of Scribal Activity and Revisions of the Text in Early Copies of
    Works by John Gower." In *New Science out of Old Books: Studies in Manuscripts and
    Early Printed Books in Honour of A. I. Doyle*, ed. Richard Beadle and A. J. Piper,
    81–121. Aldershot: Ashgate, 1995.

———. *Scribes, Scripts, and Readers: Studies in the Communication, Presentation, and
    Dissemination of Medieval Texts*. London: Hambledon, 1991.

Parkes, Malcolm B., and A. I. Doyle. "The Production of Copies of the *Canterbury
    Tales* and the *Confessio Amantis* in the Early Fifteenth Century." In *Scribes, Scripts,
    and Readers: Studies in the Communication, Presentation, and Dissemination of Medieval
    Texts*, by Malcolm B. Parkes, 201–48. The essay originally appeared in *Medieval
    Scribes, Manuscripts and Libraries: Essays Presented to N. R. Ker*, ed. M. B. Parkes and
    Andrew G. Watson (London: Scolar, 1978), 163–210.

Partridge, Stephen. "Minding the Gaps: Interpreting the Manuscript Evidence of
    the *Cook's Tale* and the *Squire's Tale*." In *The English Medieval Book: Studies in
    Memory of Jeremy Griffiths*, ed. A. S. G. Edwards, Vincent Gillespie, and Ralph
    Hanna, 51–85. London: British Library, 2000.

Patterson, Lee. *Chaucer and the Subject of History*. Madison: University of Wisconsin
    Press, 1991.

Pearsall, Derek. "Authorial Revision in Some Late-Medieval English Texts." In *Crux and Controversy*, ed. A. J. Minnis and Charlotte Brewer, 39–48. Cambridge: D. S. Brewer, 1992.

———. *The Canterbury Tales*. Boston: G. Allen & Unwin, 1985.

———. "Gower's Latin in the *Confessio Amantis*." In *Latin and Vernacular: Studies in Late-Medieval Texts and Manuscripts*, ed. A. J. Minnis, 13–25. Wolfeboro, NH: D. S. Brewer, 1989.

———. *The Life of Geoffrey Chaucer*. Oxford: Blackwell, 1992.

———. "Towards a Poetic of Chaucerian Narrative." In *Drama, Narrative, and Poetry in the Canterbury Tales*, ed. Wendy Harding, 99–112. Toulouse: Presses Universitaires du Mirail, 2003.

Portnoy, Phyllis. "The Best-Text/Best-Book of Canterbury: The Dialogic of the Fragments." *Florilegium* 13 (1994): 161–72.

Prendergast, Thomas A., and Barbara Kline, eds. *Rewriting Chaucer: Culture, Authority, and the Idea of the Authentic Text, 1400–1602*. Columbus: Ohio State University Press, 1999.

Purdie, Rhiannon. *Anglicising Romance: Tail-Rhyme and Genre in Medieval English Literature*. Cambridge: D. S. Brewer, 2008.

———. "The Implications of Manuscript Layout in Chaucer's *Tale of Sir Thopas*." *Forum for Modern Language Studies* 41 (2005): 263–74.

Robinson, Pamela. "Some Aspects of the Transmission of English Verse Texts in Late Mediaeval Manuscripts." B.Litt. thesis, Oxford University, 1972.

Rouse, R. H., and M. A. Rouse. "*Ordinatio* and *Compilatio* Revisited." In *Ad Litteram: Authoritative Texts and Their Medieval Readers*, ed. Mark D. Jordan and Kent Emery Jr., 113–34. Notre Dame, IN: University of Notre Dame Press, 1992.

Rust, Martha. *Imaginary Worlds in Medieval Books: Exploring the Manuscript Matrix*. New York: Palgrave Macmillan, 2007.

Ryan, Noel J. "The Assumption in the Early English Pulpit." *Theological Studies* 11 (1950): 477–524.

Salisbury, Eve. "Remembering Origins: Gower's Monstrous Body Poetic." In *Re-Visioning Gower*, ed. R. F. Yeager, 159–84. Asheville, NC: Pegasus, 1998.

Saul, Nigel. "Richard II and the Vocabulary of Kingship." *English Historical Review* 110 (1995): 854–77.

Scanlon, Larry. *Narrative, Authority, and Power*. Cambridge: Cambridge University Press, 1994.

Scattergood, V. J. "Chaucer and the French War: *Sir Thopas* and *Melibee*." In *Court and Poet*, ed. Glyn S. Burgess, 287–96. Liverpool: Francis Cairns, 1981.

———. "Misrepresenting the City: Genre, Intertextuality, and William fitzStephen's *Description of London* (c. 1173)." In *London and Europe in the Later Middle Ages*, ed. Julia Boffey and Pamela King, 1–34. London: Centre for Medieval and Renaissance Studies at Queen Mary and Westfield College, University of London, 1995.

———. "Perkyn Revelour and the *Cook's Tale*." *Chaucer Review* 19 (1985): 14–23.

Schwartz, M. "Kleine Publicationen aus der Auchinleck-MS." *Englische Studien* 8 (1885): 427–64.

Seipp, David J. "*The Mirror of Justices*." In *Learning the Law: Teaching and the Transmission of Law in England, 1150–1900*, ed. Jonathan A. Bush and Alain Wijffels, 85–112. London: Hambledon, 1999.

Shonk, Timothy A. "A Study of the Auchinleck Manuscript: Bookmen and Bookmaking in the Early Fourteenth Century." *Speculum* 60 (1985): 71–91.

Skemer, Don C. "Reading the Law." In *Learning the Law: Teaching and the Transmission of Law in England, 1150–1900*, ed. Jonathan A. Bush and Alain Wijffels, 113–31. London: Hambledon, 1999.

Smyser, H. M. "The List of Norman Names in the Auchinleck MS. (Battle Abbey Roll)." In *Mediaeval Studies in Honor of J. D. M. Ford*, ed. U. T. Holmes Jr. and A. J. Denomy, 257–87. Cambridge, MA: Harvard University Press, 1948.

Staley, Lynn. "Gower, Richard II, Henry of Derby, and the Business of Making Culture." *Speculum* 75 (2000): 68–96.

———. *Languages of Power in the Age of Richard II*. University Park: Pennsylvania State University Press, 2005.

Stanley, E. G. " 'Of This Cokes Tale Maked Chaucer Na Moore.' " *Poetica: An International Journal of Linguistic-Literary Studies* 5 (1976): 36–59.

Stemmler, Theo. "Miscellany or Anthology? The Structure of Medieval Manuscripts: MS Harley 2253, for Example." In *Studies in the Harley Manuscript: The Scribes, Contents, and Social Contexts of British Library MS Harley 2253*, ed. Susanna Fein, 111–21. Kalamazoo, MI: Medieval Institute Publications, 2000. This is a revised version of "Miscellany or Anthology? The Structure of Medieval Manuscripts: MS Harley 2253, for Example," *Zeitschrift für Anglistik und Amerikanistik* 39 (1991): 231–37.

Strohm, Paul. "Politics and Poetics: Usk and Chaucer in the 1380s." In *Literary Practice and Social Change in Britain, 1380–1530*, ed. Lee Patterson, 83–112. Berkeley and Los Angeles: University of California Press, 1990.

———. "Saving the Appearances: Chaucer's *Purse* and the Fabrication of the Lancastrian Claim." In *Chaucer's England: Literature in Its Historical Context*, ed. Barbara Hanawalt, 21–40. Minneapolis: University of Minnesota Press, 1992.

———. *Social Chaucer*. Cambridge, MA: Harvard University Press, 1989.

———. *Theory and the Premodern Text*. Minneapolis: University of Minnesota Press, 2000.

Stubbs, William, ed. *Annales Londonienses and Annales Paulini*. Vol. 1 of *Chronicles of the Reigns of Edward I and Edward II*. Rolls Series, vol. 76.1. London: Longmans, 1882.

Suggett, Helen. "A Letter Describing Richard II's Reconciliation with the City of London in 1392." *English Historical Review* 62 (1947): 209–13.

Sutherland, Donald W. *Quo Warranto Proceedings in the Reign of Edward I.* Oxford: Clarendon, 1963.

Sutton, Anne F. *The Mercery of London: Trade, Goods, and People, 1130–1578.* Aldershot: Ashgate, 2005.

———. "Merchants, Music and Social Harmony: The London Puy and Its French and London Contexts, circa 1300." *London Journal* 17 (1992): 1–17.

———. "The *Tumbling Bear* and Its Patrons: A Venue for the London Puy and Mercery." In *London and Europe in the Later Middle Ages*, ed. Julia Boffey and Pamela King, 85–110. London: Centre for Medieval and Renaissance Studies at Queen Mary and Westfield College, University of London, 1995.

Symes, Carol. *A Common Stage: Theater and Public Life in Medieval Arras.* Ithaca, NY: Cornell University Press, 2007.

Taylor, Andrew. *Textual Situations: Three Medieval Manuscripts and Their Readers.* Philadelphia: University of Pennsylvania Press, 2002.

Taylor, Paul Beekman. "Time in the *Canterbury Tales*." *Exemplaria* 7 (1995): 371–93.

Tinkle, Theresa. "The Wife of Bath's Textual/Sexual Lives." In *The Iconic Page in Manuscript, Print, and Digital Culture*, ed. George Bornstein and Theresa Tinkle, 55–88. Ann Arbor: University of Michigan Press, 1998.

Turner, Marion. *Chaucerian Conflict: Languages of Antagonism in Late Fourteenth Century London.* Oxford: Oxford University Press, 2007.

Turville-Petre, Thorlac. *England the Nation: Language, Literature, and National Identity.* Oxford: Clarendon, 1996.

Vale, Juliet. *Edward III and Chivalry: Chivalric Society and Its Context, 1270–1350.* Woodbridge: Boydell & Brewer, 1982.

Vale, Malcolm. *The Princely Court: Medieval Courts and Culture in North-West Europe, 1280–1380.* Oxford: Oxford University Press, 2001.

van den Neste, Evelyn. *Tournois, joutes, pas d'armes dans les villes de la Flandre à la fin du Moyen Age.* Paris: École des Chartes, 1996.

Vincent, Catherine. *Les confréries médiévales dans le royaume de France: XIIIème à XVème siècles.* Paris: A. Michel, 1994.

Wallace, David. *Chaucerian Polity: Absolutist Lineages and Associational Forms.* Stanford, CA: Stanford University Press, 1997.

———. "In Flaundres." *Studies in the Age of Chaucer* 19 (1997): 63–91.

———, ed. *The New Cambridge History of Medieval English Literature.* Cambridge: Cambridge University Press, 1999.

Warner, Michael. *The Letters of the Republic: Publication and the Public Sphere in Eighteenth-Century America.* Cambridge, MA: Harvard University Press, 1990.

Watt, Diane. *Amoral Gower.* Minneapolis: University of Minnesota Press, 2003.

Wetherbee, Winthrop. "Latin Structure and Vernacular Space: Gower, Chaucer, and the Boethian Tradition." In *Chaucer and Gower: Difference, Mutuality, Exchange*, ed. R. F. Yeager, 7–35. Victoria, BC: University of Victoria, Department of English, 1991.

Williams, Gwyn. *Medieval London: From Commune to Capital*. London: Athlone, 1970.

Wimsatt, James I. *Chaucer and His French Contemporaries*. Toronto: University of Toronto Press, 1991.

———. *Chaucer and the Poems of "Ch" in University of Pennsylvania MS French 15*. Cambridge: Boydell & Brewer, 1982.

Wood, Chauncey. *Chaucer and the Stars*. Princeton, NJ: Princeton University Press, 1970.

Wormald, Patrick. "*Quadripartitus*." In *Law and Government in Medieval England and Normandy: Essays in Honor of Sir James Holt*, ed. George Garnett and John Hudson, 111–47. Cambridge: Cambridge University Press, 1994.

Wright, Glen. "Modern Inconveniences: Rethinking Parody in *The Tale of Sir Thopas*." *Genre* 30 (1997): 167–94.

Yeager, R. F. "Did Gower Write *Cento*?" In *John Gower: Recent Readings*, ed. R. F. Yeager, 113–32. Kalamazoo: Medieval Institute Publications, 1989.

———. "Gower's French Audience: The *Mirour de l'Omme*." *Chaucer Review* 41 (2006): 111–37.

———. "John Gower's Audience: The Ballades." *Chaucer Review* 40 (2005): 81–104.

———. "John Gower's French." In *A Companion to Gower*, ed. Siân Echard, 137–51. Woodbridge: D. S. Brewer, 2004.

———. *John Gower's Poetic: The Search for a New Arion*. Woodbridge: D. S. Brewer, 1990.

INDEX

Note: If the authorship of a text is known, the author's name follows the title in parentheses. Where there is no such indication, the author is anonymous. Page numbers followed by the letter *t* indicate tables.